Brief Therapy Approaches to Treating Anxiety and Depression

Brief Therapy Approaches to Treating Anxiety and Depression

Edited by

Michael D. Yapko, PH.D.

BRUNNER/MAZEL, *Publishers* • New York

Library of Congress Cataloging-in-Publication Data

Brief therapy approaches to treating anxiety and depression/edited by
   Michael D. Yapko.
      p.   cm.
   Based on the proceedings of the Fourth Annual San Diego Conference on
Hypnotic and Strategic Interventions, March 4–6, 1988; sponsored by the Milton H.
Erickson Institute of San Diego.
   Includes bibliographies and index.
   ISBN 0-87630-508-7
   1. Anxiety—Treatment—Congresses. 2. Depression, Mental—Treatment—
Congresses. 3. Psychotherapy, Brief—Congresses. I. Yapko, Michael D. II. San
Diego Conference on Hypnotic and Strategic Interventions (4th: 1988) III. Milton H.
Erickson Institute of San Diego (Calif.)
   [DNLM: 1. Anxiety—therapy—congresses. 2. Depression—therapy. 3. Psycho-
therapy, Brief—congresses. WM 420 B8532 1988]
RC531.B75   1989
616.85'2230651—dc20
DNLM/DLC
for Library of Congress   89-15746
                                                                          CIP

Copyright © 1989 by Michael D. Yapko, Ph.D.

Published by
BRUNNER/MAZEL, INC.
19 Union Square
New York, New York 10003

MANUFACTURED IN THE UNITED STATES OF AMERICA

This book is dedicated to
Jeffrey K. Zeig,
with appreciation, affection, and respect.
His knowledge of gliding and boulder dodging
has proved to be most inspirational.

Contents

Preface   *ix*
Conference Overview and Objectives   *xiii*
Acknowledgments   *xv*
About the Milton H. Erickson Institute of San Diego   *xvii*
Conference Faculty and Presentation Titles   *xix*

SECTION ONE: KEYNOTE ADDRESS

1. Explanatory Style: Predicting Depression, Achievement, and
   Health   5
     Martin E. P. Seligman

SECTION TWO: INTERVENTIONS FOR DEPRESSION

2. Consciousness, Emotional Complexes, and the Mind–Gene
   Connection 35
     Ernest L. Rossi
3. A Renaissance Paradigm 50
     John J. Koriath
4. Treating Achilles' Heel: Differentiation of Depressive States
   and Clinical Intervention with the Depressed Patient 64
     Waleed Anthony Salameh
5. Disturbances of Temporal Orientation as a Feature of
   Depression 106
     Michael D. Yapko
6. The Multidimensional Application of Therapeutic Metaphors
   in the Treatment of Depression 119
     Brita A. Martiny
7. No More Monsters and Meanies: Multisensory Metaphors for
   Helping Children with Fears and Depression 150
     Joyce C. Mills
8. Therapeutic Diagnosing in Cases of Childhood Depression
   Ronald M. Gabriel 171

9. Integrating Ericksonian Strategies Into Structured Groups
   for Depression 184
      Brent B. Geary

   SECTION THREE: INTERVENTIONS FOR ANXIETY

10. From Panic to Peace: Recognizing the Continua 207
      Russell A. Bourne, Jr.
11. A Hypnotherapeutic Approach to Panic Disorder 226
      Harriet E. Hollander
12. Anxiety as a Function of Perception: A Theory About
    Anxiety and a Procedure to Reduce Symptoms to
    Manageable Levels 245
      David L. Higgins
13. Trance-Forming Anxiety: Hypnotic and Strategic
    Approaches to Treatment 264
      Christopher J. Beletsis

   SECTION FOUR: THERAPEUTIC APPROACHES FOR ANXIETY
                    AND DEPRESSION

14. The Treatment of Anxiety and Depression in Pain States . . . 281
      Robert Schwarz
15. Hypnotic Treatment of Depression with the Use of
    Dissociation and Submodalities 303
      Norma Barretta
      Philip Barretta
      Joseph A. Bongiovanni
16. When Doesn't the Problem Happen? 314
      Jane E. Peller
      John L. Walter
17. The Therapist as Variety Generator: Developing Solutions
    with Depressed Clients 327
      Stephen G. Gilligan

   Name Index 349

   Subject Index 353

Preface

The Milton H. Erickson Institute of San Diego conducted its *Fourth Annual Conference on Hypnotic and Strategic Interventions*, March 4–6, 1988, on scenic Mission Bay in San Diego. The three prior conferences had been successful in promoting an awareness of and interest in hypnosis and briefer psychotherapies, but none of them had a specific focal point. (The edited proceedings from the first conference are contained in a volume entitled *Hypnotic and Strategic Interventions: Principles and Practice*, edited by Michael D. Yapko, Ph.D., and available from Irvington Publishers.) For the fourth conference, it was decided that awareness of general principles and techniques of hypnosis and brief therapy had grown sufficiently to warrant developing a focused attention on specific clinical disorders. The idea was to promote advances in clinical practice by exploring new, innovative ways to address the problems that clinicians routinely face.

Recent survey data from the National Institute of Mental Health suggested that among the most common disorders from which Americans suffer are anxiety and mood disorders. Of course, this is not news to the practitioner. One is likely to be in clinical practice only a few minutes before the first client is seen who presents anxiety and/or mood disturbances as part or all of the presenting problem. Yet as common as these disorders are, treatment remains largely a "hit or miss" proposition.

The field of psychotherapy is undoubtedly going through a marked change. Many of the dogmatic principles in which we were academically trained are falling by the wayside as an emphasis on pragmatism emerges. The increasing interest in doing therapy that not only *works* but works as reliably as possible is rooted in a practical, outcome-oriented framework. There are many controversial aspects to promoting outcome-oriented, briefer approaches to therapy. For one, the area can become a therapeutic *Name That Tune* game where one therapist competes against another by challenging, "I can name that cure in three notes (sessions)."

I am actually quite conservative in my considerations of brief therapy, knowing that many therapies will inevitably be long and difficult.
However, I also know that many of the problems that we in this profession have treated as "long and difficult" are not. Rather, the approaches used have focused on nonsalient dimensions of the client's
experience, or have even unwittingly reinforced the most dysfunctional aspects of the client's problem. An obvious example is the therapist who offers depressed clients endless opportunities to describe
their emotional pain and terrible life histories. Therapy has traditionally emphasized verbal expression of one's feelings, and so this seems
a reasonable intervention. However, knowing what we now know
about depression, thanks to people such as Martin Seligman, Aaron
Beck, and Gerald Klerman, we understand that such a passive and
past-oriented approach delays or even prevents recovery.

Thus, the focus of the March 1988 conference became *"Brief Psychotherapies in the Treatment of Anxiety and Depression."* This title reflects a
commitment to expanding the range of interventions that can be applied for the benefit of the client, and emphasizes the reality that good
work can be done briefly. It seems imperative to continue to grow as
a field through challenges. I do not think therapy could have advanced
as much as it has in the past decade had it not been for the individual
thinkers who have had the audacity to ask "Why?" when they were
told how therapy "should" proceed. The faculty of this important conference obviously agree, because each presents a different way of conceptualizing and treating the clients for whom anxiety and depression
are problems.

There are at least two ways for the reader to respond to the valuable works contained in this volume. One is to take them at face value
and attempt to duplicate described approaches. However, this is less
preferable than the second way, which is to see them as examples of
ways to identify and challenge one's own assumptions about the nature of therapy. What should a therapist *always do?* What should a
therapist *never do?* When should one take a passive approach? A directive one? Growth comes from stepping outside one's usual frame of
reference. Thus, these contributions are offered with an implicit suggestion to evolve a willingness to explore and discover practical alternatives in the context of conducting psychotherapy.

As a field, we have not yet come to terms with the recognition that
whatever has the ability to be therapeutic has an equal ability to be
antitherapeutic. Doing therapy on the basis of either traditional formu-

las or nontraditional intuitions is a reliable way to avoid making real contact with the subjective world of the client. The common emphasis of the skilled practitioners who are making their work available here is on the individual client. This is a vital focus that I think will have significant impact on the growing awareness that therapy can be conceived and practiced as an outcome-oriented, directive process emphasizing a strong and positive alliance between therapist and client. I hope this volume motivates, enlightens, and challenges you, the reader.

Michael D. Yapko, Ph.D.
San Diego, California

Conference Overview and Objectives

The Fourth Annual San Diego Conference on Hypnotic and Strategic Interventions was a three-day conference featuring highly acclaimed presenters addressing the subject of brief, directive psychotherapies in treating anxiety and depression. The conference featured workshops, short courses, and original papers by acknowledged experts in the fields of strategic psychotherapy, communication, and clinical hypnosis.

The conference—which was organized and administered by the Milton H. Erickson Institute of San Diego—was of great interest to those practicing mental health professionals and students of human behavior especially involved in designing and delivering briefer and more efficient problem-solving therapeutic interventions.

The program featured 28 leading practitioners of hypnosis and strategic psychotherapy. Participants had the opportunity to (1) learn practical methods for use in their own clinical practices, (2) observe demonstrations of the presenter's clinical techniques, and (3) ask questions and discuss points of particular interest. The program's emphasis was on the treatment of anxiety and depressive disorders, which represent the most common disturbances clinicians are asked to treat. The main objective was to share active and innovative ways of intervening in such problems. With the exception of the keynote address, multiple events were scheduled at all times in order to provide a choice of activities for participants to attend.

The Institute continues to hold annual conferences. Write or call the Institute if you would like to be notified of future events.

The Milton H. Erickson Institute of San Diego
2525 Camino Del Rio South, Suite 265
San Diego, Ca. 92108
(619) 295-1010

Acknowledgments

Until you have experienced what it is like to organize and run a conference where 200 not-so-easily entertained professionals gather to focus on the less-than-uplifting subjects of depression and anxiety, you can only guess what goes into making it as successful as this conference was. It takes a great deal of organizing and reorganizing, and the efforts of many people. These people deserve to be acknowledged.

My associates at the Institute are the ones who helped define "grace under pressure." The individual who is most often thrown into the center of the conference storm is my administrative assistant *Linda Griebel*. Linda is a unique woman with a perspective on life that can only be called "different." She is a very skilled organizer, and the conference literally could not have been a success without her.

David L. Higgins was and continues to be quite exceptional in his ability to orchestrate that which needs to be done. His computer wizardry came in very handy on several hundred occasions. *Brita A. Martiny* is the strong, wonderful, silent type who knows what needs to be done and goes about doing it without much fanfare. Her many contributions did not go unnoticed, however, and are gratefully acknowledged.

My wife, *Diane Yapko*, is an exceptional woman who seems to suspend all else to make room in her busy schedule for our annual conferences. Her single-minded devotion to my efforts is invaluable to me, and is greatly appreciated. My good friend *John Koriath* lent his mind as well as his back to help make this conference happen, and as always, he did it with class.

Our volunteer staff helped out in so many ways that their contributions were indispensable. *Deanna Dahl, Marianne Friedman,* and *Karen Stolz* gave generously of their time and energy, for which I am grateful.

I would especially like to thank *Jeff Zeig* and *Ernie Rossi*. They have attended all four of our conferences and have generously given their time and energy, the value of which I cannot state in words. On both personal and professional levels, these men have contributed to me, and my appreciation is boundless.

Finally, I would like to thank *Natalie Gilman*, my editor, for doing such a thorough job on a difficult project. Coordinating multiple authors' responses and writing styles is no easy job even though she made it look that way.

M.D.Y.

About The Milton H. Erickson
Institute of San Diego

The Milton H. Erickson Institute of San Diego was established in 1983 by Michael D. Yapko, Ph.D., under the guidelines of its parent organization—The Milton H. Erickson Foundation in Phoenix, Ariz. The Institute was formed for the general purpose of promoting and advancing the important contributions of Milton H. Erickson, M.D. In that regard, the Institute performs the following functions:

- Conducting the annual meeting in San Diego each March, in which well-known experts present their most recent innovations in the practice of directive psychotherapy.
- Providing clinical training to qualified professionals (e.g., M.D., Ph.D., M.A., etc.) in the use of clinical hypnosis and directive psychotherapies. The Institute is authorized by the California Board of Behavioral Science Examiners to provide the required hypnosis education and supervision to California marriage, family, and child counselors who want to become certified to use hypnosis in their clinical practices. Training workshops are offered on a scheduled basis locally, and on an on-demand basis elsewhere, both nationally and internationally.
- Providing high-quality clinical services to the community of which we are a part.
- Stimulating research in hypnosis and brief psychotherapy.

Conference Faculty and Presentation Titles

KEYNOTE ADDRESS

Martin E. P. Seligman, Ph.D.   Philadelphia, Pa.
Optimism and Pessimism: Depression, Lyndon Baines Johnson, and the Harvard Class of 1939

INVITED WORKSHOPS

Raymond A. Fidaleo, M.D.   San Diego, Calif.
Cognitive Therapy of Depression

Stephen G. Gilligan, Ph.D.   Encinitas, Calif.
Reorganizing Attentional Strategies with Anxious and Depressed Clients

John J. Koriath, Ph.D.   Phoenix, Ariz.
Michael D. Yapko, Ph.D.   San Diego, Calif.
The Up Side of Being Down

Joyce C. Mills, Ph.D.   Los Angeles, Calif.
No More Monsters and Meanies: Multisensory Metaphors for Helping Children with Fears and Depression

Ernest L. Rossi, Ph.D.   Los Angeles, Calif.
The Psychobiology of Affective Disorders

Jeffrey K. Zeig, Ph.D.   Phoenix, Ariz.
Values in Ericksonian Approaches

INVITED SHORT COURSES

Norma Barretta, Ph.D.
Philip Barretta, M.A.   San Pedro, Calif.
Reframing Anxiety and Depression Through the Use of Submodalities

Christopher J. Beletsis, Ph.D.   La Jolla, Calif.
Trance-Forming Anxiety: Hypnotic and Strategic Approaches to Treatment

Paul Carter, Ph.D.   Encinitas, Calif.
Reframing Depression

David L. Higgins, M.A.   San Diego, Calif.
Anxiety as a Function of Perception: Treatment as a Perception of Function

Irving S. Katz, Ph.D.   Del Mar, Calif.
Critical Incident Process and Treating Depression

Brita A. Martiny, Ph.D.   San Diego, Calif.
The Use of Symbolic and Metaphorical Communication in the Treatment of Anxiety and Depression

ACCEPTED PAPERS

Russell Bourne, Jr., Ph.D.   Ashland, Va.
From Panic to Peace: Recognizing the Continua

Pamela Duffy-Szekely, M.A.   La Jolla, Calif.
Utilization of Creative Cognitive Strategies: Reframing the Pain Experience

Ronald M. Gabriel, M.D.   Regina, Sask., Canada
Childhood Depression

Brent B. Geary, Ph.D. (Cand.)   Phoenix, Ariz.
Integrating Ericksonian Strategies in Structured Groups for Depression

Paul Genova, M.D.   Portland, Me.
The Utilization Approach in Depression: Two Case Reports

Harriet E. Hollander, Ph.D.   Piscataway, N.J.
Hypnotherapeutic Approaches to the Treatment of Panic Disorder

Allan Jacobson, Ph.D.   Greenbrae, Calif.
Treatment of Depression: An Ericksonian-Strategic Approach

Sandi Janson-Selk, M.A.   San Diego, Calif.
Tapping Inner Resources in the Service of Positive Change

Lynn E. Seiser, M.A.
Karen Cauffman, M.A.   Long Beach, Calif.
   Treatment of Anxiety and Depression in Child Abuse Victims

Robert Schwarz, Ph.D.   Philadelphia, Pa.
The Treatment of Anxiety and Depression in Pain States

Christie Turner, L.C.S.W.   San Diego, Calif.
   Depression and Dysfunctional Families

John L. Walter, M.S.W.   Chicago, Ill.
Jane E. Peller, M.S.W.
   When Doesn't the Problem Happen?

MODERATORS

David L. Higgins, M.A.	San Diego, Calif.
Brita A. Martiny, Ph.D.	San Diego, Calif.
Hugh Pates, Ph.D.	San Diego, Calif.
Marian J. Richetta, M.A.	San Diego, Calif.

Brief Therapy Approaches to Treating Anxiety and Depression

SECTION ONE

Keynote Address

Chapter 1

Explanatory Style: Predicting Depression, Achievement, and Health

Martin E. P. Seligman

Martin E. P. Seligman, Ph.D., is a Professor of Psychology at the University of Pennsylvania. As the originator of the "Learned Helplessness" model of depression, he remains one of the most knowledgeable and generative researchers and theorists in the field of psychology.

Michael D. Yapko: Martin Seligman is a name that I am sure virtually all of you recognize. I do not think you can take even an introductory level psychology class without being exposed to Dr. Seligman's theories and the research that he has done for over twenty years now. He has been so influential in shaping perspectives about the nature of depression that you really cannot read about the subject without his name coming up repeatedly. Dr. Seligman received his Ph.D. from the University of Pennsylvania in 1967 and he has been on its faculty in the psychology department since 1972. When we started talking about putting together this book, Dr. Seligman sent me his vita thick with the list of his publications, which are generally related to his "Learned Helplessness" model of depression. Over the course of the last few years, he has been revising the Learned Helplessness model. The area of interest that he has recently developed is one he calls "attributional style." It is rooted in the recognition that reality is ambiguous. How we interpret the world is not a reflection of the way the world really is. Life is an ambiguous stimulus, it's an "experiential Rorschach," and basically

5

what we do is project onto it our understanding of things. The relevant question is, "How do these understandings that we develop either help or hurt us?" Dr. Seligman calls this "explanatory style" or "attributional style," and this is the topic he will be addressing.

Martin E. P. Seligman: I want to start out with a projective test. I want you all to take a projective test right now, but you don't have to tell me the answer to it. It's an unusual projective test—it's one none of you has ever taken before. As Michael was introducing me, what was the word in you heart about what I was going to say and what it would do for you? Was it "no," or was it "yes?"

I want to suggest to you that it's a meaningful question, but that we don't often frame our interactions with people in this way, believing that we carry around a word in our heart. When a patient walks through your door for the first time, there is a word in his or her heart. Is it "no?" Is it "yes?" Can you detect it? Can you measure it? Can you change it? When you received your high school diploma and you walked up to the podium, what was the word in your heart when the principal or the guest speaker shook your hand? Was it "no," or was it "yes?" Well, that's what I'm going to be talking to you about today. I'm going to suggest to you that there really is such a thing. It's a lifelong habit, it's measurable, well quantifiable and there is a science of the word of the heart. I'm also going to suggest to you that it can be changed, although not easily.

What are the long-term consequences of the word in your heart being "no?" Conversely, what are the long-term consequences of the word in your heart being "yes?" There are three arenas in which I'm going to talk about the consequences. I'm first going to talk about *depression.*

I'm going to suggest to you that people who are pessimists, believe projectively that when a bad event occurs, "It's me. It's going to last forever. It's going to undermine everything I do," aka internal, stable, and global. If you are one of those people, if the word in your heart in that sense is "no," then you may be okay now, but your risk for depression is much greater than the person sitting next to you. So, first I'm going to look at the effect of pessimism on depression.

Then I'm going to ask the parallel question for *achievement.* I'm going to ask if you believe, "It's me. It's going to last forever. It's going to undermine everything I do," then what happens to your achievement over a lifetime? What happens to your high school grades and to your college grades, to your productivity? Then I'm going to ask some far-out kinds of achievement questions about Presidents of the United States and the like.

Then, finally, I'm going to ask some questions about *ill health*. Do pessimists get sick more easily? Do their immune systems function more poorly? Do they die younger? These are the things about which I'll be talking. Last, I'm going to tell a joke.

Let me tell you how I got interested in the question of optimism, pessimism, and its effects on depression, achievement, and health.

About twenty-five years ago, I became interested in the phenomenon which has come to be called "Learned Helplessness." I worked for about ten years with animals and humans on what the consequences were of receiving uncontrollable events in the laboratory (Maier & Seligman, 1978) such as: inescapable shock, inescapable noise, unsolvable cognitive problems, and Bill Cosby records that went on and off regardless of what you did. We found over the years, both in animals and humans, that when you gave these inescapable events to them, there were a set of symptoms that occurred that looked very much like the symptoms of depressed patients who walked into my office with. Such uncontrollable events produced passivity, cognitive retardation, a lowering of self-esteem, sadness, anxiety and hostility, diminished aggression, diminished appetite, and a variety of brain changes that look very similar to those brain changes that are evident in naturally occurring depression. We're not going to talk about physiology, but I mention it because I could never get all the people and animals to do what I wanted them to do.

There was always about one out of ten, people and animals, who walked into the laboratory, and became helpless before I even gave them inescapable noise, just by being told "I'd like you to be in a laboratory experiment." There were other people, one out of three on average, who, no matter what I did to them, did not become helpless. So, what I started to worry about over ten years ago was the question, "What does a person bring to, or project onto, a situation that either makes him or her invulnerable to helplessness or supervulnerable to helplessness?" I'm going to suggest that the way that people habitually think about tragedy in their lives is an important determinant of who collapses immediately when in the face of inescapable events, versus those who bounce back instantly.

Let's begin with the theory of chronic habits of construing causality (Abramson, Seligman, & Teasdale, 1978). When we began to worry about the systematic ways in which we think about good events and bad events, it occurred to us that there were three dimensions that made a difference for depression. The first is one you all know about; it's the traditional "internal–external" dimension. It's the question, "If a bad event strikes, did I cause it, or was it caused by other people or circumstances?" So, if you're rejected by someone you love, you might say, "I'm unlovable, I'm worthless." That's an internal event. On the other hand, you might say, "He's a bastard!" That's an external event—it's he who is doing it. That's the most obvious dimension and by far the least important. The only reason it's even in the theory is that it has to do with self-esteem. The theory says that if you face a major bad event and you habitually believe that you cause bad events, then you're going to show low self-esteem, worthlessness, and self-blame. If, on the other hand, you habitually blame bad events on others, then you're going to show the constellation of depression and helplessness, but you're going to show it without the self-blame, low self-worth, or low self-esteem.

You can pretty much ignore this dimension from now on—I'll be considering it again, but the important dimension is "unstable-stable." I want you to think about the question of hopelessness for a moment, because what you're really reading about is a "Hopelessness Theory" for depression. What do we mean when we say someone is hopeless? When we take our present misery, i.e., our present bad situation , and we project it endlessly into the future, that's half of hopelessness. That's the unstable-stable dimension. The other half of hopelessness is the "specific-global" dimension. If, for example, I believe that the hostility of an audience to which I am giving a talk is not only going to occur with every audience I face over the next ten years (that would be stable), but is also going to face me everytime I interact with people, whether it be in the form of a speech, a cocktail party, or a date, then that's global. I suggest to you that what *hopelessness* is, is taking your present helplessness, and *projecting it far into the future*, projecting it across *all endeavors of your life*.

Unstable-stable addresses the question, "Is the cause of this present bad event something that is transient?" If you fail an examination, for example, you might say, "I was tired. I was hung over." Those are causes that go away in time. Some people have the habit of making those kinds of causal statements. On the other hand, you might fail and say, "I'm stupid." "I have a hang over" and "I'm stupid" are both internal. But, stupidity abides. It's the kind of cause that's going to hurt you far into the future, on later examinations. That's the reason that this dimension is important.

If, for example, you have a patient who's a tax accountant, and she's been fired from her job, it's important to know whether or not she's going to start looking for another job soon or whether she's apt to be knocked out for a long time. The unstable-stable dimension tells you that. If she chronically believes that bad events are stable, then she's not going to be resilient from depression. If, on the other hand, she believes they're unstable, then she's going to bounce back more quickly.

Now, let's move to "specific-global." That involves the question, "Is it going to hurt me just in this one situation? Or, is this something that will undermine all my endeavors?" For example, if you take an examination and you fail it you might say, "I'm stupid," which is global.

You might say, "I'm stupid at math," which is specific because it's just about that one kind of subject matter. If you're rejected by a woman you love, you might say, "She's a bitch," which is just about her. Or, you might say, "Women are impossible!" which is about women in general. Now, take your accountant. You want to know where her depressive symptoms are going to show up. Is she going to be unable to look for a new job, and not do her own income tax? Or, will she also lose her sense of humor, lose her libido, and not go to social gatherings anymore? The theory says that to the extent that she makes habitually specific explanations to that event, she'll just not do her income tax or look for another job. To the extent that she believes that bad events are caused by global factors, depressive symptoms are going to occur across the board.

That's the theory, basically. If you put these three dimensions together and ask yourself, "What is the worst way of walking around the world as far as predicting depression goes?", it is people who say, chronically, "It's me. It's going to last forever. It's going to undermine everything I do." Such people should, in this theory, be at highest risk for depression when they come across bad events.

So, the theory we're going to look at is a simple one. It says that if you can identify these people, and then look at depression, achievement, and ill health, you can predict that these are the people who are most at risk for depression, most at risk for not living up to their potential, and most at risk for getting physically ill. Conversely, people who say, "You did it to me. It's going to go away quickly," and "It's just this one thing," should be the people most resistant to depression, most likely to live up to their potential in achievement, and most likely to be physically healthy.

Well, given that theory, we now ask, "How do you *measure* the word in the heart? Is there a way you can quantify attributional or explanatory style?" So, we did what all of you would do, we devised a questionnaire. It's called the Attributional Style Questionnaire (ASQ) (Peterson, Semmel, von Baeyer, & Seligman, 1982). It's a 20-minute questionnaire. On this questionnaire, there are 12 different scenarios. This is a projective test in the classic sense of projective; it gives you 12 hypothetical situations that might have happened to you, and you're asked, "If this did happen to you, what would the most likely cause of it be?" Six of the scenarios are good ones, and six of them are bad. I will consider just the bad ones here.

One of the questions is, "You've been looking for a job quite unsuccessfully for some time. Think for a moment. If that happened to you, what would the most likely cause be?" Well, you might write down, "There are too many psychologists in California." Then you're asked to answer questions about the internal, stable, and global dimensions of the cause you gave. So, the first question is, "Is the cause of your unsuccessful job search due to something about other people or circumstances," (which is a 1 on the scale), "or totally due to you" (which is a 7)? Well, "too many psychologists in California" is attributing it to other people or circumstances. But, *you* chose to be a psychologist, so you might give that a 1, 2, or 3. Then you're asked, "In the future, when looking for a job, will this cause again be present?" Is this glut of psychologists something that's going to continue far into the future, or is it going to change? "Well, economic trends and fashions in Ph.D.'s come and go. So, on a scale from "will never again be present" to "will always be present," you're probably going to give that a 4.

Finally, the global-specific dimension. "Is the cause of too many psychologists in California something that just influences looking for a job, or does it also influence other areas in your life?" It is rated from, "It influences only this particular situation" to, "It influences all situations in my life." Well, "too many psychologists in California" probably just affects your professional life and doesn't affect your love life or athletic life. So, you'd probably give that a 1, 2, or 3. What you then do with the questionnaire is take all the bad items, average them together, and you get a profile. I won't bore you with the psychometrics, but they're decent, and as you'll see, the scale seems to do what it is supposed to do.

About seven years ago, after we had done 50 studies on the questionnaire, it occurred to us that there are quite a number of people whose behavior, achievement, depression, and whose longevity we wanted to predict, who won't answer questionnaires. Presidents of the United States, athletic celebrities, and the dead, are all examples of people who won't do that. No, *that's* not the joke! So, we asked the question, "Could you validly measure the word in the heart by reading something that someone wrote or listening to something that someone said?" This is what I spend most of my time doing these days—looking at archival documents: therapy transcripts, diaries, presidential press conferences, nomination speeches and the like, and asking, "Can you quantify the optimism and pessimism?"

Let me show you how we do this. Imagine that you're an undergraduate rater and you're reading through a therapy transcript. Your job is to find a bad event and then find causal statements in which the person tells you what caused the bad event. So, let's consider part of a therapy transcript from a depressed patient in Minnesota undergoing cognitive therapy. She says, "About four months ago, he called me on the telephone from where he's been working. He told me our relationship was over." Underline the bad event ". . . our relationship is over."

Now you scan the transcript for the cause. What does she think is the cause? "I felt devastated." No, that's a consequence. "I tried to argue, but what could I say? I still flipped out." Now, she gives you the cause: "I guess I'm just no good at relationships. I've never been able to keep a man interested in me." So, what you do is you take that event and the cause, and you put it on an index card and you give it to a panel of raters. The panel of raters is blind to who this is, what else this person has said, and even to what study it's from. They just have a bulk pack, basically, in which therapy statements, presidential statements, and statements from cancer patients are all shuffled together. Here's what the judges do. It's the judges' job to treat the item on the index card as if it were a questionnaire item and to rate it on the three dimensions on the 1 to 7 scale.

First they have to rate whether it was a good or bad event. "Our relationship is over" is, to this woman, clearly a bad event. Then she says, "I'm just no good at relationships, I've never been able to keep a man interested in me." You have four raters. To what extent is that attribution external—i.e., not due to the person? Or, to what extent is that internal? She says, "*I'm* just no good at relationships." The judges give it 6s and 7s.

Then, on the next dimension, which is unstable-stable, she says, "I've never been able to keep a man interested in me." She uses the word "never." The judges have to rate for stability. Is this cause something that goes away in time? Or, is it something that's going to go on far into the future? Well, the tense of the verb and the word "never" tells us it's stable. She believes it's going to last for a long time, so all judges give that 7s.

Finally, is "not being able to keep a man interested in me, not being good in relationships," something that hurts you just with men, or is it something that hurts you across all domains of your life? The judges give that 1s, 2s, and 3s. So, what you do then is take all the causal statements, put them together, and form a profile for the person's explanatory style. It turns out that the profile coincides pretty well with what a person would have done on the questionnaire. Thus, from now on, I will refer to the results from natural speech—we call this "CAVE" (Content Analysis of Verbatim Explanations) (Peterson, Luborsky, & Seligman, 1983)—and to the results of the Attributional Style Questionnaire interchangeably. Those are the two ways of identifying attributional style.

Now, I want to offer a brief discussion of *depression*. The proposition we'll be looking at is that people who chronically believe that bad events are internal, stable and global—even if they're not depressed now—when they come across bad events, are at significant risk for becoming depressed. That is, an internal, stable, and global attributional style is a risk factor for depression in exactly the same way smoking cigarettes is a risk factor for lung cancer. To begin to address this question, we gave the questionnaire to a bunch of students, looked at their depressive symptoms, and asked the question, "Are people who have depressive symptoms also pessimistic on the explanatory style questionnaire?" The study shows that depressed students are more likely to believe, "It's me, it's going to last forever, and it's going to undermine everything I do," than are non-depressed students. There are a number of studies that bear this out.

After a little while, we began to ask the question, "Is this also true of severely depressed patients (i.e., the suicidal, unipolar depressed patients who show you the same internal-stable-global attributional style profiles)?" There are about 30 studies on patients now. The latest one has 45 unipolar depressed patients, ten manic-depressives during the depressed phase, and a large number of controls. What it tells you is that both unipolar depressed and bipolar depressed patients are significantly more pessimistic than are controls. In addition, what the high correlation tells you is that the more depressed they are, the more pessimistic they are. There's one other thing worth mentioning about this kind of data: If you want to predict statistically the length of the episode of depression from when a patient walks into your office, you look at the stable dimension. How stable bad events are generally in her life is correlated about 0.65 with length of episode. So, as the theory suggests, the length of the depressive episode is well predicted by the stability dimension.

One of my main interests these days is prepubescent children (Nolen-Hoeksema, Girgus, & Seligman, 1986). There is an Attributional Style Questionnaire for children. It's a forced choice questionnaire in which, if they did well on a test, they're asked, "Is the cause because you're smart, or because you're smart at math?" They get to pick a response. Now, this is a group of children who self-report depressive symptoms from a childhood depression inventory. They take the childhood scale, and, indeed, depressed children are more internal, stable, and global than are non-depressed children.

About two years ago, someone undertook a meta-analysis of 104 studies involving 15,000 subjects of the question of what the relationship of attributional style is to depression (Sweeney, Anderson, & Bailey, 1986). It was found that the style, "It's me, it's going to last forever, and it's going to undermine everything I do," is very reliably correlated in a moderate-sized effect across these large numbers of studies. One of the things calculated is the "File Drawer Statistic." That's a cute statistic that tells you how many negative results, i.e., research papers, would have to be sitting unpublished in peoples' file drawers in order to overturn the results. It would have to be about 10,000 or so! So, that suggests that this is indeed a fact—that when you're depressed, you're more internal, stable, and global about bad events.

That really is not a very exciting fact, if you think about it for a moment. The interesting hypothesis is that having this way of looking at bad events, "It's me, it's going to last forever, and it's going to undermine everything I do," *precedes* and *puts you at risk for* depression. But, these are all correlational studies that merely show you that when you're depressed, you're also pessimistic. Now, there are a lot of possibilities other than the risk factor possibilities compatible with these data. One is that you're optimistic, you suddenly become depressed, and depression makes you a pessimist. So here, causation goes the other way. Another possibility is that there may be some third variable, like the way you handle anger, or your catecholamine level that makes you *both* pessimistic and depressed. The worst possibility of all is that it's just a tautology.

Part of the way we diagnose whether or not people are depressed is that they tell us, "It's me, it's going to last forever, and it's going to undermine everything I do." In the jargon, it's just "common method variance." All the rest of the studies I'm going to talk about are studies that separate out the interesting causal possibility, i.e., the risk factor possibility, from all the other uninteresting possibilities. They're all studies of the form in which you first measure a person's optimism or pessimism, and you measure their depression. Then you try to predict what's going to happen to them in the future from the earlier style. Now, the ideal way of doing such a study is called an experiment of nature. Get a town on the gulf coast of Mississippi, measure everyone's explanatory style and measure everyone's depression, and then wait until the hurricane hits. Then, see if you can predict who's going to lie there in the mud versus who is going to get up and rebuild the town. Now, there are ethical and funding problems to studies of this sort.

I was stymied as to how you would actually test this theory until one of my undergraduate students said, "Gee, Dr. Seligman, there are natural disasters that hit your classes twice a year!" Those are my midterm and final examinations. I'm the last person in my university to curve at "C." My examinations are very hard, and it seemed that this was a good way in which to test the theory. In the first natural disaster experiment, when people came to my class in September, they filled out depression inventories and Attributional

Style Questionnaires (Metalsky, Abramson, Seligman, Semmel, & Peterson, 1982). Six weeks later in October, as the midterm approached, we asked them, "What would count for you as a failure on the midterm?" Students said "B+," on the average. That was very good, because what it meant was that almost everyone was going to be a subject in this experiment! A week later, they get their midterm, and they moan and groan. A week after that, they get their midterm back with their grade, along with the Beck Depression Inventory to fill out. Then, six weeks later, they get all this stuff again. Here, we're looking at large changes in depression. We're asking the question, "Who becomes clinically depressed?" following failure on a midterm in their own eyes.

The probability of showing strong changes in depression, given that you fail the midterm in your own eyes, is about 30 percent. What's the probability of becoming depressed, given that you're a pessimist in September? That probability is also about 0.3. Now, the crucial probability is the probability of becoming depressed given that you *both* failed the midterm in your own eyes, and you were a pessimist to begin with. That's about 0.7. So, that tells you that statistically you can predict in advance who is most vulnerable to developing depressive symptoms when they fail in the classroom— it's the pessimists.

Let's go to another experiment of nature. Several of us are doing a five-year longitudinal study of four hundred children that was started when they were in the third grade at age eight (Nolen-Hoeksema et al., 1986). There are 700 parents involved as well. Every six months the children get the Kiddie Attributional Style Questionnaire, depression ratings, popularity ratings, and life event ratings. Their parents do similar ratings. What we're trying to do here is predict which children will become depressed over the course of the next five years, and which children will do poorly in school, at least more poorly than they should. These are results from the first few waves of the study. If you're a third grader and you come into school in September and you're not depressed, and you're an optimist, the chances are you're going to remain non-depressed. If you come into school in September and you're a pessimist and you're not depressed, the chances are that you're going to get depressed. If you're an optimist and you come in depressed, the chances are you're going to get better. If you're a pessimist and you come in depressed, the chances are you're not going to recover.

That's what that data tells you statistically. Next is a similar study with college students in which you measure depression and explanatory style over time. Here, you measure another variable which will interest those of you who are interested in anxiety. The additional variable here is a variable called "rumination" (Zullow, Oettingen, Peterson, & Seligman, 1988). Rumination is the tendency to wring your hands, talk to yourself, and worry about events as opposed to making action-oriented statements. When I talk about Presidential elections later, I'll talk a little bit more about this. The theory underlying this is that if you're a pessimist but you're not the kind of person who talks to yourself a lot, then the pessimism is not going to have any significant effect, because what mediates this is actually what you say to yourself. So, here you're looking at people who are both pessimists and ruminators. As with the children, you can predict who is going to become depressed. It's the pessimists who tend to become depressed over time. In addition, the worst you can be is *both* a pessimist and a ruminator. People who are both pessimists and ruminators are people who become depressed and stay depressed. If you're depressed and you're a pessimist, but you're not a ruminator, you tend to get better.

What is the relationship between getting better and changing from being a pessimist to an optimist? What is the relationship between relief from depression and change of attributional style? Well, if you're getting tricylic therapy, you may get better, but your attributional style doesn't change for the better. As a matter of fact, it changes negatively. You don't become more of an optimist under tricyclic therapy even though you get better.

Those people who get both cognitive therapy and tricylics get better at about the same rate. But, there's a relationship—a correlation of 0.25—between how much better they get and how much more optimistic they become. If you have cognitive therapy alone, the correlation between how much better you get and how much your attributional style changes is 0.44. So, there are different modalities that work reliably in depression, but drug therapy works in a different way than does cognitive therapy. Cognitive therapy seems to change the way you think about the causes of events, and the more it changes, the better you get. Tricyclic therapy probably works in another way: My suggestion to you is that it works by energizing people and getting them engaged with their environment.

The final thing to know about these studies may be useful to you therapeutically. If you look at patients at the end of therapy and consider those peoples' explanatory style who are no longer depressed, and you ask the question "Who relapses?" (Evans et al., submitted for publication), it turns out it's the people whose explanatory style has not changed. If they remain pessimists, then they are most at risk statistically for relapse. So, that suggests to me, even after depressive symptoms disappear, to keep therapy going until explanatory style has also reached a satisfactory level of change.

Okay, that's what I wanted to say about depression. Let me summarize my points. For depression, I've argued that pessimists are more at risk for depression when bad events strike, and that by changing explanatory style from an internal, stable, and global one to the reverse, as is done in cognitive therapy, you may be doing effective therapy for depression and effective prevention of relapse. Now, I want to ask the same question we asked before, except about *achievement* (Seligman, Kamen, & Nolen-Hoeksema, 1988). The prediction here is that when people who say, "It's me, it's going to last forever, it's going to undermine everything I do" come across bad events, they will do less in their work life than people with the opposite explanatory style. The place we started to ask this question was with our third grade children. We looked at classroom performance and at California Achievement Tests. We found that children who are pessimists do more poorly on the California Achievement Test and show more helplessness in the classroom as blindly rated by the teacher. So, this suggests that if you have a child who is doing badly at school, it may not be because the child is stupid, rather it may be because the child is depressive or predepressive. That's something that's going to hurt academic performance.

We then asked the same question for college students. I was talking to the Dean of Admissions at Penn about five years ago, and he said, "Marty, we make real mistakes in our student admissions. Some students have terrific college board scores and grades, but then they do very badly when they get to college. Other people, and there are more of these, are predicted to be mediocre, and they become stars. Can you help us refine our predictions?" To put this more systematically, when you apply to the University of Pennsylvania, the admissions committee actually generates a regression equation. They take your college boards, your high school rank in class, and your achievement tests. Then they give you a number like 3.3, and that predicts what your grades are supposed to be in the Freshman year. So, we randomly gave the Attributional Style Questionnaire to one third of the incoming class that year when they arrived, and then we followed them for the first semester. We asked them what their grades looked like relative to the admission committee's predictions. There were 83 students who did one standard deviation better than they were predicted to do. There were 17 students who did one standard deviation worse than they were predicted to in their college grades. Indeed, those who did better are significantly more optimistic before all this happens than are those who did worse. That tells you that holding constant high school grades and SAT's, that within the college domain optimists get higher grades than pessimists, at least statistically.

The next thing we did was to ask in real work, in real life, "Can you predict achievement from explanatory style?" What I wanted to use to test this was a job in which there's a lot of rejection, frustration, and failure. The theory says that it is in that kind of a job that optimism and pessimism are going to matter. I wasn't sure of what to do until one evening I got one of those calls you frequently get from life insurance salespersons. I hung up on him. As I was hanging up, I said, "That must be a very difficult job to have." You probably make twenty to thirty calls a day, and practically everyone you call hangs up on you! I wonder who could succeed at that? So, I talked to an acquaintance of mine who is the head of Metropolitan Life Insurance Company, and I asked him about this. He said "Marty, we have a terrible problem with this. The industry hires tens of thousands of new people a year. It costs $30,000.00 to train each person, and within four years 80 percent of them have quit, industry wide." It's an enormous financial waste, and if you also think about the human misery of being in a job you're not suited for in terms of personality, it's terrible. So, we have done a series of studies with them (Seligman & Schulman, 1986). In the initial study, we took the first hundred people who were hired in Pennsylvania in January, 1984. We gave them the Attributional Style Questionnaire and an industry personality profile test that matches your profile to that of successful life insurance salespersons. After they took both tests, we followed them for a year and then looked at who stayed and who quit. It turned out that half the people quit in the first year. The people who scored very well on the attributional style test quit at one third the rate of the pessimists. Within that study, it looked like the optimists both survived longer and sold about 35 percent more life insurance.

We then did this on a larger scale. We tested 15,000 applicants to Metropolitan Life. These people took both the Career Profile test and the Attributional Style test. Then we did two things with them. One thousand of them were hired in the usual way—that is, those are the people who passed the Career Profile test. We merely followed them for about two years to see how they did. In addition, Metropolitan Life formed a special force of 129 insurance salespeople who failed the industry test. No one will hire them, but those who are extremely optimistic scored well on our test. We now followed these people for a few years. The optimists in the regular force sell significantly more than the pessimists. Most interesting, the special force outsells everyone. The effects get larger over time. In the first year, there's a 10–20 percent difference, and in the second year there's a 50–80 percent difference. This suggests that within the real work place of challenging jobs, one's survival or well-being can be predicted not only by alleged talent, but by the word in the heart.

The next couple of things I'm going to tell you about are quite speculative, but they are timely. I'm going to ask about achievement, not of ordinary mortals like ourselves, but American presidents. Let me begin with the question of for whom we vote. Hofstadter (1963) proposed about twenty years ago that Americans are anti-intellectual in their voting preferences. In particular, they don't like candidates who doubt, who see both sides of an issue, and who are pessimistic. Can you predict who is going to win presidential elections by looking at attributional style and the factor of rumination?

In particular, what Harold Zullow, et al. (1988) did was the following: We took the last ten presidential elections, starting with Dewey and Truman. We wanted a standard speech to CAVE, so we took the two nomination acceptance speeches. Every time there was a causal statement, we put it on index cards and gave it to raters. Every sentence is rated for the presence of rumination versus action-orientation. This is done blindly. We then ask the questions, "Who won the election? Could you predict who won the election?" In nine of the last ten elections, the pessimistic ruminator loses. The one election that's not predicted was Nixon/Humphrey in 1968;

Humphrey is somewhat more optimistic than Nixon, but the Chicago riots occur at the Democratic convention. Humphrey starts off 17 percent behind in the polls and closes to within less than one percent. So, that election wasn't predicted, but nine out of ten were. Take the two candidates and look at the difference in their degree of pessimistic rumination. The larger the difference, the bigger the win. There is a hefty correlation, about 0.8, between how much more of a pessimistic ruminator you are than your opponent and how much you lose by. In the landslides, like Eisenhower versus Stevenson, it turns out Eisenhower is much more of an optimistic nonruminator than Stevenson. In the close elections, like Carter and Ford, there's a small difference and the victory is small. You might think the reason you're optimistic and nonruminating is that you're ahead in the polls at the time of the nomination and so you might think you're going to be the winner. If you partial out both incumbency and standing in the polls at the time of the speeches, the correlation between the pessimistic rumination differences and the amount you win by is 0.89. That tells you that within the last ten elections, since the advent of television at least, the amount of pessimism you convey to the voter in your nominating speech predicts pretty well how many votes you're going to get.

Now, even more speculatively, there are people whose fingers are on the button, and it would be very nice to be able to predict whether or not they are about to become bold and risky or they're about to become passive and helpless. There is a prediction in the theory that when the President of the United States is making pessimistic statements, he is not going to do much in the way of risky and bold things. But, if he's making very optimistic statements, then that's the time to watch out. What we are doing is the following: We take major events, things such as when the *New York Times* has a headline involving a Presidential decision. Then we go backward in time to a past press conference and we CAVE the press conference. We examine the relationship between earlier optimism and pessimism in press conferences and the subsequent presidential decision. We give it to political scientists who don't know what we're up to, and they rate how bold the Presidential decision was on a scale from one to ten from "not decisive at all" to "very bold, risky, and decisive."

I'll just run you through one example, and that's Lyndon Johnson. This was the first study of this that we did. Peggy

Hermann, a Lyndon Johnson expert at Ohio State, picked out a bunch of press conferences from Lyndon Johnson's career. The first group of press conferences was from shortly after the Kennedy assasination. We took those press conferences and we gave them to our raters (the raters are blind, of course), and as it turns out Johnson's baseline was about average for an American man at that time. Six months later, as some of you will recall, it is alleged that North Vietnamese ships attacked American ships in the Gulf of Tonkin. Johnson uses this as a *causus belli* and greatly escalates the monetary and troop commitment to Vietnam. So, we CAVE the press conferences before the Gulf of Tonkin incident has occurred, and it turns out Johnson's style has gone down into the range we see with manic patients—i.e., wildly optimistic. He's not talking about the Gulf of Tonkin, of course, because that hasn't happened yet, but if you take his statements, they're down in the very optimistic range. The Gulf of Tonkin incident occurs a couple of weeks later, and then after it's over, Johnson goes back to his normal level. A year later, Westmoreland comes home and asks Congress to double the troop commitment from three hundred thousand to six hundred thousand men. There's a period of about two weeks where Johnson hems and haws, gives press conferences, but the public doesn't know what he's going to do; we CAVE those press conferences, and again Johnson is down in the manic range. He then doubles the troop commitment. Right after that decision, Johnson goes into the range you see in severely depressed patients. When we look at the Tet offensive and when Johnson gives up the Presidency, we find that he is in the depressive range. What this seems to say, at least for Lyndon Johnson, who is just one President at this point, is that the pessimism or optimism prior to press conferences is at least a *harbinger* of risks to come. And, indeed, it's beginning to look as if when you look at prior press conferences statistically, they do correlate with activity or passivity.

I'm now going to turn to the final question, which is, "Can future *health* be predicted statistically by pessimism?"

We didn't choose this question at random—the reason that we got interested in health is because I've been involved in a series of studies in which we looked at the immune system consequences of animals getting inescapable shock. It turns out if you're a rat who is made helpless by inescapable shock, you grow tumors at twice the normal rate, you rail to reject implanted tumors, your t-lymphocytes don't proliferate, and your natural killer cells don't kill (Visintainer, Volpicelli, & Seligman, 1982). The effect of helplessness in animals seems to be to weaken the immune system and make animals more susceptible to disease. In addition, if you've followed what has been said, the main effect of helplessness is to produce passivity. So, you might think that someone who is a pessimist, i.e., someone who is more susceptible to helplessness would be less apt to follow medical regimes; if you believe that nothing matters, then why should you give up smoking or seek out social support? If you're passive, you get less social support. The less social support, the more illness. If you're helpless and pessimistic, it turns out bad events roll over you more than if you're optimistic and try to do things to get out of them and avoid them. The more bad life events you have, it turns out statistically, the worse your health. So, we asked the question, "Could you predict from optimism early in life what physical health would be like later?"

Chris Peterson and colleagues (1988) did the first study of this. He took about 130 Virginia Tech undergraduates and he gave them the Attributional Style Questionnaire. He measured for one month how much infectious illness they had and how many times they visited the doctor, and then he followed them for a year. It turns out that the pessimists had about twice as many doctors' visits in the next year as the optimists, and about twice as many infectious illnesses. If you partial out prior infectious illnesses and prior doctors' visits, it turns out the same relationship pertains. We are now working on more serious illnesses. Sandy Levy looked, in 1980 and 1981, at 34 women who entered the National Cancer Institute with their second bout of breast cancer. As you know, after you've had breast cancer twice, your chances of living long afterwards are not very great. These women are interviewed, we CAVE the interviews for optimism and pessimism, and we ask "Can you predict how long the women are going to live?" It turns out by now that 30 of the 34 women are dead. The women who are pessimistic tend to die more rapidly. In addition, we know the physical situation here; that is, we know the number of sites that are cancerous, and we know the natural killer cell activity. Over and above the physical manifestation of cancer known at that time, we ask, "Can you predict how long they're going to live from a psychological variable?" And again, at a marginal level, the pessimists tend to die sooner over and above the amount of cancer and the amount of natural killer cell activity.

We then asked the question, "Is the immune system what's at issue here?" Kamen, Rodin, Dwyer, and Seligman (unpublished) conducted a longitudinal study of several hundred old people. These people are interviewed once every three months about their nutrition and their grandchildren, and about once a year blood is drawn and the immune system is examined. We examined the "helper–suppressor ratio," a measure of how well your t-lymphocytes are doing as a function of optimism or pessimism. We content analyze the interview before the blood draw for optimism or pessimism, and then we look to see how your t-lymphocytes do. It turns out that among the optimists, t-lymphocytes do a much better job than among the pessimists. We partial out both depression and health at this time, and there's still this effect of optimism on the immune system.

There are about 20 studies that have this basic correlational form in the literature and each indicates that depression or pessimism or helplessness is associated with poor immune function in human beings. If you think for a moment about those studies, they're all flawed in the following way: You don't know that the psychological variable, e.g., helplessness, depression, bereavement, pessimism, or whatever, is causal. Let's say your wife dies and you're bereaved, and your immune system goes down. Well, it could be that you sleep less, you don't take care of yourself, you smoke more. There are any number of third variables which could be producing the lowered immune system. As it turns out, the only way to test a direct psychological effect is to do an experiment with human beings. Leslie Kamen has just done the right experiment. She took groups of undergraduates and injected them under the skin with allergens—your routine allergy patch test. You put in yeast, mumps, and tetanus allergens, and then you wait for a couple days and see if the arm swells up. If the arm gets red and swells up, the test tells you that your immune system is functioning well. If it doesn't swell up, then it's not functioning very well. In addition, one of the things she did was to divide the subjects into thirds and give them either inescapable noise, escapable noise, or nothing. She made one third of them helpless, and to one third she gave mastery, and one third of them were given nothing. It turned out that the arms of the people who were made helpless didn't swell up. So this is the first demonstration experimentally that the psychological state and not any of these other third variables seems to be directly producing an immunological change.

Well, this brings us to the final question to ask: "Might it be the case that your optimism and pessimism as a young person predicts what your course of chronic illness is going to be like?" To ask this question, you first have to know whether attributional style, the word in your heart, is stable. If you want to predict whether optimism at age 25 predicts health at age 65, you have to ask, "Do you carry this around with you?" So, we did a 52-year longitudinal study of this variable (Burns & Seligman, unpublished), and the way we did it was simple. We advertised in old peoples' journals for people who kept diaries when they were teenagers. We got 30 people who kept diaries. We asked them to write essays about their grandchildren, their health, and their life today. We then blindly content analyzed both the diaries and the essays. Across over 50 years, there's a 0.54 correlation between pessimism in your early 20s and pessimism in your 70s. The women who, when they're 17 years old and the boys don't go out with them, say, "I'm unlovable" will 50 years later, when their grandchildren don't visit, also say, "I'm unlovable." This tells you that what you're dealing with here is a fairly stable trait.

It brings us to the final study, which is the attempt to predict health across the lifespan. In this study, we worked with George Vaillant (Peterson, Seligman, & Vaillant, in press), who's the custodian of the Grant study of the members of the Harvard classes of 1939 to 1944. Five percent of those classes were chosen for lifetime study on the basis of being in excellent physical health, getting good grades, and a few other criteria. So, these are supposed to be the best-functioning Harvard students. They've been followed now for over 40 years with no dropouts—they are very cooperative. For our purposes, what's important is that every five years they get a physical checkup and their health is quantified. In 1946, they come back from the war and they write about what they did during the war. We content analyze these essays from 1946, and in them the authors say things like, "The ship went down because the Admiral was so stupid." Everytime they say that, our undergraduates content analyze it, and then we ask the question, "Can you predict physical health for the next 40 years?" At age thirty and age forty, you can't predict anything from psychological variables about physical health. That's because physical health at age 25 basically predicts your health until you're 40. Starting at my age, 45, and continuing through age 60, the pessimists start to get sick. When middle-age occurs, the psychological differences rear their head. Those people who show themselves to have had a pessimistic explanatory style start to develop chronic illnesses earlier, and this continues through the end of middle-age. These men are now starting to die, so in a few years we'll be able to tell you something about mortality.

Let me summarize. I've suggested to you that the word in your heart, "no" or "yes," is a powerful determinant of depression, achievement, and health. Within the envelope of events that happen to prosperous Americans, to all of you, I think we roughly have about the same amount of tragedy in the course of our lives. People we love reject us, our stocks go down, we give bad speeches, we write bad books, our patients drop us, and the like. But, what I've said here suggests that it's not the number of bad things that occur to you, but instead what you project from yourself onto those bad events that has impact. Those of you who chronically believe that those bad events are your fault, that they are going to last forever, and will undermine everything you do, seem to be at greater risk for depression, poor achievement, and ill health. It might be the case that changing attributional style might produce less depression, more achievement, and better health.

Now, I promised I'd tell you a joke. A Texan is visiting Ireland, and he's driving around the back country. He comes to an Irish dirt farm and gets out of the car and starts talking with the Irish farmer. It turns out that the Texan is also a farmer back in Texas. The conversation rolls around to the question of the conditions of farming in Texas and in Ireland. The Irish farmer asks the Texan, "Back in Texas, how big is your land?" The Texan puffs up and says, "Well, I'll tell ya, if I take my car to one end of my land at dawn, and I wait for the sun to come up, when it comes up I start to drive, and I drive and I drive, and I drive all day long. Sometimes, but not always, by nightfall I can reach the other end of my land." The Irish farmer looks at his pocket handkerchief-sized plot of land and says, "You know, I once had a car like that!"

Now we have time for questions:

Q: Have there been studies of attributional style and its relationship to catecholamines and the vegetative symptoms of depression?

A: There are no studies that I know of that look at attributional style and catecholamines. There are plenty of helplessness studies in animals that look at it, but no one has done it in humans as far as I know. There are some studies of attributional style in vegetative symptoms of depression, and it turns out that the vegetative symptoms of depression are just as well predicted as the cognitive or behavioral symptoms of depression by pessimism. So, you might have thought, and in fact it was our hunch initially, that there might be a cognitive way to be depressed and a somatic way to be depressed and that pessimism would only predict cognitive depression, i.e., low self-esteem and thinking the future is bleak, but it wouldn't predict loss of appetite, sleep disturbance and the like. It turns out it's promiscuous in this way—it predicts both the somatic and the cognitive symptoms about equally. But I know of no one who has done the relevant biological studies.

Q: When you're dealing with a family, you might have a pessimistic and depressed child or patient and an optimistic spouse or mother. The optimistic spouse is very critical, good at problem-solving, generally upbeat, and the like, and he or she may actually aggravate the situation. How do you deal with this?

A: What I want to comment on about the question, other than its acuteness, is the value judgment that I put on optimism. I should not be mistaken for saying that I think optimism is a good thing across the board. What I've said is that if you're interested in curing depression, producing more achievement, and producing better health, then there is reason to think that you should be on the side of optimism. But, that's not all there is in life; life is buying and selling. Pessimism has some costs, and it probably has some benefits, but optimism has its costs as well. Just as one example, take the example given in the question, that it could be the optimist who makes the pessimist depressed. That's one possible cost.

Another possible cost has to do with reality and knowing what the truth is. There is mounting reason to believe that optimists, nondepressed people, systematically distort reality in a benign direction. I don't really have time to tell you about the massive amount of evidence about this. But to my dismay as a therapist, and I'll tell you why "dismay," there has been mounting evidence that nondepressed, optimistic people believe they have more control than they actually do (Alloy & Abramson, 1979). They believe that more good events happened to them than actually did, and that they had fewer bad events than they actually did. For example, 80 percent of American men believe they are in the upper half of social skills, meaning they believe they have more skill than they actually do. In contrast, depressed people are much more accurate transducers of reality. That suggests that one of the costs of optimism is that it moves you systematically away from knowing the truth. As a therapist, this disturbs me, because when I first started as a therapist, I used to believe that when I was dealing with a depressed patient, I was both the agent of happiness and the agent of reality. There's this dogma in therapy since Freud and the ego's "reality principle," that part of our job as therapists is to bring the patient closer to reality—that's what "good ego functioning" is supposed to be. But this data strongly suggests that when you bring depressed people closer to reality, you make them more depressed. If you want to get rid of the depression, what you have to do is nurture and support a set of benign and romantic illusions. So, there may be antagonism between being an agent of reality and doing therapy against depression. This suggests to me that if one cares about notions like wisdom, love, and friendship, as opposed to selling insurance, not being depressed, and your t-lymphocytes functioning well, that these may well be antagonistic. There is a cost of optimism; the kind of people we want to run our companies, and the kind of people who are going to live long, may not be the kind of people who have great wisdom or be the kind of people we want to be our partners in life.

Q: There are four points to my question. The first is a question of tautology. Is finding a relationship between optimism, depression, achievement, and health merely a tautology? Second, is there a relationship between American values and optimism? Third, can you speak to a more global question about cultural differences and their effects? Fourth, can you address the notion of religion, hope for the future, an afterlife, and its effect on depression?

A: Let me answer your questions one at a time. The simple one for me to handle is the questions of tautology. That was our worry at first, and that's why we design our studies in such a way that we *first* look at pessimism and optimism, partial out present depression, and then we try to predict future depression, partialling out present depression, future poor achievements, and future ill health. What you're predicting is from pessimists now who are among people who are nondepressed, as to who will become depressed. That's not a tautology, it is genuinely predicted.

As for your second question, "Is this peculiarly American?," let me strengthen this point. You didn't say this, but I'll caricature it, if I may. It could be said that the concern with personal control, helplessness, and optimism are very American creatures. What we have here when we find the relationship of variables like helplessness and pessimism to depression are not *general* human laws. Rather, it is what happens in a culture that is very achievement-oriented and which has both "Madison Avenue" and "The Puritan Ethic." If you look cross-culturally, for instance, at Buddhist cultures that don't value achievement and optimism in the same way that Americans do, you might see a very different set of consequences. I think there's a lot to this, but I would add one serious qualifier to it; I spent a lot of my life looking back and forth between animals and humans, and what the consequences of helplessness and the like are in both. It turns out that our animal kin are relevant here, because if you give them inescapable events, i.e., you make them helpless, you produce the same effects, e.g., depressive t-lymphocyte consequences, as you do with humans. That suggests to me that when you see something from American middle-class people that is also seen in animals, you may be dealing with a more general principle. When you see cultures that don't show you depression when they become helpless and pessimistic, it may have more to do with the consequences of three or four thousand years in which two out of three of their children died before the age of five, than with the consequences of "Madison Avenue" and "The Puritan Ethic." Optimism may have been beaten out of them. I want to suggest that there might be some universality among humans about the value of not being helpless, and that helplessness might be a bad thing across the board.

Now, the question of cultural differences actually interests me greatly; it's something I work on actively. We became interested in the question of whether or not two cultures could be characterized in the way that we characterize individuals and whether or not that characterization might be meaningfully related to depression. As you do cross-cultural studies, for example, if you compare optimism of Bulgarians to Navajos, and you find out that Bulgarians are less pessimistic than Navajos, that's basically uninterpretable because there are so many variables. You just don't know what it means. Also, the manifestations of depression in Bulgarians and Navajos are very different.

So, we tried to do a study in which we matched two cultures for as many third variables as possible and we chose East and West Berlin, because East and West Berlin are in the same place, they have the same weather, and they speak the same language. They differ *only* in the political system since 1945 and its consequences. The first thing we wanted to do was measure both depression and optimism in East and West Berlin. Well, the way you want to do that, of course, is to go into East Berlin and hand out Attributional Style Questionnaires, and of course you can't do that! So, what Gabriele Oettingen (Oettingen, Seligman, & Morawska, 1988) did was to take the entire reportage of the East Berlin and West Berlin newspapers for the 1984 Sarajevo Winter Olympics. There are about one thousand causal statements in there, and she basically content analyzed them for attributional style. You may recall that the East German team in the 1984 Olympics was the best or the second best team, depending on how you count. The East German team won 26 medals, and the West German team won four medals. So, on these grounds, we thought the East Germans would turn out to be more optimistic. In addition, we're content analyzing state-run newspapers, and we're assuming that they have official cheerleading functions. As it turns out, the East Berlin reportage is much more pessimistic than the West Berlin reportage. Oettingen then asked the depression question, and to do that, she also had to be quite inventive. She went to 31 bars matching them across the Wall from each other. These are bars where workmen go to drink beer after a day of work in heavy industry. She sat in the corner and measured the number of smiles, the number of laughs, the number of "illustrators," (i.e., nondepressives who gesture a lot as with big arm movements) versus "adaptors," which are associated with depression. She found much more depression in East than West Berlin. Within the example of East versus West Berlin, indeed it looks like there's much more optimism in West Berlin and it also looks like there's less depression. I bring this up as a methodological answer to your question. I'd very much like to know the answer to cross-cultural questions about optimism and depression and their consequences, and until Oettingen did this work, I didn't even know how to go about it. Now I think we can ask across culture and across time, are there ages of despair? Are there ages of hope? Are there cultures of despair? Are there cultures of hope?

Q: What maintains optimism and pessimism? Where does it come from, and what leverage does the therapist have?

A: There's no more important question than that one. Let me say something about where I think it comes from, and just a tiny bit about how it can be changed. I have three very superficial things to say about where it comes from, and then one thing to say that isn't superficial.

Just to say two words about where it comes from, those two words are "your mother." If you look at parent versus child attributional style, there's a correlation between mothers' attributional style and children's of either sex (Nolen-Hoeksema et al., 1986). It looks as though you sit around listening to your primary caretaker talk and you get some of your attributional style that way. Secondly, there's evidence that as you listen to your teachers when they criticize you, you start to internalize [the kinds of criticisms they make of you.] Third, there is some evidence that the reality of the first bad event that hits you may form the "cookie cutter" that shapes your attributional style on later bad events.

Now, I think those are really shallow answers to deep questions. The reason I think that is because when I look at my own optimism and pessimism, and the pessimism of patients and people I love, there is another aspect which is not captured. It looks to me like attributional style is our theory of the world and our theory of our place in the world, and it's not altered very easily at all. If you think about your political theory for a moment, your liberalism or your conservativism, it's remarkable to me how you can live through exactly the same events, like the Vietnam War, and take every major event as confirmation for either theory. If you bomb the North Vietnamese and the war doesn't end, the conservatives say, "That just shows that we didn't bomb them enough!" and the liberals say, "That shows you can't bomb a gallant people into submission." So, it's self-confirming. The major theories about our own lives have the same properties of self-confirmation. I believe attributional style is nothing less than a theory of yourself and your place in the world. It's not just a superficial variable. I don't know how our theories gel, but one place I think they gel is in important autobiographical incidents. Things happen at the right time. I'll just tell you one. I'll tell you a positive one, but each of you could probably imagine a negative one like it. There's a lovely essay by John McPhee about Thomas Hoving called "A Room Full of Hovings." Hoving was the curator of the Metropolitan Museum of Art, and it was at a very young age that he was chosen for this awesome position. As curator, you go around the world with lots of money and you separate fraudulent art from the real thing and then you invest the museum's money into it. He was chosen to do this in his late

20s, and it was a very surprising event for him. Hoving describes himself, up to age 20, as being timid, with no self-confidence. In fact, at age 20, he was a sophomore at Princeton who was flunking out, ectomorphic, pimply, and couldn't say two words without shutting up. He was about to drop out when he decided he'd have a last try, so he took a sculpture course and he went to his first precept. A precept at Princeton is when seven juniors and seniors sit around with the professors and talk for an hour. Hoving was the only sophomore in it. The professor brought in this chromium and steel object with arms, symmetrical, lovely, and shiny. He put it on a pedestal and asked the class to comment on its aesthetic merits. One of the seniors started off and said, "mellifluous fluidity"; another one said, "harmony of the spheres." It got around to Hoving, and he said, quaking, "This isn't art, it's too functional; it's too symmetrical, and it's too cold." And it turned out the object was an obstetrical speculum!

Hoving said, "After that, there was no stopping me!" Now, that's a critical incident in which confidence is gained. All of you, from your own and from your patients' experience, can probably name the reverse incidents. When sexual abuse happens to you as a child, for example, it colors forever your theory of the world. I think attributional styles evolve from the idiosyncratic life history of critical events, but I don't know how to study it.

As for change, there is mounting evidence that cognitive therapy works by changing attributional style. It does so reliably and stably—patients, after cognitive therapy, have their attributional style permanently altered.

REFERENCES

Abramson, L. Y., Seligman, M. E. P., & Teasdale, I. (1978). Learned helplessness in humans: Critique and reformulation. *Journal of Abnormal Psychology,* No. 1, *87,* 49–59.

Alloy, L. B., & Abramson, L. Y. (1979). Judgement of contingency in depressed and nondepressed students: Sadder but wiser? *Journal of Experimental Psychology: General, 108,* 441–485.

Burns, M., & Seligman, M. E. P. Explanatory style across the lifespan: Evidence for stability over 52 years. *Journal of Personality and Social Psychology,* 1989, 56.

DeRubeis, R. J., Hollon, S. D., Evans, M. D., Garvey, M. J., Grove, W. M., & Tuason, V. B. (1988). Active components and mediating mechanisms in cognitive therapy, pharmacotherapy, and combined cognitive-pharmacotherapy for depression: III. Processes of change in the CPT project. Manuscript submitted for publication.

Hofstadter, R. *Anti-intellectualism in American Life.* New York: Vintage Books, 1963.

Hollon, S. D., DeRubeis, R. J., Evans, M. D., Wiemer, M. J., Garvey, M. J., Grove, W. M., & Tuason, V. B. (1988). Cognitive therapy, pharmacotherapy and combined cognitive-pharmacotherapy in the treatment of depression: I. Differential outcome in the CPT project. Manuscript submitted for publication.

Kamen, L., Rodin, J., Dwyer, C., & Seligman, M. E. P. Pessimism and cell-mediated immunity. Unpublished manuscript, University of Pennsylvania.

Levy, S., Morrow, L., Bagley, C., & Lippman, M. Survival hazards analysis in first recurrent breast cancer patients: Seven-year follow-up. *Psychosomatic Medicine.* In press.

Maier, S. F., & Seligman, M. E. P. (1978). Learned helplessness: Theory and evidence. *Journal of Experimental Psychology: General, 105,* 3–46.

Metalsky, G. I., Abramson, L. Y., Seligman, M. E. P., Semmel, A., & Peterson, C. (1982). Attributional styles and life events in the classroom: Vulnerability and invulnerability to depressive mood reactions. *Journal of Personality and Social Psychology, 43,* 612–617.

Nolen-Hoeksema, S., Girgus, J., & Seligman, M. E. P. (1986). Learned helplessness in children: A longitudinal study of depression, achievement, and explanatory style. *Journal of Personality and Social Psychology, 51,* 435–442.

Oettingen, G., Seligman, M. E. P., & Morawska, E. T. (1988). Pessimism across cultures: Russian Judaism versus Orthodox Christianity and East versus West Berlin. Unpublished manuscript. University of Pennsylvania.

Peterson, C., Luborsky, L., & Seligman, M. E. P. (1983). Attributions and depressive mood shifts: A case study using the symptom-context method. *Journal of Abnormal Psychology, 92,* 96–103.

Peterson, C., Seligman, M. E. P., & Vaillant, G. (In press). Pessimistic explanatory style as a risk factor for physical illness: A thirty-five year longitudinal study. *Journal of Personality and Social Psychology.*

Peterson, C., Semmel, A., von Baeyer, C., Abramson L. T., Metalsky, G. I., & Seligman, M. E. P. (1982). The attributional style questionnaire. *Cognitive Therapy and Research, 6,* 287–300.

Seligman, M. E. P., Kamen, L., & Nolen-Hoeksema, S. (1988). Explanatory style across the life-span: Achievement and health. In E. M. Hetherington, R. M. Lerner, and M. Perlmutter (Eds.), *Child Development in Life-Span Perspective.* Hillsdale, N.J.: Erlbaum, 91–114.

Seligman, M. E. P., & Schulman, P. (1986). Explanatory style as a predictor of performance as a life insurance agent. *Journal of Personality and Social Psychology, 50,* 832–838.

Sweeney, P. D., Anderson, K., & Bailey, S. (1986). Attributional style in depression: A meta-analytic review. *Journal of Personality and Social Psychology, 1986, 50,* 974–991.

Visintainer, M. A., Volpicelli, J. R., & Seligman, M. E. P. (1982). Tumor rejection in rats after inescapable or escapable shock. *Science, 216,* 437–439.

Zullow, H., Oettingen, G., Peterson, C., & Seligman, M. E. P. Pessimistic explanatory style in the historical record: CAVing LBJ, presidential candidates and East versus West Berlin. *American Psychologist, 1988, 43,* 673–682.

Interventions for Depression

Chapter 2

Consciousness, Emotional Complexes, and the Mind-Gene Connection

Ernest L. Rossi

Ernest L. Rossi, Ph.D., is a clinical psychologist who has authored, coauthored, and edited 14 books in the area of psychology. He is the editor of The Collected Papers of Milton H. Erickson on Hypnosis, *and is currently the editor of the journal* Psychological Perspectives. *His most recent book, coauthored with David Cheek, M.D., is* Mind-Body Therapy: Ideodynamic Healing in Hypnosis *(New York: W. W. Norton, 1988).*

It has been almost five years since the author first proposed the "mind-gene connection" at the Second International Ericksonian Congress in 1983 (Rossi, 1985). What was an emotionally intuitive notion at that time is rapidly becoming a reality today. One can hardly pick up a newspaper or magazine without reading about yet another breakthrough in molecular biology, genetics and their relationship to many forms of intellectual (e.g., Huntington's, Alzheimer's disease), emotional (e.g., manic-depressive), and psychosomatic problems. For those of us who have been out of school for more than a few years, this new research appears to be beyond any background we were offered; it involves an entirely new order of information and understanding.

A basic difficulty in grasping this new order of information is its vast scope; it requires at least a general familiarity with the fundamentals of genetics and molecular biology, the neurobiology of memory and learning, and 100 years of clinical and phenomenological research in hypnosis, psychoanalysis, and psychosomatic medicine. Is there any common concept that can unite these apparently diverse levels of understanding? A number of researchers over the past few decades

believe there is; they believe it is the concept of information and, in
particular, the process of *information transduction* (Delbruck, 1970;
Rossi, 1986b [Part II]; Weiner, 1977). Information *transduction* refers to
the process by which information is changed from one form into another. In this chapter, we will explore what is known about three
stages of the process in mind-body information transduction: (1) how
sensory-perceptual, emotional, and cognitive information on the phenomenological level of mind is transduced into the neural information
of the brain; (2) how neural information of the brain is transduced into
the molecular information of the body; (3) how molecular information
of the body accesses our genome and transduces genetic information
back into the neural information of the brain and the phenomenological experience of mind.

Most readers will recognize that this three-stage outline is essentially a cybernetic loop of communication or information transduction
between mind and body on a molecular level. In order to understand
this process of communication, we need some background in the new
theory of information substances and their receptors in emotions and
mind-body healing.

INFORMATION SUBSTANCES AND THEIR RECEPTORS IN
MIND-BODY COMMUNICATION

For over 100 years it had been an article of faith in the field of
pharmacology that drugs evoked their physiological responses by first
binding to hypothesized receptors on the cell walls of the nerves and
tissues of the body. Finally, in the 1970s, a series of investigators
demonstrated the physical reality of the insulin receptor (Cuatrecasas,
1971), the opiate receptor (Goldstein, Lowney, & Pal, 1972; Pert, 1976;
Pert & Snyder, 1973a, b), and the peptide molecules that bind to these
receptors (Hughes, 1975). The revolutionary significance of these discoveries was in the recognition of a new principle in molecular biology, endocrinology, and psychopharmacology: Peptides and their receptors are a general class of messengers in biological systems that
mediate intercellular communication at the molecular level. This con-
ception was recently expanded upon by Schmitt (1984). He introduced
the term "informational substances" to designate all of the newly discovered types of "messenger molecules" and their receptors that
modulate brain, body, and behavior. It is interesting to note that

Schmitt, who has long been regarded as the founder of modern molecular neuroscience, now finds that an essentially mentalistic concept such as "informational substance" is necessary to understand the biological dynamics of what were previously called "neuroactive substances."

Within this new category of informational substances, Schmitt included the following: *classical neurotransmitters* (acetylcholine, dopamine, epinephrine, serotonin, etc.); *steroid hormones* (estrogens, androgens, glucocorticoids, etc.); *peptide hormones* (all the hypothalamic, pituitary, and endocrine hormones, such as ACTH, B-endorphin, luteinizing hormone, thyroid, insulin); and the *neuropeptides* (substance P, the angiotensins, bradykinin, cholecystokinin, vasointestinal peptides, etc.). He also included *growth factors* (such as nerve growth factors and epidermal growth factors), *instructive factors* that are involved in gene expression, and *certain proteins*, such as messenger RNA and glycoproteins, that are involved in memory and learning. The common denominator of these information substances is that they all trigger receptor proteins located on either the cell walls, the cytosol within the cells, or the genes themselves within the nucleus of the cell. Once triggered, these receptor proteins initiate the cascade of metabolic processes that account for the special characteristics of each cell, tissue, and organ of the body.

Information substances and their receptors thus integrate all the major homeostatic and regulatory systems of mind, brain, and body that were previously thought to function in an autonomous manner: The peripheral and autonomic nervous systems, the endocrine system, and the immune system are now known to modulate each other's actions on the molecular level. Because many of these molecules can play overlapping roles as neurotransmitters, neuromodulators, growth factors, and the like, the more generic term of *information substances* is now needed to cover their multiple communication functions throughout the mind-brain-body (Iversen, 1984; Nieuwenhuys, 1985; Pert, Ruff, Weber, & Herkenham, 1985; Ruff, Pert, Weber, Wahl, Wahl, & Paul, 1985a; Ruff, Wahl, Mergenhagan, & Pert, 1985b; Ruff, Farrar, & Pert, 1986).

A second major point made by Schmitt is that many information substances modulate neural activity by triggering receptors that are located on many parts of the nerve cell rather than only at the synaptic junctions portrayed by conventional neurology. He summarized this new principle of *parasynaptic information transduction* as follows (Schmitt, 1986, p. 240):

(1) Neurons may chemically intercommunicate by the mediation not only of the dozen-odd classical neurotransmitters but also by peptides, hormones, "factors," other specific proteins, and by other kinds of *informational substances* (ISs), a term that seemed more generally applicable than "neuroactive substances" that was previously used.

(2) Alongside of, and in parallel with, synaptically linked, "hardwired" neuronal circuitry, that forms the basis for conventional neurophysiology and neuroanatomy, and that operates through conventional synaptic junctions, there is a system that I call "parasynaptic." In parasynaptic neuronal systems, ISs may be released at points, frequently relatively remote from target cells, which they reach by diffusion through the extracellular fluid. Such a system has all the specificity and selectivity characteristics of the conventional synaptic mode; in the parasynaptic case, the receptors that provide the specificity and selectivity are on the surface of the cells where they can be contacted by, and bind to, the IS ligands diffusing in the extracellular fluid.

The "hardwired" neuronal circuitry is fairly fixed in its anatomical structure; it does not change its characteristics easily but it is very rapid in its speed of information transmission (on the order of milliseconds). The IS-receptor system "software," by contrast, is in an ongoing process of flexible change, but it is slower in its rate of information transmission. Figure 1 illustrates the earlier classical view of a neural network where communication is mediated in a relatively narrow band of linear information flow between one neuron and the next by the classical neuro*transmitters*. Figure 2 illustrates how these classical neurotransmitters are now known to be supplemented by information substances of the parasynaptic system that flow through the extracellular fluid (ECF) in a broader, nonlinear pattern.

The author has described in detail how these information substances that are contained and transmitted throughout the ECF of the brain can serve as the molecular mechanism for encoding and transducing the flow of the information between the phenomenology of mind and the neural structure of the brain. There is now clear experimental evi-

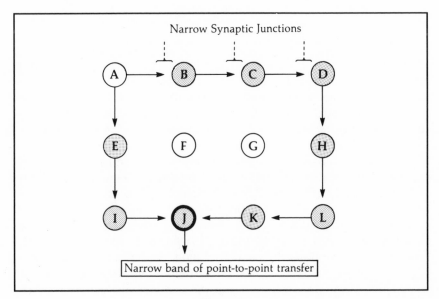

Figure 1

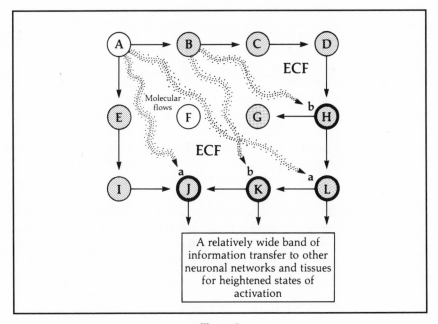

Figure 2

dence in animals (goldfish), for example, that the diffusion of information substances (glycoproteins) between brain cells is responsible for encoding memory, learning, and behavior (Shashoua, 1981). The rate of release of these information substances into the extracellular fluid is increased during intensive learning experiences. This training results in long-term memory and learning that is abolished when the information substances are removed from the extracellular fluid by administration of antisera that block the ISs' ability to bind to neural receptors. This means that memory and learning are states dependent upon the presence or absence of these information substances that encode experience in the neuronal networks of the brain. There is a vast body of historical and contemporary experimental and clinical research that supports the hypothesis that many forms of memory and learning can now be conceptualized as either overtly or covertly state-dependent (Rossi, 1986b; Rossi & Ryan, 1986). This suggests that our currently developing conceptions of the modulation of the entire mind-brain-body by IS-receptor communication systems will enable us to devise new types of experimental studies of the relationships between behavior, genes, and molecules. Schmitt noted the relationships that require more study when he wrote (1984, p. 994):

> The brain contains all the types of steroid hormones. . . . As ISs, they exert a duplex action: (1) a relatively fast (minutes) direct action on synaptic properties, regulating impulse traffic in particular neuronal nets, and (2) a slow (hours) indirect effect involving specific gene activation leading to the synthesis of essential proteins, e.g., specific receptors. Steroid hormones regulate behavioral patterns involved in reproduction, territorial defense, mood and other affective states [McEwen, 1981; McEwen et al., 1982]. For present purposes, the steroid hormones illustrate the integrative control of both the fast bioelectrical events involving the passage of impulses through neuronal nets (i.e., the neurophysiological processes that underlie specific behavior patterns), and the slow gene-activated processes that lead to the synthesis of proteinaceous material which, like specific receptors, form the molecular substratum of behavioral patterns.

The implication of this passage is that the entire class of information substances and their receptors may be important modulators of the fundamental mechanism of memory, learning, emotion, and behavior on the molecular level.

EMOTION, MOTIVATION, AND PSYCHOSOMATIC MEDICINE

Theories of emotion, motivation, and psychosomatic medicine have tended to merge with one another as we have learned more about their biological basis. For example, during the past 50 years a series of investigators has established through the methodologies of neuroanatomy (Livingston & Hornykiewicz, 1978; Maclean, 1970; Papez, 1937), neuroendrocrinology (Scharrer & Scharrer, 1940), electrophysiology (Nuwer & Pribram, 1979), and psychophysiology (Mishkin & Petrie, 1984; Olds, 1977) that the limbic-hypothalamic system of the brain is the locus for the generation and modulation of many of the classical phenomena of emotion, motivation, and psychosomatic medicine. More recent studies find that the IS-receptor systems of the brain also have their highest levels of concentration in the limbic-hypothalamic system (Nieuwenhuys, 1985; Pert et al., 1985). This is the basic type of *prima facie* evidence that implicates IS-receptor systems in the generation and modulation of emotion and motivation on the molecular level. Pert (1986, 1987) generalized this research into a new theory of the molecular basis of psychosomatic medicine.

An overview of the entire process of information transduction on the molecular level from mind to gene is presented in Figure 3. The three-stage outline of cybernetic communication between mind and body alluded to earlier is clearly evident in Figure 3 as (1) the mind-brain connection, (2) the brain-body connection, and (3) the cell-gene connection that produces and releases information substances back into the bloodstream where they can modulate many other body processes, as well as the manifestation of mind (memory, learning, imagery, emotion, and behavior) when they reach the neuronal networks of the brain.

By far the most difficult to understand of these three stages of mind-body communication is the mind-brain connection. There may be a couple of reasons for this: We are all rather vague about what we mean by "mind"; our scientific-materialistic-deterministic world view since the time of Descartes has led us to believe that mind and body are two separate realms that may or may not interact. Because of these philosophical difficulties it might be wise, for now, to acknowledge

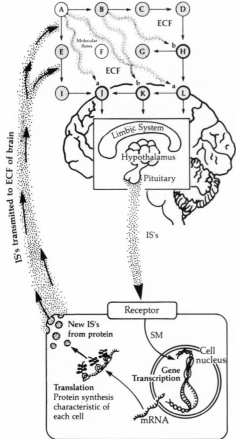

I   THE MIND-BRAIN CONNECTION

1. Neural networks of the brain's cortical-limbic systems encode state-dependent memory, learning and behavior of "mind" (words, images, sensations, perceptions, etc.) with the help of cybernetic information substances from cells of the body.

II   THE BRAIN-BODY CONNECTION

2. Neuroendocrinal information transduction in the limbic-hypothalamic-pituitary system of the brain. The information in neural networks of the brain is transduced into molecular (hormonal) information substances of the body.

3. Information substances (IS's) travel to cells of body with appropriate receptors.

III   THE CELL-GENE CONNECTION

4. Cellular receptors binding IS's

5. Intracellular secondary messengers (SM) lead to activation of "house-keeping" genes

6. Transcription of genetic information into mRNA

7. Translation: protein synthesis characteristic of each cell.

8. New IS's from proteins flow to brain to cybernetically encode state-dependent aspects of mind and behavior.

Figure 3

that the scope of this resolution of the "mind-body problem" presented in this paper is restricted to the practical interests of the therapist in mind-body healing. It is important for scientific researchers and clinicians to have a theoretical model of how mind and body communicate in health and disease so they can test the new hypothesis generated by the model. In a recent volume on the theory, practice, and research of mind-body healing, Rossi and Cheek (1988) outlined 64 such research projects in order to assess the validity and parameters of the general model illustrated in Figure 3.

CONSCIOUSNESS AND PSYCHOLOGICAL COMPLEXES

The general model of mind-body communication presented in Figure 3 may still seem so remote from the daily concerns of the practical psychotherapist as to be almost worthless. Let us, therefore, turn to at least one area where we already have enough information about the model to illustrate its potential usefulness for a new psychotherapy of the future. Figure 4 illustrates how the general model might be applied to the relationships between information substances and the state-dependent encoding of consciousness, emotional states, and psychological complexes. Although Figure 4 applies primarily to women, analogous processes are currently under study in men (Rossi & Cheek, 1988).

A glance at the chart of a woman's continually changing concentration levels in the blood of the four major hormones regulating menstruation and ovulation (progesterone, estrogen, luteinizing hormone, and follicle-stimulating hormone) in the shaded portion of Figure 4 illustrates the psychobiological basis of the mood and mentation movements that modulate the normal rhythms of feminine consciousness. These four major hormones are in turn controlled by neuroendocrinal protohormones and hormones of the limbic-hypothalamic-pituitary system. Many of these hormones have been implicated as the types of information substances that modulate state-dependent memory, mood, and learning.

Depth psychologists, such as C. G. Jung, have long recognized the rhythmic or "wave like" biological basis of "psychological complexes" and emotional life in general. In his essay "A Review of the Complex Theory," Jung wrote (1960b, pp. 96-98):

> What then, scientifically speaking, is a "feeling-tone complex"? It is the *image* of a certain psychic situation which is strongly accentuated emotionally and is, moreover, incompatible with the habitual attitude of consciousness. This image has a powerful inner coherence, it has its own wholeness and, in addition, a relatively high degree of autonomy, so that it is subject to the control of conscious mind to only a limited extent, and therefore

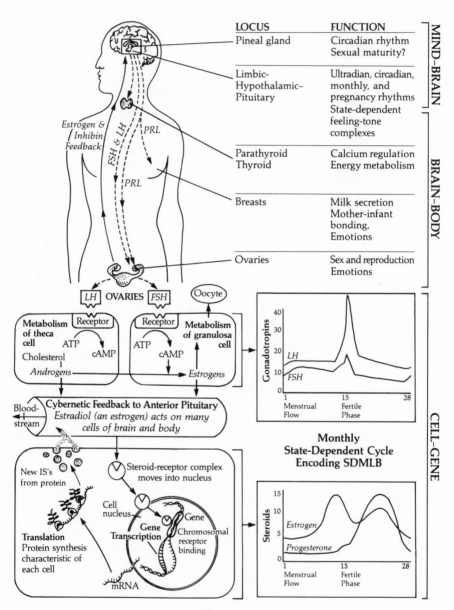

Figure 4.

behaves like an animated foreign body in the sphere of consciousness. The complex can usually be suppressed with an effort
of will, but not argued out of existence, and at the first suitable
opportunity it reappears in all its original strength. *Certain experimental investigations seem to indicate that its intensity or activity
curve has a wavelike character, with a "wave-length" of hours, days, or
weeks.* (author's emphasis). This very complicated question remains as yet unclarified. . . .

The phenomenology of complexes cannot get round the impressive fact of their autonomy, and the deeper one penetrates
into their nature—I might almost say into their biology—the
more clearly do they reveal their character as *splinter psyches*. . . .
Today we can take it as moderately certain that complexes are in
fact "splinter psyches." The aetiology of their origin is frequently
a so-called trauma, an emotional shock or some such thing, that
splits off a bit of the psyche. Certainly one of the commonest
causes is a moral conflict, which ultimately derives from the
apparent impossibility of affirming the whole of one's nature.

I believe that Jung's "very complicated question" can now be clari-
fied: Psychological complexes, in essence, are state-dependent memory, learning, and behavior (SDMLB) systems that are encoded by
many information substances during normal psychobiological events
such as menstruation and childbirth, as well as so-called trauma, and
emotional shock (Rossi & Cheek, 1988).

The most ordinary activities of everyday life can also encode memory and learning; cholecystokinin, which is an information substance
released into the bloodstream from the intestinal mucosa during the
digestion of fatty and amino acids, for example, has been found recently to be responsible for the enhancement of memory and learning
(Flood, Smith, & Morley, 1987). One can easily imagine how such a
psychological mechanism had survival value: When good nutrients
were found, it would certainly facilitate survival for the organism to
remember where they were found. *Perhaps the state-dependent encoding
of memory, learning, emotions, and behavior by information substances and
their receptors was one of the major mechanisms shaping the evolution of
consciousness itself !*

A striking illustration of how state-dependent mood, memory, and
behavior modulated by hormones can encode a psychological complex
is the role of oxytocin, which recent investigators (Weingartner, 1986)

have found to be responsible for the amnesia that usually cloaks a woman's memory of her experience of giving birth. Oxytocin is an information substance that is released in massive amounts from the uterus during labor, and by the posterior pituitary after delivery to regulate lactation and maternal behavior. Many women feel depressed by their memory loss of one of the most significant events of their lives. This sense of loss may have particular significance for some women. Thomas Insel of the National Institute of Mental Health recently implicated oxytocin in mother-child bonding. Consequently, many women have consulted hypnotherapists for help in recovering their experiences of giving birth.

In one remarkable case recorded verbatim (Erickson & Rossi, 1979, pp. 282–313), the woman recovered not only the experience of giving birth but also many earlier traumatic and amnesic memories that had become associated with it. In only a few hypnotherapeutic sessions, she experienced a very deep process of personality maturation that apparently occurred spontaneously when she recovered her lost traumatic memories. This type of clinical outcome implies that psychotherapeutic processes in general, and hypnotherapeutic processes in particular, can access and reframe the state-dependent memory and learning systems (Jung's "feeling-toned complexes") that were originally encoded by information substances on a purely biological molecular level. State-dependent memory and learning systems may be regarded as the common denominator between mind and body. They can be created, accessed, and modulated by purely biological as well as psychological processes. Their experiential activation is usually a continually varying coordination between the biological and psychological levels that we call "psychobiological."

The apparently deterministic outline of Figure 4 does not mean that hormones completely govern personal experience as a naively reductionistic and behavioristic approach might maintain. Careful research has repeatedly documented that there is no simple one-to-one relationship between hormones and emotional life. The cyclic fluctuations illustrated in Figure 4 do suggest, however, that women who are truly sensitive to themselves can experience daily oscillation in the sensations of their mind-body. How women interpret this continually changing pattern of sensations depends on the personal meaning they give to them. When women are conditioned by their culture to take a negative view of these inner changes, then, of course, they will interpret the sensations as pain and dysfunction. However, when women are given an opportunity to create a positive frame of reference for interpreting these sensory changes, their experience can have healing and life-enhancing effects.

Elsewhere I have outlined how similar psychobiological rhythms that take place within all of us on a 90-minute basis can be utilized to enhance self-awareness as well as healing (Rossi, 1986 a, b, c). I now call this the Ultradian Healing Response. It provides us with an opportunity to optimize self-hypnosis, meditation, and "inner work" of all varieties on a deep psychological level at least half a dozen times a day when we experience a natural psychobiological need to "take a break."

SUMMARY

This chapter has outlined a new theory of the psychobiological basis of consciousness, emotional complexes, and mind-body healing. The novelty and scope of this new theory is the outcome of integrating a wide range of research and clinical observation from the earliest foundation of psychoanalysis to modern genetics. The molecular encoding of state-dependent memory, learning, and behavior by information substances and their receptors is regarded as the common denominator that bridges the Cartesian dichotomy between mind and body. This new view, which purports to trace a complete path of cybernetic information transduction from mind to molecule, can be of heuristic value to researchers and clinicians who are seeking new hypotheses to test and new therapeutic methods to explore in their daily work with mind-body relationships.

REFERENCES

Cuatrecasas, P. (1971). Insulin-receptor interactions in adipose tissue cells direct measurement and properties. *Proceedings of the National Academy of Sciences, U.S.A., 68,* 1264–1269.

Delbruck, M. (1970). A physicist's renewed look at biology: Twenty years later. *Science, 168,* 1312–1314.

Erickson, M., & Rossi, E. (1979). *Hypnotherapy: An Exploratory Casebook.* New York: Irvington.

Flood, J., Smith, G., & Morley, J. (1987). Modulation of memory processing by cholecystokinin: Dependence on the vagus nerve. *Science, 236,* 832–834.

Goldstein, A., Lowney, L., & Pal, B. (1972). Stereospecific and nonspecific interactions of the morphine congener levorphanol in subcellular fractions of the mouse brain. *Proceedings of the National Academy of Sciences, U.S.A., 68,* 1742.

Hughes, J. (1975). An endogenous ligand for the morphine receptor. *Brain Research, 88,* 295.

Iversen, L. (1984). Amino acids and peptides—fast and slow chemical signals in the nervous system? (The Ferrier Lecture). *Proceedings of the Royal Society of London, Series B—Biological Sciences, 221,* 245–260.

Jung, C. (1960b). *The Structure and Dynamics of the Psyche. Vol. III. The Collected Works of Carl G. Jung.* (R. F. C. Hull, Trans.) Bollingen Series XX. Princeton, N.J.: Princeton University Press.

Livingston, K., & Hornykiewicz, O. (Eds.) (1978). *Limbic Mechanisms.* New York: Plenum.

Maclean, P. (1970). The triune brain, emotion, and scientific bias. In F. Schmitt (Ed.), *The Neurosciences: Second Study Program* (pp. 336–349). New York: The Rockefeller University Press.

McEwen, B. (1981). Endocrine effects on the brain and their relationship to behavior. In G. Siegel, R. Albers, B. Agranoff, & R. Katzman (Eds.), *Basic Neurochemistry* (pp. 775–799). Boston: Little, Brown.

McEwen, B., Biegon, A., Davis, P., Kerry, L., Luine, V., McGinnis, M., Paden, C., Parsons, B., & Rainbow, T. (1982). Steroid hormones: Humoral signals which alter brain cell properties and functions. In R. Greep (Ed.), *Recent Progress in Hormone Research, 38,* 41–85. New York: University Press.

Mishkin, M., & Petrie, H. (1984). Memories and habits: Some implications for the analysis of learning and retention. In S. Squire & N. Butters (Eds.), *Neuropsychology of Memory* (pp. 287–296). New York: Guilford.

Nieuwenhuys, R. (1985). *Chemoarchitecture of the Brain.* New York: Springer-Verlag.

Nuwer, M., & Pribram, K. (1979). A role of the inferotemporal cortex in visual selective attention. *Electroencephalography & Clinical Neurophysiology, 46,* 389–400.

Olds, J. (1977). *Drives and reinforcements: Behavioral Studies of Hypothalamic Functions.* New York: Raven Press.

Papez, J. (1937). A proposed mechanism of emotion. *Archives of Neurology and Physiology, 38,* 725–744.

Pert, C. (1976). The opiate receptor. In R. Beers, Jr., & E. Bassett (Eds.), *Cell Membrane Receptors for Viruses, Antigens and Antibodies, Polypeptide Hormones, and Small Molecules.* New York: Raven Press, pp. 435–450.

Pert, C. (1986). The wisdom of the receptors: Neuropeptides, the emotions, and bodymind. *Advances, 3*(3), 8–16.

Pert, C. (1987). Neuropeptides: The emotions and bodymind. *Noetic Sciences Review, 2,* 13–18.

Pert, C., Ruff, M., Weber, R., & Herkenham, M. (1985). Neuropeptides and their receptors: A psychosomatic network. *The Journal of Immunology, 135*(2), 820s–826s.

Pert, C., & Snyder, S. (1973a). Opiate receptor: Demonstration in nervous tissue. *Science, 179,* 1011–1014.

Pert, C., & Snyder, S. (1973b). Properties of opiate-receptor binding in rat brain. *Proceedings of the National Academy of Sciences, U.S.A., 70,* 2243–2247.

Rossi, E. (1985). Unity and diversity in Ericksonian approaches: Now and in the future. In J. Zeig (Ed.), *Ericksonian Psychotherapy.* (Vol. I.) (pp. 15–30): *Structures.* New York: Brunner/Mazel.

Rossi, E. (1986a). Altered states of consciousness in everyday life: The ultradian rhythms. In B. Wolman (Ed.), *Handbook of Altered States of Consciousness* (pp. 97–132). New York: Van Nostrand.

Rossi, E. (1986b). *The Psychobiology of Mind-Body Healing: New Concepts in Therapeutic Hypnosis.* New York: W. W. Norton.

Rossi, E. (1986c). Hypnosis and ultradian rhythms. In B. Zilbergeld, M. Edelstein, & D. Araoz (Eds.), *Hypnosis: Questions and Answers.* New York: W. W. Norton.

Rossi, E., & Cheek, D. (1988). *Mind-Body Therapy: Ideodynamic Healing in Hypnosis.* New York: W. W. Norton.

Rossi, E., & Ryan, M. (1986). *Mind-body Communication in Hypnosis. Vol. 3. The Seminars, Workships and Lectures of Milton H. Erickson.* New York: Irvington.

Ruff, M., Farrar, W., & Pert, C. (1986). Interferon Y and granulocyte/macrophase colony-stimulating factor inhibit growth and induce antigens characteristic of myeloid differentiation in small-cell lung cancer cell lines. *Proceedings of the National Academy of Sciences, U.S.A., 83,* 6613–6617.

Ruff, M., Pert, C., Weber, R., Wahl, L., Wahl, S., & Paul, S. (1985a). Benzodiazepine receptor-mediated chemotaxis of human monocytes. *Science, 229,* 1281–1283.

Ruff, M., Wahl, S., Mergenhagan, S., & Pert, C. (1985b). Opiate receptor-mediated chemotaxis of human monocytes. *Neuropeptides, 5,* 363–366.

Scharrer, E., & Scharrer, B. (1940). Secretory cells within the hypothalamus. *Research Publications of the Association of Nervous and Mental Diseases.* New York: Hafner.

Schmitt, F. (1984). Molecular regulators of brain functions: A new view. *Neuroscience, 13,* 991–1001.

Schmitt, F. (1986). Chemical information processing in the brain: Prospect from retrospect. In L. Iversen & E. Goodman (Eds.), *Fast and Slow Signaling in the Nervous System.* New York: Oxford University Press, pp. 239–243.

Shashoua, V. (1981). Extracellular fluid proteins of goldfish brain. *Neurochemistry Research, 6,* 1129–1147.

Weiner, H. (1977). *Psychobiology and Human Disease.* New York: Elsevier.

Weingartner, H. (1986). Memory: The roots of failure. *Psychology Today,* January, 6–7.

Chapter 3

A Renaissance Paradigm

John J. Koriath

John J. Koriath, Ph.D., is a research psychophysiologist and therapist. His teaching, writing, and research emphasize experiential learning and a participatory view of health. Dr. Koriath consults in this capacity with individuals, groups, and organizations. He serves on the faculty of Arizona State University and as President and founding participant in the Turtle Island Project.

> The rock loosed by frost and balanced on a singular point of the mountainside, the little spark which kindles the great forest, the little word which sets the world a fighting, the little scruple which prevents a man from doing his will, the little spore which blights all the potatoes, the little gemmule which makes us philosophers or idiots. Every existence above a certain rank, has its singular points: the higher the rank, the more of them. At these points, influences whose physical magnitude is too small to be taken account of by a finite being, may produce results of the greatest importance. All great results produced by human endeavour depend on taking advantage of these singular states when they occur—*Maxwell, 1882, p. 443*
> Timing is crucial—*Zeig, 1986, p. 253*
> Everything said is said by someone—*Maturana & Varela, 1987, p. 27.*

This chapter suggests a participatory model of health. Its aim is not to treat the particular seeds which grow and develop into the symptomatic patterns of anxiety and depression. Rather, its purpose is to influence the soil from which those seeds are able to sprout into conscious experience. A singular state such as that described by Maxwell (1882) in the above quote has been sensed by therapists for over two decades. This transitional point in world views has been described in various ways as the emergence of holistic thinking (Russell, 1983), the dawning of an Aquarian or New Age (Hills, 1977), the utilization of a

50

systems approach (Segal, 1986), and the growth of an organismic view (Koriath, 1986). Regardless of the descriptive phrase, the content generally focuses on the limitations of the Cartesian grid, Newtonian mechanics, and linear thinking for describing the dynamics of complex systems. For therapists, these limitations combine in a general recognition that the domain of objective reality is not independent from subjective experience. Simply put, the measurer influences what is being measured, and the observer influences what is being observed. We participate in constructing reality. On all scales of human experience—from physiological, emotional, and cognitive processes, to relationships of self, family, and nations—the nature of our personal participation modulates the flow of daily consciousness we come to call living.

The boundary separating subject from object, and persons from the events that occur in their lives, is permeable. To pass through such a boundary requires the resolution of paradox. The paradox is resolved in an awareness that opposing points of view share commonalities. This chapter describes such a passage in terms of the cycles of experience in the author's career in the field of healing. It is a vision of health—a view generated from the recursive learning process of ongoing participation in the field of health.

Yapko (1988) pointed out that the life events associated with the experience of depression are recurrent. Transitions in personal relationships, shifts in career, and issues of personal growth continue throughout life, with some facets that can be anticipated and others that remain uncertain. Although an effective treatment of depression (Yapko & Koriath, 1988) will often focus on a person's immediate problems, the treatment can only be considered complete if it also helps to reshape the nature of an individual's personal response to life events. Such reshaping "enriches the soil" of a person's life and liberates those resources that can prevent the experience of depression from being associated with similar events that will occur. This chapter clarifies such an effort and highlights its importance as an essential aspect of an effective therapeutic treatment for anxiety and depression.

NOW MINUS TEN YEARS

When I began working with cancer patients a little more than a decade ago, the therapeutic goal was clear: to help transform a life-threatening illness into a life-challenging event. At that time there was a general framework. When a person was diagnosed as having some form of neoplastic disease, the focus, with only few exceptions, was on the statistical probability of eliminating the tumor without eliminating the host. The statistic was based on averages calculated from treating large populations, designed to remove the variability of individual cases. A rough sense of the statistics can be grasped by creating a ratio: Take the average number of successes, divide by the total number of cases, and reduce the fraction. The chance of surviving a particular type of cancer: one out of _____ .

This framework is well known by many and reflects an approach that views disease as the presence of dysfunctional parts, in this case abnormal cells, to be removed from the body, so that the machine can once again function normally. A patient diagnosed using this approach is given *a chance*, often minimal, and is then expected to await the outcome.

It is not surprising that such a scenario leaves a person treated in this manner with a perception of threat and a reactive response, usually submission. Emotions are generally depressed and characterized by hopelessness and helplessness. Cognitive style is structured in confusion. An approach skewed so grossly toward objectivity and resting so heavily on reductionism filters out the presence and participation of the person in treatment. To a humanistic, systems-oriented therapist, it is not surprising that such an approach is far less than dramatically successful in restoring health.

A decade ago, the therapeutic approach applied by my colleagues and myself emerged from a paradox of sorts. Our rationale was intuitive. It surfaced from an awareness that the will to live exerts a powerful shaping influence on the dynamics of living systems as a whole. Direct empirical evidence was largely anecdotal. "Spontaneous remission" served as a general category to house the more dramatic cases of uniqueness. Indeed, the health-care system as a whole was largely involved in categorizing people on the basis of their disorders, with few database sorts directed at generating a view of a person's involvement in the healing process.

A movement in that direction was beginning from the clustering of earlier investigations that related stress to physiological processes. Hans Selye's research (1956) provided elaborate evidence to indicate that chronic stress produces hormonal imbalance and suppresses the immune system. Samudzhen (1954) and Turkevich (1955) were among early animal researchers who demonstrated a relationship between stress and accelerated tumor development. By 1969, Friedman (1969) had suggested to the New York Academy of Sciences that no further animal research was necessary to demonstrate that resistance to infectious and neoplastic disease was modified by "environmental factors of a psychosocial nature" (p. 392).

The stream of relationships linking stress with the disruption of physiological cycles joined what appeared to be a historical "meandering" of reports that tied depression and emotional postures to physiological dysfunctions. Physicians could trace the stream back to Galen in the second century A.D. and note the anecdotal accounts of Gendron (1701), Burrows (1783), Nunn (1822), Walshe (1846), Bernard (1865), and Paget (1870). The strength of statistical corroboration began to emerge with a 250-patient study by Snow (1893), and a subsequent study by Evans (1926). Leshan (1977) intensified a recognition of the dimension of emotional posture in studies of over 500 cancer patients whose histories of emotional despair, loss, and "bottled up" emotions intertwined with the functional integrity of the immune system. Thomas and Duszynski's (1973) 30-year prospective study of 1,300 John Hopkins medical students highlighted the relational etiology of dysfunctional cell growth and emotional patterns that portrayed a lack of closeness to parents, a minimal demonstration of strong emotions, and a "low gear" approach to living.

For those whose intuitive sense of the importance of personal participation in health had at least been sparked (and, for a few, ignited), a step toward credibility emerged from a growing research base. Schmale and Iker (1971) demonstrated that they could discern trends of a "helplessness-prone personality" (p. 99) in 73 percent of a group of women biologically predisposed to cervical cancer. Kissen (1969) observed that "poorly developed emotional outlets" (p. 545) distinguished between heavy smokers who developed lung cancer and those who did not. Group trends such as these easily branched off earlier findings (Blumberg, 1954; Klopfer, 1957) that associated rapidly growing tumors with blocked emotional outlets and rigid loyalty to a person's own framework of reality.

Though a number of cutting-edge clinicians were able to synthesize these intimations of the significance of "subjective" posture (also read *will* or *choicefulness*) into patterns of treatment, a great deal of attention was given to the approach popularized by the Simontons (1978). They emphasized relaxation and mental imagery as therapeutic techniques in the treatment of life-threatening illnesses and associated depression. Their program focused on stressful events that left a person susceptible to illness, secondary gains that resulted from dysfunction, and the process of goal forming to disrupt dysfunctional patterns and reinforce new belief systems.

The author's therapeutic adaptation of the Simonton strategies, available research findings, and personal intuition, highlighted the two principles most comfortably nested in the cutting-edge consensus of health care at that time. One principle focused on the notion of personal responsibility for one's health. The other principle focused on the significance of stressful events in shaping a person's overall health. Both principles shape the framework of possibilities applied to an effective treatment of anxiety and depression.

Personal Responsibility and Control

The concept of personal responsibility and control served as a powerful turnaround response to the "one out of ____ " chance scenario that characterized health-care delivery and stripped the individual of involvement in the healing process. In application, however, limitations emerged. It encouraged an overburdening sense of guilt for disruptions in well-being. Though permeable and changing, boundaries exist that constrain physiology, emotions, relationships, and the social organization of our lives. Personal responsibility and control for one's health also tended to create a distorted sense of independence (and at times isolation) for some. It ignored the systemic connections that join each of us to family, community, and larger ecologies. This became increasingly clear in the author's work with cancer patients. Patients formed a variety of goals to channel the will to live. Yet, individuals in the supportive environment of a residential retreat often encountered obstacles when these goals were pursued in the extended cultures of family, friends, and work.

The Significance of Stressful Events

Linking stressful events to disruptions of health was a significant research accomplishment. When integrated into practice, however, interesting twists emerged. Although stress was associated with events that disrupted health and resulted in the experience of depression, the stress did not appear to be in the event itself. Rather, stress emerged from the nature of a person's response to an event.

How a person responds to events is seldom clear simply from behavioral observations. Observing behavior generally only indicates "what" a person is doing in response to an event. When someone diagnosed with cancer routinely practices relaxation and mental imagery in order to enhance immune function, yet regards it as another "treatment" to increase chances of survival, the nature of his or her dysfunctional response remains largely unchanged. The expectation that "something will make me better—" in this case a relaxation technique—remains the same. The boundary between subjective posture and objective reality remains uncrossed, and therefore adaptive capacity is not expanded. The person's behavior has changed, but not the nature of his or her response patterns. The dynamics of stress remain intact.

Evolving a sense of the constraints that shape issues of personal responsibility and control in practical application has led to the current view of a participatory model of health. Similarly, a shift of focus that highlights the *nature* of a person's response to life events is emerging from an earlier recognition of the important dynamics of stress.

NOW

The opportunity to change the nature of our response is the singular point at which the will to live can transform physiological and psychological soil. At this point, a person can choose to mobilize energy that transcends the domain of *chance*. The boundary between subjective experience and objective reality is reshaped. Existential psychologists have emphasized an intuitive sense of the creative response (May, 1975). The story can be told scientifically as well in the context of psychoneuroimmunology (PNI) (Rossi, 1986).

A general scenario emerges (Frankenhauser, 1980). Consider an event that places demands on our adaptive capacity, for example, a job with new and uncertain responsibilities, a child coming into the teen years with new expectations of personal freedom, a relationship entering a phase that requires redefinition. When the nature of our response is *reactive*, one that relies heavily on old learning patterns, one that is perceived as limiting possibilities, our perception tends to be characterized by feelings of threat. This psychological climate has a corresponding physiological climate (Frankenhauser, 1980; Rossi, 1986). A general arousal of the autonomic nervous system is expressed by a surge of sympathetic activity. Epinephrine and norepinephrine are released from the medulla of the adrenal gland. The hypothalamus, a center for emotional processing in the brain, expresses threat with the release of corticotropin-releasing factor (CRF). CRF initiates increased release of adrenocorticotropic hormone (ACTH) from the pituitary gland. A current of ACTH flows through the bloodstream and alters the wavelike release of glucocorticoids from the adrenal gland. The climate shifts. Glucocorticoid flow resembles a storm and function of the immune system erodes.

A *creative* response to the same event, one that is open to new possibilities and learnings that employ new patterns and is characterized by the perception of challenge, is associated with a different physiological climate (Frankenhauser, 1980; Rossi, 1986). The organismic arousal expressed by the sympathetic branch of the autonomic nervous system occurs, but without the storm of glucocorticoid activity associated with the reactive response and the perception of threat.

Rossi (1986) provided an elaborate conceptual view of how the nature of a person's response becomes encoded in the cellular structure of the body. He detailed practical techniques for therapeutically restructuring that encoding by employing Ericksonian approaches and the principles of state-dependent learning and memory. Yapko (1988) outlined in detail numerous strategies for therapeutically altering the nature of response patterns on multiple dimensions of experience. The next section of this chapter will describe the use of ceremony as a technique for accessing the boundary between the reactive and creative response.

Ceremony as an Agent of Change

Ceremony can be conceptualized as a general technique to integrate significant events in the lives of individuals and groups. Although ceremonies evident throughout human history share this characteristic, the particular structure of ceremonies employed by various cultures rests heavily on the world view of those who use the ceremony. Most of us have been a part of ceremonies that reflect the view of Western religions and industrial society. In that context, our general role in ceremonies is narrowly defined and expressively constrained. In this chapter, ceremony is presented in the context of a participatory model of health. The goal is to integrate persons with the events that occur in their lives by resolving the paradox that connects subjective experience with objective reality.

Ceremony can function as an experiential metaphor and generate a context that reshapes personal communication style. An individual's experience in a ceremony can simultaneously disrupt patterns associated with the experience of depression and frame life-style patterns associated with the experience of health. *All learning is experiential.* The ceremonies discussed in this section "work" by generating an experiential context. The context is one that integrates an experimental attitude with an existential longing. In a framework of psychoneuroimmunological theory, the experiential learning that ceremony serves to frame modulates the dynamic flow of the vast array of neurotransmitters circulating in the bloodstream and touching each and every cell of the body. Metaphorically and functionally, the dynamics of this circulation can be thought of as "a stream of consciousness" in which "experience is medicine."

Three ceremonies will be described—the water ceremony, the talking circle, and the making of the mask. The structure of these ceremonies attracts the creative response of the will to live by requiring participants to make a paradox-resolving agreement. The assumption underlying these ceremonies is that a group can share a common vision, yet each individual within that group sees and expresses that vision uniquely. Inherent in this view is a personal acknowledgment that "no individual sees things as they are." Individuals see themselves and their world in the context of their own life experience. Participation in the ceremony affirms that each person's view has something to teach every other person and that each person needs to learn what every other person needs to teach.

The Water Ceremony

The water ceremony creates a general focus for a participatory vision of health and allows the particular needs of each participant to surface. Oral tradition suggests that some form of this ceremony originated in the discipline of the Sufis.

Participants are gathered in a circle in silence. The person conducting the ceremony explains that the ceremony will be used to facilitate communication and that the word communication itself can be thought of as an integration of the words "common" and "unique." The conductor gives each person a clear glass and explains that it will serve as a symbolic container for their experience. A pitcher of water is held up to the group and a statement is made that highlights the literal and metaphorical significance of water. Water is a fundamental substrate for all life on this planet, essential to survival, and a catalyst for our most basic functions. As the conductor proceeds around the circle, pouring a small amount of water into each person's glass, participants are informed that their presence in the circle signifies that a particular need regarding their health exists. Each person is encouraged to allow that need to rise into his or her conscious mind and, in silence, symbolically to project that need into the glass. They are informed that each specific concern will surface in a unique way. It may relate to their physical health, their emotional health, or their way of thinking. It may reflect some aspect of their personal relationships, a memory, or a dream.

When each person, including the conductor, has had the opportunity to become consciously aware of what he or she holds in his or her hand, the conductor moves around the circle once again and asks each participant to pour the water back into the pitcher. A statement is then made that the pitcher is a common vessel into which each person's unique concerns have blended in a way that transcends boundaries. A pinch of salt is added and the conductor expresses the concept that our individual and collective concerns exist in a medium that represents the interrelated ecology of our planet and the unbroken chain of life. The conductor then makes a final pass around the circle, once again pouring a small amount of water into each participant's glass. Participants are asked to take a moment to appreciate the significance of what they hold in their hands, to take a sip of the water, and with the awareness of their experience, to continue the communication of the therapy session.

The Talking Circle

The talking circle serves a function similar to the water ceremony, but provides each participant with the opportunity for verbal expression. This ceremony has been used for countless generations in the Native American culture and reflects an awareness that all beings are alive, interrelated, and governed by an ecological imperative.

The person conducting the ceremony gathers participants in a circle to signify that, for the moment, a system of "relatives" is being formed.

When this ceremony is conducted in a manner that reflects Native American culture, a candle is lit in the center of the circle to represent the nurture and support that fire provides for humans, and to provide a point of focus. The dancing flame is a concrete reminder of the variety of infinite expressions that can emerge from a common source. Cedar and sweetgrass are burned in an abalone shell. The conductor moves around the circle, fanning the fragrant aroma on each participant with an eagle feather. This serves as a silent invitation to each participant to enter a space in which he or she feels free to express and is open to hear the song of the heart.

The conductor then tells a story or two that reflect the interrelated dynamics of life. These stories may highlight the autonomous nature to be seen in humans, animals, or the phenomena of nature. A sense of respect and awe for the principles of nature within us and nature around us are interwoven in each story and used to attract the creative response of each individual in the circle.

The person conducting the circle presents the simple ground rules. It is assumed that each person holds the truth of his or her own life experience and the resources for healing in the subconscious. The conductor explains that each participant will have the opportunity to express that truth without interruption, interpretation, or discussion from any other member of the circle. A person may speak for as long or as short a period as desired. When a participant is finished, he or she passes an eagle feather (or some other symbolic anchor) on to the next person and says "to all my relations." It is explained that speech often reflects the song of the mind, but that in the talking circle the song of the heart is sought. Each participant is encouraged to allow that song to be sung spontaneously while holding the eagle feather as a symbolic source of strength. The author has discussed elsewhere a conceptual view (Koriath, 1986) and empirical evidence (Koriath & Lindholm, 1986; Koriath, Lindholm, & Landers, 1987) for the functional integration of heart and brain, which parallels the metaphorical representation of "mindsong" and "heartsong" in this ceremony.

The conductor may begin. For the therapist, this is the singular point in the ceremony, the point at which professional training and experience are turned toward self. The therapist spontaneously expresses the personal range of emotions and thoughts that surround a significant event in his or her own life. The therapist is challenged to bring forth the creative response from within and offers that personal effort of self-healing as a gift to the group. Participants have the opportunity to learn experientially how to be therapists in their own lives. Repeated participation in this ceremony shapes and refines the skill. Participation in this ceremony also protects the therapist from the common experience of "burnout" by requiring a truthful involvement and expression of self in daily work. When the conductor/therapist feels his or her expression is complete, the feather is passed to the next participant. This process continues until the eagle feather has made its journey around the circle of "relatives." The conductor thanks each participant for the expression of his or her personal truth. The candle is then extinguished. The ceremony is closed by having all of the participants turn around to face the outer boundary of the circle. Hands are clasped and a statement is made by the conductor to affirm that as this talking circle is disbanded, the experience shared together within the circle can now be carried to the other circles of each participant's life.

With continued participation, the talking circle serves to reshape personal communication style. When a person is assured that no interruption, interpretation, or discussion of his or her expression will occur, an open integration of thoughts and feelings begins to emerge. Similarly, when people are aware that they will not provide analysis, interpretation, or discussion of what someone else is saying, a new quality of listening develops. As time passes, these patterns of an evolving communication style surface in relationships with family, friends, and the extended cultures of daily life.

The Making of the Mask

The making of the mask is a ceremony that highlights the personal boundary between appearance and spirit. The experience allows each participant to explore the nature of the creative response in a personal way. It is an intimate ceremony that two participants perform as partners.

The person conducting the ceremony presents the context to participants. The conductor explains that one person will make the mask on the other, and that roles will then be reversed. The mask is to be considered symbolically. Once formed, the mask will be an identical replication of the face. The inside of the mask is the impression of one's appearance as it is presented to the world. The outside of the mask is the reflection of one's spirit. Taken as a whole, the mask represents the boundary at which one discovers the nature of the creative response.

During the ceremony, meditative music is played. The person on whom the mask is being made lies comfortably on the floor. The mask maker spreads a thin layer of vaseline on the entire surface of his or her partner's face. The mask maker then creates a mask by placing strips of plaster impregnated surgical gauze on the partner's face. Each gauze strip is dipped in water and placed on the face, forming a criss-crossed pattern that covers the entire face and leaves only the nostrils exposed. The intimacy of touch and the art of creation is shared by both partners as forehead, cheeks, chin, eyes, and mouth are slowly masked in the ceremonial process. As the music plays, participants have the opportunity to focus on the impression of one's appearance, the reflection of one's spirit, and the uniqueness of the boundary between the two. The mask hardens fairly quickly. The mask maker then slowly lifts the mask off the partner's face, and each person now has the opportunity to see in a new way.

The ceremony is performed once again with the roles exchanged. Following the ceremony, partners are given the opportunity to walk together and share the nature of their experience. Materials are gathered and both people decorate the mask to reflect their experience with the spirit. The mask serves as both reminder and discovery of those internal movements that initiate the creative response uniquely in each individual.

NOW PLUS TEN YEARS

This chapter suggests a participatory model of health as a "Renaissance paradigm," a way of seeing that can utilize that singular point in the transitional boundary between world views. This way of seeing suggests that the will to live can initiate a creative response that transcends the rules of chance alone. Where might such a view lead?

The mission of a Renaissance paradigm is the transformation (also read *trance—formation*) of culture, beginning with the awakening of the creative response within each individual and moving with the force of attraction through the successive scales of family, community, nation, and planet. For some, such a mission must seem "non-sensical." Certainly this was the case centuries ago when it was proposed that the earth orbits the sun, or, more recently, that humans might fly to the moon. As the Renaissance emerged in Europe following the Dark Ages, it must have seemed fantastic to consider the system of science transcending centuries of civilizations built upon systems of authority.

The mission of a Renaissance paradigm, however, seems to make sense to many in light of a growing recognition of the principles that govern the integrity of living systems (Gleick, 1987; Maturana & Varela, 1987; Segal, 1986; von Foerster, 1984):

1. Living systems are self-organizing.
2. Living systems are interrelated.
3. Livings systems function recursively.

These principles appear to be universally present in the dynamics of complex systems and provide a potential structure to house the mission of a Renaissance paradigm. Many branches of science are applying these principles to model events in a new paradigm. Together they present a singular view. There is order in chaos and a mechanism that allows for free will within a world governed by deterministic laws (Crutchfield, Farmer, Packard, & Shaw, 1986).

Choice is the gift of this paradigm. Will is its strength and directing force. Will is emerging as the creative response that can move humanity into a domain beyond chance happenings. It suggests the mission of a Renaissance paradigm as a conscious choice by a generation committed to participatory health. Is such a choice worth making when the outcome lies in a field of uncertainty? Each of us makes that decision alone in our uniquely singular context of intuition, reason, and passionate longing. For those who choose the creative response, the poignant sense of an enhanced aliveness provides an answer and a direction.

REFERENCES

Bernard, C. (1865/1978). *Experimental medicine*. In O. Simonton, S. Simonton, & J. Creighton (Eds.), *Getting Well Again*. Los Angeles: Tarcher.

Blumberg, E. M. (1954). A possible relationship between psychological factors and human cancer. *Psychosomatic Medicine, 16*(4), 276–286.

Burrows, J. A. (1783/1978). A practical essay on cancer. In O. Simonton, S. Simonton, & J. Creighton, *Getting Well Again*. Los Angeles: Tarcher.

Crutchfield, J., Farmer, J., Packard, N., & Shaw, R. (1986). Chaos. *Scientific American, 255* (6), 46–57.

Evans, E. (1926). *A psychological study of cancer*. New York: Dodd, Mead.

Frankenhauser, M. (1980). Psychobiological aspects of life stress. In S. Levine & H. Ursin (Eds.), *Coping and Health*. New York: Plenum.

Friedman, S. (1969). Psychosocial factors modifying host resistance to experimental infections. *Annals of the New York Academy of Sciences, 164*, 381–393.

Gendron, D. (1701/1978). Enquiries into nature, knowledge, and cure of cancers. In O. Simonton, S. Simonton, & J. Creighton, *Getting Well Again*. Los Angeles: Tarcher.

Gleick, J. (1987). *Chaos: Making of a New Science*. New York: Viking.

Hills, C. (1977). *Nuclear Evolution*. Boulder Creek, Calif.: University of the Trees Press.

Kissen, D. (1969). A further report on personality and psychological factors in lung cancer. *Annals of the New York Academy of Sciences, 164,* 535–545.

Klopfer, B. (1957). Psychological variables in human cancer. *Journal of Projective Techniques, 21,* 331–340.

Koriath, J. (1986). Milton Erickson in an age of therapy. Paper presented at the Third International Congress on Ericksonian Approaches to Hypnosis and Psychotherapy, Phoenix, Ariz.

Koriath, J., & Lindholm, E. (1986). Cardiac related cortical inhibition during a fixed foreperiod reaction time task, *International Journal of Psychophysiology, 4,* 183–195.

Koriath, J., Lindholm, E., & Landers, D. (1987). Cardiac related cortical activity during variations in mean heart rate, *International Journal of Psychophysiology, 5,* 289–299.

Leshan, L. (1977). *You Can Fight for Your Life.* New York: M. Evans & Co.

Maturana, H., & Varela, F. (1987). *The Tree of Knowledge.* Boston: New Science Library.

Maxwell, J. C. (1882/1969). *Science and Free Will.* Reprinted in L. Campbell and W. Garnett (Eds.), *The Life of James Clerk Maxwell* (p. 443). London: Johnson Reprint Co.

May, R. (1975). *The Courage to Create.* New York: Norton.

Nunn, T. (1822/1978). Cancer of the breast. In O. Simonton, S. Simonton, & J. Creighton, *Getting Well Again.* Los Angeles: Tarcher.

Paget, J. (1870). *Surgical Pathology* (2nd ed.). London: Longman's Green.

Rossi, E. (1986). *The Psychobiology of Mind-Body Healing.* New York: Norton.

Russell, P. (1983). *The Global Brain.* Los Angeles: Tarcher.

Samudzhen, E. (1954). Effect of functionally weakened cerebral cortex on growth of innoculated tumors in mice. Meditsinskii Zhurnal. Akademiia Nauk Ukranian SSR, 24(3), 10–14.

Schmale, A., & Iker, H. (1971). Hopelessness as a predictor of cervical cancer. *Social Science and Medicine, 5,* 95–100.

Segal, L. (1986). *The Dream of Reality.* New York: Norton.

Selye, H. (1956). *The Stress of Life.* New York: McGraw-Hill.

Simonton, O., Simonton, S., & Creighton, J. (1978). *Getting Well Again.* Los Angeles: Tarcher.

Snow, H. (1893). *Cancer and the Cancer Process.* London: Churchill.

Thomas, C., & Duszynski, D. (1973). Closeness to parents and the family constellation in a prospective study of five disease states: Suicide, mental illness, malignant tumor, hypertension, and coronary heart disease. *The John Hopkins Medical Journal, 134,* 251–270.

Turkevich, N. (1955). Significance of typological peculiarities of the nervous system in the origin and development of cancer of the mammaries in mice.*Voprosky Onkologii (Leningrad), 1*(6), 64–70.

von Foerster, H. (1984). On constructing a reality. In P. Watzlawick (Ed.), *The Invented Reality.* New York: Norton.

Walshe, W. (1846/1978). *Nature and Treatment of Cancer.* In O. Simonton, S. Simonton, & J. Creighton, *Getting Well Again.* Los Angeles: Tarcher.

Yapko, M. (1988). *When Living Hurts.* New York: Brunner/Mazel.

Yapko, M., & Koriath, J. (1988). The up side of being down. Workshop presented at the Fourth Annual San Diego Conference on Hypnotic and Strategic Interventions.

Zeig, J. (1986). Motivating patients to follow prescriptions. In B. Zilbergeld, M. Edelstein, & D. Araoz (Eds.), *Hypnosis: Questions and Answers.* New York: Norton.

Chapter 4

Treating Achilles' Heel: Differentiation of Depressive States and Clinical Intervention with the Depressed Patient

Waleed Anthony Salameh

Waleed A. Salameh, Ph.D. (University of Montreal), is a licensed clinical and consulting psychologist in private practice in San Diego, Calif., and the developer of Integrative Short-Term Psychotherapy (ISTP). His professional interests include applying his approach to psychotherapeutic work with individuals, families, and groups; conducting professional training experiences in different mental health settings; and clinical writing.

In 1985, Salameh was awarded the Milton H. Erickson Institute of San Diego Award in recognition of his contributions to the field of strategic interventions. He is the co-editor of The Handbook of Humor and Psychotherapy-Advances in the Clinical Use of Humor. *His publications include over 80 clinical handbooks, invited chapters, articles, and presentations in the areas of psychotherapy and effective communications. Salameh is currently working on a forthcoming book,* Integrative Short-Term Psychotherapy (ISTP): The Origination of Human Change.

> I have been fighting the powers of darkness lately. Still they prevail with me. But I have more or less got my head out of the inferno, my body will follow later. How one has to struggle, really, to overcome this accursed blackness. It would do me so much good if I could kill a few people.—D.H. Lawrence (From "Selected Letters")

In the *Iliad*, Homer reported that the great Greek warrior Achilles was vulnerable only in his heel. Consequently, the term Achilles' heel is often used to describe a vulnerable point in an individual or system. In this sense, depression can be seen as the Achilles' heel of human emotion, a common vulnerable point that, in its psychopathological form, can cripple the everyday functioning of many individuals, causing significant distress, demoralization, and personal pain. The purpose of this chapter is threefold: First, an analytical look will be taken at how depression presents itself clinically in different patients. Second, some of the therapist's stumbling blocks in treating depressed patients will be identified and addressed. Third, a specific eight-step program for clinical intervention with the depressed patient will be presented.

THE FACES OF DEPRESSION—DIFFERENTIATION OF DEPRESSIVE STATES

The work in this chapter essentially pertains to the disorder known as major depression, as distinguished from either the organic affective syndrome or the depressive phase of bipolar disorder. The chapter refers solely to adult patients presenting with a nonpsychotic unipolar affective disorder, with no known history of a manic episode. The revised third edition of the *Diagnostic and Statistical Manual of Mental Disorders*, (DSM III-R) of the American Psychiatric Association (1987) describes major depression according to the following diagnostic criteria.

At least five of the following symptoms have been present during the same two-week period and represent a change from previous functioning; at least one of the symptoms is either (1) depressed mood, or (2) loss of interest or pleasure. (Do not include symptoms that are clearly due to a physical condition, mood-incongruent delusions or hallucinations, incoherence, or marked loosening of association.) (1) depressed mood (or can be irritable mood in children and adolescents) most of the day, nearly every day, as indicated either by subjective account or observation by others (2) markedly diminished interest or pleasure in all, or almost all, activities most of the day, nearly every day (as indicated either by subjective account or observation by others or apathy most of the time) (3) significant weight loss or weight gain when not dieting (e.g., more than 5% of body weight in a month), or decrease or increase in appetite nearly every day (in children, consider failure to make expected weight gains) (4) insomnia or hypersomnia nearly every day (5) psychomotor agitation or retardation nearly every day (observable by others, not merely subjective feelings of restlessness or being slowed down) (6) fatigue or loss of energy nearly every day (7) feelings of worthlessness or excessive or inappropriate guilt (which may be delusional) nearly every day (not merely self-reproach or guilt about being sick) (8) diminished ability to think or concentrate, or indecisiveness nearly every day (either by subjective account or as observed by others) (9) recurrent thoughts of death (not just fear of dying), recurrent suicidal ideation without a specific plan, or a suicide attempt or a specific plan for committing suicide.* (p. 222)

The *Dictionary of Psychology* (Chaplin, 1975), defines depression as follows: "1. In the normal individual, a state of despondency characterized by feelings of inadequacy, lowered activity, and pessimism about the future. 2. In pathological cases, an extreme state of unresponsiveness to stimuli, together with self-depreciation, delusions of inadequacy, and hopelessness." *Webster's New Collegiate Dictionary* (G. & C. Merriam Co., 1980) defines depression as: "1. A state of feeling sad, dejection. 2. A psychoneurotic or psychotic disorder marked by sadness, inactivity, difficulty in thinking and concentration, and feelings of dejection." A female patient described her depression as follows: "I feel rotten, like I'm not up to it. I cry too much. I look at myself in the mirror every morning and tell myself I am old, fat and ugly. When I drive on the freeway, I feel I'm going to have a car accident. People compliment me, but I don't believe what they tell me. I feel like a parasite. I just want to crawl into a hole and be left there."

A consistent picture of the clinical symptomatology associated with depression emerges from the above descriptions, namely, a lowness of spirits, lowered activity, unbalancing or deregulation of usual activities and interests, inability to concentrate or think clearly, lack of motivation, social withdrawal or misinterpretation of social feedback given by others, unresponsiveness to stimuli, self-deprecation coupled with a breakdown of the patient's sense of self-esteem, suicidal ideation, and feelings of inadequacy. Many authors agree that depression

---

*Reprinted with permission from the *Diagnostic and Statistical Manual of Mental Disorders, Third Edition, Revised*. Copyright 1987, American Psychiatric Association.

has recognizable clinical symptoms, and with varying levels of exacerbation can lead to increasingly severe levels of personal dysfunction. Depression is described as having somatic, cognitive, affective, and behavioral levels of symptom expression (Beck, 1967, 1973, 1983; Miller, 1984).

The clinical literature on depression offers various models for understanding the phenomenon of depression, and some indications for its treatment. Depression has been theorized to be a consequence of "learned helplessness," where the individual feels personally helpless in the face of perceived "uncontrollable" events with concomitant attribution of blame to oneself (Seligman, 1974, 1975, 1983). Depression has also been explained as a cognitive distortion of reality involving erroneous generalizations based on negative cognitive schemata, which must be rationally disputed in order to lift the depressive affect (Beck 1973, 1983; Beck, Rush, Shaw, & Emery, 1979; Ellis, 1973; Ellis & Whiteley, 1979).

Given the preceding important conceptions of depression, we might now ask: How can we gain a further understanding of depression? The answer to this question ultimately lies in analyzing how depression presents itself clinically in different patients. The clinical picture of depression suggests that, in conjunction with a vertical continuum of symptomatic severity, there exists a second horizontal continuum of differential depressive manifestations. Figure 1 illustrates the interaction between symptomatic severity and differential clinical states in depression. Along this horizontal continuum, a purebred depression is rarely observed. Rather, what is more commonly seen in the consulting room or hospital is a pathological cohabitation between depression and other psychological disorders, creating different and clinically distinguishable strains or faces of depression. What emanates from clinical work is that it would be more faithful to clinical phenomena to speak of "depressions" instead of "depression."

Along the horizontal line of depressions, the clinician can observe clinical symptoms that would squarely fit within the description of depression, yet are in continuous and active interaction with other clinical symptoms that consistently cohabit with depressive symptoms, thus resulting in multiple faces of depression. This section proposes and differentiates some depressive states along this continuum. These include: (1) oppositional depression, (2) defeatist depression, (3) narcissistic depression, (4) hysterical depression, (5) parentified depression, (6) borderline depression, (7) anxiolitic depression, and (8) secondary depression. Each of these will be described and illustrated with a

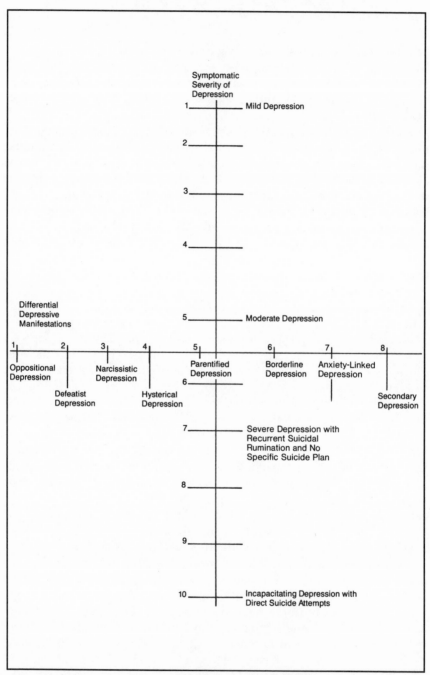

Figure 1. Interaction between symptomatic severity and differential clinical states in depression

brief clinical vignette clarifying the associated clinical features. In keeping with the ethical requirement of patient confidentiality, secondary case details have been changed and all personally identifying information has been removed from the vignettes. The patients discussed in this section exhibit the classical symptoms of depression described above and would have a diagnosis of major depression under DSM III-R criteria. The focus in this section will be on the interaction between the depressive symptoms and other psychopathological states superimposed on the depression.

This section begins by identifying four categories of depression related to anger. In this group of depressions—namely, oppositional depression, defeatist depression, narcissistic depression, and hysterical depression—the predominant mood state related to depression is usually anger. The anger may have varying levels of intensity, coupled with some form of accusation toward others for perceived injustices.

Oppositional Depression

This category refers to those patients whose depression is characterized by anger, turned both inward and outward. In addition to their depression, these patients present with a clear oppositional quality expressed both directly and indirectly. Symptoms include work inefficiency, inability to complete tasks on time, feeling disrespected by the "system," automatically refusing constructive suggestions offered by others, feeling invalidated by others and thus having to "struggle" to present their point of view, inability to express rage or disagreement in a straightforward manner, lack of assertiveness, and feeling overly responsible for other individuals' issues while simultaneously resenting such responsibility. These patients' mood states typically fluctuate between depression and anger. Characteristic behavioral indicators for this depressive category include frequent changes in career path, relationship failure including divorces, longstanding dependency relationships with parents, and conflicts with supervisors. Some of the oppositional depression symptoms may overlap with symptoms described in DSM III-R for passive-aggressive personality disorder.

> *Clinical Vignette—Oppositional Depression:* A 39-year-old occupational therapist requested treatment with the author, complaining of severe depressive symptoms, including overeating, lack of motivation to form life goals, and social withdrawal. The patient had been married but was divorced and had not been dating for the year prior to seeking treat-

ment. She was engaged in a change of career and was enrolled in a
graduate program to obtain a degree in management. However, she was
having interpersonal conflicts with one of her teachers and could not
bring herself to finish a class paper that would have secured her successful completion of her graduate degree. The patient recounted that she
would sit at her desk and try to complete her paper, but would be
flooded by thoughts of personal inadequacy and the futility of her pur-
suits. She would then furtively leave her house and not do any work on
her paper.

The patient was a psychotherapy veteran. During the preceding ten
years, she had been in long-term treatment with both a Gestalt therapist
and Rogerian therapist, with no significant relief of her symptoms in either instance. She was sophisticated enough in her knowledge of psychological jargon to justify her depression to herself as well as to oppose
any viewpoint presented to her by others, including the therapist. For
example, when the therapist offered an interpretation, or attempted to
focus her on her feelings, she would become tearful and respond negatively with expressions such as: "That's not part of my reality," or "For
me it's not like that." The patient reported that during a recent telephone
conversation with her mother, her mother was extremely critical and
judgmental toward her. In reaction, the patient felt very depressed,
began to cry during the conversation, and responded with the sarcastic
comment, "Thanks for sharing." In summary, she would vacillate emotionally between feeling depressed for rehashing her emotional inade-
quacies and feeling angry toward others for mistreating her. She seemed
stuck with feelings of anger, but did not have the ability to give voice to
her specific feelings. Her anger would then become indirect and generalized and would cause her to sabotage herself in many areas while opposing and distancing herself from others.

Defeatist Depression

This face of depression refers to patients who have become "professional losers." They create life scenarios in which they end up de-
feated, rejected, or helpless. They continuously snatch defeat from the
jaws of victory, as if dedicated to proving that they can fail in any
situation. They are differentiated from oppositionally depressed patients in that they have no previous history of personal success, and
their rage is much more readily observable. They not only oppose
feedback from others, but they also become quite angry that others do
not concur with their defeatist scenario. They usually initiate interactions by directly or indirectly asking for sympathy and understanding
for their defeats. However, they quickly elicit anger because of exaggerated expressions of helplessness and hopelessness. The anger they

elicit from others in turn feeds into their feelings of depression and dejection. Nonetheless, they seem unaware of how they provoke anger and are quick to accuse others of being insensitive and harsh while depicting themselves as misunderstood, unloved, and rejected. They refuse to acknowledge their own contribution to their personal problems. However, their depression is frighteningly real with what they report to be almost unbearable and consistently negative ruminations.

These patients' mood states tend to fluctuate between depression and a high level of rage at self and others. Characteristic behavioral indicators for this depressive strain include stubbornness, the projection of rejection while interacting with others, feelings of suspiciousness or bigotry toward others, interpretation of the suggestions of others as condemnations, deflection of interpersonal feedback, psychological rigidity, a clear history of repeated work and interpersonal failures, refusal to acknowledge their own contribution to personal difficulties, and a pernicious cycle of defeatist scenarios. Some of the defeatist depression symptoms may correspond with symptoms described in DSM III-R for paranoid personality disorder.

> *Clinical Vignette—Defeatist Depression:*   A 23-year-old man was referred to the author in desperation by another therapist who stated that he was exasperated because he was unable to achieve meaningful results with the patient after three years of weekly individual psychotherapy sessions. The patient presented with many depressive symptoms, including suicidal ideation. Self-employed, he cleaned cars, but reported that he had numerous conflicts with his clients who "are too picky and don't understand me." He stated that he had many problems, had seen many therapists, and that "none of them have really helped me." His description of his difficulties converged around the themes of being unsuccessful at most endeavors, and being rejected by others. His speech was characterized by a preponderant use of the word "no." He would respond to most comments with such responses as: "I don't think so", "I've never been in touch with my feelings all my life", "I don't know what I feel." He would readily avow his helplessness and state to the therapist, "I don't know how to . . . You're supposed to help me figure things out." Yet it became increasingly clear that he would react to feedback by using his defeatist hammer to destroy what was offered him as he responded with answers such as, "I've already tried that," or "That doesn't work."
>
> The patient reported that he was in total social isolation and did not have any friends. However, he had developed an elaborate system to explain his isolation, relating it to the "differences between people in New York and California." The patient had moved to California from New York approximately eight years earlier. He insisted that: "People

are much friendlier in New York than in California. I had many friends in New York. People in New York are easy to talk to, but in California no one will talk to me." He persisted in this belief despite a recent vacation in New York during which most of his "friends" would not return his calls. In his view, his interpersonal difficulties were totally unrelated to him and were due to the problems of other persons who reside in California. In summary, this patient had developed a means for ensuring defeat in most endeavors. He invested so much energy in developing defeatist scenarios that he ended up feeling exhausted and had no energy left to explore or enjoy life. He was deeply absorbed in his defeatist scenario, with the result that he was interpersonally isolated and personally limited, unable to recognize or meet his own needs. In this state, he could not even begin to fathom the needs or wishes of others.

Narcissistic Depression

In narcissistic depression, the patient experiences a severe depressed state mixed with unbridled rage. In addition to their clinical depression, these patients exhibit a sense of grandiosity and feelings of entitlement. They feel deeply injured when others do not acknowledge their sense of self-importance, yet they refuse to reciprocate by extending similar privileges to others. They experience frequent indignation in their perception that others are "indifferent" to them, followed by explosive rage toward others for not attending to them, followed by feelings of guilt and depression before eventually reverting to indignation for a repetition of the cycle. Their relationships with others tend to oscillate between short-lived periods of overidealization and utter incrimination, that is, another person may seem to be the greatest specimen of humanity to them on one day, and be persona non grata the next day.

When they feel emotionally wounded by others, their feelings of entitlement and their self-preoccupation are used to justify a retaliatory response. In these instances, they tend to relate to others with impeccable cruelty and sang-froid. Their expression of rage might then be displayed by exploding at others publicly or by intentionally developing schemes for shaming or embarrassing the intended victim of their rage. In their virulent self-righteousness, they exhibit a lack of empathy for the other person's position. Once their rage has been detonated, it is usually followed by feelings of guilt leading either to despair or to an unsuccessful attempt to make amends with the person at whom the rage was directed. Their patterns persist regardless of the presence or absence of situational stressors. Subsequently, their interpersonal world is deserted as they provoke feelings of fear and apprehension in others. They complain about the cruelties and traumas inflicted upon them by others, yet fail to see these same aspects in themselves. Their emotional states fluctuate among rage, guilt, and depression, thus conveying moodiness and emotional unpredictability.

Characteristic behavioral indicators for this category include a consistent history of relationship failures (including divorces and alienation from the members of one's own family), a history of persistent suicidal ideation, and numerous accidents attributable to "dangerous hobbies" such as reckless driving, drug usage, or collecting and using dangerous weapons. Job-related difficulties are not uncommon, and these individuals may end up being either "impossible bosses" who cannot develop group cohesiveness with their employees or problem employees who project a negative image of the organization they represent. Some of the narcissistic depression symptoms may intersect with symptoms described in DSM III-R for narcissistic personality disorder.

> *Clinical Vignette—Narcissistic Depression:* A 50-year-old chair of a university chemistry department requested therapy, complaining of severe depression and interpersonal problems. The patient had been appointed to the chairmanship of the chemistry department by the dean of the faculty at his university two years earlier despite faculty opposition to his appointment. He described his colleagues as "insensitive, stupid, and unable to follow departmental regulations." Upon further investigation, it became clear that the patient himself was insensitive. As examples, he would fume at the department secretaries for making insignificant typing errors, or he might storm out of departmental meetings ranting and raving at various colleagues and slamming doors. He felt entitled to many privileges and courtesies from his colleagues, yet accorded them none. He would make a point of incriminating his colleagues publicly, saying such things as, "I told you this before," or, "If you do this again, I will have to take disciplinary action against you." He would report such clearly inappropriate behaviors to the author with a tone of sheer self-justification and the expectation of support for his pronouncements. The patient simultaneously stated that he felt desperate over his troubled relationships and lack of friends. He had engaged in an affair with a colleague, whom he described as "my madonna, a very special person." This affair went sour when the woman became disenchanted with his feelings of entitlement, his moodiness, and his lack of regard for her needs. Eventually, she ended the relationship. He responded to this by severely berating his "Madonna" in public and attempting to have her demoted from her departmental post. He then experienced a period of depression which led him to express his anger

by driving recklessly. He caused an accident in which he rear-ended another vehicle, resulting in severe hand and facial injuries to himself. The patient's difficulties were compounded by an antagonistic relationship with his teenage daughter who had run away from home. She was facing legal difficulties due to drug dealing and car stealing incidents. The patient felt extremely guilty about his daughter's behavior and vacillated between the extremes of wanting to protect her and being enraged by her behavior. His daughter refused to see him on numerous occasions, which caused further depression. He appeared to be constantly teetering on the edge of chaos, using his rage as a fuel to continue his fights with the world, while simultaneously feeling emotionally bankrupt, dissatisfied, and dejected.

Hysterical Depression

The features of this disorder approximate what is called "agitated depression" in the literature. Clinically, hysterical depression has many psychopathological elements. It can manifest a manic aspect with the patient engaging in a flurry of activities that do not meet the full criteria for bipolar disorder. It can have a paranoid element with extreme interpersonal suspiciousness and the development of different "schemes" to protect oneself from feared attacks by others. It can have a dissociative component with feelings of derealization and depersonalization from which the patient quickly recovers. It can also exhibit a psychosomatic feature with numerous physiological complaints. Moreover, it can involve a sociopathic and borderline aspect with unpredictable rage at certain persons and the intent to get revenge for misperceived "injustices." In summary, the only predictable element in hysterical depression is its unpredictability. These patients are clearly very difficult to treat, and they usually have difficulty in complying with therapeutic recommendations. They seem to live in a constant state of emotional agitation, perpetually depressed and also perpetually anxious and enraged. Their emotions are invariably amplified, exaggerated, and multiplied to a higher degree than reflects their true proportion. Their emotional world resembles a volcano in constant eruption, with depression being the most frequent type of lava spouted. They tend to convey an impression of unyielding emotional edginess, as if an ominous event of gigantic and tragic proportions was soon to befall them. Consequently, they quickly succeed at provoking edginess and anxiety in others. As a result of the interpersonal emotional ambiance they create, they end up being isolated, with few, if any, friends. In certain instances, they may have an unusual or "magnetic" quality that initially attracts others to them. However this magnetic attractiveness fades quickly when others begin to perceive the shallowness, lack of genuineness, suspiciousness, and rage exhibited by these patients. Other interpersonal disturbances include demandingness toward others coupled with a continuous need for attention and praise, interpersonal manipulations, and exaggerated dependency needs. Suicide threats and suicidal gestures are not uncommon and they typically orchestrate false attempts to manipulate and frighten others. These patients show an erratic work history, and tend to hold jobs in the service industries where they can have superficial interactions that are not self-threatening. They may have conflicts at work with supervisors or peers, and can end up switching jobs frequently or quitting work for long periods of time. Additional behavioral indicators for this condition are marital as well as familial conflicts (both with members of one's immediate family and with one's extended family), in which the patient feels deeply wronged or used by relatives or immediate family members. The feeling of being exploited by others may permeate the daily interactions of these patients. The lack of intimacy in their lives is a predominant feature of their functioning. Feelings of emptiness and lack of direction may also be seen, together with rebelliousness concerning recommendations for change. A history of failed treatments with multiple transfers from one therapist to another and reassignment to different therapeutic programs or modalities often occurs with these patients. Finally, numerous psychosomatic complaints with no physical base are present, together with a belligerent attitude toward the medical system for not "curing" them.

> *Clinical Vignette—Hysterical Depression:*   A 36-year-old real estate broker requested treatment, complaining of a crippling depression that she stated was preventing her from performing at work and was causing interpersonal difficulties with her husband and son. The patient seemed rather flamboyant and agitated, with a somewhat flowery and exaggerated verbal style. She stated, "I have changed therapists as frequently as I have changed my socks. None of them have been able to help me whatsoever." When further questioned on her previous treatments, it became evident that she had effectively sabotaged her prior therapeutic work by wanting to self-treat, refusing to comply with therapeutic recommendations, and feeling suspicious toward and betrayed by her therapists even though they had made energetic efforts to help her. She terminated treatment impulsively whenever she perceived the therapist to be "mishandling" her issues. These interpersonal conflicts extended beyond the

therapeutic arena to the overall pattern of the patient's interactions with others. For example, the patient showed exaggerated distrust of her husband, her son, and her co-workers, whom she felt were all exploiting her. She would interpret differences of opinion as put-downs or rejections, and gestures of good faith extended by others toward her were seen as lies or fake overtures. She seemed extremely critical of others and of herself. She expressed righteous indignation at the medical system for its failure to cure various psychosomatic symptoms she had experienced since early adulthood, yet it seemed that she did not know exactly what she wanted from the system (besides dueling with the clinicians from whom she had chosen to seek treatment). She appeared unable to self-examine, and showed little insight with respect to others' motives or even her own. She appeared to be edgy and unpredictable, with a high degree of bitterness for misperceived wrongs committed by entities or others toward her. Furthermore, she was intolerant of any differences of opinion or unfamiliar alternatives presented to her, and would see such presentations as personal rejections since she had not thought of them first.

In many instances, it seemed that her anger was a disguised request for affection and acceptance from others, since she did not know of any other way to express her needs. She often seemed flooded by her own emotions, and incapable of decoding exactly what she felt. Her overall clinical presentation involved many feelings simultaneously displayed in a dramatic fashion without allowing any of these emotions to be explored in depth. While undoubtedly depressed, she could show in quick succession a fit of anger, a fit of laughter, a fit of tears, followed by a return to a neutral emotional tone before leaving the consulting room. Her ability to disconnect from one emotional state and rapidly move into another seemed to represent a disconcerting armor behind which she perpetually shielded herself from others.

Parentified (or Parent-Identified) Depression.

In recent years, the mental health field has had to grapple with the increasing prevalence of child abuse, sexual or otherwise. Child abuse has not received proper consideration in the mental health field due, perhaps in part, to a shortcoming in psychoanalytic theory. Sigmund Freud theorized that children have active sexual fantasies about their parents (Freud, 1959, 1953/1974). The reality of child sexual abuse indicates that, in fact, it is the parents who have active sexual fantasies about their own children or other children. These are carried out, in some instances, in the form of sexual molestation. The discovery of this important reality has brought about strong reactions in psychoanalytic circles (Masson, 1985), but has also further sensitized clinicians to the recognition that child abuse can extend beyond sexual abuse. There may be emotional, physical, financial, or other forms of abuse inflicted by parents or parental figures upon children.

Emotionally ill parents leave many emotional casualties behind them. Their abuse of their children sows the seeds of psychopathology as the children later become, in turn, emotionally dysfunctional adults. Such patients include adults molested as children (AMACs), adult children of alcoholics (ACAs), adults emotionally abused as children, adults who have been physically abused or neglected as children, adult children of drug-addicted parents, and adult children of severely mentally ill parents, as well as other adults who have suffered different forms of sustained parental abuse during childhood. There is an important and growing literature (Bradshaw, 1988a, 1988b; Miller, 1981, 1983, 1984, 1986; Minuchin, 1974; Satir, 1967, 1976, 1978, 1988) addressing the psychodynamics and treatment of adults who were abused or abandoned as children of dysfunctional families.

The term "parentified" has been used to describe the childhood experience of these patients. The term implies that the child is expected by the parent to take on a sexual, physical, or emotional adult role that a child would not realistically be equipped to handle. In being forced to take on a "parentified" role, the child, in essence, becomes a parent to his or her own parents. For instance, the child may be expected to fulfill the role of a fully responsive sexual adult, to digest emotional material that is clearly beyond the scope of his or her emotional development, to carry out physical chores that surpass his or her physical abilities, to endure physical hardships and suffering that would incapacitate even an adult, or to carry out other adult responsibilities that do not fall within the realm of usual childhood experiences.

Severe depression seems to be a common denominator for most adults who have been abused and parentified as children. Therefore, the term "parentified depression" has been coined by the author to describe a particular form of depression relating to adults who have been abused and parentified as children. These patients present with a similar cluster of clinical symptoms. They are paralyzed by continuing self-doubts and a negative self-concept. They typically engage in abusive relationships that perpetuate the cycle of abuse they were forced to live through as children. Such relationships may cast them in the role of the continuing victims or perpetrators of abuse through disabling relationships that tend to replay the dysfunctional childhood patterns that are most familiar to them. These patients repeatedly feel "victimized" by the world. Their childhood experiences give them a valid "angle" from which they perceive the world as a threatening, fearsome place where calamities will assuredly befall them and where they will eventually be betrayed, mistreated, invalidated, and victimized. They tend to feel overly responsible for problems or tragedies that do not belong to them and to which they have not contributed in any way. They may feel an exaggerated sense of obligation to make the impossible possible, or to sacrifice themselves in a "martyrized" fashion in order to take care of unfeeling, unresponsive others they may encounter. In effect, they may self-destruct in the hope of pleasing the rejecting god/parent representative. They may have alcohol or drug addiction problems. They may devalue themselves by behaving in self-demeaning ways in order to provoke scorn or rejection. They may feel undeserving of success in life and may sabotage their own talents and accomplishments in order to fail. They are unable to recognize or express their needs to others in their current interactions since as children they were expected to have no needs. They lack social skills and relate to others in accommodating, passive, or at most, passive-aggressive ways. They are afraid of anger, yet have a deeply buried and adamantly denied rage at the way they have been treated throughout their lives.

The predominant mood states that these patients exhibit are depression mixed with fear and anticipatory anxiety, reflecting the anticipation of negative outcomes in most situations. Characteristic behavioral indicators for this condition include problems in sexual behavior as manifested in sexual dysfunctions (e.g., vaginismus, anorgasmia, lack of sexual desire, premature ejaculation, and impotence); sexual promiscuity encompassing a range of psychosexual disorders and unusual sexual acts; phobias with or without panic attacks; repeated nightmares involving gruesome cruelty and pain perpetrated upon the patient; long-term exploitation at work through submission to the demands of unappreciative and abusive employers; a history of divorces or failed relationships with abusive others where the patient typically overstays in the relationship against all indications that the relationship is detrimental to him or her; lack of age-appropriate social skills with the adoption of a passive or passive-aggressive stance in interactions; inability to express personal needs directly with feelings of guilt for having any needs or desires; psychosomatic complaints such as intermittent headaches, "pins and needles," or burning sensations throughout the body; self-demeaning behavior (calling oneself stupid or incompetent, readily submitting to demeaning treatment in social situations); and a pattern of obsessively blaming oneself for disasters or calamities (e.g., plane crashes, world hunger) not directly related to one's behavior.

Clinical Vignette—Parentified Depression: In order to illustrate the complexity of this syndrome, two case examples are provided. The first case illustrates emotional abuse by both parents. The second case illustrates sexual abuse by a father and emotional abuse by a paranoid mother.

> A 34-year-old woman requested psychotherapy complaining of marital difficulties with her husband, recurrent nightmares, feelings of anxiety, career dissatisfaction, recurrent and uncontrollable crying spells, and feelings of inadequacy. The patient seemed to be overly attached to her three-year-old daughter, and would refuse to retain a babysitter so that she and her husband could go out together. She stated that she did not trust babysitters, fearing that they might abuse or otherwise negatively affect her daughter. The patient's father was a police officer who also ran his own business when he was not on duty. Therefore, he was seldom at home and the patient had rarely seen him when she was a child. When her father was at home, the patient felt that he wanted either to sleep or to get ready for work. If she approached her father for affection or attempted to engage him to play with her, he would look at her threateningly and wave his finger, warning her to stay away from him. The patient's mother had worked full-time since the patient was eight years old. At that young age, the patient was expected to take over the household responsibilities and the care of her two younger sisters. For example, when the patient came home from school, her mother would call her from work and give her instructions about preparing dinner for the family. The patient was responsible for the preparation of meals for her family until she was 14 years old. Moreover, her mother expected her to clean the house, including her sisters' rooms as well as her own. The patient recounted that on many occasions she was forced by her mother to make her sisters' beds while her sisters played outside, despite the fact that her sisters were only one and two years younger than she was. She felt that her sisters understood early on that they could manipulate their mother so that the patient would be blamed for any conflicts or problems among them. Therefore, the patient received an inordinately high proportion of the blame for everyday conflicts or problems. She reported that she was physically more attractive than either of her two sisters, but her mother turned this positive aspect into a negative one by calling her a "dumb belle." In addition, her mother repeatedly conveyed to her the contradictory message that "your looks will help you get whatever you need in life."

The patient related an incident that poignantly captures the flavor of her childhood experiences. The incident occurred when the family cat was killed by an automobile. The three sisters were all deeply grieved by the cat's death. However, the patient tearfully reported that she spent a long time nurturing and consoling her sisters for the cat's death, yet no one in the family took the time to reciprocate. She indignantly stated, "It was my cat, too!' In summary, she felt repeatedly overtapped for her resources during childhood. The emotional framework of feeling "overtapped" was replayed in her current role with a husband who also had two jobs, was frequently away from home, and expected the patient to be "efficient" without allowing her to express her emotional needs. Furthermore, the patient idealized her relationship with her daughter, and had irrational fears regarding harm that might befall her child. She emphatically stated: "I want to protect my daughter from what I lived through as a child. I want her to have a happy childhood."

The second case of parentified depression pertains to a 54-year-old woman who presented herself for treatment complaining of driving phobia (especially when driving over bridges or intersections), fears related to her adult children dying in automobile accidents, nightmares, and frequent panic attacks. The patient was severely depressed and had difficulty sleeping at night. She faced a distressing work situation in which an exploitive employer demanded that she work unrecorded and uncompensated overtime hours. The patient was also engaged in clearly exploitive relationships with her children and with others whom she considered friends, who seemed to abuse her resources both emotionally and financially. She had been married five times, each time to a man who constantly criticized her, encouraged her dependency and passivity, and invalidated her emotional needs. She experienced a particularly cruel form of emotional abuse at the hands of one of her husbands. He would surreptitiously hide the medications she was taking and then accuse her of losing her mind when she could not find where she left them.

The patient stated that she suffered from longstanding migraine headaches, and was prone to uncontrollable crying spells, which lasted approximately 20 minutes. She could not attribute these episodes to any recognizable environmental trigger. She was the oldest child in her family, with one brother who was three years younger. Her parents had divorced when she was nine years old, and her mother remarried three years later. She reported that her mother became highly suspicious of her after she remarried. After the patient's stepfather moved in to live with the family, the mother established a series of extremely severe rules governing the patient's interactions with her stepfather. For instance, the patient was not allowed to look at her stepfather directly in the face during normal conversation; she was expected either to look away from him or to turn her chair the other way when she was talking to him so that they would not see each other face to face. Moreover, the patient's mother ordered her to go straight to her room upon returning from school each day, without engaging in any interactions whatsoever with her stepfather. The patient was sequestered in her room most afternoons and evenings, and had dinner alone in her room, separate from the other family members. After everyone had retired to their individual rooms at night, the mother expected her daughter to come downstairs, wash the dishes, and clean the house. On the stepfather's birthday, the mother would ask the patient to cook his favorite dish for him, and she would then ask her daughter whether she "minded" if she, the mother, claimed credit. The patient had to abide by her mother's rules from age 12 until the time she left home at age 18. She stated that, throughout this period, she would notice her mother constantly watching her to verify that she was not associating with her stepfather. The mother would also become infuriated if her husband looked at the patient or violated the unwritten code that she had established for the family. Fifteen years after the patient had left home, her mother became physically handicapped and moved from another city to live in the same neighborhood as the patient. She expected the patient to assume full nursing responsibility for her, which the patient dutifully carried out for ten years thereafter.

As mentioned earlier, the patient's biological parents divorced when she was five years old. When she was nine years old, she and her mother and brother moved to California. Her father, who already resided in California, came to visit his two children for the first time after a four-year absence. The patient was evidently very happy to see her father again. Around that time, however, she needed to enter the hospital for a tonsillectomy. She clearly remembered that her father took her to the hospital as her mother was working that day. After her operation, she was sent to a private hospital room to recuperate while still under anesthesia. Her father accompanied her to her room following the operation. The patient repeatedly stated that "something wrong" happened between her and her father in that room yet she had a complete emotional and memory block regarding the nature of the incident.

This patient had subsequently refused to submit to anesthesia in any operation during her adult life, and had an unexplainable fear of hospitals. Moreover, she mentioned that, whenever she went to visit her father as an adult, her father would greet her by kissing her on the lips and touching her chest with his hands. The patient's emotional and memory block regarding the incident with her father after the operation persisted for the first nine months of treatment. The clinical puzzle was finally resolved when the patient came in for a session in a state of total emotional exhaustion. She reported that she had watched a television movie the previous evening in which a nine-year-old girl who was committed to an institution was given a soporific drug by one of the institution's employees, who raped the child while she was under its effect. The patient's state of high emotional activation following the movie gave her the key to what had happened to her. By piecing together the available elements of the clinical puzzle, it became clear that the patient believed she had been sexually molested by her biological father at age nine while under anesthesia after her tonsillectomy. The patient was emotionally devastated by this realization, especially as she began to unblock and remember the details of the molestation. She was severely depressed following this breakthrough. She realized that both of her parents had violated her in different ways, and that her life was bereft of genuine affection. The stark absence of emotional support in her life was further highlighted by the fact that both of her parents were especially affectionate toward her younger brother throughout their lives, continuously showering him with attention and gifts. Over time, her brother had developed a demanding relational pattern toward her, expecting her to "help him" when he was having difficulties. In summary, the patient felt shackled by her lifelong abuse. Due to the numerous emotional traumas to which she had been subjected, she felt unable to reconstruct an emotionally stable visage. She felt tormented by the emotional quicksand into which she was thrust as a child and into which she continued to fall as an adult. She was fighting a war of self-attrition with no end in sight. The depth of her depression could only be equalled by the depth of her buried rage.

Borderline Depression

This strain of depression is predominantly seen in patients suffering from a borderline personality disorder. In borderline depression, the predominant mood state related to depression is fear, which causes patients to project a "frozen image" where their emotional reactions are not shown to others. These patients may also experience periods of suspiciousness of varying intensity that may take on paranoid proportions under certain circumstances. When severely depressed, they may have brief psychotic episodes with both delusions and hallucinations during which they are unable to carry on with everyday activities and may threaten or attempt suicide. Their depression is characterized by a "mute" flavor whereby most of their pain and suffering is internalized and experienced subjectively and is not evident or observable to others around them. The muting of their depression may be related to their fear of others and their basic belief that others cannot understand their feelings. They typically do not socialize with others in any meaningful way, and would tend to project socially as loners. Their depression is the result of a ruthless self-examination, the invariable result of which is that they do not deserve to be approached by others or to be successful in life. Therefore, they mostly withdraw from their environment except for essential or necessary interactions. Subsequently, their behavior becomes rather predictable along the axis of withdrawal from emotional or behavioral participation with others. Characteristic behavioral indicators for this condition include a history of shallow relationships and oversensitivity to being hurt by others, a chaotic career history including holding jobs that are below their intellectual potential, difficulties in clearly expressing themselves, disastrous judgment in interpersonal relationships with an inability to distinguish genuine offers of intimacy from false ones, the potential or actual presence of suicidal attempts and brief psychotic breakdowns including delusional thinking and hallucinations, and the "frozen" image described above.

Clinical Vignette—Borderline Depression: A 31-year-old woman requested treatment complaining of severe depressive symptoms. The patient was living with her brother at the time, whom she described as a chronic alcoholic with an explosive temper. She had been emotionally coerced by her parents to live with her brother and to play a quasi-nursing role with him. However, the situation had reached an unmanageable level because of her brother's extensive alcoholic binges and his emotional and physical abuse toward her. The patient had previously engaged in other abusive relationships, including a marriage to a physically abusive husband as well as a recent relationship in which she was emotionally exploited by an oblivious, married man. The patient's father was employed in a position that required him to travel extensively during the patient's childhood. He was a distant, withdrawn figure in her life. She stated that her father was physically absent for such long periods of time that she actually believed he had died at one point. When her father was present, he engaged her in a type of interpersonal debate in which he quizzed her and simultaneously took the opposite position to whatever she said. She reported that her father made a point of "showing her" that she was wrong on most of her answers. She was not allowed to discuss how she felt about different situations because her father had repeatedly said that feelings were "useless."

The patient's mother was a passive-aggressive woman who played a martyr role in the family and manipulated the patient into doing what the mother felt "should be done," such as taking care of her alcoholic brother. Moreover, the patient was having problems at work with an exploitive supervisor, who asked her to do most of the hard work and then took credit for it. The patient's relationship with her brother, which was the presenting problem, caused her much emotional suffering over the years. She reported that her brother, three years younger, neglected her during most of her childhood. She stated, "I became invisible for him for most of our childhood." For example, though the patient and her brother attended the same school, he would not speak to her if he saw her in the school hallways. Moreover, her brother had been physically violent toward her on many occasions, including episodes of locking her in a closet and throwing away the key, pushing her in front of a car on a street, playing dangerous childhood "games" with her such as having her insert a metal implement into an electric socket, and attempting to drown her in the family pool.

Though the mother was at home during the patient's childhood, she was totally oblivious to the patient's complaints regarding her brother and would disregard her daughter's reports that he was physically endangering her. The current living arrangements were such that the patient was again thrust into the same situation of being physically endangered by her brother. Just as before, her parents did not heed her complaints regarding her brother's behavior, and expected her "to keep quiet and take care of him." The patient stated that she was having difficulty sleeping at night and was having nightmares and delusions about shadows moving in the dark outside her house or entering her room. She experienced active suicidal ideation, and projected a "frozen" emotional expression reflecting the depth of her paralyzing underlying depression. She spoke with a lisp, which became accentuated when she was tense. It was also difficult to decode her communication since she communicated in a type of "word salad" that included multiple reactions and feelings regarding disparate issues. She frequently went off on tangents when she attempted to answer a question. She seemed to be verbally and emotionally immobilized by her fear and its concomitant self-contained depressive stance. The flavor of the patient's condition is perhaps best conveyed by a recurrent nightmare, which she called "the rat dream." The patient would invariably wake up perspiring, breathless, and terrorized every time she had this nightmare, in which rats invaded every inch of her room and squirmed all over her bed. The patient described the core of her nightmare as follows:

> "Slowly, I turn my head to the right, very slowly, and look towards my toes. I freeze on the spot. There are rats all over my bed. The panic comes up and almost takes over; I will myself not to move in spite of it. The rats are so close that I can see every detail on their ugly faces, I can see the coarse hair sticking out of their fur, the claws on their toes. But their faces are the worst, red beady eyes, long whiskers, and big teeth with pink gums. I want to close my eyes, but I can't because I am too afraid to. I'm having trouble breathing but I make myself. My head starts to spin inside with panic. I make it stop. I have to be able to think. I push the fear down into a little spot and seal it off. I can't move because the movement makes the rats angry. The rats are happy because no matter what I do they will win. I'm dead either way. I start to scream in my head. I don't dare to scream out loud."

Anxiety-Linked Depression

In this disorder, the essential depressive symptoms seem to be triggered by a deep-seated anxiety that permeates the patient's world. These patients experience continuous worries about most current events in their lives, mingled with non-specific feelings of apprehension about the future without any specific reason. They tend to be brooding, uneasy, highly ambivalent in their decision making, and self-doubting. Overall, they appear to feel "hassled" by others and by the world. Their depression feeds on feelings of being harassed and overburdened. Therefore, they tend to ride an emotional roller coaster; at one extreme, they feel depressed and exhausted, and at the other extreme, they feel anxious and harrowed. Their relationships with others are unproductive because they feel interpersonally threatened and put-upon by others' "undue demands." They also feel distressed in the presence of others, and are unable to establish intimate relationships, due to the mixture of interpersonal frostiness and withdrawal that they exhibit. When vexed by what they perceive to be discourteous behavior, they tend to take a punishing stance toward others' "misbehavior." The punishing aspect of their negative interpersonal evaluations leads them to cut others off emotionally when feeling intimidated or irritated. This attitude perpetuates their feelings of alienation. The dysfunctional interpersonal patterns that prevent them from achieving intimacy cause them to leave behind a trail of unfinished relationships with different unresolved issues that are not addressed in actuality or in retrospect. Any attempt to discuss important emotional issues with them is met with hypersensitivity and the threat of discontinuing all contact. The threat escalates as the other person persists with the request for meaningful emotional communication. Characteristic behavioral indicators for this condition include anxiety-related tics or habits such as picking at one's face, nail biting, or muscle jerking. Furthermore, there may be a history of inability to control eating and excretion habits. The somatic symptoms exhibited by these patients include panic attacks, heart palpitations, choking, chest tightness, trembling, faintness, sweating, or increased pulse rate. Relationship and marital difficulties are frequent in these patients, with the distinguishing characteristic of having successive brief relationships that end in emotionally traumatic ways with unfinished emotional business between both partners. There may also be job-related difficulties as the individual feels alienated from peers on the job, or as he or she feels besieged by institutional requirements.

Clinical Vignette—Anxiety-Linked Depression: A 36-year-old engineer requested treatmeAt complaining of severe depression following a recent divorce. He also reported that he had interpersonal difficulties at work with his colleagues, whom he felt berated him and ignored his needs. Furthermore, the patient stated that he had "problems" with his supervisor because he had difficulty in carrying out some of his job duties. He had noticed that his supervisor was observing him closely in order to ensure that he was fulfilling his responsibilities. This provoked the patient's anger toward the supervisor, whom he felt was hassling him. In short, the patient had come to perceive his job as an annoyance and believed that his peers and his supervisor were treating him in an insensitive manner. Except for his marriage, which had lasted approximately two years, the patient had a relational style of dating women for brief periods—usually about two months. Typically, he would have three or four dates with different women in the same week, with all of them ending in failure and disappointment. He attributed his relational failures to his belief that, "I just couldn't get my point across."

He appeared to be rather guarded and interpersonally defensive, and would automatically interpret any differences of opinion between himself and others as a personal rejection, which would make him angry with the alleged perpetrator of the rejection. His negative sense of self-esteem usually led him to believe that the women he dated did not value him as a person. Therefore, he would endeavor to dazzle them, inviting them to dinner at expensive restaurants, but then invariably blaming them for his overspending.

The patient had come from an emotionally dysfunctional family with a highly dominant mother and a passive father. His mother had the habit of regularly calling him to chastise him for "not keeping in touch," which enraged him. He did not voice his angry feelings to her, which gave her implicit permission to continue calling him. Although the patient was submissive toward his mother, he tended to be punishing and intolerant toward others who disagreed with him, reacting rudely to any perceived rejection. The patient reported that he was subject to long depressive bouts during which he would unhook the phone, crawl into bed and pull the covers over his head, and feel extremely depressed. During these episodes, he had an active fantasy of his mother coming to take care of him. Another interesting feature of this patient's presentation was his body posture. He would thrust his upper body in front of his legs when walking as if running ahead of himself. When stressed, his anxiety also showed in various body tics, including uncontrollable nose twitching, shaking of both hands, and an overall rigid sitting posture with his gaze fixed on an object away from his interlocutor. The most striking common denominators of his different life situations were his reenactment of the same dysfunctional interpersonal pattern of high expectations followed by a feeling of being misunderstood and hassled by others, coupled with the nagging feeling that he was on the verge of breaking through emotionally to others, and yet for some reason "just could not get his point across."

Secondary Depression

This type of depression is commonly seen in successful individuals who do not suffer from major psychopathology but who present with an unyielding feeling of sadness and discontentment. The predominant mood state is related to a constant dissatisfaction with one's accomplishments and a feeling "that one has not yet arrived." Patients suffering from secondary depression are usually high-functioning professionals who have achieved well in their respective professions. They are clearly perfectionistic and have used their perfectionism to hone their skills and abilities in a particular field of endeavor. In that sense, their perfectionism serves a constructive purpose. The dysfunctional aspect of their perfectionism is that it prevents them from accepting their accomplishments and relaxing enough to enjoy their successes. They tend to live in an idealized world where everything has to be "just so." Their relationships with others tend to be invaded by their perfectionism as they look for the perfect friend or emotional partner. They are disappointed by the shortcomings they perceive in others, and cannot overcome their disappointment to see the overall constructive aspects of others.

When hurt by others, they tend to exaggerate the hurt, and refuse to continue in the relationship and learn from the hurtful episode. They tend to use their work as a protective barrier to ward off intimacy with others, and look on their own achievements with some degree of scorn. They are embarrassed by the compliments or recognition others may offer them, and have difficulty in allowing others to get to know them at a personal level. Their failures tend to be concentrated in the interpersonal area, with an ongoing history of relational difficulties. However, they do not have much difficulty in launching new relationships due to their good verbal skills and high degree of professional success. They are usually excited at the outset of a new relationship, and then tend to gradually lose interest in the other person.

As they are unable to accept failure, they do not learn from the emotional lessons that accompany it. They are oversensitive to any form of constructive feedback or criticism, and may experience shame or embarrassment with respect to things that would seem customary to others (such as being given instructions or a protocol on how to address a sensitive situation with which they are unfamiliar). The predominant mood state that accompanies depression in these patients is a sense of dissatisfaction and a tension surrounding the themes of "wanting more" and "getting more." Characteristic behavioral indicators for this condition are a history of high professional or business achievements coupled with a history of relational failures and obsessive rumination regarding work-related items that are used as a smokescreen to fill an emotional void. A further behavioral indicator is that these patients allow their work time to slowly creep into their personal time with the justification that, "I must make sure that this is done smoothly by the deadline."

Idealistic expectations of others are also present, together with an idealized way of looking at the world. Another sphere of stark contrast highlighted in secondary depression is that these patients show great responsibility in intellectual and work areas together with marked irresponsibility in emotional and relationship areas. They appear to be more concerned with the appropriateness of the interpersonal image they project than with the more authentic emotional image that reflects their human needs, vulnerabilities, and frailties. In this sense, they seem strikingly inept at voicing personal needs in a constructive way.

> *Clinical Vignette—Secondary Depression:*   A 47-year-old corporate executive presented himself for treatment complaining of multiple relationship failures and interpersonal problems with his executive secretary, whom he felt was overly domineering and insensitive to his needs. He showed an outstanding record of career achievement with successive promotions. He had been married once and had a daughter from that marriage. He experienced conflicts with his ex-wife over her not allowing him to see his daughter as much as he wanted. He could not effectively assert himself with his ex-wife to directly express what he wanted in terms of visitation times and privileges. Subsequent to his divorce, he led an active social life and engaged in numerous relationships. In these relationships, he would be impressed by the beauty or intelligence of his companion, and would idealize her attributes. This preceded a second phase in the relationship in which he would begin to notice certain "defects" or "shortcomings" in the woman he was dating. As examples, he might complain that the woman did not know how to conduct an active conversation in social settings, did not know how to dress appropriately, was too quiet, or did not exactly fit his particular image of feminine beauty. The predictable third phase of the relationship would occur when the patient would gradually withdraw from the relationship, which would provoke anger and withdrawal on the part of his companion. Eventually, this would lead to a breakup and the later initiation of a new relationship by the patient with a reenactment of the idealization/ disappointment/withdrawal phases. Upon the dissolution of each of these relationships, the patient experienced a severe depressive episode with symptoms of insomnia, psychosomatic problems, blurred vision, lack of motivation for work, and a feeling that he would soon die. His relationship with his secretary was most unsatisfactory for him and a major source of depression in his life. His secretary was a domineering woman who had worked for him for 15 years. She had her own way of

conducting his business and would not respond to his indirect requests for changes at the office. For instance, he would write notes concerning certain items, which she would not answer. Their interaction consisted of a dizzying barrage of questions thrown at him by her on how she should handle different business matters. She would typically choose to ask him these questions during his lunch break, when he was simply trying to have a sandwich in his office. He expressed anger toward her, yet confessed that he would be totally helpless if she left him. He felt doubtful that he could replace her with another secretary who would be as "competent" as he perceived her to be. In actuality, the patient had created a rather unbearable work situation for himself with his secretary, yet saw himself as having no options but to perpetuate his dissatisfaction and put up with her.

The patient described himself as "Living in a Museum of Disappointed Emotions," and he once verbalized the metaphor of his life as "visiting a wax museum called the Museum of Disappointed Emotions." In this fantasy, he pictured himself as speaking to the wax figures at the museum with none of them responding, and then feeling deeply depressed as a result of the unresponsiveness. The image of the Museum of Disappointed Emotions clearly reflected the patient's idealization and rigidity, and the heavy toll of emotional alienation concurrent with his way of being.

COMMON THERAPIST STUMBLING BLOCKS IN THE TREATMENT OF DEPRESSION

Having delineated the different faces of depression in the first section, the next two sections focus on the treatment of depressive patients. Some of the common stumbling blocks that the clinician may encounter with depressive patients are reviewed. It is important for the clinician to maintain self-awareness regarding these blocks since their insidious effects, when unchecked, can vitiate the psychotherapeutic process. The therapist working with a depressive patient can encounter the following five countertransference blocks:

1. *Taking on a caretaker or enabler role.* This block consists of the therapist feeling sorry for the depressed patient, then taking on increasingly greater responsibilities for the patient's welfare outside of the therapeutic session. Since depressive patients are quite adept at eliciting sympathy or enabling behaviors from others, therapists may quickly find themselves engaging in such behaviors, including reducing or eliminating professional fees for treatment rendered, ignoring or excusing the patient's lack of motivation, extending themselves to the patient outside of the therapeutic context beyond customary and reasonable practice, or taking sides with the patient against others. The

therapist must keep in mind at all times that a major goal in treating depression is to change the patient's attitude of helplessness and to facilitate his or her gradual movement in the direction of self-responsibility. Too much empathy can be as deleterious to the patient's welfare as too little empathy. The therapist must examine his or her own motives in order to take a supportive stance toward the patient without enabling him or her to perpetuate the stance of helplessness. The therapist needs to encourage self-sufficiency instead of promoting self-deficiency.

2. *Losing perspective of the therapist-patient boundaries.* The therapist may become incapable of distinguishing his or her feelings, thoughts, or responsibilities from those of the patient. The therapist may also come to believe that he or she can control the patient's behavior and thus attempts to do so, which may lead to becoming indispensable to the patient. Depressive patients challenge the therapist's objective ability to understand where therapist responsibility stops and where patient responsibility begins.

3. *Elicitation of the therapist's own depression.* Depressive patients may elicit a feeling of ineffectiveness and depression on the therapist's part due to the bottomless pit of their own feelings of ineffectiveness. The therapist must contain his or her own depression and seek supervisory consultation should this depression persist. Being entrapped in the swamp of a mutually depressive ambiance does not advance the patient's treatment. The therapist must maintain a concrete focus, aiming for small and measured therapeutic goals that slowly help pull the patient out of the depressive pit.

4. *Feeling angry at the patient's lack of movement.* Certain strains of depression, especially those related to anger and hysterical depression, can provoke the therapist's anger in response to the patient's rage and or stubbornness. In addition, the therapist may become an identified target of the patient's rage since he or she is proposing new alternatives for approaching situations to replace the ineffective ones entrenched within the patient's maladaptive belief system. The therapist needs to monitor his or her anger and seek consultation for its resolution as indicated. Moreover, the therapist's anger can be brought into the psychotherapeutic process when appropriate, perhaps by pointing out how the patient's interpersonal style provokes frustration in relationships with others. Using examples from both psychotherapeutic sessions and real-life situations to illustrate how the frustration is provoked may prove useful.

5. *The limits of catharsis.* In some instances, depressed individuals can use tears as a cathartic passport to other feelings. Crying becomes a unidimensional outlet for a multidimensional range of emotions. The therapist can help the patient to gain awareness of how crying can mask other emotions, and slowly encourage him or her to express the complexity of feelings without using the mechanism of tears. However, the therapist also needs to keep in mind that the expression of sadness, when it is actually the underlying emotion, is an essential ingredient in processing therapeutic material that relates to either the historical origins or current manifestations of depressive affect. In this respect, the therapist must work with the patient to give sadness and crying its appropriate place, without allowing the tears to take over the patient's overall emotional horizon throughout psychotherapeutic work.

CLINICAL INTERVENTION WITH THE DEPRESSED PATIENT

In this final section, an eight-step treatment program for working with depressed patients is presented. It is subject to modification depending upon the clinician's judgment regarding each patient's unique needs and the particular strain of depression presented by the patient. The eight steps of the treatment program are presented together with a definition of tasks, possible assignments, and a metaphor or story that can be used for each step. The therapist can use his or her clinical judgment in adapting the interpretation of the metaphor to the patient's personal needs and dynamics. The purpose of the assignments, metaphors, and stories is to achieve a reassociation of the patient's experiences. As Musetto (1986) indicated, Erickson believed that cure came from the reassociation of the patient's experiential life. Metaphors and assignments address the unconscious level of functioning by helping the patient dissociate from negative patterns and associate with either already experienced positive patterns or newly discovered patterns offered by the therapist.

Step 1—Resolution of Original Conflicts

Depressive affect may originate from the leftover feelings experienced by the patient in interaction with parental figures during childhood. These feelings are exacerbated by current events that patients interpret as further confirmation of the way their parental figure(s) perceived or treated them. Depression can originate in childhood interactions with emotionally unavailable, condemning, abusive, depressed, or otherwise psychologically dysfunctional parents, who convey an inadequate perception of self, others, and the world to the patient. Later on, it becomes extremely difficult for an individual to surpass these limitations and achieve a satisfying self-perspective. The patient keeps returning to the same emotional frame of reference developed when he or she was growing up. During step 1, the therapist's task is to help patients make the necessary linkages between their past experiences (Archeological), their presenting problems (Contemporary), and their style of interaction with the therapist during psychotherapeutic sessions (Immediacy). This author has proposed (Salameh, 1986, 1987, In progress) a process model within the Integrative Short-Term Psychotherapy (ISTP) approach which provides the therapist with the necessary structure for making therapeutic linkages. This model is presented in Figure 2. In following this model, the therapist can link the patient's past experiences with contemporary experiences, both of which are further linked with the immediate manifestation of

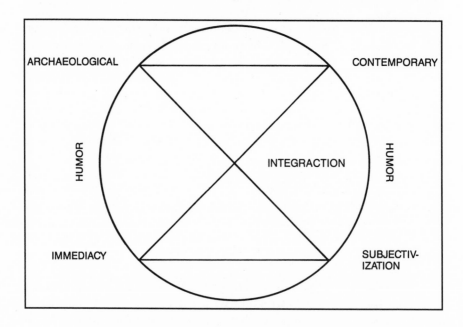

Figure 2. Integrative short-term psychotherapy process model

these patterns or experiences during interactions with the therapist. Once the patient is aware of Archeological/Contemporary/Immediacy the linkages (ACI), he or she would then enter the subjectivization stage, consisting of the expression of emotional material that relates to "unfinished emotional business" connected with such linkages. The subjectivization stage is then followed by an "Integraction," where patients can integrate their insights with their emotions, and act in concrete ways to initiate behavioral changes. Humor can be used with sensitivity and judiciousness by the therapist to help lubricate the entire process.

ACI Assignments. Different assignments can be used to help in establishing the linkages. Such assignments may include role playing using an "empty chair technique" whereby the patient dialogues with one or more parental figures with whom there is unfinished emotional business. The role playing would involve the patient sitting in the empty chair, and at different points in the dialogue taking on the role of the parental figure with whom there are unresolved issues. It can be reasonably assumed that the patient has incorporated many of the parental figure's patterns within his or her self-concept, and can therefore play the parent rather accurately. In those instances when the parental figure is deceased, some patients may feel the need to visit the parent's grave site following the role playing and attempt to pursue an emotional resolution with the parent if they feel ready for such an assignment. Writing an unaddressed letter to a parent can either replace or complement the role playing.

Metaphor. A friend of mine has a wise old grandmother who has witnessed many events in her lifetime. Grandmother has a favorite saying, which she frequently repeats: "You don't have to pay for the same dinner twice."

Step 2—Working Through Unresolved Grief

One way of gaining a theoretical understanding of depression is to interpret it as a prolonged unresolved grief reaction. Depressive patients may feel unresolved grief over love offered yet rejected by others, mistreatment, failed dreams, and other concerns that may be of crucial relevance to the patient. The therapeutic task at this step is to help process unresolved grief reactions that the patient may still be harboring. This work could overlap with the work delineated in step 1. The grief needs to be exhausted and "worked through" in order for the patient's emotional life to be filled with other options. Depressive patients can learn that they do not need to react uniformly with grief to different life situations. In another sense, grief needs to be placed in its proper perspective. The patient can be helped to reach the realization that grief is entwined with life itself, and yet that life is more than grief. Paradoxically, the acceptance of grief as a normal reaction allows for the acceptance of joy and happiness as well. Depressive patients often feel that they do not have the right to grieve for the sad occurrences in their lives, thus forcing themselves to carry the unresolved grief as a perpetual refrain in their everyday life.

Assignments.   Assignments for working through grief resemble those used in step 1. Other assignments may include keeping a journal, writing a farewell poem, designing an emotionally cathartic role-play situation with the patient whereby the grief can be constructively processed, and other symbolic ways of saying goodbye.

Metaphor.   The following may be told to the grieving patient: Every tear you shed is like a testimonial to the intensity of your love for _____. Presence is not synonymous with death (or separation). The care of your loved one and the memories of what you lived with them will be with you although you are no longer with this person physically. No one can take those memories and love from you. Here is a poem about grief that I have written and would like to share with you.

Through the Fire

Tonight
I held you through the fire
Tonight
Our tears became rivers
And flooded the earth
Tonight
I saw behind the mask
Tonight
I knew
That death cannot erase presence
That love cannot be killed
Tonight

I reached to your spirit
As we soared toward pure acceptance
Tonight
The moon was your glowing heart
Pulsating gently, strongly
Always there
Tonight
I knew I never lost you
And never will
Tonight
The power of our love
Shook the distant mountains.

Step 3—Expression of Anger

Many depressed patients experience a chronic state of anger, with
the distinguishing feature that their anger is turned inward. They
swallow their anger and end up feeling resentful toward themselves,
binding up much of their motivational energies into a pool of self-di-
rected hostility. The therapeutic task at this step is to faciliate the outward expression of anger in constructive ways. The anger may have
historical targets (e.g., disliked parental figures or traumatic childhood
events), or there may be an ongoing target for the anger related to
current events and frustrations.

Assignments.   Assignments for anger expression may include encouraging the patient to be more directly critical of situations he or she
dislikes. For instance, a depressed patient in group psychotherapy was
asked to voice one valid criticism of each group member, including the
therapist, without apologizing for her critical comments. Another assignment could be for the patient to learn how to rephrase what others
are communicating to him or her in order to gain a foothold on the
theme of responsiveness to others (e.g. "So if I understand you cor-
rectly, you are saying that . . . "). A third assignment would consist of
encouraging the patient to role play, asking the person with whom he
or she is angry to leave the consulting room in a fantasy situation, and
then escorting the person out of the office. The object of anger could
be asked to part ways with the patient, and to not disturb him or her
anymore. In another variation, the object at whom the anger is targeted may be asked, in fantasy, to move to an adjacent room during a

therapy session. The patient would then be encouraged to address the anger target through the wall and freely express any unvoiced resentments or dislikes with any level of intensity with which the patient feels comfortable.

Metaphor.   There is a story about a Chinese emperor who was feeling very depressed. A famous doctor was brought in to cure the emperor. He told the emperor: "I can cure your Highness but I will ask for your Highness's mercy not to kill me." The emperor promised that he would not kill the doctor. The doctor then left the emperor's court and promised to return the next day. However, the doctor did not show up to see the emperor the next day or on the four following days. The emperor was furious at the doctor for ignoring him. Finally, the doctor came in on the sixth day. The emperor was so enraged that he ordered him to be put in a big pot of boiling oil. As the doctor was being lowered into the pot, he reminded the emperor of the emperor's promise not to kill him if he was cured of his depression. The emperor ordered that the doctor's life be saved and seldom felt depressed again.

Step 4—Debunking of Myths Held by Depressive Patients

Those clinicians who espouse the cognitive therapy model for the treatment of depression (Beck, 1973, 1983; Beck et al, 1979; Ellis, 1973; Ellis & Whiteley, 1979) have identified many erroneous beliefs held by depressive patients, which cause perceptual distortions resulting in depression. Such erroneous beliefs include overgeneralization from one instance to all instances, negative "I" statements (e.g., "I am ugly"), and other distortions. The therapeutic work at step 4 focuses on debunking any erroneous beliefs or myths held by depressive patients that allow them to perpetuate their condition. Some of the myths commonly observed by this author include (1) "My misery is eternal." Depressive patients must be educated to the effect that every problem or difficulty has a beginning, a middle, and an end. Therefore, no misery is timeless. Whatever situation has triggered the depressive affect will eventually reach its end and exhaust itself. (2) "I am unhappy because others don't do things the way I want them to." Depressive patients must be trained to dissociate their own unhappiness from the behavior of other individuals. What others do or do not do needs to be dissociated from what the depressive patient does or does not do. The depressive patient has to give up the role of the "emotional police officer," constantly taking responsibility for others' behavior or equating the behavior of others with his or her personal worth. Focusing on one's own issues and what one can do to change personally is more likely to lead to productive outcomes. The responsibility for improving one's situation has to be shifted from being another individual's responsibility to being the patient's responsibility. (3) "I must prove to others how wrong they are by suffering personally." The martyrdom complex shown by many depressed patients needs to be debunked. They can learn to express their disagreements directly without using the medium of personal suffering to express dissent.

Assignments. Assignments at this step include asking the patient to write down his or her most common negative thoughts or beliefs, and then examining each belief with the patient to establish its degree of validity. Other assignments would encompass training the patient to stop looking at situations dichotomously, i.e., in terms of "right" and "wrong" or "They are good—I am bad/I am good—they are bad." The therapist can usually detect all these myths in operation by paying attention to the patient's statements and pointing out when such myths are either being voiced or implied by the patient.

Metaphor. There is a Chinese proverb that states "You cannot prevent birds of sorrow from flying over your head, but you can prevent them from building nests in your hair."

Step 5—Reduction of Perfectionism and Accumulation of Efforts

Depressed patients are often strikingly perfectionistic. Such perfectionism prevents them from achieving worthwhile goals, since they refuse to engage in any endeavor if it does not evolve flawlessly and lead to perfect results. They refuse to see the world within a realistic framework, and because of their assessment that they will always fall short of perfection, or that others will not meet their standards, they end up mired in a negative status quo. Therapeutic work at step 5 aims at pointing out how perfectionism cripples the patient from acting constructively, while the therapist attempts to reduce the patient's perfectionistic world view to realistic proportions. The pertinent equation in this regard is that the patient needs to decrease his or her expectations of self and others while increasing his or her personal efforts. The accumulation of small efforts along the way will eventually get the patient closer to the desired goal(s). Usually, if the expectations are too high, then the efforts will decrease due to discouragement over the amount of effort to be extended. On the other hand, if the expectations are decreased, the goals become more feasible and therefore, the efforts will be increased. Depressive patients frequently have a difficult time taking small steps. They expect to make giant steps and consequently end up being immobilized.

Assignments.   Numerous assignments can be used to anchor the notion of accumulation of efforts coupled with the reduction of perfectionism. The patient needs to be trained to break tasks or goals into small digestible units. For example, patients can be asked to develop a list of small daily efforts they would commit themselves to in order to reach a certain goal. Patients can be asked to walk a quarter of a mile or around the block each day, make one telephone call to a friend per day, attend one social activity or meeting each day, or read one article in the daily paper. A depressed patient who had to complete one paper in a course in order to obtain her graduate degree could not bring herself to stay long enough at her desk to complete her paper. She felt that the paper was too overwhelming for her to complete. She was asked to spend only 15 minutes working on her paper every day, which, in her own opinion as well as the therapist's, was a small amount of time. She followed this prescription and was able to complete her paper, for which she received an "A," within four weeks. She subsequently stated to the therapist that this experience helped her become more aware that she could gain control over her helplessness through the accumulation of successful efforts. Another area where perfectionism impedes effective functioning is in the interpersonal arena. Perfectionists relate to others on the basis of the "right answers" that others should provide, as opposed to simply finding out what others really feel or want. One depressive patient had difficulty getting dates because he expected the woman whom he approached to give him the "right answer," which meant agreeing to go out on a date with him in the evening. Anything short of an evening date was not good enough. He was coached to ask the women he liked about their interests and what activities they enjoyed, and then offer to join them in their activities rather than ask for an evening date. He was also encouraged to begin the dating interaction with smaller steps, such as having coffee or lunch together, and gradually getting to know each other in this way before going out on a longer evening date.

Metaphors.   1. Antiperfectionism metaphor: "Best is the enemy of good." A friend of mine related this story to me. When he was a child, he enjoyed hiding himself under a pile of dead autumn leaves and daydreaming. For him, this was a perfect pastime. However, he also told me that he seldom found a nice pile of dead autumn leaves to hide in that did not have a little dog poop in it. He learned to accept that it was okay for nice piles of dead autumn leaves to have a little dog poop in them.

2. Accumulation-of-efforts metaphor: There is a story about the king of a vast territory who had only one son to inherit his kingdom. It broke the king's heart that his only son, the successor to this throne, was a hunchback. On his 16th birthday, the prince asked his father for an unusual birthday gift—a life sized statue in his own likeness that depicted him in an upright standing position, without his humpback. The king was chagrined by his son's request, and yet honored his wishes. The prince asked that the statue be installed in his private quarters. Every morning, when the prince woke up, he would walk up to the statue and attempt to correct his posture to imitate the statue's posture for a few minutes. Five years later, when the prince reached his 21st birthday, everyone was surprised to notice that he was no longer a hunchback.

Step 6—Redirecting Motivation

Some depressed patients seem to restrain their motivational energies to the circumference of depression and its accompanying behavioral correlates. For instance, they may be well-motivated to isolate themselves, ruminate over all the negative aspects they experience on a given day, prevent themselves from taking risks to change their situation, and subsequently feel helpless and hopeless once the depressive state has set in. The therapeutic task at step 8 is to change the direction of motivational forces away from depression and guide it into other items or activities. The motivational energy needs to be channeled into constructive projects.

Assignments.   Before prescribing assignments to redirect motivation, the therapist can directly acknowledge that he or she is impressed by the patient's strong motivation related to depression and its companion states. The therapist can then inquire whether the patient would be willing to put one-tenth of this motivation into a nondepressive project. For example, a depressed patient employed as a bread delivery man spent the major part of his working day in a van by himself delivering bread to different locations. His ongoing internal dialogue involved making negative statements about himself and his job performance. He was asked to interrupt himself one out of every two times whenever he caught himself making derogatory self-statements. On every other utterance of negative self-talk in his van, he was instructed to tell himself in a loud, firm voice: "Stop it! Stop it!" In another instance, a depressed woman was asked to take a self-defense class twice a week as a way of getting active and simultaneously learning discipline.

Metaphor.   As a child, I was fond of watching the television series "Lost in Space," which recounted the travels and adventures of the Robinson family as they journeyed through outerspace. You might have watched some episodes of this series yourself. There is one episode of "Lost in Space" I still vividly remember because it particularly impressed me. In this episode, a monster invades the Robinsons' spacecraft and attempts to take it over. This monster derives its physical energy from the fear it elicits in others. Therefore, as the monster invades the ship, it gradually becomes more and more powerful as it sucks more energy from different members of the Robinson family, who become frightened upon seeing it and then pass out. The only person left on the ship that the monster has to face is Will Robinson— the Robinsons' youngest child. When the monster confronts Will Robinson, Will tells the monster: "I am not afraid of you. Your only power is the power I give you. You feed on the fear that you provoke in other people." When Will confronts the monster in this way, the monster begins to shrink in size until it becomes a small puddle, and then completely disappears.

Step 7—Emotional Education

Depressed patients often lack skills in the area of emotional expression. They may need to be educated to give a voice to all their emotions as opposed to the monosyllabic expression of emotion through depression. Depression need not be the tunnel through which they enter the world of emotions. Ineptitutde for expressing emotions is sometimes manifested through the following emotional patterns:

1. *Emotional overdramatization.* In this instance, the patient exaggerates his or her sadness and uses a "Poor me, all the horrible things

that have happened (are happening) to me" stance to prevent himself or herself from differentiating emotions.

2. *Delayed emotional reaction syndrome.* This consists of delaying one's reaction to an emotionally loaded situation instead of voicing one's immediate reaction to the situation.

3. *Emotional obligation.* Many depressed patients feel that if they directly express their feelings to others, they will be somewhat obligated to appease, to overexplain or, to take responsibility for others' feelings. They need to be educated that they can express their feelings without any sense of obligation other than expressing the feeling itself. In fact, expressing feelings can liberate individuals from obligations and promote better understanding of self and others.

4. *Denial of the right to feel.* Parallel to the previous theme of an obligation attached to expressing emotions, many depressed patients believe they have no right to acknowledge their feelings and that they are condemned to emotional self-containment. Therefore, in many situations, they tend to prevent their feelings from unfolding in a natural manner. They need to allow their feelings to take their course, and to mark time with such feelings until the feelings exhaust themselves. There is a self-validation that comes from owning one's feelings and respecting both their timely expression and eventual dissolution.

5. *Surpassing the moodiness.* Many depressed patients choose to express their emotions through a channel of moodiness. Being in a "bad mood" can be seen as an amorphous or impotent way of saying: "I am angry/I am sad/You hurt me/I feel lonely." Depressed patients often need encouragement to reduce their moodiness and increase their emotional visibility to others.

Assignments. The assignments for this step fall within the parameters of increasing the frequency of assertive behavior on the patient's part. For example, a depressed patient had developed a peculiar style of interaction with her elderly mother in which she would offer her mother to join her in different activities. Her invitations were consistently declined. Instead of persisting in asking her mother to accompany her, the patient was instructed to visit her mother and to ask her about the details of the patient's early childhood years, how she grew up, what her favorite colors were, and what type of child she was. The mother was delighted to tell the patient all the details of her childhood years, instead of being asked repeatedly to take part in activities that she did not particularly favor. The patient told her mother during the conversation that the invitations were simply a way of telling the mother that she (the patient) loved her. The mother responded with similar expressions of love, and asked her daughter to sit down, have some tea, and just talk. In this way, the patient was able to put an end to her passive interactive stance with her mother by joining her mother's frame of reference. Her fear of openly talking to her mother had to be processed and subsequently dissipated through the assignment of asking her mother about the details of her childhood years.

In another instance, a depressed sales agent had a sales contract with a grocery store owner who was rude and derogatory toward him. Whenever the patient went to the grocery store to service the account, the owner would make fun of him and act in an insulting and demeaning manner. The patient was afraid that he would lose the account if he confronted the store owner on his inappropriate behavior. He was encouraged to voice his dissatisfaction with the way the business owner addressed him the next time he went to the store to service the account. His assignment was simply to express his feelings and wait for an explanation or reply from the other party. The patient was pleasantly surprised that, upon being confronted with his rude behavior, the business owner apologized for his derogatory comments and began dealing with the patient in a more respectful way.

Metaphor.   A well-known African proverb states: "Unless you call out, who will open the door?" Another African proverb states: "He who conceals his disease cannot expect to be cured."

Step 8—Fantasy Reseeding

Depressed patients seem to suffer from "fantasy pollution," i.e., their fantasies are basically negative in nature and are derived from the premise that "nothing works for me." The therapeutic task at stage 8 is to change the content of the patient's fantasies from negative to positive and to eventually alleviate negative fantasies. Fantasy reseeding can take place either under hypnosis, while using imagery training techniques, or through the use of indirect communication techniques such as humor and other forms of metaphoric communication (Salameh, 1986). The goal at this step is to provide the patient with a technology that can enable him or her to relanguage his or her reality.

Assignments.   The assignments used at this step are usually im-
agery-related assignments in which the patient is trained to incorporate new imagery in order to reduce and replace depressive imagery.
The following three imagery assignments illustrate the fantasy reseeding process: (1) A depressed patient who felt submerged by negative
depressive statements and depressive images was given a fantasy in
which her destructive thought patterns became garbage items that she
needed to throw into the trash. She was told that, when throwing out
the garbage, she could not simply toss these items into the trash.
Rather, she must first dismantle and crush them, take them apart, and
make them unusable so that they cannot operate again in her life. She
became actively engaged in this fantasy task of dismantling the old
destructive thought patterns and images. She successfully imaged
breaking them down into small pieces, like shattering a glass mirror,
and then dumping the whole lot into the trash. (2) In another instance,
a patient who harbored many depressive worries was asked to liken
his worries in imagery to a heavy overcoat he no longer needed to
wear. He was instructed to imagine how heavy and burdensome the
overcoat was, and then to imagine the immense relief and sense of
freedom he would experience when he took the heavy overcoat off
and threw it away. (3) A female patient whose depressive associations
were related to feeling "left out in the cold" (i.e., abandoned) was
instructed to imagine that within herself there was an inner sun that
would always shine and provide her with feelings of warmth and
nurturance whenever she felt depressed.

Metaphor.   "When the vine entwines your roof, it is time to cut it
down."

SUMMARY

This chapter has examined the different faces of depression, and
how it manifests itself in conjunction with other dysfunctions. Some of
the stumbling blocks commonly found in working with depressed patients have been reviewed. An eight-step intervention program has
been delineated for the treatment of depression. In essence, psychopathological depression represents a global dysfunctional response
pattern to the events in one's life. Ultimately, it is not other people or
life's circumstances that tend to cause an individual the most psycho-

logical harm. Rather, it is the repetitive application of the same dysfunctional patterns in *reacting* to different individuals or situations that results in the highest level of emotional damage to the individual. The use of the same negative patterns guarantees the same negative results. Negative patterns eventually destroy the individual's emotional and interpersonal adjustment. Therapeutic work with depressed patients aims at helping them break the global pattern of psychopathological depression. Once the purposeless suffering is removed from depression, depression can serve as a vehicle for greater emotional openness, vulnerability, and self-awareness. The Greek gods meant for Achilles to have a vulnerable point in his heel lest he become insensitive and overconfident, and thus lose perspective on his humanity. A penetrating Korean proverb states: "The earth is firmer after the rain."

REFERENCES

American Psychiatric Association (1987). *Diagnostic and Statistical Manual of Mental Disorders* (Third Edition, revised). Washington, DC: American Psychiatric Association.

Beck, A. (1967). *Depression*. New York: Harper & Row.

Beck, A (1973). *The Diagnosis and Management of Depression*. Philadelphia: University of Pennsylvania Press.

Beck, A. (1983). Negative cognitions. In E. Levitt, B. Lubin, & J. Brooks (Eds.), *Depression: Concepts, Controversies, and Some New Facts* (2nd ed.). (pp 86–92). Hillsdale, NJ: Erlbaum Press.

Beck, A., Rush, J., Shaw, B., & Emery, G. (1979). *Cognitive Therapy of Depression*. New York: Guilford Press.

Bradshaw, J. (1988a). *Bradshaw on: The Family*. Deerfield Beach, FL: Health Communications, Inc.

Bradshaw, J. (1988a). *Bradshaw on: Healing the Shame That Binds You*. Deerfield Beach, FL: Health Communications, Inc.

Chaplin, J. P. (1975). *Dictionary of Psychology—Revised Edition*. New York: Dell.

Ellis, A. (1973). *Humanistic Psychotherapy: The Rational-Emotive Approach*. New York: McGraw-Hill.

Ellis, A., & Whiteley, J. M. (Eds.). (1979). *Theoretical and Empirical Foundations of Rational-Emotive Therapy*. Monterey, CA: Brooks/Cole.

Freud, S. (1953/1974). *The Standard Edition of the Complete Works of Sigmund Freud* (translated by James Strachey). London: Hogarth Press.

Freud, S. (1959). *Collected Papers of Sigmund Freud*. (Vols. 1–5). New York: Basic Books.

Masson, J. M. (1985). *The Assault on Truth: Freud's Suppression of the Seduction Theory*. New York: Penguin.

G & C Merriam Co (1980). *Webster's New Collegiate Dictionary*. Springfield, Mass.: G & C Merriam Co.

Miller, A. (1983). *For Your Own Good: Hidden Cruelty in Childrearing and the Roots of Violence*. New York: Farrar, Strauss, and Giroux.

Miller, A. (1986). *Pictures of Childhood*. New York: Farrar, Strauss, and Giroux.

Miller, A. (1981). *Prisoners of Childhood*. New York: Basic Books.

Miller, A. (1984). *Thou Shalt Not Be Aware: Psychoanalysis and Society's Betrayal of Children.* New York: Farrar, Strauss, and Giroux.

Miller, H. (1984). Depression: A specific cognitive pattern. In W. Webster (Ed.). *Clinical Hypnosis: A Multidisciplinary Approach* (2nd ed, pp. 421–458). Philadelphia: Lippincott.

Minuchin, S. (1974). *Families and Family Therapy.* Cambridge: Harvard University Press.

Musetto, A. P. (1986). Ericksonian approaches to strategic psychotherapy. In P. E. Keller & L. G. Ritt (Eds.). *Innovations in Clinical Practice: A Source Book.* (Vol. 5, pp. 45–58). Sarasota, Fla: Professional Resource Exchange.

Salameh, W. A. (1986). Humor as a form of indirect hypnotic communication. In M. Yapko (Ed.), *Hypnotic and Strategic Interventions: Principles and Practice* (pp. 133–188). New York: Irvington.

Salameh, W. A. (1987). Humor in Integrative Short-Term Psychotherapy (ISTP). In W. F. Fry, & W. A. Salameh (Eds.). *Handbook of Humor and Psychotherapy: Advances in the Clinical Uses of Humor* (pp. 195–240). Sarasota, Fla.: Professional Resource Exchange.

Salameh, W. A.: *Integrative Short-Term Psychotherapy: The Origination of Human Change.* (in press).

Satir, V. (1967). *Conjoint Family Therapy.* Palo Alto: Science & Behavior Books.

Satir, V. (1976). *Making Contact.* Berkeley: Celestial Arts Publications.

Satir, V. (1988). *New People Making.* New York: Scribner Books.

Satir, V. (1978). *Your Many Faces.* Berkeley: Celestial Arts Publications.

Seligman, M. (1974). Depression and learned helplessness. In R. Friedman & M. Katz (Eds.), *The Psychology of Depression: Contemporary Theory and Research.* Washington, DC: Winston.

Seligman, M. (1975). *Helplessness: On Depression, Development, and Death.* San Francisco: Freeman.

Seligman, M. (1983). Learned helplessness. In E. Levitt, B. Lubin, & J. Brooks (Eds.), *Depression: Concepts, Controversies, and Some New Facts* (2nd ed.), (pp. 64–72). Hillsdale, NJ: Erlbaum.

Chapter 5

Disturbances of Temporal Orientation as a Feature of Depression

Michael D. Yapko

Michael D. Yapko, Ph.D., is Director of the Milton H. Erickson Institute of San Diego. He is well known for his writings on hypnosis and psychotherapy, having written Trancework *and* When Living Hurts: Directives for Treating Depression. *He is editor of* Hypnotic and Strategic Interventions: Principles and Practice, *and of the Milton H. Erickson Foundation* Newsletter. *He is founding member of the Editorial Board of the Ericksonian Monographs, and has been a frequent presenter at national and international meetings sponsored by the Milton H. Erickson Foundation, the International Society of Hypnosis, and the American Society of Clinical Hypnosis. A clinical psychologist, Yapko maintains a clinical practice in San Diego, where he is also on the faculties of National University and United States International University. An international trainer in brief therapy methods, Yapko has conducted workshops in Australia and Europe.*

PSYCHOTHERAPY AND THE CONCEPT OF TEMPORAL ORIENTATION

The emphasis of this book is on the use of brief therapy methods in the treatment of anxiety and depression. Brief therapy as a class of methods has many characteristics that distinguish it from other approaches to psychotherapy. One such distinguishing feature is the role of time in the treatment process. Brief therapy has usually been defined either in terms of the number of therapy sessions involved or the duration of the treatment process (Haley, 1973; Zeig, 1987). Since a primary objective in the treatment process for many clinicians is to

106

help catalyze therapeutic changes as rapidly as possible, it has become increasingly necessary to evolve clearer conceptualizations of the dynamics of specific mental disorders, and more efficient methods for addressing those dynamics.

Specific psychotherapy approaches have often been described as existing somewhere on a continuum where the polar extremes are characterized as "past oriented" and "here and now-oriented" (O'Hanlon, 1987; Zeig, 1987). They have also been described as existing somewhere on a continuum where the polar extremes are characterized as "insight-oriented" and "change oriented" (O'Hanlon, 1987; Zeig, 1987). Brief therapy methods are undoubtedly "change-oriented," and may best be described as *future* oriented rather than as past or present oriented. The emphasis of such approaches is a consideration of ways the psychotherapist might intervene in order for the client to experience a therapeutic alteration of some dysfunctional pattern. Although there is little or no consideration of the past or how the client came to have the problem in the course of the therapy (i.e., minimal emphasis is placed on talking about the past), the problem's underlying dynamics and etiology will most likely be considered in the formation of therapeutic strategies (contrary to popular misconceptions about brief therapy methods). Simply put, such approaches can consider and make use of underlying dynamics in a client's problem, but do not emphasize spending time talking about or cultivating insights about the past. Milton H. Erickson, M.D., stated succinctly the dominant view representing brief therapy methods when he said:

> Insight into the past may be somewhat educational. But insight into the past isn't going to change the past . . . Your patient has to live in accord with things of today. So you orient your therapy to the patient living today and tomorrow, and hopefully next week and next year (Zeig, 1980, p. 269)

Havens (1987) suggested that Erickson's unique approaches to brief psychotherapy can best be understood as rooted in attempts to orient the patient to the future. Erickson metaphorically described the role of his farming background as influencing his tendency to think in terms of future growth from therapeutic seeds planted today (Zeig, 1980). It is apparent that conceptualizing future possibilities clearly and orienting one's thoughts, feelings, and actions in the direction of those possibilities are vital to their eventual achievement. Not all people, how-

ever, are able to relate to each of the dimensions of time with equal
clarity and skill. The impact of one's ability to relate to past, present,
or future seems to be quite profound in shaping one's life. The relationship appears to be reciprocal, since one's life experiences (as
Erickson's farming background may demonstrate) seem equally capable of influencing one's relationship to past, present, and future.

Consider this temporal orientation factor relative to a psychotherapist's choice of therapeutic modality. The distinction is made between
approaches to therapy that, by their very nature (i.e., independent of
the presenting disorder), require a lengthy period of time before sub-
stantive changes may become evident, and those approaches that attempt to catalyze changes in a relatively short period of time. The
merits of all approaches to psychotherapy are evaluated according to
numerous criteria, of which the length of treatment time is only one.
Clearly, a consideration (i.e., subjective value) of time as a factor in the
treatment process plays a pivotal role in a psychotherapist's choosing
an orientation that will serve as a framework for the interventions he
or she makes. Why does one psychotherapist prefer a past-oriented
approach to treatment whereas another prefers a "here-and-now" approach? What relationship is there between the psychotherapist's temporal orientation (i.e., one's best related to dimension of time) and the
therapy he or she performs *independent* of the client's needs?

The answer to these questions can be critical to the success or failure of the therapy. If a client's dominant temporal orientation is not
diagnosed, the clinician can unwittingly reinforce the client's most
dysfunctional patterns (Yapko, 1988). For example, using a past-oriented approach with a client already too preoccupied with past traumas does little or nothing to create positive future possibilities. Thus,
such an exclusive approach would be contraindicated.

The issue of a past, present, or future orientation in treatment is an
important one. Much of what has come to be known about effective
treatment in recent years has been a direct consequence of the increased interest in the work of solution-oriented psychotherapists.

Erickson, in particular, made a unique contribution to psychotherapy with his orientation to the future and delineation of tactics one
might use in order to produce therapeutic changes.

What exactly is a "temporal orientation," and what specifically is a
"future orientation?" For the purposes of this chapter, a temporal orientation is defined as a more well-developed awareness of and relationship to a particular sphere of time, either past, present, or future.

"Awareness of and relationship to a particular sphere of time" means that consciously and / or unconsciously, one is inclined to think about, react to, and use as a valued frame of reference for interpreting ongoing subjective experience and guiding personal choices one dimension of time to a greater extent than the others. (By analogy, in the same way that one may have a preferred sensory modality, called the "primary representational system," one may likewise have a preferred relationship to time.) A "future orientation," then, is when the preferred or best-developed time relationship is one with events or experiences that have not yet happened. Similarly, a "present orientation" indicates a preference for current experience, and a "past orientation" reflects a greater involvement with previous experience.

One cannot be so oriented to one dimension of time that one's ability to relate to another dimension of time is precluded without severe consequences. Thus, each person can relate to each dimension of time, but with varying degrees of cognitive clarity and affective impact.

TEMPORAL ORIENTATION AND QUALITY OF EXPERIENCE

How one organizes internal experiences around subjective perceptions of time plays a major role in daily living. For example, the ability to plan for the future by establishing and working intensely toward a specific goal is desirable only to the extent that the goal is worth achieving. However, if the individual with the goal is consumed by that goal to the point of making daily living chronically uncomfortable, then such a strong future orientation has become dysfunctional. Similarly, a commitment to maintaining stability of a relationship over time is a worthy endeavor, but if such an orientation to maintaining the past ways of relating precludes dynamic growth in new directions to the relationship's detriment, then such a past orientation is dysfunctional.

It is interesting to note the role of a dysfunctional temporal orientation in various emotional disorders. Habit disorders, for example, often reflect a strong present orientation that precludes any meaningful relationship to predictable negative consequences (e.g., eating the cheesecake *now* is all that matters; forget how unhappy I'll be when I weigh in tomorrow). The negative consequences that may come later are simply no match for the strength of the impulse of the moment. Offering the suggestion to curb an impulse by saying, "Stop and think before you act," is asking the client to do exactly what he or she does not know how to do. (If he or she did, impulsivity would not be a problem!) Another example is anxiety disorders, where the dread of anticipated problems (future orientation) is a common feature. Clearly, in this example, the person is demonstrating negative and too strong a future orientation. Offering the suggestion to "Enjoy today and stop and smell the roses along the way," again is asking the client to do exactly what he or she does not know how to do.

DEPRESSION AND DISTURBANCES OF FUTURE ORIENTATION

A tendency toward negative expectations is well known and described in the clinical literature on depression (Beck, 1967, 1973, 1983; Seligman, 1974, 1975, 1983). Obviously, expectation implies a degree of future orientation. As proposed here, the cognitive clarity and emotional significance of one's expectations are of central importance in determining their degree of influence over current experience.

Aaron Beck, in his well-developed cognitive theory of depression, described a "negative triad" of experience that represents classical features of depression (Beck, 1967, 1983). The triad consists of negative self-evaluation, helplessness, and negative expectations. Martin Seligman, in his theories on depression involving "learned helplessness" and negative attributional style, described the extensive role of pessimism in depressives (Seligman, 1974, 1975, 1983; Trotter, 1987). Clearly, a dysfunctional relationship with one's sense of the future plays a significant role in depression.

In a previous book, *When Living Hurts* (Yapko, 1988), the author identified a generalized tendency in depressed clients to have a past temporal orientation. In calling it a generalized tendency, the implication is that not all depressed individuals will reflect such an orientation. In fact, a specific depressed individual may be oriented to *any* of the time dimensions in a way that is somehow imbalanced and dysfunctional. The wary clinician, in using temporal orientation as a diagnostic tool, can more readily identify such an imbalance, and provide therapeutic directives to facilitate a more functional balance.

The depressed client's tendencies toward a past orientation are manifested in a number of ways. These include:

1. A limited (usually moderate to severe) ability to make future projections of any kind at all. The client simply has a very difficult time

thinking about the future, usually because the *current* level of emotional pain rooted in past hurts is so absorbing.
2. An impaired ability to make future projections that are beyond a simple extrapolation or continuation of current experience. Simply put, the individual believes that the future is "just more of what is happening right now."
3. A diminished ability to shift perspectives from past experiences when projecting for the future.
4. Nonspecific (global) expectations of a negative nature. The client simply believes that the future is only going to pose more opportunities for being overwhelmed and hurt.

As with any individual, the depressed client can only rely on his or her own frame of reference for relating to ongoing experience. When the depressed client's personal history includes negative and dysfunctional learnings affecting the ability to think and problem-solve rationally (i.e., without the cognitive distortions Beck described) and make accurate attributions regarding blame and controllability (i.e., without the global, internal, and stable attributions Seligman described), how can the client *not* be depressed? If and when the depressed person looks to the future and anticipates either nothing at all or else just more pain, depression seems a likely consequence. The disturbance (i.e., impairment) of one's future orientation that negatively distorts one's view of the future is an obvious precursor to the negative expectations, hopelessness, and apathy so typical of depressed clients.

The major point of this chapter can now be stated succinctly. The negative expectations and pessimism described by Beck and Seligman may be better understood as a deficit in the depressed client's ability to relate to a future orientation. Other or self-generated projections into the future are lacking either in cognitive clarity (i.e., ambiguous or hazy thoughts) or positive affective strength (i.e., either little or no emotional significance or else only negative in quality). The imbalance of temporal orientation permits the existence of the negative perceptions, misguided attributions, preoccupations with past hurts, and lack of a sense of ability to change. The individual experiences life according to a rigid personal frame of reference at the expense of a positive future orientation.

The disturbance of a future temporal orientation implies an overreliance on past or present experience to a dysfunctional degree. The inability or diminished ability to establish meaningful expectations for the future is hurtful to *any* type of therapy. The role of positive expectations is well known in successful treatment outcomes. With depressed clients in particular, even greater attention must be paid to this aspect of treatment.

GOALS IN THE TREATMENT OF DISTURBANCES OF TEMPORAL ORIENTATION

In describing negative expectations and pessimism as closely related to an impairment of a sense of future orientation, it becomes apparent that an early goal of treatment must be to enhance the depressed client's ability to orient meaningfully to the future. The necessity for making this an early goal of treatment may be apparent, given the difficulties often associated with first getting depressed clients into treatment and then engaging them meaningfully in the ongoing therapy process. If the client has no positive expectation that therapy can help, or that *anything* can help, the hopeless "Why bother to try?" attitude emerges unchallenged from within. Thus, the depressed client will often require some fairly immediate *experiential* evidence that positive changes can be accomplished. The therapeutic goals in building or enhancing a positive future orientation can be described as follows:

1. Make future possibilities concrete, cognitively clear, and emotionally impactful enough to provide the experience(s) that will operate as a frame of reference for making the choices most likely to lead to worthwhile outcomes.
2. Enhance the client's ability to create and follow plans leading to positive future possibilities.
3. Enhance the client's ability to identify as objectively as possible (delineating specific criteria for doing so) both the locus of control and the locus of responsibility in establishing future expectations in order to either prevent or minimize any sense of personal failure or personal helplessness if specific expectations are not realized.
4. Teach the client specific goal-planning strategies by breaking global goals (often experienced as overwhelming tasks) into a linear sequence of specific attainable steps. Care must be taken to make sure that each step falls within the realm of the client's true abilities to succeed.

5. Teach autohypnosis techniques with an emphasis on experientially relating to outcomes generalized by current actions in order to determine whether current actions are likely to lead to the best (however "best" is defined) possible outcome(s).

Milton Erickson, in a lecture on time reorientation (In Rossi & Ryan, 1985), had a unique way of thinking about the value of an enhanced future orientation in psychotherapy:

> You know, one of the most informative aspects of human behavior is this matter of hindsight. Hindsight is so awfully important, and you wonder why you didn't use this knowledge based on hindsight in the form of foresight. How often have you said to yourself, "If I had only known things would work out this way! I had all the data available to me beforehand, so why didn't I realize it would work out this way?" And in the practice of medicine and psychiatry, you need to speculate on how things are going to work out, and on how to use the available information. (p. 196)

The concept of using hindsight as a basis for foresight as a general goal of treatment can allow the creative clinician the opportunity to use future-oriented techniques for the client's benefit.

FUTURE-ORIENTED APPROACHES TO TREATMENT

Any approach that encourages the client to develop a closer and more positive relationship with the future has the potential to help depressed clients showing evidence of an impaired future orientation. Use of hypnotic approaches may permit the development of a stronger experiential frame of reference. Coupled with nonhypnotic approaches, they can afford more comprehensive, multidimensional interventions. The approaches may be divided into three general categories: (1) age progression approaches involving formal hypnosis, (2) anecdotal approaches involving therapeutic and experiential metaphors, and (3) task assignments involving "real world" assignments constructed so as to expand limiting (i.e., depressogenic) frames of reference. Each of these categories is discussed briefly in this section.

Age Progression

Erickson's encouragement for his patients to "speculate upon future if they viewed it as the past" (Erickson in Rossi & Ryan, 1985, p. 198) is an intriguing concept. He described such future-oriented work in his lecture on time reorientation in *Life Reframing in Hypnosis.* The following description is from that lecture.

> The technique that I'm going to describe now is one which I have used for a good many years. The first step in the technique is this matter of the induction of a hypnotic trance—and usually a deep trance is employed. Then I ask the patient to reorient himself in time. Now that doesn't mean that I change calendar time or worldly time, but I ask the patient to alter his subjective understandings of time. We all have a general idea of what we will be doing next Christmas. We don't know exactly what we will be doing next Christmas, but we have certain general expectations. So I ask my patient to *forget the immediate present* [italics the author's] and feel himself oriented instead to next Christmas or next year, so that he then can look back upon the "past." (Bear in mind that patients can be regressed in time or they can be progressed in time—both techniques can be employed toward this utilization of their capacities to think in various ways.) Then I ask the patient who has altered his time orientation to think comprehensively about stressful matters—about those things that worry him and make him fearful in his current life situation. And since he can look upon those things from his reoriented vantage point as having occurred in the past, he now can employ hindsight in their resolution! You see, hindsight is often no more than a focalization and utilization of the understandings that were available at the time the event occurred. (p. 196)

The use of age-progression techniques in ways such as Erickson described can have profound impact. Havens (1987) also described his successful use of future-orientation methods and observed that "once people have envisioned a pathway into a desirable future and have imagined themselves carrying out the necessary steps, there is a remarkable tendency to actually respond to events in a manner consistent with these outcomes" (pp. 8–9). In effect, the psychotherapist is using hypnotically-based age-progression interventions to manipulate the mechanism of self-fulfilling prophecies, much as the manipulation of the mechanism of repression is accomplished with the use of hypnotically based amnesia. The use of age progression in another related way was described by Erickson in his 1954 article, "Pseudo-Orientation in Time as a Hypnotherapeutic Procedure." Here he described cases in which he age-progressed clients to a later time at which they could experience their problems as resolved. He asked each to describe the events that led to recovery, and then provided suggestions of amnesia for their having done so. He then carried out the treatment plan the clients had provided! The role of expectations, particularly at unconscious levels, in influencing life experience cannot be overstated. Age-progression approaches can be most effective in instilling positive expectations at those levels.

Therapeutic and Experiential Metaphors

Metaphors have been well described in the literature for their effectiveness in introducing ideas and possibilities in a relatively nonthreatening manner (Zeig, 1980; Lankton & Lankton, 1983). For the purpose of facilitating an enhanced future orientation, metaphors are used to impart messages in a more symbolic, less threatening form than direct communication. A number of future-oriented metaphors specifically for depressed clients are described in *When Living Hurts* (Yapko, 1988). When the metaphors also provide direct experiences of antidepressant messages, they can be called "experiential metaphors." Erickson (in Zeig, 1980, pp. 148–153) described such an intervention with a severely depressed woman named Betty, who worked at a hospital where Erickson conducted a demonstration. In procuring her help as a volunteer subject for the demonstration, Erickson had found out beforehand about her depressed condition. While seeming merely to be demonstrating various hypnotic phenomena, Erickson was, in fact, taking Betty through a variety of life-enhancing experiences. He hoped to impart to her a message that said her future could change as her value for life (i.e., especially her own) evolved. Erickson described the interaction this way:

> Now when I went to the arboretum and had her hallucinate the arboretum, what was I talking about? Patterns of life: life today; life in the future; blossoms; fruit, seeds; the different pattern of each leaf for each plant. We went to the zoo and I was again

discussing life with her—youthful life, mature life, the wonders of life—migration patterns. And then we went to the seashore where countless generations in the past had found pleasure, where countless generations in the future would find pleasure, and where the current generation was finding pleasure . . . I named all the things worthwhile living for. And nobody knew I was doing psychotherapy except me. (pp. 152–153)

Anecdotes and experiential metaphors have the capacity to alter the client's frame of reference by establishing new, more adaptive associations. As a tool for enhancing a positive future orientation in depressed clients, new and positive associations to future possibilities can replace negative expectations or depressogenic perceptions of being "trapped."

Task Assignments

Another vehicle for facilitating the balance of temporal orientations and an enhanced sense of a future orientation is the task assignment. When the clinician assigns the client the task of altering a usual (but dysfunctional) sequence of behavior, or engaging in a new pattern altogether, the task assignment creates the opportunity for a shift of one's frame of reference. Many such task assignments specifically for depressed clients are described in *When Living Hurts* (Yapko, 1988), and often involve the breaking down of complex patterns of behavior into more easily identified patterns that can be exaggerated or minimized. For example, requiring a dysfunctionally rigid person needing to develop some flexibility to go to the zoo and report on diverse evolutionary adaptations that permit survival may encourage some insight into the value of adapting oneself to life's demands. The analogical message that depression may be a by-product of rigidity that precludes developing a sense of changing future trends and the need to adapt to them may be more memorable a realization in the zoo than from direct verbalization. A carefully constructed task assignment can make use of real-world contexts that lead the client to acquire relevant learnings.

SUMMARY

The major premise of this chapter is that the negative expectations and pessimism commonly found in depressed clients are predictable consequences of a disturbed future orientation. Unlike therapeutic interventions that emphasize past or current considerations as the vehicle of the therapy, the author is promoting the idea that instilling a stronger sense of future orientation is central to the effective treatment of depressed clients. Goals and techniques for facilitating a strong future orientation in depressed clients were described in this chapter, with an emphasis on the value of experiential learnings that can broaden and enhance the client's frame of reference.

Currently, it is not common practice to treat depressed clients with a future orientation. However, based on the framework of temporal orientation presented here, it seems advisable to incorporate the future into the present as soon as possible to effect change. It is a hope for changing the future that leads a client into therapy in the first place. The *therapist's* ability to orient to positive future possibilities is therefore as important as, and perhaps even more important than, the client's ability. By considering this dimension of therapeutic intervention, it is hoped that depressed clients will get the efficient help they require.

REFERENCES

Beck, A. (1967). *Depression*. New York: Harper & Row.
Beck, A. (1973). *The Diagnosis and Management of Depression*. Philadelphia: University of Pennsylvania Press.
Beck, A. (1983). Negative cognitions. In E. Levitt, B. Lubin & J. Brooks (Eds.), *Depression: Concepts, Controversies and Some New Facts* (2nd ed., pp. 86–92). Hillsdale, N.J.: Erlbaum.
Erickson, M. (1954). Pseudo-orientation in time as a hypnotherapeutic procedure. *Journal of Clinical and Experimental Hypnosis, 2,* 261–283.
Erickson, M. (1985). *Life Reframing in Hypnosis*. (E. Rossi, & M., Ryan, eds.). New York: Irvington.
Haley, J. (1973). *Uncommon Therapy*. New York: Norton.
Havens, R. (1987). The future orientation of Milton H. Erickson: A fundamental perspective for brief therapy. *Ericksonian Monographs, 2,* 3–14.
Lankton, S., & Lankton, C. (1983). *The Answer Within: A Clinical Framework of Ericksonian Hypnotherapy*. New York: Brunner/Mazel.
O'Hanlon, W. (1987). *Taproots: Underlying Principles of Milton Erickson's Therapy and Hypnosis*. New York: Norton.
Seligman, M. (1973, June). Fall into helplessness. *Psychology Today, 7,* 43–48.
Seligman, M. (1974). Depression and learned helplessness. In R. Friedman & M. Katz (Eds.), *The Psychology of Depression: Contemporary Theory and Research*. Washington, D.C.: Winston.
Seligman, M. (1975). *Helplessness: On Depression, Development, and Health*. San Francisco: Freeman.
Seligman, M. (1983). Learned helplessness. In E. Levitt, B. Lubi, & J. Brooks (Eds.), *Depression: Concepts, Controversies, and Some New Facts* (2nd. ed., pp. 64–72). Hillsdale, N.J.: Erlbaum.

Trotter, R. (1987, Feb.). Stop blaming yourself. *Psychology Today, 21,* 31–39.
Yapko, M. (1988). *When Living Hurts: Directives for Treating Depression.* New York:
    Brunner / Mazel.
Zeig, J. (Ed.) (1980). *A Teaching Seminar with Milton H. Erickson.* New York: Brunner /
    Mazel.
Zeig, J. (Ed.) (1987). *The Evolution of Psychotherapy.* New York: Brunner / Mazel.

Chapter 6

The Multidimensional Application of Therapeutic Metaphors in the Treatment of Depression

Brita A. Martiny

Brita A. Martiny, Ph.D. (U.S. International University), is in private clinical practice at the Milton H. Erickson Institute of San Diego. She is also involved in providing training programs for mental health professionals in Ericksonian methods. She holds a degree in social work from the University of South Africa, and is on the faculty of National University in San Diego. Martiny's interest is in the area of women's issues and depression.

OVERVIEW

The growing interest in the use of therapeutic metaphors in psychotherapy may be attributed to the respect that Milton Erickson's innovative style of therapy has commanded. The strategic use of metaphors as indirect techniques to facilitate clients' accessing their own problem-solving resources has been considered a hallmark of Ericksonian therapy (Zeig, 1980 a, b, Lankton & Lankton, 1983).

Erickson's observations regarding the unconscious mind's ability to generate significant solutions to personal problems were the basis for his therapeutic use of symbolic and metaphorical communications. He seemed to perceive problems structurally, recognizing how a variety

The author would like to acknowledge Michael Yapko's generous contribution of time and editorial expertise as well as Linda Griebel's technical assistance in the preparation of this chapter.

of experiential components could either combine synergistically or operate singly in order to maintain the client's problem.

Symptoms may be seen as metaphors of a client's experience. For example, depression can be thought of as a warning signal indicating something wrong in the person's life. Looking at symptoms in this way—i.e., as messages expressing symbolically the underlying dynamics of a problem—one can see clearly the importance of employing different levels of communication (Madanes, 1984).

Multiple-Level Communication

Erickson was well known both for his perceptiveness in pacing the client's experience with multilevel communication and for expanding the client's awareness of his or her inherent creative potential in the therapeutic process. The purpose of this chapter is to illustrate how metaphors may be used to address aspects of each of the multilevel aspects of depression (Beck et al., 1979, Seligman; 1983; Yapko, 1988). The advantages of such a multilevel approach are numerous. First, this approach provides a broad perspective of the primary problem components, allowing them to be more clearly distinguished from the background of secondary issues. Second, the client's multilevel communication, which may be seen in the nuances of behavioral responses to the therapist in the session, reflect patterns and interactional styles the client engages in outside the therapy session. Erickson used his acute perceptiveness to identify key patterns maintaining core issues so that when faced with a difficult problem, he could focus on its pattern or design as either a usable catalyst or a target for intervention (Erickson, Rossi, & Rossi, 1976; Yapko, 1985a). From this knowledge, Erickson molded his communication to that of the client's experience, and in so doing established the rapport needed to maintain the momentum of therapy. Third, a multilevel perspective provides the foundation from which one can manipulate a variety of therapeutic variables in order to provide the necessary shifts in unconscious patterns that would be self-reinforcing patterns for change. Fourth, such an approach emphasizes the value placed on each person's inherent ability to grow and change in ways that are meaningfully determined by the client's own frame of reference. In Erickson's case, even though many of his metaphors were based on the vast repertoire of his own life experiences, his anecdotes were structurally designed to relate to purposeful communication, commonly found as a basis of myths and legends. Rosen (1982) identified Erickson's tales as following arche-typal patterns that incorporate a theme of purposeful intention.

General Uses of Metaphors

Metaphors provide therapeutic ground that can be used for excavation (i.e., identifying etiology and historical factors) as well as for development (i.e., seeding, developing a future orientation). Using metaphors for diagnostic purposes presumes the clinician's ability to notice which dynamic elements in the metaphor trigger responses in the client, and to verify this information in other, structurally similar metaphors. When used therapeutically, metaphors function as a medium from which injunctions for change may be presented directly as directives or indirectly in the form of embedded suggestions. The degree to which the client consciously comprehends the metaphor's meaning is not considered a necessary prerequisite to change occurring. This de-emphasis on insight and the acknowledgment that change may occur on an unconscious level is a basic tenet of Ericksonian therapy (Bandler & Grinder, 1979).

When incorporating metaphors as an integral part of the naturalistic Ericksonian approach, treatment is structured around the client's frame of reference so that the client may be encouraged to build associations and assimilate change as part of a natural and evolving process. By joining the client's frame of reference, the clinician can lead the client to discover alternative ways of thinking, feeling, and behaving (Yapko, 1988).

Many proponents of Ericksonian therapy have discussed the therapeutic use of metaphors, including Carol Lankton and Steve Lankton (1983), Sidney Rosen (1982), and David Gordon (1978). Jeffrey Zeig (1980) identified the following advantages to using anecdotes in psychotherapy:

1. Anecdotes are nonthreatening.
2. Anecdotes are engaging.
3. Anecdotes foster independence. The individual needs to make sense out of the message, and then come to a self-initiated action.
4. Anecdotes can be used to bypass natural resistance to change. Anecdotes can be used to present directives and suggestions in such a way as to maximize the possibility that they will be accepted.
5. Anecdotes can be used to control the relationship. The listener can-

not use habitual ways of controlling relationships when he or she is forced to listen to an anecdote.

6. Anecdotes model flexibility. Erickson was devoted to creativity. He used anecdotes as a way of expressing his interest in subtlety and creativity.

7. Erickson used anecdotes to create confusion and promote hypnotic responsiveness.

8. Anecdotes tag the memory; they make the presented idea more memorable.

Rossi's research on creative thinking (Rossi, 1986, pp. 25–26; Rossi & Ryan, 1985) suggested that creative problem-solving can occur on an unconscious level of experience fully independent of conscious involvement. Thus, the primary functions for using metaphors as an indirect treatment modality are to bypass conscious resistance and to allow for the emergence of novel solutions from the client's unconscious. Yapko (1988) introduced the concept of using metaphors to provide depressed clients with a positive future temporal orientation. Using the client's life experience as a continuum for change, metaphors can be used to bridge an established problem-solving ability (i.e., having made changes in the past) to the present experience of paving the way for future changes.

Indications and contraindications for using metaphors

Though metaphors have a versatility that may be used in all types of therapy and at any stage of therapy, their use is especially indicated when there is evidence of resistance constellated around a problem area. A fundamental guideline in using metaphors relates their use to the degree of defensiveness associated with the problem. The greater the perceived resistance, the greater is the need for indirection (Zeig, 1980a). Metaphors are thus best indicated in instances where it is therapeutically beneficial to bypass conscious awareness and any associated resistance, thereby creating the opportunity for the client to access and utilize unconscious resources. Zeig (1980a) suggested that metaphors be used to model flexibility in a nonthreatening way and to encourage independence in clients who can generate and "own" the solutions to their problems.

Often, metaphors used to engage the client's attention in a nonthreatening way are introduced with a statement such as "Once I had a client who, like you . . . ." In the case of depression, metaphors that attempt to model to the client other peoples' success with similar problems may be contraindicated if the client is operating from a position of feeling personally helpless to change (Yapko, 1985b). Such metaphors may entrench the cognitive distortion that "I can't do what others can do" and "I can't achieve what others can achieve." This contributes to increased feelings of hopelessness and helplessness and thus is contraindicated.

Metaphors may be contraindicated in cases where the degree of indirection is not matched to the level at which the client's problem needs to be addressed, i.e., if the metaphor is so indirect that the client cannot meaningfully associate it with his or her personal experience of depression. In such cases, the loss of rapport may actually exacerbate the feelings of depression as the client may feel either invalidated or that the problem is so great as to be beyond the scope of the therapist's ability to deal with it effectively. With depressed clients in particular, metaphors that are used to facilitate unconscious change without conscious awareness may increase feelings of worthlessness and dependence, primarily because the client does not feel personally responsible for making changes. Thus, it may be necessary to bolster the hypnotic work done (delivering metaphors in trance) with more concrete task assignments (experiential metaphors) that are better matched to the client's level of concrete thought. It is generally a sound practice to pace the typically concrete nature of depressed clients with metaphors that can be meaningfully assimilated into the client's frame of reference. The level of abstraction of metaphors must vary according to the individual abstraction capabilities of each client.

In general, there are no known contraindications for metaphors that are appropriately and sensitively used in a treatment plan. However, as in all therapeutic endeavors, the timing and sequencing of treatment modalities are crucial to maintaining the client's engagement in therapy. If employed successfully, they can motivate the kind of therapeutic risk-taking that will enlarge the client's capabilities in order to make the necessary changes.

Alternative Frames of Reference for Describing Metaphors

Erickson's unorthodox and creative use of language combined with his strategic use of direct and indirect communication styles resulted in a variety of attempts by various authors and clinicians to analyze the form and content of his communications, as seen in the following examples.

From the neurolinguistic programming standpoint, the viability of metaphors is found in a structural analysis of Erickson's anecdotal communication style, including digital and analogical components (Bandler & Grinder, 1975, 1979). In addition to the meaningful suggestions embedded in the story, Erickson marked therapeutic points in the metaphor by using pauses, voice-tone changes, the patient's name, or other devices that would make sufficient impact on the client's awareness (Bandler & Grinder, 1975; Grinder, Delozier, & Bandler, 1977).

In a strategic therapy view, Haley's (1963, 1973) interactional view distinguished between Erickson's verbal use of metaphors, which may be used both in and out of formal trance, and task or action metaphors that serve to establish an experiential basis for the therapy.

Watzlawick's (1976) interpretation of Erickson's therapeutic use of metaphors related it to the accessing of right-hemisphere experience, analogical communication, and symbolic processing. The right hemisphere is thought to be the center of the client's creative potentials for problem solving.

Metaphors in Treating Depression

This chapter explores how metaphors can be designed to address themes that are based on the client's ongoing subjective experience and underlying depressive dynamics. Such themes are identified in relation to existing depressive patterns evident in the client, and simultaneously serve as a means to implement the proposed treatment strategy. One can generally assume that by the time a depressed client seeks treatment, depressive patterns have already been established. One can further assume that attempts to deal with the depressogenic issues have been unsuccessful, resulting in feelings of frustration and anxiety. Seligman's (1974, 1975, 1983) research on depression linked one's experience of personal helplessness to inaccurately perceiving no options; the client assumes that nothing he or she can do will effectively change the hurtful situation. A goal of treatment, then, is to enhance the client's sense of independence and control over life events by teaching the client how to identify and carry out the necessary steps in the process of effective problem-solving.

Erickson (Zeig, 1980a) considered rigidity in thinking, feeling, or behavior as a basis for pathology, as it reflects the client's restricted ability to adapt to changing situations and generate appropriate responses. Depressogenic patterns become entrenched when clients maintain a rigid homeostasis. For example, with the average depressed client, the clinician can anticipate that a realistic and linear sequence of priorities will need to be established in order to counteract the client's cognitive deficits of distorted and global thinking. The goal is to facilitate the development of a degree of mastery in problem solving. This goal acknowledges the fact that depressed clients tend to be so internally absorbed that they use their own (negative) frame of reference to evaluate external situations, and consequently transform their inability to effectively problem-solve into a belief that the situation cannot be resolved.

The implications for how metaphorical approaches might be used effectively in the treatment of depression lie in the utilization of dormant client resources. Specifically, one can employ a general framework in which the client's positive resources (e.g., problem-solving skills, feelings of comfort) are accessed, and then the expectation that these resources can be extended on a temporal dimension into the realm of future possibilities is seeded. By allowing a client to experience himself or herself differently in a trance state, and by retrieving or creating feelings that could be experienced as "enjoyable," there is a sharp contrast to the experience of depression that preceded it. Not all of Erickson's metaphors were for the purposes of accessing and extending resources, however. Many of his metaphors were designed to clarify and reframe the specific, negative aspects of the client's situation in order to stimulate a more functional emotional association to experience (Rosen, 1982).

In the treatment of depression, metaphors may be used to seed positive change, enabling clients to anticipate a more positive future. This addresses hopelessness, a key aspect of depression (see Seligman's chapter in this volume). By building a positive expectancy—i.e., that change is possible—the client is therapeutically maneuvered into a position where using a positive orientation toward the future serves as a fulcrum for change. This enables clients to (1) establish positive behavioral expectations for themselves; (2) realistically anticipate events that are likely to unfold; (3) plan and follow through on goal-oriented behavior; (4) project specific future outcomes on the basis of current behavior or trends; and (5) accurately extrapolate to later situations on the basis of current data (Yapko, personal communication, 1988).

Yapko's (1988) Multiple Dimension Dissociative Model of depression listed eight interrelated dimensions of experience. These may be hierarchically structured according to the degree to which they represent portions of the client's ongoing experience. These eight dimensions on which symptoms arise are physiological, cognitive, behavioral, affective, relational, symbolic, contextual, and historical. The diverse range of symptomatic variables identified in the model illustrate the importance of recognizing and treating depression as a product of multi-dimensional interrelated experiences, rather than as being due to a single dimension cause. Furthermore, it suggests life-style risk factors, not only diagnosable pathology. Although many of the dimensions can and do operate synergistically to maintain depression, the distinct style an individual has in experiencing his or her depression is often reflected on a single, conscious dimension. In other words, although the client may have symptoms evident on all eight dimensions of experience, he or she may only be aware of and present symptoms on a single dimension while the others remain dissociated and out of awareness.

Throughout the remainder of this chapter, examples of how clients represent problems on each of the dimensions are provided. How the client's subjective experience can be identified and incorporated into treatment is elaborated. Then, sample transcripts of therapeutic metaphors addressing each dimension are provided in order to illustrate their use. Additionally, examples of task assignments, which may be viewed as *experiential* metaphors, are provided, with an emphasis on their ability to complement metaphors delivered to the client in a trance state. When the shift in perception resulting from the use of therapeutic metaphors (with or without formal hypnosis) is complemented by the use of experiential (task) metaphors, the client can better achieve the psychological momentum necessary to alter depressogenic patterns.

THE DIMENSIONS OF DEPRESSION

Having established that depression is a complex disorder manifested on multiple dimensions of experience, the clinician is faced with the task of deciding at which dimension(s) treatment should be aimed. Because of the interrelated nature of the dimensions, treatment focused on one will serve as a catalyst for modifying established depressogenic patterns on others. How the clinician decides which dimension to intervene on is determined by the client's representation and perception of the depression. Prior to intervention, the clinician should strive to develop an appreciation of the client's frame of reference, particularly regarding on which dimension(s) the depression is most clearly experienced. This understanding not only can increase rapport, but can give the clinician information about the degree of resistance and insight the client has regarding symptoms. Choice points for intervention on a particular dimension will depend on three factors: (1) how much resistance is associated with conscious awareness; (2) how acute or life-threatening the symptom is; and (3) the degree to which the client's social functioning has been impaired (Yapko, 1988).

The Physiological Dimension of Depression

Assessing relative prominence in the client's experience

The physiological dimension of depression is represented primarily by the following symptoms: sleep disturbances (hypersomnia or insomnia); appetite disturbance (hyper- or hypophagia); high fatigability; marked change in body weight; sex-drive disturbance (hyper- or hyposexuality); anxiety; vague or specific physical complaints with no apparent organic etiology; and magnification or persistance of physical symptoms with no known organic etiology (Yapko, 1988; p. 29).

The following client presentation illustrates how this dimension of experience may be represented as prominent in depressive symptomatology:

> My physician referred me to you because I have symptoms he hasn't been able to figure out a cause for. All the medical tests I have had during the past two years have come up negative. Yet my weight has increased by almost 50 pounds; my body feels so heavy. I move around and have these sharp pains in my chest. I have consulted many physicians and there is no evidence of anything physically wrong, and yet I am in frequent pain. Am I burdened to suffer without a definition for this agony? I seem to cry either for no reason or for the slightest reason. I have even thought of killing myself to escape from always feeling so bad.

Although I am so tired, I can't sleep, and when I do eventually fall asleep, I never manage to sleep through the night. I feel exhausted all the time; during the day I am so tired that I can't think clearly and want to sleep. At night when I should be sleeping, my mind is racing with so many thoughts that I have difficulty falling or staying asleep. I always wake up early and can't fall back asleep. I feel so anxious and my heart pounds. I can't even be bothered to dress and go out anymore—I just don't have the energy to move from home. I used to enjoy working at the animal shelter, but now I have lost interest in that as well. I'm so focused on how bad I feel. My doctor thinks it's depression, but I think that's silly—after all, the problem is clearly physical.

In this brief example, the following physiological symptoms were manifested: sleep disturbance, excessive weight gain; a high level of fatigue; crying spells; suicidal ideation; specific physical complaints of chest pain with no organic etiology; and anxiety. The client's inability to modify these symptoms independently had resulted in an exacerbation of the feelings of frustration and anxiety.

Metaphorical intervention

From the client's description of her experience, it was apparent that she had been frustrated in her attempts to obtain medical confirmation of an organic problem. Furthermore, she rejected the diagnosis of depression in favor of thinking that an as-yet-unidentified organic problem exists.

Due to the amount of resistance constellated around her symptoms, evidenced by her flat rejection of a psychological basis for her problems, the use of therapeutic metaphors was indicated. Having determined that the dimension of experience most prominent in her awareness was physical, a metaphor was delivered in trance intending to modify a prominent physiological symptom, namely the sleep disturbance. A general metaphor encouraging a better relationship with her body may also have been employed, but sleep was focused on as a key symptom pattern to interrupt. This is strictly a matter of clinical judgment. In this case, the purpose of the metaphor was to provide a context in which the client could reframe her experience of her body in order to see it in a more positive light. It attempts to introduce a shift in the established pattern of early morning waking by introducing Erickson's use of the concept of "arithmetical progression" (Rossi & Ryan, 1985).

The concept of arithmetical progression was favored by Erickson in the treatment of insomnia. It is a technique in which the client's sleep is extended by seconds, i.e., from three hours and two minutes to three hours, two minutes, and one second; then three hours, two minutes, and two seconds. Suggesting such small increments of change is usually easy for the client to accept. Once the client has accepted and applied the concept, then the extra seconds could be replaced by minutes and then hours. Eventually, a reasonable time frame for sleeping could be established. Erickson considered the therapeutic turning point to be the client's acknowledgement that sleeping the extra second was a "therapeutic victory." In order to maximize the benefits of potential analogical transfer, the metaphor was structured to parallel the client's physiological experience, and to lead the client into an alternative way of dealing with this. In this client's case, of all the physical symptoms named, sleep disturbance was viewed as the most malleable on a short-term basis. Thus, an early success from interrupting the anxiety that interfered with sleep could help launch a momentum to the therapy that could later allow her to address her other symptoms as well. In the author's experience, sleep disturbance symptoms are quite responsive to hypnotic interventions. In this client's case, the following metaphor was utilized:

Cycles

There are so many issues that you are dealing with now, and no words seem to adequately express how you are feeling inside . . . and you may enjoy knowing that right now there is nothing you have to say . . . or do . . . not even think about how your breathing and pulse rate have slowed down . . . as you continue to quietly enjoy developing comfort now . . . or perhaps in 32 seconds time . . . and you can enjoy knowing that you can choose to extend that comfort a second at a time . . . comfortably allowing the seconds to build up into substantial minutes of enjoyable comfort . . . and I wonder if you will discover that tonight or if it will be tomorrow night . . . and while you explore ways within yourself to deepen that experience . . . in a way that is balanced . . . because balance is the essence of being able to enjoy life's possibilities . . . consider how nature works in balanced cycles of activity and rest, day and night . . . and that the balance of nature is orderly in allowing for the vitality of spring to precede the abundance of summer activity . . . and that each falling leaf signals the time when nature can enjoy taking a rest . . . quietly and peacefully . . . inside and outside . . . and you can recall a time when as a child you had played yourself into being so tired . . . and recall how good it felt then to climb into bed and feel the comfort of sleep as your head touched the pillow . . . and you can fully enjoy that memory now as you extend that comfort into the present . . . and you can recall how it felt then when you woke up early for school . . . and then realized it was a day you could sleep late . . . and how good it felt to continue comfortably sleeping a second at a time . . . allowing time to enjoy having sweet dreams and hours to enjoy them. . .

Acknowledging the client's own experience of anxiety associated with the symptoms of sleep disturbance increased her involvement with the story, and prepared her for the therapeutic lead into a restructuring and reframing of the client's experience from her present negative association of sleep to the possibility of comfortably re-experiencing sleep in an age-regressed state. The purpose of using age regression was to depotentiate the negative anxiety-provoking elements of the symptom of disturbed sleep by accessing and extending contrasting past positive experiences. This indirect approach to treating the symptom offers the client the opportunity to use her own past learning creatively to modify the symptom (Rossi & Ryan, 1985).

The effect of using a time bind (i.e., "I wonder if it will be tonight or tomorrow night") presupposes that change will occur. If accepted, it also allows the client to determine when the change will occur from within the limits of the time frame, thus providing a sense of control over the symptom and the process of change.

In addition to the use of the above trance metaphor, a task assignment was used to make it more desirable to sleep than carry out the tasks. The purpose of assigning such an "ordeal task" (Haley, 1984) is to make it more inconvenient to carry out the symptomatic behavior than to let it go. Such task assignments might use a pointless or boring task to make sleep a desirable escape, i.e., making an index of the number of names and the number of times they occur in the local telephone directory. In contrast, counter-therapeutic task assignments would be ones that include any activity that would impair sleep and contribute to insomnia, i.e., late night physical exertion.

The Cognitive Dimension

Assessing relative prominence in the client's experience

The cognitive dimension of experience includes the following depressive symptoms: negative expectations (hopelessness); negative self-evaluation; negative interpretation of events; suicidal ideation; indecision; confusion; primarily internal focus; diminished concentration span; primarily past-temporal orientation; global thinking style; victim mind-set (helplessness); cognitive distortions (erroneous patterns of thinking), rumination, perceptual amplification or minimization; and rigidity (Yapko, 1988, p. 29).

The following is an example of how a client's thought patterns may be viewed as the primary dimension of symptomatic representation:

> I wish you could help me end this agony. If it's acceptable to put a suffering animal out of it's misery, then why not me? I will never be able to succeed in life, and I am tired of fighting against failure. I have a history of repeated failures and nothing will ever change that. I am a burden to myself and to everyone who has the misfortune of being in a relationship with me. I deserve to be punished for the pain I bring to myself and others. I am trapped in a relationship that is destructive, and yet I can't seem to pull myself out of it. My job is a dead end as there is no future for me there. I don't know why I even bother to think life could be different. Perhaps Sartre's legacy of *No Exit* is my inheritance as it seems there is no way to escape from feeling like this . . . that I can't talk about it and at the same time I can't not talk about it . . . as my thoughts continue to spin around on a macabre carousel of pain and despair, agony and futility . . .

The above example illustrates the extent to which the depressed client tends to adhere to rigid and distorted perceptions of events that are linked to increased feelings of helplessness. The symptoms manifested on this dimension were: negative expectations; negative interpretations of events; internal focus; global thinking style; and cognitive distortions with rumination.

Metaphorical intervention

The following metaphor was used to address the client's experience by dissociating her thoughts from depressed affect, and by suggesting a linear progression of thought (i.e., with a beginning and end) to contrast with the cyclical self-defeating nature of her distorted cognitions.

The Circus

Have you ever been surprised to find that one day you suddenly notice a new building that seems to have magically appeared? And yet you know you just never noticed it before? I'm not sure just when you will become aware of how differently you can experience yourself . . . knowing that change is inevitable . . . and how suddenly gradual changes can be noticed. Now, I don't know if you ever had the experience of seeing a circus parade . . . in real life or in a book . . . {Client nods head.} Then you can recall how all the townsfolk would line the street to watch the parade come into town . . . and how people would stand on the side and watch the procession go by . . . but they were only observers . . . and they could watch things go by without getting caught up in them . . . you could enjoy standing apart at a comfortable distance, and fully appreciate the skill of the jugglers, clowns, trapeze artists, the elephants, dancing dogs, and plumed horses . . . and after the parade, the tents were set up . . . and the rides alongside it . . . with the big ferris wheel that spun around and around . . . where the view from the top was so different . . . from that at the bottom . . . and at the top you could see way beyond the circus . . . so far ahead . . . and feel the air moving past as you moved forward . . . just as you can now become aware of the winds of change . . . and I don't know just which people you will put into your circus parade . . . who the clowns are . . . some with sad eyes and painted smiles . . . others whose life is an endless performance and parade . . . and I wonder who the geeks are . . . in all spheres of life . . . and which thoughts you can watch pass by . . . and enjoy seeing how they become specks on the horizon . . . so far away there . . . while you experience yourself so comfortably here . . . from this soothing distance . . . and you may find that discomfort is made up of many distinct parts . . . just as the circus parade is . . . and it's not important for you to identify the parts now . . . what is important is that you can enjoy knowing that you have the ability to stand back and watch the parade of painful experiences pass by . . . and that you can experience yourself so comfortably here while it moves further away over there . . . and you can really become aware of how much you can value yourself and appreciate yourself over here . . . and extend this into the future . . . while the painful procession over there continues to march comfortably far away into the past . . . and you can continue to breathe in the comfort of standing apart and to breathe discomfort out over there . . .

The circus metaphor was used to provide the client with a means to dissociate affect from thought. A key aspect of the metaphor was to access and establish the ability to "stand on one side and watch things go by without getting caught up in them." This strategy utilizes the client's ability to dissociate as a resource for distancing one's emotions from one's ruminations. Dissociation is also utilized as a basis for using age progression to extend an awareness of self-worth into the future, and to minimize focus on the painful experiences of the past.

In conjunction with the use of therapeutic metaphors, the clinician may suggest a symptom prescriptive task assignment. For example, the client may be told to ruminate from 3:10 P.M. to 4:25 P.M. every afternoon while standing in the bathtub. As an underlying resistance is brought to the surface, assuming there is one in order for such an assignment to be appropriate, the client builds a negative association with ruminating, allowing its diminution.

The Behavioral Dimension

Assessing relative prominence in the client's experience

The behavioral symptoms of depression include disturbance in activity level (hyper- or hypoactive); aggressive or destructive acts; crying spells; suicide attempts; slow or slurred speech; substance abuse; generalized impulsivity; behaviors inconsistent with personal values; destructive, compulsive behavior; psychomotor agitation or retardation; acting-out behavior; giving-up behavior; perfectionistic behavior (Yapko, 1988, p. 30).

The following is a transcript of a depressed client's presentation in which symptomatic behavior patterns may be identified:

> I wish I could stop crying so that I could speak properly now. Well, I don't suppose talking would help anyway, because I am so agitated that I fidget constantly and can't sit still. There only seems to be one way to end this hell, and that is to die. I've tried to kill myself twice—once with an overdose of valium and alcohol, and once by slashing my wrists. My husband ended up finding me both times and took me to the hospital. Everything I do is badly done, I couldn't even kill myself properly. Whenever I see a knife, I still think about cutting my wrists. If it weren't for the valium that holds me together, I'd probably do it. Sometimes, though, I actually do make little cuts on myself. It somehow makes me feel better. See my scars?

The client's suicidal ideation and history of suicide attempts are strong indications that the client required immediate intervention. In this brief example, the following behavioral symptoms were manifested: disturbance in activity level (hyperactivity), destructive acts, crying spells, suicide attempts, substance abuse, psychomotor agitation, and "giving-up" behavior.

Suicide represents the most serious risk for therapists working with depressed clients. The therapist's role is to assess suicide potential and whether the client needs to be hospitalized for his or her own protection, or needs to be placed on antidepressant medications.

Metaphorical intervention

The following transcript demonstrates how a direct approach could be used to deal with the seriousness of the suicidal client. Indirect treatment techniques such as metaphors are contraindicated in crisis situations as clients are presumed to be experiencing uncertainty and the purpose of therapeutic interventions is to reduce this.

Seeds
I know that you must be feeling very badly inside in order to have seriously considered suicide . . . and how desperate you

must have been to consider that course of action as if it were your only alternative . . . but now it seems that there must be an element of hope in you somewhere . . . because you're here . . . and you can hear . . . that you can experience life differently . . . since you have made the effort to seek therapy . . . and this hope must have a life of its own to survive being surrounded by so much . . . but suffering takes on meaning when it affirms living . . . and perhaps you may consider how inevitable it is that in the cycles of nature life is born from death, light from dark . . . and that hope, like a seed, may lie dormant in the earth waiting for the right time to grow . . . and growing pains of the seed breaking open precede the growth that follows so naturally . . . comfortably . . . so that the scars of progress can be seen proudly as symbols of growth . . . where the focus is on growth as part of a natural cycle . . . and growing pains a natural prelude to life . . . and the seeds of change are already in you . . . the seed of desire for things to change . . . the seeds of motivation to learn new ways to handle old situations . . . the seeds to change that grow when you do things differently . . . and nurture and care for those seeds for change planted within you with each skill you learn for managing your life well . . .

In the above transcript, acceptance of the client's genuine suicidal feelings is demonstrated. Facing her pain and confusion contributes to establishing the rapport which is essential for crisis intervention. The process of leading into the possibility of feeling differently had to be tailored to the client's needs so as not to run the risk of devaluing the present experience with promises of the pain being too easily overcome.

Metaphorically reframing the client's pain as prerequisite to growth builds a mind set of hope and compliance since the client now can see herself as having already engaged in the first steps of positive change. The next step is seeding the development of increased feelings of comfort that accompany growth and expansion. Suggesting that growth is part of a natural and inevitable cycle may enhance the client's increased flexibility in adapting to change.

A task assignment involving the client in a concrete representation of growth may involve planting seeds and observing their growth cycle, not unlike Erickson's prescription to the "African Violet lady" (Zeig, 1980a).

The Affective Dimension

Assessing relative prominence in the client's experience

The affective dimension of depression includes the following symptoms: ambivalence; loss of sources of gratification; loss of sense of humor; poor self-esteem; feelings of inadequacy, worthlessness; loss of emotional attachments (apathy); dejected mood; sadness; excessive or inappropriate guilt; sense of powerlessness; high or low emotional reactivity; increased irritability and anger; loss of motivation; anhedonia. The focus is primarily on depressed feelings (Yapko, 1988, p. 30). A client who presents primary symptomatology on this dimension might sound like this:

> I feel angry and desperate because the constant unhappiness I feel seems endless. I feel hopeless about ever being able to feel happy like other people. There are so many things I see that make me feel even worse. Just seeing other people laughing hurts me because I am so cut off from feeling that way. I am scared that I will hurt someone or myself when I get angry. The feeling is so strong that I can't think clearly, and I feel as though I will lose control if I start to let even a small amount of the anger out.

In this brief example, the following affective symptoms were manifested: loss of sources of gratification; loss of sense of humor; poor self-esteem; feelings of inadequacy, worthlessness; dejected mood, sadness; high emotional reactivity; increased irritability, anger; anhedonia.

Metaphorical intervention

Therapeutic metaphors that acknowledge feelings yet deal with their deceptive nature (i.e., the cognitive distortion called "emotional reasoning" described by Beck, 1967) may provide the client with insight into how feelings may distort one's perceptions of reality. One might initiate a discussion about Hollywood techniques for arousing peoples' feelings, such as violins and sympathy ploys. This may illustrate how easily feelings can be manipulated by external cues designed to elicit predictable emotional responses, encouraging the client to come to the understanding that feelings are only one way of relating to experience, and may not always be the best or most reliable way. For clients who typically elevate their feelings to the level of greatest importance, often to their own detriment, this can be a powerful reframing regarding emotions.

In designing metaphors to address the affective dimension, the underlying goal is to offer the client viable ways to be less absorbed in negative emotions and even be more objective. This would allow them to create optimal distance between themselves and their feelings in order to "reality test" more accurately. It would further permit the client to learn to respond to salient specific details of problem solving rather than the overwhelming global nature of the problem.

Anger is generally a consequence of frustration resulting from the client's being blocked in attaining desired outcomes. The task of the clinician is to help the client be a better problem solver, in order to reach desired outcomes more frequently and efficiently.

Dealing directly with the above client's anger that is so readily accessible may actually hinder the therapy. Increasing the client's awareness of anger by focusing on (and thus amplifying) this single dimension that he or she is experiencing does not create alternatives (Yapko, 1988). The client presented an inability to feel good as well as feelings of anger toward others who do. The theme of the following metaphor is to limit the experience of frustration (and consequently anger) through successful living. Metaphors may instead be used to positively integrate angry feelings in a way that will contribute to a positive valence within the client. This transcript is an example of how associations among feelings can bridge the psychic energy in anger with that of problem solving.

Artists

And you can discover so many different ways to go into trance . . . consciously *wondering* what words I am going to use and what images I'm going to paint on your imagination . . . and enjoy knowing that your unconscious will respond autonomously and wisely . . . appreciating and making good use of past learning and experience . . . and I can describe an artist who deliberately used watercolors to create the effect he wanted . . . and he enjoyed knowing that he had a variety of choices for how to express himself . . . a variety of outlets for communicating his feelings . . . he could choose to use oils or inks if he so desired . . . and he was aware that *there are a number of possible ways to create something valuable* . . . and in the selection of colors . . . he enjoyed knowing that he could use any color he wanted . . . and in the process of painting and engaging himself in his own creative process, he would stand back from the canvas . . . *get enough distance* here to see the context of the work over there . . . make each brush stroke meaningful and deliberate . . . a valuable contribution to the whole . . . and to enjoy knowing that he could see so differently here . . . about feeling so differently there . . . from a comfortable distance . . .

The above metaphor addresses the need for the client to develop an awareness of the possibility of making use of a range of alternatives in dealing with her feelings. By introducing options as resources, the therapist can help the client to discover her ability to act selectively and autonomously in contrast to reacting in a limited and restricted way. Task metaphors to increase flexibility in problem solving may include creating the same image in a variety of different media—clay, oil, ink, watercolors. Another task assignment would be directing the client to stand in a closet for an hour and to repeat, "I'm trapped. I'm trapped." This task is an example of a symptom prescriptive technique that encourages resistance to the symptom by amplifying it (Yapko, 1988).

The Historical Dimension

Assessing relative prominence in the client's experience

This dimension accounts for the specific etiological factors of depression found in the client's life experience. The following depressogenic patterns may be found on this dimension: a history of significant losses; a history of aversive, uncontrollable events; inconsistent demands, expectations, and environments; and a narrow range of personal experiences (Yapko, 1988, p. 32).

The following example illustrates how a client may represent the above symptoms:

I'm an ACA (Adult Child of an Alcoholic) and because of this family history, I face so many challenges in trying to cope with life. My parents used to fight constantly and never had any time for me. I was very alone as a child, and I have felt unloved and sad for as long as I can remember. Both parents used to hit me when they were drinking and so I used to lock myself in my room and wait until they were asleep. Nothing I ever did seemed to be good enough, and I could just as easily be slapped or hugged for being around them. One thing I realize now is how scared I was that *they* would be hurt. I used to stay at home most of the time even though I hated it, because I was scared that if I was not there to look out for them, something terrible would happen to them.

In this brief example, the following historical symptoms were manifested: history of aversive uncontrollable events; inconsistent demands, expectations, and environment; and a narrow range of personal experience.

The information gained from exploring the extent to which depressogenic factors have existed on the historical level has an obvious value in providing perspectives about the client. However, the clinician operating within the strategic model uses discretion in determining the extent to which historical information is considered necessary to review in forming an intervention for the client's current dysfunctional patterns of experience. The following transcript indicates how the clinician may use the historical dynamics presented above in developing a therapeutic metaphor.

Metaphorical intervention

Journey

. . . I once knew someone whose situation was not unlike your own in some important respects . . . He had been awarded a full scholarship to study at Harvard, but he decided he could not meet up to such high expectations . . . He felt so sad, knowing that he was not accepting the challenge of a golden opportunity to move ahead . . . and he felt so unhappy, knowing that he should be happy . . . he felt so unworthy of the recognition he had worked so hard for . . . it seemed to him as though his life had been a long struggle . . . and that the path he was on had been full of obstacles . . . but now as he looked back along the rocky road of his life he realized that he could see things differently . . . that his past was not the same as his future . . . and so he imagined putting on a secure coat of comfort . . . and going back to places alongside the road where he could safely leave painful memories . . . places in the past where they belonged . . . and as he did so . . . he began to see how comfort could emerge from pain . . . how someone could succeed in leaving the ghetto he grew up in to move on in life . . . how dreams of the past may become realities of the present . . . he felt his step become lighter as the load of painful memories was restored to the past . . . and he knew where they belonged and where to find them if he ever had reason to do so . . . and he enjoyed the comfort of knowing that his life journey would take him ahead where there be more safe places to leave old unwanted memories . . . and more opportunities to pick up new meaningful ones . . .

The above metaphor illustrates how the client's feelings about painful traumatic past experiences can be acknowledged while simultaneously placing them in the context of not belonging in the present. The symbolic and cliched use of a life journey provides the client with a momentum for sequencing a temporal framework, i.e., the past necessarily leads into the present, which in turn leads into the future. Thus, the metaphor provides a natural opportunity to seed the possibility of positive future changes occurring that relate to having a greater purpose beyond the current depression.

The goal of the metaphor is to amplify the need for the client to recognize that the past is not the present. A related task assignment would be to have the client "live in the past" for a week without using any form of modern technology, i.e., no electricity. Ignoring present or future capabilities in order to stay "stuck" is amplified and made a magnet for resistance to maintaining such a pattern.

Symbolic Dimension

Assessing relative prominence in the client's experience

This dimension represents the client's internal experience symbolically in ways that are consciously acceptable to the client. The symptoms that may occur on this level are: destructive fantasies or images; recurring nightmares; bothersome images; symptoms as metaphorical representations of inner experience; the client's interpretation of the meaning of depression; healing images; and spiritual involvements and interpretations (Yapko, 1988, p. 31).

An example of how this dimension may be represented by the client follows:

> I feel trapped in a web of despair. It is as if I can't ever get out of it and the more I struggle, the tighter the web holds me. It feels as though this depression is like a great big black spider's web that is always holding me back from the rest of the world so that I can't enjoy life like other people can. I am trapped and I don't even have any strength left to continue struggling.

In this brief example, the following symbolic symptoms were manifested: destructive and bothersome images; interpretation of the "meaning" of depression; and the symptoms as metaphorical representations of inner experience.

Metaphorical intervention

The symbolic representation of the client's experience as a spider web may be used to form the basis of a metaphor. In the metaphor, the clinician transforms the web's incapacitating attributes to a view of the web providing a structure from which one can initiate action. The goal is to parallel the client's experience by accepting and utilizing imagery from her frame of reference, and then lead into a solution-oriented approach.

The Web

You know all too well just how it feels to be trapped . . . and how tired this can make you feel . . . but you can give yourself permission to stop struggling now . . . and work smarter, not harder . . . and have you ever had the sensation of being suspended in a hammock . . . or perhaps on a swing . . . having your body safely supported by the structure beneath you? . . . and as you continue to grow even more relaxed . . . you can focus your thoughts on how intricately a hammock is knotted together . . . and that something strong enough to hold you down can also be used to pull you up . . . to make it strong enough for you to relax in . . . and you may imagine how much skill is involved in the craft of making lace so that each thread is artfully linked to the next . . . and to the next . . . and how you could trace its weave from any point to any other point . . . each thread combined with another to form a strong structure so that you can safely and effortlessly climb out . . . and stand up . . . you can see how something that can hold you down can also be used to pull you out . . . and you may not know just yet where to start the process for yourself in your own experience . . . but isn't it interesting to notice how small and far away a little black spider looks?

The above metaphor illustrates how the client's imagery may be utilized as a basis for reframing her experience in terms of problem resolution. How the problem is conceptualized generally determines the degree of success or failure that can be anticipated in future outcomes. By therapeutically manipulating the client's internal representation of the problem (i.e., images and associated thoughts), the therapist can encourage the client to predict the future positively. This strategic maneuver creates the opportunity for the client's self-generated imagery to be the precursor to success. Through the process of pacing the client's imagery, the clinician may lead the client into thinking differently and consequently acting accordingly in living out positive predictions (Sherman, 1988).

A task assignment to highlight the process necessary to achieve outcomes could be instructing the client to read a magic book and learn an escape trick. Through subsequent assignments in which the client performs the escape for others, social contact is encouraged and the fact that what appears to be a magical escape is actually a step-by-step process that is learnable is demonstrated.

Contextual Dimension

Assessing relative prominence in the client's experience

This dimension relates to situational variables that may synergistically interact to result in the following depressive symptoms: generalized, predictable, restricted responses in particular situations; depressogenic situational cues (anchors) involving specific people, specific places, specific objects, specific times of day (month and year), ambiguity regarding situational demands, responsibilities; ambiguity regarding situational locus of control; situational diffusion or rigidifying of boundaries; and situational violation of personal values and ethics (Yapko, 1988, p. 32). An example of how this may be presented by a client follows:

> I feel like giving up whenever I think about still having two more years to plow through before I get my master's degree. When I first started studying, I felt fortunate in having the opportunity to attend school and develop myself professionally. Now, I look at the time spent sitting in class as a waste. I think the school regulations are archaic, and I am aware of writing bland papers to please bureaucratically bound professors, rather than because I find them personally enriching. I am generally feeling angry and resentful and I am having a hard time controlling my feelings. It's depressing. I tend to express myself sarcastically and have little tolerance for other students' idealisms about reforming the world. It takes all the energy I have to sit through classes. My level of motivation is nonexistent and I don't even know why I bother to carry on or how long I can carry on with this farce. I feel so trapped and fear I'll never finish.

This example reflects the client's sense of hopelessness, worthlessness, ambivalence, and ambiguity regarding personal standards, and in meeting up to the specific expectations of a school program.

Metaphorical intervention

The client's generalized depressive response relates to specific depressogenic situational cues, such as attending class and dealing with the school's professors. In response, the clinician may use a metaphor designed to reframe the client's negative perception of his situation into a more positive one.

Einstein
. . . It seems important for you to know the value of your feelings about school . . . and how these feelings are associated with your ability to learn more about yourself . . . so that you may become aware of your increasing capability to use these valuable feel-

ings . . . to grow in unexpected and surprising ways . . . taking your time to discover what you need to know in varying degrees . . . and in learning to discover, you may find that what did not seem purposeful at one time, may seem purposeful at another time . . . and this reminds me of a story I once heard about Albert Einstein, the legendary physicist who claimed that space and time were not what they seemed to be . . . on a personal level, it took a long time for him to find the space that he needed to be creative . . . in his early years, he recalled how confined he felt attending school . . . how different he felt from the other students . . . and how differently he thought . . . he was considered to be a backward and introspective child . . . and that this experience made him see the world about him in a very different way . . . and when he later recalled those years, looking back at the time when he felt as though school fostered a stance of personal opposition . . . much like you are experiencing now . . . he later felt that it was the catalyst that enabled him to question the assumptions that so many other people took for granted . . . and it was his ability to use negative feelings positively as a creative challenge, that led him to discover the theory of relativity . . . and it seems as though feelings that may not seem purposeful at one time can indeed become very purposeful at another time. . . And I wonder just how it is, and in what way you will be able to use the feelings you now have . . . to creatively think differently . . . and be able to make some personally significant discoveries of your own . . . and why not be just angry enough to grow beyond the simple demands of a school you didn't design? . . .

Metaphors such as the one above can be of value in helping the client to detach his feelings from the context in which they occur in order for him to be actively goal-oriented in meeting school requirements. The metaphor's purpose is to develop the client's receptivity to accepting the limitations of the situation, thus avoiding the frustration he might experience in holding on to unrealistic expectations. The effect is to facilitate the client's ability to meet the prescribed demands effortlessly by not internalizing problems over which he has no control. Task assignments designed to increase acceptance and clarify issues of control may be to redesign the school or to ask friends for something that they definitely do not have and have no way of providing (Yapko, 1988).

Relational Dimension

Assessing relative prominence in the client's experience

Depressive patterns found on the relational dimension typically involve the following symptoms: victim relational style; marked dependency on others; high reactivity to others; social secondary gains; social withdrawal and isolation; social avoidance, apathy; excessive approval-seeking patterns; self-sacrificing martyrish patterns; over-responsible for others; inappropriate scapegoating of self or others; passive-aggressive patterns; diffuse or rigid personal boundaries; power-seeking or avoiding; incongruent patterns of relating; hypercritical of others; and a narrow range of communication skills, i.e., identifying and expressing feelings (Yapko, 1988, p. 31).

The depressed client who has a "victim" relational style typically has difficulty in setting limits and in dealing with issues of responsibility. Generally, the client is either under or overresponsible in regard to relationships with others. The underresponsible client tends to be self-negating and placating, whereas the overresponsible client lives with the illusion of having created and being responsible for all adverse circumstances in his personal setting (Yapko, 1985b). The feeling of being taken advantage of evident in the underresponsible client is connected to symptoms on the relational dimension such as poor self-esteem. This results in the client feeling apprehensive about expressing personal feelings for fear of abandonment (Yapko, 1985b). An example of how this might be represented by the client follows.

My wife had a very unhappy childhood and when I married her 20 years ago, I believed that I could make up for the past. I mean, I really wanted to make her happy. At first, I enjoyed giving her all the things she never had, both materially and emotionally. But eventually, the pleasure turned to worrying about her safety when I was not there. I worried about what she would do if I was not there to give her advice and support. Now, I realize that no matter how much I do for her there will always be even more that I could do. As our nursery became more successful, I had to spend more time at the business and less time with her. I feel so guilty about that. When she gets upset, she drinks too much and becomes verbally aggressive and blames me for not being a good husband. When that happens, I think about all that I have done for her in these past 20 years and how much I have had to give up doing for myself to take care of her. I can't leave her because she will not be able to manage on her own; and yet, I can't help feeling resentful about her not appreciating how much I have sacrificed for her.

In this example, the following relational symptoms were manifested: self-sacrificing, martyrish patterns; overresponsibility for others; and power-seeking.

Metaphorical intervention

In the above transcript, the client's increased level of stress and depression was associated with his excessive sense of responsibility for taking care of his wife. It was apparent that his initial motivation in providing for his wife was that it fulfilled needs within him by giving him a purpose. He made it his objective to actively change life circumstances so that she could be happy. The following metaphor addressed the client's unrealistic commitment to being solely responsible for his wife's happiness. It illustrates how personal growth in relationships depends on *both* partners synergistically meeting their own needs as well as the needs of their partner.

Symbiosis
. . . And there are so many different ways you can find to create balance internally just as there are so many different examples for you to see it externally . . . and you can explore ways to create your own experience of comfortably balancing what you give with what you take in relationships and sometimes it's easier to distinguish giving from taking when we take pleasure in giving . . . but there are times when giving protection stunts the growth of the other person . . . and then one has to take back the protection in order to give growth . . . and isn't it ironic how what is meant to be help can eventually hurt . . . and now you can know deeply that the best way to help sometimes is not to help . . . now, a perfectly natural example may be found in your own nursery of experience . . . where you know how a plant's growth may be stunted if it grows in the shade of a larger

one . . . and so often the protective shade may be moved to another place where it can be enjoyed . . . enabling the smaller, less robust plant to build its own strength in its own patch of sunlight . . . and to grow into being wonderfully robust . . . and what a difference it is for both plants to have the opportunity to grow independently . . . beautiful together, yet separate . . .

The above metaphor illustrates how his own personal growth and development as well as his wife's may be inhibited by overprotection and overresponsibility. This analogy creates the bind that in order to help his wife, and himself, he should create enough space for her to have the freedom to grow in her own right.

The client's awareness of responsibility issues may be fostered by assigning the tasks of choosing a plant to continually (and inconveniently) check on and dote over, and asking his wife every 15 minutes, "Is there anything I can do for you? Command me." The resistance to such excessive responsibility can be channeled in the direction of achieving a more functional autonomy in both relationship partners.

SUMMARY

Therapeutic metaphors represent a vivid and colorful way of facilitating clients' ability to generate problem-solving solutions and establish internal associations that may be both long term and personally significant. The ability to identify dysfunctional patterns and personal themes in the client's experience and to incorporate these elements into a sound treatment plan is a major advantage of using this technique. The clinician who is committed to the task of developing creativity in problem solving with his or her clients may find that metaphors may be used flexibly throughout the treatment process and in a wide variety of therapeutic situations. Treatment may be better focused by conceptualizing the broad context of depressogenic experience within a framework of specific interrelated dimensions. From this perspective, the clinician can aim therapeutic metaphors at resolving specific issues on specific dimensions. The treatment can then be extended through experiential metaphors that can build experiences that will integrate the benefits of therapy into everyday life situations.

REFERENCES

Bandler, R., & Grinder, J. (1975). *Patterns of the Hypnotic Techniques of Milton H Erickson, M.D.:* (Vol. I). Cupertino, Calif.: Meta Publications.

Bandler, R., & Grinder, J. (1979). *Frogs into Princes.* Moab, Utah: Real People Press.

Bandler, R., & Grinder, J. (1982). *Reframing: Neuro-Linguistic Programming and the Transformation of Meaning.* Moab, Utah: Real People Press.

Beck, A., Rush, J., Shaw, B., & Emery, G. (1979). *Cognitive Therapy of Depression.* New York: Guilford Press.

Beck, A.T. (1967). *Depression: Clinical, Experimental, and Theoretical Aspects.* New York: Hoeber. (Republished (1972) as *Depression: Causes and Treatment.* Philadelphia: University of Pennsylvania Press.)

Erickson, M. H., & Rossi, E. L. (1979). *Hypnotherapy: An Exploratory Casebook.* New York: Irvington.

Erickson, M. H., Rossi, E. L., & Rossi, S. I. (1976). *Hypnotic Realities.* New York: Irvington.

Gilligan, S. G. (1987). *Therapeutic Trances: The Cooperation Principle in Ericksonian Hypnotherapy.* New York: Brunner/Mazel.

Goldsmith, S. (1986). *Psychotherapy of People with Physical Symptoms: Brief Strategic Approaches.* New York: University Press of America.

Gordon, D. (1978). *Therapeutic Metaphors: Helping Others Through the Looking Glass.* Cupertino, Calif.: Meta Publications.

Grinder, J., Delozier, J, & Bandler, R. (1977). *Patterns of the Hypnotic Techniques of Milton H. Erickson, M.D.* (Vol. II). Cupertino, Calif.: Meta Publications.

Haley, J. (1963). *Strategies of Psychotherapy.* New York: Grune & Stratton.

Haley, J. (1973). *Uncommon Therapy: The Psychiatric Techniques of Milton H. Erickson, M.D.* New York: W. W. Norton.

Haley, J. (1984). *Ordeal Therapy.* San Francisco, Calif.: Jossey-Bass.

Lakoff, G., & Johnson M. (1980). *Metaphors We Live By.* Chicago: University of Chicago Press.

Lankton, S. R. (1980). *Practical Magic: A Translation of Basic Neuro-Linguistic Programming in Clinical Psychotherapy.* Cupertino, Calif.: Meta Publications.

Lankton, S., & Lankton, C. (1983). *The Answer Within: A Clinical Framework of Ericksonian Hypnotherapy.* New York: Brunner/Mazel.

Madanes, C, (1984). *Behind The One Way Mirror.* San Francisco, Calif.: Jossey-Bass.

Rosen, S., (1982). *My Voice Will Go with You: The Teaching Tales of Milton H. Erickson, M.D.* New York: W. W. Norton.

Rossi, E. L. (Ed.) (1980) *The Collected Papers of Milton H. Erickson, M.D.* (Vol. I) *The Nature of Hypnosis and Suggestions.* New York: Irvington.

Rossi, E. L. (1986). *The Psychobiology of Mind-Body Healing.* New York: W. W. Norton.

Rossi, E. L., & Ryan, M. O. (Eds.) (1985). *Life Reframing in Hypnosis.* New York: Irvington.

Seligman, M. (1974). Depression and learned helplessness. In R. Friedman & M. Katz (Eds.), *The Psychology of Depression: Contemporary Theory and Research.* Washington, D.C.: Winston.

Seligman, M. (1975). *Helplessness: On Depression, Development, and Health.* San Francisco, Calif.: Freeman.

Seligman, M. (1983). Learned helplessness. In E. Levit, B. Lubin, & J. Brooks (Eds.), *Depression: Concepts, Controversies, and Some New Facts* (2nd. ed., pp. 64–72). Hillsdale, N.J.: Erlbaum.

Sherman, S. J. (1988). Ericksonian psychotherapy and social psychology. In J. Zeig & S. K. Lankton (Eds.), *Developing Ericksonian Therapy: State of the Art* (pp. 59–90). New York: Brunner/Mazel.

Watzlawick, P. (1976). *How Real is Real?* New York: Vintage Books.

Watzlawick, P. (1978). *The Language of Change.* New York: Basic Books.

Watzlawick, P. (1983). *The Situation Is Hopeless, but Not Serious.* New York: W. W. Norton.

Yapko, M. D. (1981). A comparative analysis of direct and indirect hypnotic communication styles. *American Journal of Clinical Hypnosis, 25,* 270–276.

Yapko, M. D. (1984). *Trancework: An Introduction to Clinical Hypnosis.* New York: Irvington.

Yapko, M. D. (1985a). The Erickson hook: Values in Ericksonian approaches. In J. Zeig (Ed.) *Ericksonian Psychotherapy,* (Vol. I, pp. 266–281). New York: Brunner/Mazel.

Yapko, M. D. (1985b). Therapeutic strategies for the treatment of depression. *Ericksonian Monographs, 1,* 89–110. New York: Brunner/Mazel.

Yapko, M. D. (1986). Depression: Diagnostic frameworks and therapeutic strategies. In M. Yapko (Ed.) *Hypnotic and Strategic Interventions: Principles and Practice* (pp. 215–259). New York: Irvington.

Yapko, M. D. (1988). *When Living Hurts: Directives for Treating Depression.* New York: Brunner/Mazel.

Zeig, J. (Ed.) (1980a). *A Teaching Seminar with Milton H. Erickson, M.D.* New York: Brunner/Mazel.

Zeig, J. (Ed.) (1980b). *Ericksonian Approaches to Hypnosis and Psychotherapy.* New York: Brunner/Mazel.

Zeig, J. (Ed.) (1985). *Ericksonian Psychotherapy* (Vols. I & II). New York: Brunner/Mazel.

Zeig, J., & Lankton, S. (Eds.) (1988). *Developing Ericksonian Therapy: State of the Art.* New York: Brunner/Mazel.

Chapter 7

No More Monsters and Meanies: Multisensory Metaphors for Helping Children with Fears and Depression

Joyce C. Mills

Joyce C. Mills, Ph.D., is in private practice in Encino, Calif., where she is a consultant to medical, educational, and media organizations. She has integrated traditional psychotherapy and Ericksonian hypnotherapy into her own innovative approach. Mills has also presented widely at professional meetings, including the Third and Fourth International Ericksonian Congresses, and has been published in numerous journals. She is currently expanding her outreach of therapeutic work with children and their families into national television and video. Mills is also coauthor, with Richard J. Crowley, Ph.D., of Therapeutic Metaphors for Children and the Child Within *and of a therapeutic comic book for abused children entitled* Gardenstones: Fred Protects the Vegetables, *published by Childhelp USA.*

In examining a framework for creating and utilizing effective multisensory metaphors for children, it is common to focus on the didactic steps involved in doing so (Lankton & Lankton, 1986; Mills & Crowley, 1986). Of equal or perhaps greater importance is a focus on what might be called the invisible "metaphorical atmosphere." This atmosphere is synthesized from the therapist's conscious and unconscious beliefs, attitudes, and values that coalesce into an inner state of

The author would like to acknowledge the editorial assistance of Margaret Ryan on this paper.

being. This inner state of the therapist is crucial to the creation of any kind of therapeutic metaphor because it also functions as a metaphorical statement or indirect communication to the child.

Part I of this chapter explores two key areas that can adversely influence the atmosphere created by therapists: the conscious or unconscious use of diagnostic labeling, and expectations of change in the form of "giant leaps" rather than in smaller, subtler shifts. Part II explores the development of a variety of metaphorical interventions in terms of a "braiding process" by which the child's problem (fear and/or depression), the child's unique inner resources, and the metaphorical task (the idea or behavior to be learned) are woven into a solution or resolution. This braiding process, which becomes the vehicle through which the child transforms his or her own problem, can thrive only in an atmosphere that is free of labeling and misdirected expectations.

PART I: THE INVISIBLE METAPHORICAL ATMOSPHERE

Beyond Diagnosis and Labeling

It is my belief that treating children who are experiencing fears and symptoms of depression cannot begin from a primary focus on diagnosis. With such a focus, the child too often *is* the diagnostic label, and the disorder or presenting problem becomes the dominant, if not the sole, focus of attention. To the extent that a diagnostic label sets up a preconceived set of expectations and associations, it can become a roadblock to successful therapeutic intervention. Worse, it may even function iatrogenically in a negative direction (Mills, 1988).

The shift away from diagnostic labeling was reflected in the field of psychotherapy through the emergence of the whole new "strategic" approaches to the therapeutic process (Erickson, 1980; Haley, 1973; Madanes, 1981; Satir, 1972; Watzlawick, 1978; Zeig, 1982, 1985, 1987). Yapko summarized this new focus as follows (1988, p. 19):

> In the practice of strategic psychotherapy, the de-emphasis of reliance on specific theoretical constructs is encouraged, and instead the emphasis is placed on developing a refined awareness for and acceptance of the subjective frame of reference of the client. The client is not viewed as pathological, or sick, but rather as a victim of his or her own inability to have access to the capabilities or tools necessary for effective living. When the individual is empowered with full access to the necessary resources and

is competent in their utilization, the therapy is considered complete.

Milton H. Erickson, M.D., was one of the earliest clinicians and physicians to deemphasize diagnosis in favor of the greater importance of viewing each patient as "utterly unique." His innovative approach of validating and utilizing the patient's presenting behavior and symptomatology pushed diagnostic, conceptual, and theoretical frameworks into the background as the therapist was taught to perceive and respond *in the moment* to the vast array of minimal cues being provided. In the following quotation, Erickson expressed his views on the iatrogenic role of the doctor (Rossi & Ryan, 1986, pp. 139–140):

> A question that has been written on periodically, for I don't know how long, is the question of iatrogenic disease—that is, disease caused by the doctor. "I think you have a rather bad heart, and you'd better watch it." So the patient promptly becomes a cardiac invalid. I have such a patient at the present time. The doctor merely said: "You may have something wrong with your heart. You'd better watch it." And the patient was bedridden for three months as a result of the remark—iatrogenic disease. While I have read a number of articles on this subject of iatrogenic disease, and heard many discussions about it, there is one topic on which I haven't seen much written about and that is *iatrogenic health.* Iatrogenic health is a most important consideration—much more important than iatrogenic disease.

Gilligan (1987) termed the process of staying present in the moment and not drawing upon diagnostic labels *experiential deframing.* In the following quote, he noted the radical shift such a perspective represents in the field (p. 14).

> Erickson repeatedly stressed that therapeutic communications should be based neither on theoretical generalizations nor on statistical probabilities, but on actual patterns distinguishing the client's present self-expression (e.g., beliefs, behavior, motivation, symptoms). This is a truly radical proposition in that it requires therapists to begin each therapy in a state of experiential ignorance. It assumes that the client's expressions are individualized models of "reality" and that the therapy is based on accepting

and utilizing these models. To do so, therapists must develop a receptive state of *experiential deframing* in which they set aside their models and become "students" to learn a new "reality" (i.e., that of the client).

The following case illustrates an approach to *deframing* an adolescent girl of her presenting label of bulimia so that she might begin to experience the considerable portion of her body and personality that were not entrenched in the problem. The intent of the approach was to facilitate her private experience of her self as a person without the limiting frame of bulimia.

Eat, and Enjoy Life.   A 16-year-old girl arrived for her session quite despondent over the diagnosis of bulimia she had recently been given by her physician. Because she had a chronic kidney disorder, her physician had referred her for relaxation and/or hypnotic training. She had already been in an eating disorder program at one of the major hospitals. There she was told that only 10 percent of the patients truly recover, and that the other patients return periodically throughout their lives. (Thus the label of bulimia had already become an entrenching life sentence for this young girl.)

After completing the program, she had been successfully free of her bulimic behavior for a short period of time (one month). Then she relapsed into her old behavior patterns and became ill once again. Her relapse could not be viewed as surprising since (1) she had been told, in effect, that whatever she learned and gained from her experience in the eating disorder program would probably not work, and (2) the unconscious pattern of thought, feeling, and behavior that fueled the bulimic response had never been addressed in her treatment program.

Since I had experienced an eating disorder problem as a child and adolescent that today would be labeled as bulimia, I decided to tell her of the experience that served as the turning point in my life. My purpose was to provide her with an anecdote that would have strong personal relevance for her. She was told the following.

"When I was a kid, I used to throw up all the time. I used to throw up after every meal and sometimes in between, depending on the circumstances. I had a 'nervous stomach,' so sometimes the vomiting would occur involuntarily, but I had also developed a pattern of inducing it so that I wouldn't throw up in public.

"When I was 17, my mother took me to a specialist, and the specialist told us that my problem could be *very serious*, that I could have *long-term effects on my health*, and that I had to be placed on a *special diet* immediately. He also warned that the fluid could come up into my throat and cause me to *choke to death* at any time. [Italics underscore highly negative suggestions given as a matter of course.]

"From then on, I was not eating well, I was not sleeping well, I got more anxious, and I threw up more than ever. I was watching my diet as the doctor prescribed, but when you're out socially as a teenager, it only makes things much worse not to be able to participate in all the eating activities.

"My mother decided to take me back to my old GP, who hadn't seen me in at least five years. After listening to me describe my symptoms and after a thorough examination, he gave me a big hug, and said there was nothing wrong with me. He told us that I had 'a little bit of a nervous stomach,' and that drinking hot water and lemon would help. He also told me to take a plastic bag, put it inside a regular brown paper bag, put it in my purse, eat anything I wanted to eat, and if I felt like throwing up and couldn't make it to the bathroom, just throw up in the bag and enjoy my life!" [This was long before "symptom prescription" was identified as an effective approach.]

"I never threw up again. I left his office and phoned my boyfriend (who is now my husband) and said, "Let's go down to Nathan's Restaurant (a wonderful restaurant in Coney Island). I want a fried shrimp sandwich right now!"

By the end of the story, we were both laughing heartily—both at the story itself, and because I clearly am not bulimic or underweight. She asked with expectant urgency in her eyes, "Can I have it work out so well, too?"

I said, "I'm 42 and I haven't had that problem in 25 years. Yes, when I get nervous I can throw up, but that's not my first choice!"

I then moved the intervention into what I later recognized as what Erickson had termed a "fractional approach to symptomatology" (Rossi & Ryan, 1985, 1986). I began a metaphorical interrogation to determine what percentage of her was actually bulimic.

"Let's say that you're 100 percent of a person, right?"

She said, "Right."

"So, how much of a percentage of you do you think throws up?"

She looked at me incredulously as I continued.

"Do your toes take part in vomiting?"

"No," she answered.

"Your ankles?"

"No."

"Your feet?"

"No."

"Your calves?"

"No."

"Your knees . . . . thighs . . . . hips . . . . hands . . . . buttocks . . . . vagina . . . . heart . . . . lungs . . . . shoulders . . . . brain . . . . back?" We determined that her stomach, esophagus, mouth, and fingers were the parts involved in creating the vomiting response.

I continued. "Let's take an overall percentage, with that information in mind. Is 100 percent of you involved in vomiting?"

"No."

"Ninety percent?"

"No."
"Eighty percent?"
"No."
She finally determined that, "Only 20 percent of me throws up."
Then I asked, "Do you mean to say that you are willing to label your entire self on the basis of a puny 20 percent? That sounds like pretty strange mathematics to me!" We both laughed, and I concluded that it might be a lot easier if we started to look at the 20 percent that needs the healing in terms of the 80 percent that knows how to live perfectly well.

If we remove the labels that are supposed to circumscribe or delineate the problem troubling the child before us, what remains is a series of ever-changing behaviors that manifest the child's inner states of being—what Gilligan (1987) termed those "multiplex experiential ideas" that color, shape and determine the child's inner phenomenological reality.

Subtle Shifts Versus Giant Leaps

Along with diagnostic labeling, *expectation* is yet another powerful force that is always present in the therapeutic atmosphere in one form or another. It can function as a source of either iatrogenic healing or illness. Often in doing short-term therapy, there is an expectation that change must occur (or be "facilitated," "provoked," "evoked," etc.) in a dramatic and rapid way (Haley, 1984; Madanes, 1984).

This expectation can come from either or both the therapist and client. When working with children, such expectations can also come from harried parents.

Although short-term and strategic therapeutic approaches are certainly powerful and efficacious, the expectation for quick and dramatic change, or what might be called "giant leaps," can be destructive as well as illusory. The expectation can be destructive when the actual change being *lived* by the client is devalued as "not good enough"; and it is illusory because it often does not endure. Quick change may even create a disturbance in the natural process of transformation that would be necessary for enduring change. Erickson's therapeutic interventions, even when focused on a symptom in an apparently circumscribed way, were actually intended to facilitate a generative level (Gilligan, 1987) of change within the client's inner experiential world (Erickson & Rossi, 1979).

For these reasons, rather than focusing on the 'how-long-will-this-take' pressure, I focus on facilitating, nurturing, and protecting those subtle shifts in behavior, feeling, or awareness that can gradually form the basis for extensive and enduring change. This issue of subtle shifts is of particular importance when working with children. They know this timetable of expectation all too well in every part of their daily lives, from toilet training to school curricula.

Frequently, I use the following "baby-step" metaphor to communicate this idea of subtle shifts indirectly to both children and adults, as well as to families. (The tone and sophistication of language are changed, of course, according to age levels.)

> When you were a baby, your parents kept a careful record of each and every new thing you learned to do or say. And they would get very, very excited about all these new things—even the tiniest ones—the first time you looked at them, the first time you smiled, the first time you blew bubbles with your saliva, the first time you grasped a spoon. Along with all of these things that your parents got excited over, another most thrilling moment came when you took your first baby step. You prepared for that first step for a long time. You held onto your parents, you held onto walls and cabinets, you held onto anything that you could find so that you could practice walking all by yourself. You fell down and got up, fell down and got up, many, many times. But then that day came, that moment when it all worked—when you took that first step, and continued walking for several more steps, all by yourself. That one step, that is really just a little baby step, was one of the most important things you ever learned to do.

Both child and adult clients can relate easily to this baby-step metaphor. It gives them permission to move slowly while removing the pressure of high expectations. Ironically, by expecting baby steps to be significant, the change that emerges is usually strongly anchored and stable. It endures, and acts like a magnet in attracting and binding new "baby steps" of change.

PART II: NO MORE MONSTERS AND MEANIES: CHANGE VIA THE BRAIDING PROCESS

This section focuses on the therapeutic process of "braiding" as it emerged in the following two cases. The first case involves Paul, a

seven-year-old boy who was experiencing fears, of going to sleep because of "monster nightmares." Paul also manifested a tough guy ex-
terior to cover up his inner fears, along with secondary symptoms of
encopresis. The second case is David, a teenager, who describes himself as being depressed because of his lack of friends, his withdrawn
behavior, and his overall feelings of inadequacy. Of particular note is
the contrast in metaphorical tasks that unfolded for the two young-
sters. For Paul, the task became an outward, tangible molding of
"Quacker Island," a wonderfully colorful and rich example of the *artistic metaphor*. For David, the task involved an inner, intangible search
and synthesis as he experienced the *living metaphor* of the crystal, while
he listened to a carefully selected *story-telling metaphor*. (For extensive
discussion of the nature and creation of each type of metaphor, see
Mills & Crowley, 1986).

In both cases, the process of *braiding (Figure 1)* provided a unifying
channel by which each major element in the therapeutic process (the
child's presenting problem, the child's unique inner resources, and the
metaphorical task) was incorporated into the resolution. Braiding allowed each child to discover a transformative solution that arose out
of the integration of all three elements. This is in contrast to approaches that seek to eliminate, extinguish, or abolish the problem
behavior or symptom.

Braiding also accorded each major element "equal power," so to
speak, so that a balanced perspective was achieved. If the presenting
problem is emphasized to the diminution, or even exclusion, of the
child's inner resources, the therapeutic perspective is going to be an
unbalanced one. Similarly, overly deemphasizing the presenting problem in favor of either the child's inner resources or the metaphorical
intervention will result in another level of imbalance.

The Monsters, The Masks, and Quacker Island.   Husky seven-year-old
Paul walked brusquely into my office and asked if I had any new toys to
play with. It had been about a year and a half since I had last seen Paul.
At that time, he had been struggling with his aggressive behavior toward other children, and with an extremely short attention span. His
teachers had found him disruptive and difficult to manage. Paul was
seen both individually and with his parents in family counseling, both at
home and in school.

After approximately three months of therapy, Paul had learned how to
express himself with words rather than with fists. His parents were sat-

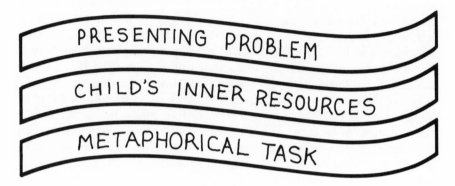

Figure 1A

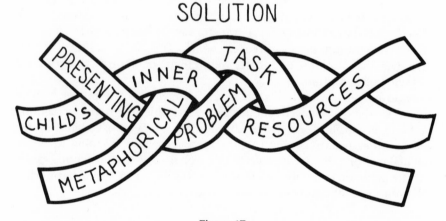

Figure 1B

Figure 1 (a & b) A diagrammatic view of the *braiding process* in which the child's presenting problem, the child's unique inner resources, and the metaphorical task are woven into a solution.

isfied with ending therapy at that time, and were given the reassurance that they could return as needed.*

Paul's return signaled a need for more learnings, as his behavior was once again indicating new turmoils. His mother reported that he wasn't sleeping very well and that he was having frequent monster nightmares. This turmoil was offset by his facade of "Mr. Tough Guy," which was, in turn, undermined by the fact that he was soiling his pants during the day.

Since Paul and I had previously established a solid relationship, he was very excited to see me and to have the chance of exploring my office again. When he walked in, his big brown eyes darted everywhere. My office is filled with many colorful pictures on the walls, puppets of all kinds in a big round basket, and a coffee table with numerous objects such as shells, coral, rocks, crystals, statues, and a Native American story doll.

After taking his time exploring the many items, he asked if we could draw "Sure," I said, and we both went over to the art table.

What his mother had told me about his "monsters" and his tough-guy attitude seemed to go together like two puzzle pieces, one fitting into the other, but separately not quite showing enough of the bigger picture. While we were drawing, I asked Paul how things were going for him.

"Oh, fine," he said, puffing himself up as if he were trying to look bigger to me. He went on and on, telling me how he was the *best* baseball player, the *best* soccer player.

I then asked Paul directly about the monsters he was experiencing. Assuming his tough-guy stance he said, "Yeh, those monsters. . . . They come out at night but they can't get me because *I'm tough.*"

"Boy," I said, "when I was a little girl I sure was afraid of monsters."

"Not me!" Paul exclaimed rather strongly. "They can't get me."

When working with children who act one way but feel another, the theme of *masks* comes to mind (Mills & Crowley, 1988). Therefore, I gave Paul a large drawing pad and asked him if he liked masks. He perked up and exclaimed, "Oh, yes, real scary ones—I love 'em!"

Delighted with his enthusiasm, I asked him to draw a picture of a terrifically scary mask. He immediately picked up a marker and began drawing. As he was drawing, he said, "There's *lots* of dripping blood! There's blood from the ears, blood from the mouth, there's blood everywhere!" He even put an eyeball in the middle of the monster's mouth *(Figure 2)*. Thinking I was moving in a therapeutically strategic direction, I then lifted that piece of paper with his first drawing of the mask and asked Paul to draw a picture of what was underneath the mask. Not expecting his answer, I was quite surprised when he replied in a boom-

---

* This "return as needed" suggestion is considered a controversial issue in many therapies. However, I feel it is important to set an atmosphere of "comfortable learning" when working with adults as well as with children—a place to which one could return if so desired, very much like one might return to college for further education.

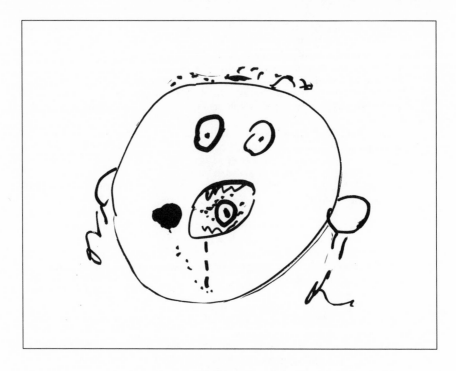

Figure 2.

ing voice, "Another mask." Then he began drawing another very scary mask on the paper *(Figure 3)*. This drawing was free of blood, but was still clearly a monster (a one-eyed one at that!).

When Paul finished, we spent a few moments commenting on this second picture. Then I lifted the paper again to expose a clean sheet, and asked Paul to draw what was underneath this mask. If you haven't guessed already, Paul snickered and said, "Another mask" and drew his third scary mask *(Figure 4)*. There was a marked difference in this mask; the face had evolved from a scary cyclop's face to one of a sad/mad little boy.

At this point, I became aware of a concern I was experiencing about the desirability of continuing with this approach. I wondered if Paul was in the process of anchoring himself to his fear by continuing to draw scary masks. Although the three drawings showed some kind of a progression, I was concerned that the focus was remaining on the sad, scary, negative aspects of his experience. What I was hoping to evoke, and expecting to see, was the emergence of clearly positive images. I now wondered if I should try to change the approach by introducing another

Figure 3.

type of intervention. With some ambivalence, I decided to allow the current intervention to continue to unfold, feeling a certain trust in Paul's inner process. I lifted the third mask drawing and, once again, asked Paul to draw what was underneath *this* mask.

Almost immediately, Paul's facial expression changed and softened. His tough-guy look melted into one of a delightful little boy as he drew his fourth picture. When he was finished, he said in a strong voice, "A happy little boy. He's a great kid!" *(Figure 5).*

Figure 4.

It became apparent by the change in Paul's affect and in *the feeling tone of interaction in the room* that he had begun to lift the masks of fear shrouding his own happiness. This session provided a safe opening into the profoundly gifted world of inner resources that were waiting to be expressed by this wonderful child.

In order to get to the happy face, Paul first had to portray three different scary masks. This reflected his particular need to focus at

Figure 5.

that point on his problem area—but in a safe, indirect, metaphorical way.

In our next session, Paul asked to work with clay. Spontaneously, he said that he wanted to make an island. We used plasticine clay to create his island and to sculpt a very special friend, "Quacker the Duck," who lived on the island. He then made a large tree with a big snake on the top of it and placed it on the island. Each week, Paul expanded his is-

---

The Braiding of Paul's Solution

Presenting problems:	Monsters at night
	Tough-guy attitude
	Daytime encopresis
Paul's inner resources:	Likes to draw
	Likes masks
Metaphorical task:	Drawing the masks
Solution/resolution:	"A happy little boy"

---

land by increasing its size, adding surrounding water, and creating many more characters.* Among the island characters were a beaver, a frog, a goose, and three other ducks. It was easy to see that Paul's personality was emerging in relation to the expansion of his island. His attention span, which was still considered to be unsuitably brief elsewhere, never wavered while he worked on this creation. For 20 minutes or more, he would sit in rapt concentration as he molded and shaped his new world.

An interesting note here is that Paul was about to begin attending a new school. Because of his previously negative experiences in school, he was apprehensive about it. While we were working on Quacker Island during our fourth session, I casually said, "Hey, guess what? *Wyland* [the name of the school] rhymes with *island!*" Laughing, we both began to say, "*Wyland–island*" over and over.

I wanted to anchor (associate) the positive feeling of his island with his response to his new school. Using an interspersed hypnotic suggestion, I said, "I just thought of something neat. Every time you hear or see the word *Wyland*, you can begin to think of your *island* and to see it in your mind." His smile broadened immediately, and I knew he was delighted with this new thought.

Paul began attending his new school with confidence and a positive attitude. His teacher reported that he was cooperative and warm with the other children. His work began to earn stars and positive comments from those who worked with him.

Paul's progress continued over the next two months. His mother reported that he was sleeping better, and that the soiling had become almost nonexistent.

After about three months of working with Paul on a weekly basis, he came into my office, looked at his island, and said, "We don't need the snake anymore. What this island needs is a rainbow."

"What kind of a rainbow?" I asked.

"A big rainbow," he replied.

---

*Paul's island initially was about four inches in diameter. When completed, it was more than ten inches in diameter *(Figure 6)*.

"Do you want some new clay?" I asked as I began to reach for the art materials.

"Nope," he answered confidently, "I'll use the snake." With that utterly profound comment, he took the snake off the tree, kneaded it into multicolored clay, and created a beautiful rainbow. He took a few more pieces of clay and decided to make a nest with eggs in it, which he then placed on top of the rainbow. I asked him if perhaps the nest might go inside the tree (I wanted to verify that his placement of it on the top of the rainbow was intentional). He answered quite emphatically, "No, the nest belongs *on top* of the rainbow." Once the nest was securely (and purposefully!) in place, he moved on to request that we make some wizards, "because every island likes wizards to live there" *(See Figure 6)*.

From our first session, which focused on scary monster masks, to his evolutionary creation of Quacker Island, Paul's transformation continues to be a source of inspiration and enlightenment to me both personally and professionally.

Figure 6. Paul's Quacker Island

Transformation: The Braid Continues

Now that we have the emergent personality behind the scary masks, the transformational process gains in momentum as Paul conceives of and crafts a populated island. This process culminates in Paul's literal transformation of the snake into the rainbow. The braiding process during this time period might be depicted as follows:

Presenting behavior:	Tentative changes in a positive direction
Paul's inner resources:	Rich inner fantasy world
	Likes to sculpt
Metaphorical task:	Creating his island
Solution/resolution:	A thriving island crowned by a rainbow, paralleled by improvements in mood, school performance, sleeping, and elimination

---

Crystal of Change.   David was a nice looking, 15-1/2-year-old boy who described himself as being depressed about his dropping grades and his lack of confidence around his peers. His parents were enormously concerned about his not having friends or an active social life. David's parents were both quite outgoing and very successful in business. His father was strong-willed and domineering; his mother was also quite assertive. David was the youngest of four children, with two older brothers and one sister. He was a quiet, sensitive youngster in a circle of extroverted family members. Although his family was close and supportive, David felt that nobody wanted to acknowledge him the way he was. They told him it wasn't "normal" to spend so much time alone, and that normal teenage boys should have lots of friends and be dating girls. Although they meant well, they were labeling David in a way that painfully invalidated his own natural personality. By the time he came for therapy, he was extremely confused about his identity. He knew that he did not want to become like everyone in his family, but he was also quite worried that he would never change. He wondered if he would be shy forever, if "that was all there was for me."

After entering my office and becoming comfortable, David became interested in a cluster of crystals that rests on a table in front of the couch. Slowly, I began to tell him about how amazing crystals are.

"When they are part of a big rock, they look like this [pointing to the craggy, rocklike surface]. But when you chip away a piece from that big rock and turn it around, look at what is inside [pointing to a protruding cluster of sparkling crystals on the other side].

Utilizing the rock crystal as a metaphor for change, I then slowly added: "It's amazing how this could look like a simple rock when it is viewed from the outside, but by turning it around and looking *inside,* look at all there is to discover." He sat back on the couch and took the crystal, holding it for the rest of the session.

I then asked David to close his eyes and let the crystal teach him something that he needed to know that could be useful in his everyday life. He did as he was asked, and with eyes closed, took a deep breath and became noticeably more relaxed. Now I began to tell him a story of an experience I had recently had on a catamaran in Hawaii. I told him about how the waters were quite choppy, and how my guide, who was completely focused on what he was doing, had a sure hold on the boat's lines. The story went on to describe many different aspects of the trip, but focused particularly on my concerned questioning of my guide:

"Leonard, how do you know when it is time to change direction?"

After a few moments, Leonard, still working the sails, turned to me and said in a soft, deep voice, "Oh, I don't know. You watch the sails and feel the wind, and you just know inside when it is time to change."

"Hmmmmm," I thought to myself, "you watch the sails and feel the wind, and *you just know inside when it is time to change.*"

Although David's trance lasted only 15 minutes, it appeared to have a profound effect on him, as demonstrated by his subsequent behavioral and emotional changes. The next week he came into my office with an entirely new haircut—one he had wanted to try but "didn't have the guts to," as he put it. In addition, he began talking more positively about what he knew he could do to improve his life with such statements as, "It's not going to happen with me hiding in my room."

I continued to see David every other week for about three months, tapering to once a month for approximately a year. I gave him *living metaphors* (Mills & Crowley, 1986) to carry out between sessions, such as finding a five-sided rock with the instructions to "hold it in your hand and let the rock teach you something important you need to know." I suggested a five-sided rock because of its parallel to our five senses. Also, David had to use his three primary senses to accomplish the assignment: Find the rock (visual), hold the rock (kinesthetic), hear the rock ("let the rock teach you something"). Although this seems like a simple and uncomplicated assignment, I have found that the results can be surprisingly dramatic. In giving it to families, it can serve as a means for improving communication, shifting awareness, and activating inner resources for change.

Another assignment I gave David was to buy a small plant and transplant it "only when you think it is time to be in the bigger pot, one where there will be more room for the roots." David very much enjoyed nature and all things connected with it; therefore, the suggestions were very much a part of his background and value structure. His interests were utilized to create both storytelling and living metaphors throughout his therapy.

David also struggled with inner dialogues telling him that he would never change. Therefore, it became important to open positive auditory channels within him. One assignment he was given to facilitate this change was to go home and arrange his music tapes in a special order. I asked him to put the music he like the best first, and his least favorite tapes at the back. This living metaphor served two purposes: (1) It helped to activate positive auditory experiences by the very nature of identifying what music he liked best—again presenting a task facilitating a "subtle shift" in David's devaluing unconscious auditory dialogue. (2) It helped to develop and broaden his awareness of choice and his ability to make changes.

David was agreeable to these suggestions and assignments. His motivation to learn other ways of dealing with his problems was high. He began speaking up for himself with his family while still maintaining his own sensitive style of communicating.

During his last session, I pointed to a tree outside my window that we had watched throughout the year we worked together. I asked David to look at it and remember, "Change is natural; you don't have to tell a tree to change—it just does, because even a tree knows when it is time to change, to let go of the leaves it no longer needs in order to make room for the new ones in the spring. Each leaf is unique and different, and each has a purpose."

When I finished speaking, I placed the crystal in his hand with the intent of reconnecting him to his initial experience of self-discovery. He paused for a moment, and as he looked down at it, a smile emerged, letting me know that the inner associations were taking place. There wasn't very much more to say. His growth process was fully launched and was moving under its own momentum. I smiled to myself and I said, "That's right, and that learning can continue in many ways."

These two cases nicely complement each other; together, they illustrate the essential overlapping of the visible and invisible levels of therapeutic work. Paul's metaphorical task was outer and quite visible,

---

The Braiding of David's Solution

Presenting problem:	Depressed, avoidant, overly shy
David's inner resources:	Appreciation of nature.
	Attraction to crystal.
	Ability to focus inward.
	Readiness for change
Metaphorical task:	Inner utilization of the crystal:
	"Let the crystal teach you something you need to know"
Solution/resolution:	Changes in behavior, awareness, and motivation

whereas David's was primarily internal and invisible. Yet both levels of work seemed to facilitate what Erickson so beautifully termed "an inner resynthesis of the patient's behavior achieved by the patient himself" (Erickson, 1980, vol. IV, p. 1). David's changes in behavior, awareness, and motivation are manifestations of this inner resynthesis, just as Paul's Quacker Island vividly represents his. The braiding process is perhaps another way to visualize or conceptualize this process of inner resynthesis, which requires a transformation, a "reorganization and reassociation," (Erickson, 1980, vol. IV, p. 1) of elements and facets already present in the personality. Nothing is eliminated; the integrity of the personality is maintained, as all of its "self" is accepted and integrated.

SUMMARY

To best elucidate the essence of this summary, a metaphor or analogy comes to mind. A "trailer" to a movie often attracts our attention and gives us a few enticing clues about the movie. However, to get the full story, we have to see the movie in its entirety. For me, the whole story, when working with children and adolescents (or a person of any age, for that matter), involves a thorough exploration of both outer (behavioral) and inner (phenomenological) dimensions. The outer behaviors generally represent a culmination or coalescence of many inner (and invisible) levels. It is to these inner levels that we must look both for clear illumination of the problem and for the strengths, resources, and positive associations that contain the healing threads of change and solution.

REFERENCES

Erickson, M. (1980). In E. Rossi (Ed.), The *Collected Papers of Milton H. Erickson on Hypnosis (4 vols.).* New York: Irvington.

Erickson, M., & Rossi, E. (1979). *Hypnotherapy: An Exploratory Casebook.* New York: Irvington.

Gilligan, S. (1987). *Therapeutic Trances.* New York: Brunner/Mazel.

Haley, J. (1973). *Uncommon Therapy.* New York: W. W. Norton.

Haley, J. (1984). *Ordeal Therapy.* San Francisco: Jossey-Bass.

Lankton, S., & Lankton, C. (1986). *Enchantment and Intervention in Family Therapy.* New York: Brunner/Mazel.

Madanes, C. (1981). *Strategic Family Therapy.* San Francisco: Jossey-Bass.

Madanes, C. (1984). *Behind the One-Way Mirror.* San Francisco: Jossey-Bass.

Mills, J. (1988). PMS: Symptom, or source of transformation. *Psychological Perspectives, 19*(1), 101–111.

Mills, J., & Crowley, R. (1986). *Therapeutic Metaphors for Children and the Child Within.* New York: Brunner/Mazel.

Mills, J., & Crowley, R. (1988). A multidimensional approach to the utilization of therapeutic metaphors for children and adolescents. In J. Zeig & S. Lankton (Eds.), *Developing Ericksonian Therapy: State of the Art.* New York: Brunner/Mazel.

Rossi, E., & Ryan, M. (Eds.) (1985). *Life Reframing in Hypnosis. (Vol. II.) The Seminars, Workshops, and Lectures of Milton H. Erickson.* New York: Irvington.

Rossi, E., & Ryan, M. (Eds.) (1986). *Mind-Body Communication in Hypnosis. (Vol. III.) The Seminars, Workshops, and Lectures of Milton H. Erickson.* New York: Irvington.

Satir, V. (1972). *Peoplemaking.* Palo Alto, Calif.: Science & Behavior Books.

Watzlawick, P. (1978). *The Language of Change.* New York: Basic Books.

Yapko, M. (1988). *When Living Hurts: Directives for Treating Depression.* New York: Brunner/Mazel.

Zeig, J. (Ed.) (1982). *Ericksonian Approaches to Hypnosis and Psychotherapy.* New York: Brunner/Mazel.

Zeig, J. (Ed.) (1985). *Ericksonian Psychotherapy (2 vols.).* New York: Brunner/Mazel.

Zeig, J. (Ed.) (1987). *The Evolution of Psychotherapy.* New York: Brunner/Mazel.

Chapter 8

Therapeutic Diagnosing in Cases of Childhood Depression

Ronald M. Gabriel

Ronald M. Gabriel, L. R. C. P., L. R. C. S., Ed., L. R. C. P. S. Glas., D. P. M., M. R. C. Psych., was born in London, England, and graduated in medicine from the University of Edinburgh, Scotland, in 1952. Gabriel subsequently trained in psychiatry, becoming a child psychiatrist with a Jungian analytic background. After a successful career directing two clinics near London, he moved to Canada. He currently has a private practice in Regina, Sask., and is on the faculty of the University of Saskatchewan. His encounter with Ericksonian hypnosis in recent years has revolutionized his already lengthy clinical experience in child psychiatry. Gabriel is also currently using Ericksonian techniques with cancer patients.

Prior to World War II, the possibility of depression in childhood was barely recognized. In the standard textbook written by the father of American child psychiatry, Leo Kanner (1957), there is no mention of the condition. As there is no reason to believe that children's characteristics have changed, it is reasonable to conclude that the symptoms of childhood depression were either not being identified or were being labeled incorrectly. One of the earliest descriptions of childhood depression was given by the English psychoanalyst Donald Winnicott (1944), who pointed out that it was not at all uncommon. He described a disorder that presented as an anxious restlessness with self-destructive behaviors that could also include hypochondriacal worry. The condition now has become far better known.

The usual adult depressive symptomatic pattern of withdrawal from involvement in life is less clearly seen in childhood. Sleep disturbances with early morning waking are also less prominent in the child. In children, the main characteristics are disorders of attention and behavior. Without a recognition of the reality of childhood depression, this syndrome can easily be misdiagnosed as a behavior disorder, a learning disability, an attention-deficit disorder, or an anxiety state. When the problem produces a listless, exhausted child, it can even be mistaken for physical disease. Of course, depression can be associated with any of these conditions, each of which can exist in its own right. More frequently, however, there are groups of symptoms that are ways in which depression can become manifest.

A model for conceptualizing depression can do much to clarify the matter. Carl Jung (1916) saw depression as an impairment in the flow of psychic energy or libido from the individual toward the outside world. In a state of good health, a balance is achieved between the amount of energy devoted to personal issues and the amount devoted to attending to the world. However, when personal issues demand excessive attention, the remaining energy often becomes inadequate to cope with simultaneous external demands. This imbalance results in a withdrawal of energy from the conscious world, giving rise to depression. Jung, borrowing the term from Janet, called this state an *abaissement du niveau mental*—a lowering of the level of mental activity. Internal demands of this nature can be produced whenever it becomes necessary for the patient to rewrite his or her world picture, either temporarily or permanently. Examples of such demands may include such problems as experiences of loss, bereavement, lack of appropriate nurturing, abandonment, environmental stressors, threats from people, threats from impending psychotic processes, or threats from impending physical disease. When the organism organizes itself to handle any of these problems, a rearrangement of the energy flow occurs, resulting in a need to put the outside world "on hold" for some period of time. To a limited degree, this is part of everyone's normal experience. The imbalance only becomes a pathological condition when the internal problem fails to be solved and the usual flow of energy fails to become rebalanced within a reasonable amount of time.

Although the pronouns "he" and "him" will be used from here on, they are intended to signify both sexes. It is noteworthy, however, that most of the cases seen are male. This may be due to the fact that there is a greater tendency for boys to produce behavioral symptoms having nuisance value, thus more effectively drawing attention to their needs.

Sometimes the symptoms of childhood depression can produce a degree of relief through their effects on the family. If the parents perceive that the child is physically sick, they may take him out of school, put him to bed, or nurse him in other ways. This parental behavior may have a regressive effect on the child and may successfully separate him from his current difficulties sufficiently to allow healing to take place. For a relatively robust child who is handling a problem reasonably well and to which he can be expected eventually to adjust, this may be all that is needed for recovery. Recurrent colds and flus often seem to be manifestations of the child who has too much with which to cope.

When the depression fails to clear quickly, clinicians may see some of the more serious pictures of pathology already described. The irritable and behaviorally disturbed child may then be faced with the additional problem of having to cope with unsympathetic or even punitive adults. Paradoxically, such harsh treatment can sometimes produce temporary relief, since the child deflects his energies toward becoming angry with the people around him. But, in such instances, he is not solving anything, and the situation becomes compounded by his despair. This is the state of affairs that is usually presented to therapists in the clinical setting. Many of these children are referred to clinicians, and they form a large proportion of the patients seen in the author's practice.

DIAGNOSING AND TREATING THE PATIENT

What follows is a suggested protocol for a diagnostic interview concerning a child of about 11 years of age. It is idiosyncratic in its detail and should be adapted to the individual style of the clinician. It should be noted that therapeutic strategies are introduced, whenever possible, from the start.

There would appear to be a strong drive for health in children. Removal of obstacles to this, such as pessimism and poor self-esteem, often result in very rapid change. For this reason, the clinician's style, when suggestive of hope and positive health, can lead to speedy improvements. These suggestions are introduced from the start.

The story of the problem is taken from the parent(s) in the presence of the child. Focusing on their main concerns will tend to ensure good cooperation. This half-hour of work should also provide a developmental history of the child and an initial evaluation of the family dynamics. It also allows the child to observe the clinician either directly or from the "shelter" of being involved in drawing a picture or reading a book. The child is assured that he will have as much individual time as is needed in due course. It is hoped that, by then, the clinician will have been perceived by the child as a trustworthy and empathetic person.

Patients come for help, so it may be unreasonable to expect them to separate history taking from the therapy. Communications during this phase are potentially extremely therapeutically significant: It must be remembered that healing can start at the very beginning of contact with patients. This has implications for all aspects of the interaction, including the design of the office, the behavior of the receptionist, and everything done and said by the clinician. Even a remark such as, "Please sit here. It's a chair where things often change for the better," may elicit little obvious response but can become a valuable seed. Making a future appointment for the child in order to "let me know how things are improving" is not lost on him or his parents. Simple gestures of this type can turn out to be excellent investments.

A very careful psychosocial history is subsequently taken from the child in the absence of the parents. This is done with the greatest of respect for the child's complaints. These usually include accounts of being teased by fellow students, not being appreciated by teachers, and being treated unkindly by one or both parents. Some of this may be true, either as a causative factor or, more frequently, as a reaction to the irritability and unpleasant behavior of the depressed child. Detailed notes are taken, partly for the record, but, perhaps more therapeutically, as a signal to the child that his reality is being believed and perceived as correct. Empathetic responses are made to draw out more of the painful story. This may appear to the child as excessive concern and can lead to the creation of an implied paradox to which something in the child may begin, unconsciously, to protest that it is not necessarily as bad as all that.

When this history is concluded, the next therapeutic intervention is introduced as though it is part of the history taking. An accessing question is constructed and then slowly delivered in the following form: "When you look back over your life . . . can you remember . . . the last time . . . you felt really . . . really happy?" At this stage, the question usually produces a number of valuable responses. The child looks inward and age-regresses, achieving a light trance associated with an intense awareness of an inner world that has usually not been attended to in any positive manner. Most children offer a "Garden of

Eden" type of response, describing an unrealistically idyllic time. Such memories exist in the fantasies of most people. For children, they are usually located in the preschool years or before some other important event, such as a parental separation or remarriage or the birth of a sibling. Maintaining the age regression, the dissociation can be deepened by taking a further history of how life began gradually to get more difficult from the post-Garden of Eden time to the present day.

During this second history taking, opportunities are taken to seed ideas of change as part of an apparently conversational set of empathetic remarks. Comments such as: "It must have been hard for you to decide how best to handle that problem" suggest that handling it is possible. Emphasizing the ability to cope is part of any psychotherapy. Within the intentionally enhanced age-regression trance, such responses may act powerfully to induce acceptance that there may be resources available inside the child to do more than just accept emotional pain and feelings of inadequacy.

The next step may be to use a variation of the well-known "Three Wishes" approach described in most standard texts (Gregory & Smeltzer, 1977), which will maintain any growth already taking place. The question may be phrased along these lines: "Can you think of any magical change in yourself that, if it could happen, would make things a little bit better?" One or more such desired changes are written down, with obvious care, into the notes. This first session usually lasts about an hour and a half. It is terminated by a sudden alteration of style in which arrangements are made with the child and parents for one or more future appointments. This is done with much practical discussion about suitable times for these, and though cutting off the trance-history experience, one can include the word "change" from time to time in an emphatic manner to characterize the next session. This is one example of Milton Erickson's interspersal technique (Erickson, Rossi, & Rossi, 1976). The point of this is to produce a degree of amnesia, at least for some of the contents of the interview (Erickson & Rossi, 1981). The positive suggestions for change are thus left to do their work in the child's mind, unimpeded by conscious notice or analysis.

Most mildly depressed children return, after a week or so, with their symptoms vastly improved. The second or third sessions in these cases are not nearly as significant as the first in terms of causing growth and reorientation. The child does not yet know it, but the main thrust of the healing process is already happening. These subsequent

sessions can be used for formal, and therefore impressive, trance induction, with the stated goal of bringing about the changes desired by
the child. A useful experience of this nature can be attained by employing the multiple embedded metaphor approach outlined by
Stephen and Carol Lankton (1983), using it to conceal amnesically a
direct change command in the style described by Jeffrey Zeig (1985).

> *Case Example 1*   Michael, age 13, was constantly in trouble for such be-
> haviors as stealing and lying. He had been diagnosed as suffering from
> temporal lobe epilepsy and was on medication. His parents were di-
> vorced, and his mother had recently remarried following the suicide of a
> former fiance. Michael, who had no memory of any joys or successes of
> his own, felt he wanted to change his personal past. While in trance, he
> was encouraged to explore all the possible meanings of the fiance's sui-
> cide, but without verbally reporting on it. In fact, amnesia was encour-
> aged for that session, which was quite long. In a subsequent session, he
> was told multiple embedded metaphors involving messages of creative
> change and a set of suggestions for handling his world more effectively.
> This appears to have been successful because his mother reported an
> immediate and significant improvement, which has been maintained for
> ten months.

Another valuable approach, appropriate for the third session, is to
review changes the child has noticed in his life. These are frequently
perceived as changes in other people instead of himself. It is necessary
to show the child that it is he, not his schoolmates or parents, who has
changed. This is done by encouraging the history-taking type of light
trance to recur by recreating the original atmosphere of the first session while inquiring into recent events. If possible, each response to
the patient can carry a message implying the child's responsibility for
the changes. Examples of this might include making statements such
as: "It probably took quite a bit of strength to ignore . . . " or "You
must have put a lot of thought into avoiding . . ." while continuing to
sustain the child's narrative.

Many depressed children, like adults, believe they are facing problems for which there are no solutions. They feel they are at a dead end
and that there is nowhere to turn. Such children may be helped by
being told about the enormous database that is their unconscious
mind. They may be told how this database has accumulated knowledge and wisdom every day of their lives, and that it surely has some
useful thoughts that could solve their problems. They are then invited
to consider a problem that has bothered them recently. The uncon-

scious mind, when asked, is likely, after a little consideration, to access the appropriate data or subroutines and to come up with an idea for handling the problem. It can then be encouraged to come up with another, and another. Computer-related metaphors about the unconscious mind generally seem to be attractive to puberty-age children. The metaphor, when well delivered, can lead to relief as the child gains a sense that solutions to his problems are possible. This is in marked contrast to the feeling of impasse in having no appropriate strategies for escape. Beyond that, the child also experiences a sense of being in charge of his destiny in a way that is exhilarating and liberating, especially as he realizes that he can use this approach to deal with future difficulties.

> *Case Example 2*   Chad, age twelve, had recently dropped from a B average to a D average at school and was in trouble with his teachers. He had been a happy boy until he was about eight years of age, when he started to become aware of his father's destructive criticism, both of Chad and of his mother. He cried when telling how his father called him "Sugarbowl" because of his large ears. Irritable and angry, Chad was plagued by piles of homework and an unhelpful attitude from both parents. Since Chad knew that life had been more successful for him when he was younger, he was conversationally age-regressed and given the idea that the younger Chad must have had some pretty useful skills for dealing with his father. This metaphoric construct proved to be very helpful to him. He is beginning to develop remarkable strengths as his depression is lifting. His grades are improving, and he is finding that he can continue to access the wisdom of his younger self—which, in this case, represents to him what we might call the unconscious. No trance has been used other than the informal one created by the absorbing style of the contents of the therapy.

Many children appreciate hypnotic imagery of the type described by William Kroger (Kroger & Fezler, 1976), such as scenes of beaches or isolated cabins that may be used to induce feelings of relaxation and health. Frequently, children will enjoy being given few enough cues that they can elaborate their own variations on such themes. This permits them to demonstrate to themselves their own creativity and ability to adapt the material to their own needs. One of the images often used by the author is that of the "room of your own design." This perfect room can be a totally free creation of the child. Other scenes should be offered in such a way as to maximize the opportunity for the child to personalize them. Indeed, if the scene is to be revisited in a later session, the child may be told that, since he is now older and somewhat changed, he may find that the scene has also changed.

To enhance these effects, the child is taught self-hypnosis and encouraged to use it in times of need and upon retiring to bed. The method that is taught is as follows. During trance, the child is told:

> Just about now, the magic word will come into your mind. It might mean something to you, or maybe not. Anyway, you'll remember that word when you need it. Whenever you want to solve some problems about your feelings, you can use it. All you have to do is close your eyes and say the magic word the right number of times, and you will know the right number of times. You will find that very soon you are in the "room of your own design." There, you can access your databases or subroutines and find some of the answers you need.

This self-induction is demonstrated and practiced in the office during the immediate posthypnotic period by suggesting that the child might like to try it out while he is still with the clinician. A formal technique, such as a short count backwards, is also given for ending a trance.

What has been outlined thus far is a possible treatment schema for a child suffering from a mild chronic depression. It is safe to use this approach in any case where depression is suspected. If things go as described, the diagnosis tends to have been confirmed by the response to treatment. Some variations in patient responses and their implications will now be discussed using the model of therapeutic diagnosis. Resulting differences in the course of the interaction with the patient is noted.

During age regression, it is often suggested to the child that one or more memories from way back may float into his mind. This may be elaborated upon in some manner such as: "Early memories are rather like snapshots and little more . . . You may find yourself noticing more than you thought you really remembered . . . Maybe you can see a little more, hear a little more or even smell something that surprises you a bit because you had not noticed it before." This, of course, increases the dissociative effect of the age regression, deepens the trance, and is particularly useful when one of the therapeutic objectives is to work with the actual early memories.

Case Example 3   David, 12 years old, was depressively enmeshed with his mother, a nurse who often worked late. He cried that he never saw his mother enough because of her work, and complained that everyone hated him. He had a severe reading disability though he was intelligent. David complained that he was a "second-class person." Referral resulted when his mother found a knife in his room, which he explained was there in case he chose to kill himself. The boy had a long history of learning and behavioral problems at school. He was taken into therapy and, in his first trance, described the feeling of a coffin coming out of the left side of his head. He became very sad when he thought about the suffering of "the younger David" who at the age of two had been deserted by his father. He later recalled feeling abandoned when in the hospital with asthma, because his mother failed to visit him for three days. In subsequent sessions, he hallucinated a number of younger Davids, and tenderly comforted them with good advice and concern. In each case, he was encouraged to help the younger Davids. His improvement significantly accelerated, however, after his mother had been age-regressed and relived some very happy school days of her own in his presence. This led to her sharing her memories with David and, at the same time, seemed to allow her to give him increased personal respect apparently so that he could make his own memories now. Mother and son began to take separate trips to visit other family members and were better able to establish some freedom from each other. About six months later, David's increasing control of his own life and less dependent relationship with his mother led to the depression clearing completely. Feeling better about himself, he was able to accept reading remediation constructively. He had a girlfriend, and enjoyed visiting a preteens' dance club with her.

From time to time, the use of hypnosis appears to produce problems for a child. He may come out of the trance or, at the end of the session, be reluctant to return for another. Handled sympathetically, some children will explain this by saying that they had experienced frightening images or feelings. Indeed, careful observation of the patient during the trance will normally show some signs of tension, so the child's account usually will not be unexpected. In these cases, the author has often found that either the child has been a victim of abuse, or that psychotic features had failed to be diagnosed. These possibilities are not mutually exclusive.

Actual abuse can usually be recalled to some degree during the post-trance period. Simply asking whether the child has ever been abused in such a manner as to imply, if possible, that one does not necessarily intend to question any further, will frequently elicit a confirming response. For example, one might say: "I have the feeling that somewhere in the past something really bad may have happened to you that you don't have to talk about unless you want to." This can be followed by a low-key reassurance of help, such as saying, as if to one-self, "Perhaps we shall have to do some work on those bad memories sometime." At the next session, a reconstruction of more positive memories or a dissociation of negative feelings from the memories may be attempted (Bandler & Grinder, 1979).

At times it will be found during the history taking that there is a complete absence of the "Garden of Eden" fantasy. This child simply cannot recall any happy period in his past. These children are usually in quite severe depressions and often have a family history of depres-sive or even manic-depressive disorders. It is very difficult for such children to benefit from a psychotherapeutic approach without also making use of medication. Low doses of an antidepressant such as clomipramine can often make the child feel better enough to be open to hypnotherapeutic experience of the types already described. The medication may act pharmacologically or may enhance suggestions of recovery. However, whichever way it acts it is possible to expect fairly rapid improvement, and it is found that the medication can be termi-nated after a few weeks in most cases without relapse. The "Garden of Eden" fantasy can then usually be evoked in a manner similar to that noted in the mildly depressed child. It would appear that this widely prevalent fantasy can survive in a mild depression but not in a severe one.

Case Example 4   Stephen, almost 11 years old, complained of loneliness, being bored at school, troubles with teachers, being bothered by other students, and suffering from headaches, which were especially bad at recess. His mother was described by her doctor as a well-controlled depressive. He had been able to talk openly about his feelings to one of his sisters, but he felt that his family needed him to "tough it out." Stephen could not recall any happy time in his past, and resisted any suggestions to age-regress. It was deemed necessary to put him on an antidepressant medication, especially in view of his mother's severe chronic mood disorder, which may have played a role in his own. Stephen soon responded to the medication and became flexible enough to participate in play therapy. He went into spontaneous trance during play and began to create a myth, which took several sessions to com-plete. Generations of difficulties appeared in the myth, which featured two women who mated with dinosaurs and then, with difficulty, had two children. The dinosaurs died, and their offspring produced a half-human child who eventually, after much searching, discovered remains of dinosaurs in his travels. Soon after creating this myth, Stephen became very affectionate toward the author and cautiously brought his stuffed bear, which had been his treasure from babyhood, to his next two sessions. It was as though he was bringing his own infancy into the therapy. In doing so he seemed to gain in maturity at home. He decided he would ask his parents for a dog and pretend it was to help him feel better. In truth, he said, it was to keep his mother company when he was at school so that he would not have to worry about her being alone. At this stage, the antidepressant was gradually withdrawn. Stephen has been in good shape and symptom-free for the past few months.

Over a period of several years of observation, many of the children with a marked family history of depressive disorders have shown relapses at about yearly intervals. These relapses have responded to further treatment, but the prognosis into later life has not been determined.

DIFFERENTIAL DIAGNOSIS OF CHILDHOOD DEPRESSION

Psychotic features need to be carefully evaluated. Thought disorder is not a characteristic of depression, and if it is observed, together with a disturbance of affect, it is more likely that the problem is early schizophrenia. Hallucinations, on the other hand, are quite frequent in childhood depressions. Children readily project their feelings into auditory and/or visual hallucinations. Hearing their thoughts occasionally, as a voice in their heads, is not unusual for many children. These thoughts may be heard as the voice of a critic making disparaging remarks about the child. The auditory hallucinations are not primarily persecutory but may be perceived by a depressed child as such. They are sometimes experienced in the same way as the usual putdown comments made by children at school. Visual hallucinations seem to be rarer, and would merit further diagnostic investigation in order to exclude organicity.

A chronic low-grade depression that resists other than very temporary improvement may indicate severe parental pathology or neglect. For example, one 12-year-old boy had to babysit three younger siblings almost every evening, and when his parents returned, he was sent off to bed with the other children regardless of the time, on the grounds that he needed his sleep. His own needs were ignored. In another case, a girl's mother had been hospitalized several times for severe depressions, precluding her from functioning as an effective parent. The child's neglect as a consequence led to childhood depression. Mother's treatment permitted her to become a model parent provided she took regular doses of antidepressant medication. As mother's depression improved, so did her daughter's. In a third case, a boy's father, who had been regularly abused as a child, beat his son cruelly whenever the boy failed to live up to the father's expectations while playing hockey. These are examples of parents who had to become the focus of therapy themselves, since, without positive parenting skills and a good home environment, a child cannot meaningfully change. In desperate cases, the child may have to be removed from the home for his own protection. Fortunately, such extreme situations are much less common than the mild depressions that, as the result of some family or environmental deficit, present as learning problems and behavior disorders.

CONCLUSIONS

In the majority of cases, hypnotically based strategies for change and for the facilitation of problem-solving abilities can be a key to more rapid and reliable therapeutic success. Since the most frequent differential diagnoses are early psychosis and neurological organic disorders, and since it is usually not difficult to distinguish these conditions, it is safe to proceed with treatment along the lines described here. If the diagnosis proves to be a condition other than depression, this will become clear quite rapidly with no harm done. What presents as irritability, attention disorder, and behavior disorder in childhood is likely to be childhood depression. In these cases, the possibility for rapid and effective improvement now exists through the application of hypnotic and strategic interventions.

REFERENCES

Bandler, R., & Grinder, J. (1979). *Frogs Into Princes.* Moab, Utah: Real People Press.
Erickson, M. H., Rossi, E. L. (1981). *Experiencing Hypnosis: Therapeutic Approaches to Altered States.* New York: Irvington.
Erickson, M. H., Rossi, E. L., & Rossi, S. I. (1976). *Hypnotic Realities.* New York: Irvington.
Gregory, I., & Smeltzer, D. J. (1977). *Psychiatry.* Boston: Little Brown.
Jung, C. G. (1916). *The relations between the ego and the unconscious.* In *Collected Works,* Vol. 7 (1953). London: Routledge.
Kanner, L. (1957). *Child Psychiatry* (3rd ed.) Springfield, Ill.: Thomas.

Kroger, W. S., & Fezler, W. D. (1976). *Hypnosis and Behavior Modification: Imagery Conditioning*. Philadelphia: Lippincott.

Lankton, C., & Lankton, S. (1983). *The Answer Within: A Clinical Framework of Ericksonian Hypnotherapy*. New York: Brunner/Mazel.

Winnicott, D. W. (1944). Transactions of the Ophthalmological Society, Vol. LXIV. In *Collected Papers* (1958). London: Tavistock.

Zeig, J. K. (1985). The clinical use of amnesia. In J. K. Zeig (Ed.), *Ericksonian Psychotherapy* (Vol. I): *Structures*. New York: Brunner/Mazel.

Chapter 9

Integrating Ericksonian Strategies Into Structured Groups for Depression

Brent B. Geary

Brent B. Geary, Ph.D. (Cand.) (Arizona State University), is a member of the inaugural clinical staff of the Milton H. Erickson Center for Hypnosis and Psychotherapy in Phoenix, Ariz. He concurrently maintains a private practice in the Phoenix area. Geary possesses an extensive background in Ericksonian approaches to hypnosis and psychotherapy tracing to his childhood. His father, Louis L. Geary, M.D., a semiretired psychiatrist residing in California, was a student of Dr. Erickson in the 1950s and 1960s, and instilled in him a deep and abiding regard for Ericksonian methods and values.

An ever-burgeoning wealth of literature exists regarding the psychotherapeutic treatment of depression, a multifaceted phenomenon that stands as one of the most common psychobiological maladies. Every major theory of psychopathology addresses the etiology of depression, and all models of psychotherapy propose modi for alleviating the affective, motoric, cognitive, physiological, or behavioral sequelae of the condition. This chapter examines one treatment modality, group psychotherapy, and advocates the joining of two therapeutic models—Ericksonian/strategic and cognitive therapies. Together, they may improve the ability to abate the suffering of depressed individuals.

The author is grateful for the technical and editorial assistance of Tim Kigin, Linda Carr McThrall, and Michael Liebman, and for the continuing encouragement and support of Jeff Zeig.

184

COGNITIVE GROUP THERAPY OF DEPRESSION

Group psychotherapy is a major treatment method that may be applied in a broad array of settings and to diverse populations (Yalom, 1985). Only recently, however, have outcome studies begun to demonstrate the benefits of group treatment of depression (Hogg, 1986). Much of the impetus for this analysis has been provided by researchers from the behaviorist school, stemming from their belief that depression arises from the lack of interpersonal skills necessary to elicit social reinforcers from the environment (Youngren & Lewinsohn, 1980). Consequently, groups are viewed as efficient vehicles for the learning and practice of social skills. Group psychotherapy from this and other theoretical perspectives that employ a multiplicity of intervention strategies has been shown to be effective in alleviating the symptoms of depression.

Cognitive therapy, developed by Aaron Beck and his colleagues, has emerged in the past twenty years as a proven approach in the treatment of depression (Beck, Rush, Shaw, & Emery, 1979). A sizable body of evidence points to its soundness in individual psychotherapy for depression. However, the principles and practices of cognitive therapy may be effectively applied in group settings as well (Roth & Covi, 1984). Cognitive group therapy of depression has been shown to be equal or superior to behavioral groups (Shaw, 1977), self-control and unstructured group therapies (Fleming & Thornton, 1980), and psychodynamically oriented groups (Stever et al., 1984) in reducing depressive symptomatology.

Cognitive groups for depression are typically highly structured in format and are designed to include a mildly to moderately depressed, homogenous membership (Hollon & Shaw, 1979). In contrast to the emphasis upon "here-and-now," member-to-member interactions seen in interpersonal process groups (Yalom, 1985), cognitive groups tend to stress "extrapersonal" factors in members' lives outside the group (Waldo, 1985). Here, intragroup transactions are used to highlight distorted cognitive patterns that are seen as contributing to members' depression. Thus, the method is essentially a successive treatment of individuals in the group context (Roth & Covi, 1984). Like individual cognitive therapy, cognitive groups are often delivered within a time-limited structure, though therapeutic delivery may also be in open-ended groups. Cognitive group therapists are active and directive, using didactics extensively to supplement the ongoing supportive atmosphere of the group (Hollon & Shaw, 1979).

The aim of cognitive groups is essentially the same as in individual cognitive therapy, that is, "to help depressed individuals to identify, evaluate, and modify their dysfunctional personal paradigm" (Covi, Roth, & Lipman, 1982, pp. 459– 460). Beck (1976) hypothesized that it is one's "construct" that forms the foundation of psychogenic depression. This contrast is a unique assumptive framework that contains an individual's negative beliefs regarding himself or herself, the world, and the future. The personal paradigm is accessible to scrutiny in therapy by examining a client's information-processing dynamics, composed of "cognitions" (ideas and images available to consciousness in a given situation) and "schemas" (assumptions or beliefs formed by early experience that guide cognitions) (Rush, 1983). Identifiable patterns of cognitive distortions maintain the pessimistic and stringent mind set that characterizes the depressive condition (Hollon & Beck, 1979). The cognitive therapy intervention model is basically comprised of cognitive restructuring and behavioral techniques (Beck, Rush, Shaw, & Emery, 1979). Depressed clients are led through a process of identifying, self-monitoring, and challenging cognitions ("automatic thoughts"), uncovering and disputing underlying schemas, and disconfirming the depressogenic cognitive structure through behavioral "experiments" in the individual's environment. Adaptive change results from the incorporation of a more balanced and realistic personal paradigm.

ERICKSONIAN AND STRATEGIC APPROACHES IN THE TREATMENT OF DEPRESSION

Although Ericksonian and strategic psychotherapies may be considered independent models of treatment, they are linked by common historical and philosophical bases (Stanton, 1981). In practice, intervention tactics from both approaches are frequently employed conjunctively. Zeig and Geary (1988) identified seven avenues of Erickson's influence on strategic therapy that represent therapeutic patterns of both. These commonalities are (1) an emphasis on brief treatment and the advocacy of a concentrated, short-term orientation to therapy; (2) the active role of the therapist, utilizing a flexible stance in which the therapist extensively uses his or her role to direct therapeutic process; (3) a focus on the presenting symptoms, seeing problems as leverage points for systemic change; (4) an emphasis on the positive characteristics of the client while deemphasizing pathology, encouraging the elicitation of strengths and resources rather than limiting the client through pejorative labeling; (5) an emphasis on utilization, therapeutically using whatever the client brings to the treatment milieu; (6) tailoring treatment and individualizing therapy through the recognition that each person is unique; and (7) the use of indirection, promoting change through multilevel communication. Inherent in the Ericksonian/strategic perspective is the postulate that each client must be considered individually and treated with interventions based on that person's phenomenological experience. Hence, no protocols for particular diagnostic categories exist.

Yapko (1985) presented ways in which Ericksonian and strategic patterns of intervention may be applied to cases of depression. A number of hypnotic approaches were described as suited for either symptomatic or dynamic treatment of depression, including pattern interruption, reframing, symptom substitution, age regression and progression, and therapeutic metaphors. Additionally, he stated that the trance phenomena of amnesia, catalepsy, dissociation, hallucinations, ideodynamic responses, sensory alteration, and time distortion can be brought to bear in an ongoing hypnotherapeutic process. Strategic approaches "are perhaps best used to rapidly and effectively resolve the impasses that so often arise in the push for therapeutic progress" (Yapko, 1985, p. 97). These may address common depression dynamics involving personal responsibility, patterns of blame, and locus of control. Practitioners may actively engage depressed clients through the use of other interventions well-documented in the strategic literature, including symptom prescription, ordeal therapies, behavioral prescriptions, double binds, and the utilization of resistance.

INTEGRATING ERICKSONIAN/STRATEGIC AND COGNITIVE METHODOLOGIES

The combined usage of Ericksonian/strategic and cognitive methodologies allows the psychotherapist to treat depression in a comprehensive manner. Ample features of commonality exist among these therapeutic systems to provide a sound rationale for applying their procedures together. The most salient themes of intermutuality include the following.

1. Active Therapist.   Practitioners in both the Ericksonian/strategic and cognitive molds assume extensive responsibility for planning and influencing change (Haley, 1973; Hollon & Shaw, 1979). Indeed, terms frequently used to describe the two approaches are remarkably similar. In cognitive therapy, therapists and clients together form a relationship based on "collaborative empiricism" (Beck, Rush, Shaw, & Emery, 1979) and Gilligan (1987) depicted the Ericksonian model as "cooperative." Both of these therapeutic schools emphasize the importance of establishing a sound therapeutic alliance with clients and discourage the deployment of their techniques until a safe and accepting environment has been engendered (Gilligan, 1987; Beck & Emery, 1985). Clinical judgment regarding the timing and level of intervention is a central attribute for Ericksonian/strategic and cognitive therapists. Rapport and clinical judgment, then, form the foundation from which therapists provide structure, guide experience, and facilitate the course of therapy.

2. Active Client.   Engagement of clients in the therapeutic process is a hallmark of these treatment models. Extrasession assignments are liberally prescribed in order to speed clients' discovery and progress. Client participation in formulating a treatment plan is explicitly stimulated in cognitive therapy, as are the scheduling of activities and the devising of *in vivo* "experiments" (or "extended self-therapy," in cognitive parlance) to disconfirm depressogenic personal hypotheses regarding the self, experience in the world, and the future (Beck, Rush, Shaw, & Emery, 1979). Erickson gained a measure of renown for the ingenious use of his patients' social environments and the often enigmatic assignments he enjoined (Zeig & Geary, 1988). Haley (1983) and others have systematized therapeutic tasks that can be incorporated into the client's environment to promote change outside of therapy. Far from the analyst's couch, the client of Ericksonian/strategic and cognitive therapies finds that the process of change is vigorous and cross-contextual.

3. Brief Treatment.   Cognitive therapists advocate the negotiation of time-limited agreements, generally 12 to 20 sessions for groups (Hollon & Shaw, 1979) and 15 to 25 visits in individual therapy (Beck, Rush, Shaw, & Emery, 1979). Erickson was one of the first to conceptualize psychotherapy as potentially brief, bucking the dominant psychoanalytic model of his day (Zeig & Geary, 1988). Haley's delineation of strategic therapy is steeped in this tradition (Stanton, 1981). Tactics such as goal setting, focusing upon symptoms, extrasession homework assignments, sequencing, and problem-solving expedite the relatively rapid resolution of depressed client's complaints and are common to both systems.

4. Reorganization of Rigid Patterns.   In emphasizing the primacy of acquired restrictions in the development of psychosocial disorders, Erickson observed:

> Patients . . . are caught in mental sets, frames of reference, and belief systems that do not permit them to explore and utilize their own abilities to best advantage. The therapeutic transaction ideally creates a new phenomenal world in which patients can explore their potentials, freed to some extent from their learned limitations. (Erickson & Rossi, 1979, p. 2)

This view is entirely consistent with the cognitive therapy premise that emotion and behavior are extensively determined by the manner in which an individual cognitively organizes the world and that negative underlying assumptions promote dysfunction (Beck, Rush, Shaw, & Emery, 1979). Ericksonian/strategic and cognitive therapies aspire to allow clients to reorganize their associational structures and operate in the world in more realistic, self-valuing ways. Trance in the Ericksonian tradition and the cognitive restructuring of cognitive therapy influence a disruption of previously formed associations and encourage new ways of perceiving, thinking, feeling, and behaving (Erickson & Rossi, 1979; Hogg, 1986).

5. Focus on Present Experience.   The "utilization approach" of Ericksonian/strategic therapy and the "collaborative empiricism" of cognitive therapy view the contemporary functioning of clients as the crux of the therapeutic process. Both systems eschew interpretation of unconscious dynamics and, rather, accept symptoms as indicators of personal organization and adjustment (Beck, Rush, Shaw, & Emery, 1979; Haley, 1967). Symptom correction is taken as the goal of therapy with little value placed on the development of insight or the discussion of past (i.e., childhood) experience, except to elucidate currently existing patterns. In fact, cognitive therapists see "intellectual insight" as a pitfall if understanding is not additionally incorporated at an emotional level (Rush, 1983) and Ericksonian/strategic therapy often purposefully avoids translation of unconscious communication into conscious awareness through the use of indirection (Zeig & Geary, 1988; Stanton, 1981). In both schools, therapy is conceived as a learning process in which clients realize that their existing resources are responsive to actively effecting desired outcomes.

6. Individualization of Treatment.   Ericksonian/strategic and cognitive therapies are models that explain how undesirable patterns may arise, but both are best portrayed as theories of change rather than theories of personality (Hogg, 1986, Zeig & Geary, 1988). Nosological systems are not employed by either model, and clear demarcations are drawn between patients and problems in order to keep intact the orientation that solutions to problems lie within the individual's capabilities. Although a categorization of cognitive distortions is used in cognitive therapy and classes of interventions are specified by each approach, the material of therapy is inherently individual-specific (Beck, Rush, Shaw, & Emery, 1979; Haley, 1967). Interventions are tailored to specific client situations and are structured to allow personally meaningful experiences. There is an expressed accentuation of positive expectancy in both schools: The process of restructuring depressogenic schema with subsequent improved mood in cognitive therapy and the position that symptoms are adaptive and malleable in the Ericksonian/strategic model.

7. Intervention Strategies.   There are a number of therapeutic tactics in the respective schools that bear resemblance to each other. Commonalities can be seen in the cognitive therapy method of generating alternative interpretations and in Ericksonian/strategic reframing. The conduct of disconfirming experiences in the cognitive approach is similar to the prescription of tasks or ordeals in Ericksonian/strategic processes. Also, many of the relaxation and imagery techniques of cognitive therapy are analogous to Ericksonian/strategic uses of metaphors, age progression, and pseudo-orientation in time (Beck & Emery, 1985; Yapko, 1985). Though the methodologies differ in explaining dynamics of how change occurs, the compatibility of the approaches is highlighted by stylistic similarities.

BENEFITS OF INTEGRATING ERICKSONIAN/STRATEGIC METHODS INTO COGNITIVE GROUPS FOR DEPRESSION

The foregoing account serves to illustrate that the blending of Ericksonian/strategic and cognitive methodologies can be harmonious and may be effected without requiring radical shifts in therapist views regarding the length of groups, treatment philosophy, client roles, and other such germane considerations. In fact, it is this author's experience that the use of a synthesis of tactics from both therapeutic schools cultivates a more powerful synergistic therapeutic effect. The use of a multi-operational approach to depression is generally warranted.

The most cogent benefits are in the form of client gain and satisfaction. Cognitive group therapy typically does not afford much consideration to group dynamics issues such as therapist-client relations, cohesion, or affective sharing (Hollon & Shaw, 1979). There are those in the cognitive movement, though, who argue for greater sensitivity to these interests (Roth & Covi, 1984). Ericksonian/strategic methods, such as trance induction and reframing, help to form a link between the external activity focus of the cognitive group and intragroup processes. Therapists who utilize Ericksonian/strategic techniques not only add maneuverability to their clinical repertoires, but are also commonly seen in a different light by group members. Therapist-client rapport can thereby grow. Increased intimacy is occasioned by the induction of trance (Gilligan, 1987), and the gentle, permissive demeanor of the Ericksonian hypnotherapist is a nice complement to the often didactic role of the cognitive therapist. Trance, metaphor, reframing, and the like instill an agreeable affective experience for group members that can supplement the thoughtful learning and behavioral ventures of the cognitive methodology.

Hypnotic strategies, like cognitive approaches, help to focus the diffuse attentional processes characteristic of depression. Dysphoric individuals tend to orient to past mistakes and failures, search their environments for remedies, generalize magnified implications from discrete events, and distort conceptions of personal responsibility and control (Beck, 1976; Yapko, 1985). Hypnosis can be utilized to seed shifts in depressed clients' orientations, that is, to suggest alternative perceptions which can be therapeutically developed later. Hypnotic seeding can implant beneficial ideas for clients regarding future possibilities, personal prowess, and realistic compartmentalization of experience. Reframing promotes personal forgiveness in the midst of a tyrannical cognitive set, and metaphors urge motivation to engage in personal solutions. Tasks and ordeals add symbolic discovery to the more detailed experimentation of cognitive homework assignments and can be acted out within the group setting. Finally, Ericksonian/strategic approaches allow clients to experience a benign and resourceful unconscious and to realize that a vast potential lies within.

RECOMMENDATIONS FOR IMPLEMENTATION

The suggested framework presented here adheres to the basic model of cognitive group psychotherapy for depression with the interspersal of Ericksonian/strategic methods into the ongoing group process. This conceptualization rests upon the incorporation of the cognitive format detailed elsewhere (Roth & Covi, 1984; Covi, Roth, & Lipman, 1982; Hollon & Shaw, 1979) and the author's experience in conducting such groups.

Several prerequisites for therapists bear mention. First, there must be a genuine belief in group psychotherapy as a viable mechanism for facilitating change. Experience in leading groups is vital, as the skills required to be effective with groups differ from those necessary for conducting individual and family therapy. A thorough grounding in cognitive therapy and the accompanying cognitive model of psychopathology is a second essential ingredient. Further, efficient application of Ericksonian patterns of communication presupposes rigorous training and extensive practice in the methodology. Finally, one should possess a comprehensive understanding of strategic psychotherapy and an awareness of when to intervene in this mode (and, conversely, when not to intervene). Although the techniques of these therapeutic approaches (as with all others) may be applied in a "gimmicky" fashion isolated from a theoretical perspective, the results in such instances are likely to be antitherapeutic.

Forming the group involves advance planning regarding a number of pertinent issues. Group size depends, to a large extent, on whether one or two therapists will be involved. Groups can be, and frequently are, conducted efficiently by one therapist when membership is limited to four to six (Hollon & Shaw, 1979); two therapists can accommodate five to ten members with seven or eight being the optimal size (Yalom, 1985). The model presented here presumes a closed group (fixed membership with no admission of new clients) with a planned duration of 12 weekly sessions lasting one and one-half to two hours each, and a homogeneous membership of mildly to moderately depressed individuals. Other formats, of course, are possible (Hogg, 1986; Yalom, 1985; Covi & Roth, 1984) but should be detailed before the inception of therapy. Psychometric evaluation and structured interviews may be employed to quantify progress and assist in defining inclusion/exclusion criteria. This author routinely uses the Beck Depression Inventory (Beck, Rush, Shaw, & Emery, 1979) in screening.

Other instruments are available and are widely applied, such as the Hamilton Rating Scale for Depression (Hamilton, 1967) and Rosenbaum's Self-Control Schedule (Simons, Lustman, Wetzel, & Murphy, 1985; Rosenbaum, 1980). Suicidal clients, the severely withdrawn, and patients manifesting psychotic and/or personality disorder features are not good candidates for group treatment using this format; Yalom (1985) presented a more thorough discussion of exclusion criteria for groups in general. Motivation, willingness to commit to a group and its requirements, and a realistic expectation for change are considered primary inclusion factors. Finally, this author's experience echoes the reports of other clinicians and researchers who have stated that group psychotherapy for depression may be well utilized as a punctuation or termination for individual therapy, as well as for clients entering treatment for the first time. One should decide the composition of groups in advance in terms of new, veteran, or mixed clients, and be aware of considerations involved in each particular choice (Roth & Covi, 1984, Hollon & Shaw, 1979).

An intake interview serves as an indispensable introduction to the group for clients. In this session, members are able to meet the therapist(s), ask questions, and have therapeutic orientations and group requirements explained to them. In his groups, the author requires that members purchase, read, and complete exercises in *Feeling Good* (Burns, 1980), attend every session with emergencies the only exceptions, agree to retain members' confidentiality, and "be open to new experiences and to taking reasonable risks." Therapists are afforded the opportunity to clarify client data, to describe the format and time frame, and to provide information regarding hypnosis and common misconceptions. The process of therapy actually begins during this session. At this point, the therapist can establish a positive expectation for change in clients and elicit a commitment for active participation in the group process. This *expectant mind set* fosters a greater potential for beneficial outcome.

To recapitulate, group psychotherapy is ready to begin when skilled and informed therapists have solidified central issues such as group size, duration, and client inclusion/exclusion criteria. Clients provide informed consent to group participation, have questions and concerns addressed, and are instilled with an attitude receptive to change. The remainder of this chapter illustrates the ways in which Ericksonian/ strategic intervention patterns can augment cognitive therapy groups for depression.

UTILIZATION OF SPECIFIC ERICKSONIAN/ STRATEGIC INTERVENTIONS

Cognitive therapy groups for depression afford ample opportunity for the infusion of Ericksonian/strategic tactics. Following is a description of some of the structures and aims of Ericksonian/strategic interventions derived from the author's experience.

Group Hypnotic Inductions

This therapeutic pattern is an especially valuable component to introduce in the first group session. A group induction at the beginning of the initial session can serve as a particularly beneficial reinforcement of the positive mind set seeded in the intake interview. Members have the opportunity to relax, to some degree, despite the anxiety they may feel as they speak in front of strangers or as they wonder whether they really will get better. Consistent with the naturalistic Ericksonian approach, such worries can be addressed in the trance experience. For example:

> And you can wonder just how much benefit you will find in the group . . . so much is new . . . new faces . . . a new experience . . . and new ways of incorporating the learnings of the past . . . and of the next few weeks. And it's nice to just relax and let some of that worry comfortably slip away as you find those new ways to trust and value yourself.

Or, to focus attention in a new and intimidating situation:

> Because you really don't know what the person on your left wants to achieve . . . and you really can't anticipate how the person on your right will change . . . but you can be left with a realization that within you exist the resources for achievements and changes that are right for you. And you can begin to really focus in on those changes that you want to make . . .

Group inductions can suggest the pride that depressed clients can rightfully feel for getting to and getting through the first session. A group induction at the close of the inaugural meeting helps to instill this pride and tie it to the anticipation of further rewards. For instance:

> You know how hard it was to get yourself here . . . through the worries, the doubts, the pain . . . and you can allow yourself to feel good . . . really feel good about yourself for accomplishing something so important to you . . . and you might wonder . . . and perhaps anticipate . . . all the other ways in which you'll feel better here in the group and elsewhere.

As groups progress, they evolve identities of their own. Each member has positive characteristics that emerge and can be highlighted by observant group therapists. Group inductions offer occasions to enhance group cohesion and highlight members' attributes, as this excerpt illustrates:

> And you can really feel the power of the group . . . the feelings of support . . . the feelings of mutuality . . . the closeness you feel . . . as you can appreciate the sensitivity of Kathy . . . the perceptiveness of Steve . . . Terry's quiet strength . . . [citing attributes of specific members] . . . and your unconscious mind can use the power of the group . . . use that support to activate those very qualities within you . . . and the growing recognition that the expression of those qualities is helping you to grow and make those changes in your life you so desire . . .

Group inductions, then, help to build group cohesion, establish a future orientation with expectations for gain, and allow recognition of members' strengths and contributions. Additionally, they introduce relaxation as a counterbalance to the anxiety that typically accompanies depression and the introduction to group therapy. Group inductions may also employ hypnotic strategies such as interspersal techniques (Erickson, 1966), pseudo-orientation in time (Erickson, 1954), age regression and progression (Yapko, 1985), and confusion (Gilligan, 1987). If two therapists work with the group, the voice of one can represent unconscious qualities (holism, acceptance, creativity, etc.) while the other can point out conscious mind functions (analysis, skepticism, linear processing, etc.). One therapist may voice "worries of the past" whereas the other speaks of "new ways of thinking" about the future; one can relate metaphors and the other can suggest deepening in a more formalized manner. Other innovative interplays are left to the inventiveness of the reader.

Individual Hypnotic Inductions

Hypnosis with individual group members should be used carefully and selectively in group psychotherapy. Pitfalls can arise from other members' perception that the hypnotized individual is monopolizing therapist resources and group time, and there might then be demands for similar experiences from other group members. But the judicious use of hypnosis with individuals in a group context can offer a host of advantages as well.

This author has been continually impressed by the benefits group clients so often harvest from what Yalom (1985) termed "spectator therapy." Almost invariably, hypnotic work accomplished with one member transfers to other members in some manner, whether in the form of insight, vicarious learning, understanding of others, acceptance, or in some other positive way. Group settings are rife with possibilities for the utilization of "My-Friend-John" techniques (Erickson, 1964), indirectly addressing the dynamics of one member while talking to another. An example can be provided from a group facilitated by the author in which one member spoke of an inability to "turn off" negative internal dialogue. Hypnosis was used, and simultaneously another member's issues were addressed in the hypnotic work. The second member had remained silent during the sessions despite the urgings of therapists and other group members to contribute. An excerpt from the session illustrates the technique:

> And, Sharon, trance can allow your body to *remain quiet . . . until you're good and ready* . . . to open yourself to new possibilities . . . and I don't know what part of your body is most ready *to speak* . . . to the problem that you've brought here today . . . but you know your hands *can converse* in certain ways . . . can *give voice to your thoughts* . . . but your hands are at rest now . . . and your thoughts can be, too . . . so that *you can carefully choose the right words* . . . words that you want to hear . . . and you can realize that *others want to hear you* as your thoughts provide you with new meanings . . . more positive meanings for your consideration.

The italicized segments represent the messages stated to the silent member, marked out in a subtle manner by head direction, gestures, and voice intonation and tempo. Aside from such strategies, many group members report that watching someone else experience hypnosis provides them with a safe introduction to the phenomenon. This allows them to be more willing to utilize trance for themselves.

Individual inductions are most appropriate when particular concerns of one member can be targeted while more general themes in the group are also engaged. Examples include trauma accured from neglectful or abusive parents, failure experiences, self-esteem issues, lack of confidence, shyness, body image, and procrastination. Other examples abound, but the important point is that therapists can remain vigilant for such common trends in the content and process of the group and may effectively employ hypnosis on multiple levels.

Reframing

Reframing is a highly effective method for transforming clients' perceptions of depression. It is generally useful to disrupt the tendency of depressed individuals to view themselves as pathological. Reframing expedites the presentation of alternative, more benign conceptions. The group format enables the strategy to be employed in a manner that deepens personal acceptance and self-understanding.

This author engages groups in a procedure he terms "reframing rehearsal." First, an explanation of the concept is offered that positive intentions may underlie even undesirable behaviors and states. Clients are afforded a broader understanding of their depression in this way, and can view their behavior as misdirected rather than "sick." Second, a prominent complaint of a particular group member is chosen to illustrate the concept. Behaviors repeatedly acted out in the group are especially useful. Third, the therapist(s) reframes the patterns by hypothesizing a positive intent. Then other members are asked to offer additional reframes in a nonevaluative atmosphere. Depressed individuals are often quite adept at inferring positive motives in others even though they seem unable to do so in themselves.

For example, one member of a group the author led complained of her lack of self-assuredness and of her tendency to frequently ask others for advice. This theme was evident in her in-group behavior. The therapist framed her motive as "the desire to consider all options thoroughly before taking action." Members then suggested these other reframes: "genuine interest in the opinions of others and the willingness to allow people to express their beliefs"; "wanting to affiliate and

be close to people"; "in the process of learning to trust herself and externally validating her beliefs"; "permitting others to feel good by
helping her"; and so forth. The member whose complaint was utilized
as the illustration was then asked to consider these propositions and,
with the help of the group, "brainstorm" more constructive behaviors
that would satisfy the original intentions. Other members of the group
then chose problems, and the process was repeated.

This method allows a three-phase process whereby members learn
reframing: (1) modeling an explanation for cognitive understanding;
(2) practice through reframing others' behaviors; and (3) incorporation
of the strategy into personal experience by reframing one's own problem states. This final step can be accomplished in a "go-around" format in which members offer at least three reframes for problematic
behaviors they evidence. The best examples are discrete behaviors
displayed within the group or from the recent past outside the group.
Integration of the strategy is heightened further when members are
given the directive to reframe everyday behaviors as a homework
assignment.

Therapists have an important dual responsibility with regard to the
deployment of reframing in groups. On the one hand, it is vital that
therapists genuinely offer reframes that could be plausible motives for
the individual's experience. That is, reframes must be offered ethically
and sincerely. On the other hand, therapists should be as certain as
possible that members do the same. Reframing can effect a potent shift
in a person's perceptual set, but the actualization of this turnabout
usually takes time. Thus, the reframing process will likely warrant
repetition. The depressive position is not easily modified and therapist
perseverence is required. As a final note on the topic, reframing must
be presented in a manner that avoids the provision of excuses for destructive or abusive behavior. Therapeutic acumen enables reframing
to differentiate positive motives from unwanted behaviors. It is not
meant to provide unwarranted justification for untoward acts.

Seeding

At a meta-level, lessons gained within the group are "seeds" that,
it is hoped, will come to fruition as beneficial changes in members'
everyday lives. True gains result when new or refined behaviors tested

in the safe atmosphere of the group are implemented in daily existence.

The entire group process is a matter of incrementally planting and cultivating seeds for change. It is important, for instance, to build upon the positive expectations established at intake. To some extent, processes inherent in group therapy for depression will support this. Members experience increased activity levels, constructive feedback, and affinity that contribute to a hopeful perspective. Additionally, the effect of proven techniques of treatment sustains positive anticipation as members begin to experience their subjective worlds differently. Active therapist participation in the seeding-actualization process is required to augment members' growth.

Tactics seed insight, and thus the role of therapists is to amplify and support learning. It is prudent for therapists to comment pointedly on client progress. Asking for emotional reactions assists in demonstrating the beneficial effects of the work of the group, as in:

> Jerry, you just talked about your ability to consider multiple options for yourself in this situation. When we started group, you portrayed yourself as someone who uses all-or-nothing, black-or-white thinking. What have we explored here that has been useful for you in making this change? Can you tell us how you feel about improving your outlook?

Commonly, one member's expression of pride serves as a seed for similar future expressions by others.

Metaphors

Zeig (1980) presented a thorough account of the potential applications of anecdotes in psychotherapy. Yapko (1985) further specified the utility of this approach in the treatment of depression. These authors illuminated the multiple purposes that can be served through the use of metaphors in both hypnotic and nonhypnotic processes.

Metaphors in a group context are best presented in a manner that encourages a range of possible responses in members. In this way, no member is without a meaningful reference point in the story. For instance, since group members will progress in therapy at different rates, any metaphor constructed to address growth or change should reflect this, as in:

> And trees grow in a variety of ways: Some add height very quickly but don't blossom or bear fruit for awhile; others flower and provide harvests all along as they grow more slowly . . . And, you know, it took Thomas Edison a long time and he performed many experiments before he got it right in creating the light bulb. Other inventions and discoveries in history, though, came quickly in flashes of insight to scientists. The important thing is that these people were open to possibilities.

Many useful metaphors are available to indirectly bolster the process of working out of depression. They may also be arranged to underscore group cohesion, boost the sense of universality in group members, and comment upon a host of other developmental dynamics of the group.

Tasks and Ordeals

The methodology of constructing and consigning appropriate tasks for clients is discussed in detail elsewhere (Madanes, 1984; Haley, 1984). The pertinent point here is that the assignment of ordeals combines agreeably with the cognitive therapy procedure of devising homework experiments that can disconfirm depressive assumptions. Strategic tasks are particularly suited to paradoxically utilize resistance and to add a symbolic and/or playful element to clients' discoveries in the world apart from the group. Ordeals may also be set up for execution within groups, as in the example of one client who was cautious and participated little in group for fear of "saying something wrong." It was suggested that he ask each group member for permission to speak, and then present a specific outline of what he proposed to say before making any statement. This task was offered facetiously and was supported by the good-natured insistence of the group that it be carried out. It required only two trials of such blatantly careful consideration before the member internalized the point and started on the road to greater spontaneity. The author advises readers to become thoroughly acquainted with cautions and contraindications before using these techniques.

Providing a Worse Alternative

This strategy is particularly advantageous in mature, working groups in which there is high cohesion and trust. It is a useful tactic for sustaining motivation and utilizing resistence. Providing a worse alternative also symbolically illustrates autonomy and the need to make choices for oneself, both of which are central issues in depression. For example, one group member complained of waking in the wee hours nightly and ruminating on negative thoughts. Another group member suggested that at such times it would be useful to apply a particular exercise from *Feeling Good*. The insomniac countered that she experienced great difficulty in completing that exercise. She was reassured that it would get easier with practice and was urged to try this suggestion. She asked, "Do I have to? It's so hard and I'm just no good at it." The therapist benignly offered, "Of course, you don't have to do it. It's your choice. You might prefer to call all the other group members who have an easier time with the exercise at 2:00 A.M. and ask them to complete it for you." The client returned the next week with copious logs and graphs and reported that all were filled out between the hours of 1:30 and 5:00 A.M. In another group, a member was told that he did not have to appear for the final interview for a job for which he appeared to be the leading candidate. Instead, a full 45 minutes of the next session would be reserved for him "to regale all of these people who care about you and are pulling for you with all the reasons why you didn't go and why you didn't deserve the job in the first place." The newly employed man returned the next week to discuss strategies for maintaining his new position.

Other patterns of Ericksonian and strategic interventions are available and, when employed sensibly, can succeed in supplementing the ongoing mechanisms of cognitive therapy procedures. The versatility of the Ericksonian/strategic approach is accentuated by the fact that it may be used either as a sole psychotherapeutic modality or as a synthesis with other models in individual, family, and group treatment.

TERMINATION OF THE GROUP

The aim of group therapy of depression is to effect changes in members' internal and external experience so that more satisfying patterns of thinking, feeling, and behaving are encountered in everyday life. Emphasis on this generalization becomes more pronounced in the last three or four sessions through the guidance of the therapist(s). Members begin to anticipate life without the support of the group, and will often lament the difficulty of transferring the gains of group therapy to outside routines. An attitude of confident reassurance on the part of the therapist(s) is beneficial, and differences in members' comportment that bespeak positive advances should be highlighted.

Though the group ends, not all clients are prepared to terminate psychotherapy. As stated earlier, the group experience might serve as an adjunct to ongoing therapy for some clients. Others will backslide or will desire greater resolution of issues that surfaced during the course of the group. Members should be informed that follow-up therapy is available and that utilization of such services in no way indicates personal inadequacy or failure of the group. Group clients often form collaborative social relationships to enhance the continuity of group gains, and therapists can point to such liaisons as valuable sources of support.

The author customarily teaches self-hypnosis to his groups in the eighth or ninth session. Many members request induction audiotapes, and these are gladly given. Both self-hypnosis and taped inductions are excellent means for providing members with transitional referrents. The natural anxiety members feel when separating from an important source of self-fulfillment may be abated by utilizing such devices. The final group session is always reserved for saying goodbye and giving feedback. Metaphorically, this is a ceremony to commemorate the bounty reaped from the seeds that were planted such a short while ago.

CONCLUSIONS

The cognitive model of depression is but one of numerous prominent theories that purport to explain the disorder. Entire treatises could be written on the incorporation of Ericksonian/strategic methods into other treatment approaches. Certainly, the hypnotic and directive procedures described could easily be seen as effecting increases in clients' self-efficacy and efficacy expectations (Bandura, 1977), though they are not depicted here as doing so. Ericksonian/strategic approaches offer potentially effective means for teaching individuals to elicit positive reinforcement from their social environments (Lewinsohn, Weinstein, & Alper, 1970). It could be reasonably argued that this is the actual mechanism of action of successful therapy when employing the model presented. The techniques described in this chapter help depressed clients modify the internal, global, and stable attributions constituting the "depressive attributional style" theorized to be at the core of helplessness and depression (Abramson, Seligman, & Teasdale, 1978). Ericksonian/strategic procedures could find their way comfortably into components of psychodynamic, self-control, self-esteem, and other treatment programs arising from a variety of perspectives.

Ultimately, though, most clinicians opt for utility and results. The cognitive-Ericksonian/strategic group psychotherapy model proposed here contains these qualities: It is highly practical for a wide spectrumof clients, and it delivers multimodal benefits. The model is structured yet malleable, individualized and at the same time broadly applicable, and consciously directed with an inherent regard for unconscious processes. However, it is not offered as a resolute panacea. Talented therapists are invited to test, modify, and add their personal touches to the evolution of this therapeutic enterprise. Clients have much to gain and nothing to lose other than the bane of depression.

REFERENCES

Abramson, L. Y., Seligman, M. E. P., & Teasdale, J. D. (1978). Learned helplessness in humans: Critique and reformulation. *Journal of Abnormal Psychology, 87*, 49–84.

Bandura, A. (1977). Self-efficacy: Toward a unifying theory of behavioral change. *Psychological Review, 84*, 191–215.

Beck, A. T. (1976). *Cognitive Therapy and the Emotional Disorders.* New York: International Universities Press.

Beck, A. T., & Emery, G. (1985). *Anxiety Disorders and Phobias: A Cognitive Perspective.* New York: Basic Books.

Beck, A. T., Rush, A. J., Shaw, B. F., & Emery, G. (Eds.) (1979). *Cognitive Therapy of Depression.* New York: Guilford Press.

Burns, D. (1980). *Feeling Good: The New Mood Therapy.* New York: Morrow.

Covi, L., Roth, D., & Lipman, R. S. (1982). Cognitive group therapy of depression: The close-ended group. *American Journal of Psychotherapy, 36*, 459–469.

Erickson, M. H. (1954). Pseudo-orientation in time as a hypnotherapeutic procedure. *Journal of Clinical and Experimental Hypnosis, 2*, 261–283.

Erickson, M. H. (1964). The "Surprise" and "My-Friend-John" techniques of hypnosis: Minimal cues and natural field experimentation. *American Journal of Clinical Hypnosis, 6*, 293–307.

Erickson, M. H. (1966). The interspersal technique for symptom correction and pain control. *American Journal of Clinical Hypnosis, 3*, 198–209.

Erickson, M. H., & Rossi, E. L. (1979). *Hypnotherapy: An Exploratory Casebook.* New York: Irvington.

Fleming, B. M., & Thornton, D. W. (1980). Coping skills training as a component in the short-term treatment of depression. *Journal of Consulting and Clinical Psychology, 48*, 652–654.

Gilligan, S. G. (1987). *Therapeutic Trances: The Cooperation Principle in Ericksonian Hypnosis.* New York: Brunner/Mazel.

Haley, J. (1967). *Advanced Techniques of Hypnosis and Therapy: Selected Papers of Milton H. Erickson, M.D.* New York: Grune & Stratton.

Haley, J. (1973). *Uncommon Therapy: The Psychiatric Techniques of Milton H. Erickson, M.D.* New York: W. W. Norton.

Haley, J. (1984). *Ordeal Therapy.* San Francisco: Jossey-Bass.

Hamilton, M. (1967). A rating scale for depression. *British Journal of Social Clinical Psychology, 6,* 278–296.

Hogg, J. A. (1986). *Comparison of Cognitive and Interpersonal Process Group Therapies in the Treatment of Depression.* Unpublished doctoral dissertation, Colorado State University.

Hollon, S. D., & Beck, A. T. (1979). Cognitive therapy of depression. In P. C. Kendall & S. D. Hollon (Eds.), *Cognitive-Behavioral Interventions: Theory, Research, and Procedures.* New York: Academic Press.

Hollon, S. D., & Shaw, B. F. (1979). Group cognitive therapy for depressed patients. In A. T. Beck, A. J. Rush, B. F. Shaw, & Emery, G. (Eds.), *Cognitive Therapy of Depression.* New York: Guilford Press.

Lewinsohn, P. M., Weinstein, M. S., & Alper, T. (1970). A behaviorally oriented approach to the group treatment of depressed persons: A methodological contribution. *Journal of Clinical Psychology, 26,* 525–532.

Madanes, C. (1984). *Behind the One-Way Mirror: Advances in the Practice of Strategic Therapy.* San Francisco: Jossey-Bass.

Rosenbaum, M. (1980). A schedule for assessing self-control behaviors: Preliminary findings. *Behavior Therapy, 11,* 109–121.

Roth, D., & Covi, L. (1984). Cognitive group psychotherapy of depression: The open-ended group. *International Journal of Group Psychotherapy, 34,* 67–82.

Rush, A. J. (1983). Cognitive therapy for depression. In M. R. Zales (Ed.), *Affective and Schizophrenic Disorders: New Approaches to Diagnosis and Treatment.* New York: Brunner/Mazel.

Shaw, B. F. (1977). Comparison of cognitive therapy and behavior therapy in the treatment of depression. *Journal of Consulting and Clinical Psychology, 45,* 543–551.

Simons, A. D., Lustman, P. J., Wetzel, R. D., & Murphy, S. G. (1985). Predicting response to cognitive therapy: The role of learned resourcefulness. *Cognitive Therapy and Research, 9,* 79–89.

Stanton, M. D. (1981). Strategic approaches to family therapy. In A. S. Gurman & D. P. Kniskern (Eds.), *Handbook of Family Therapy.* New York: Brunner/Mazel.

Stever, J. L., Mintz, J., Hammen, C. L., Hill, M. A., Karvik, L. F., McCarley, T., Motoike, P., & Rosen, R. (1984). Cognitive-behavioral and psychodynamic group psychotherapy in treatment of geriatric depression. *Journal of Consulting and Clinical Psychology, 52,* 180–189.

Waldo, M. (1985). A curative factor framework for conceptualizing group counseling. *Journal of Counseling and Development, 64,* 52–64.

Yalom, I. D. (1985). *The Theory and Practice of Group Psychotherapy* (3rd ed.). New York: Basic Books.

Yapko, M. D. (1985). Therapeutic strategies for the treatment of depression. In S. R. Lankton (Ed.), *Ericksonian Monographs (Number 1): Elements and Dimensions of an Ericksonian Approach.* New York: Brunner/Mazel.

Youngren, A. M., & Lewinsohn, P. M. (1980). The functional relationship between depression and problematic interpersonal behavior. *Journal of Abnormal Psychology, 89,* 333–341.

Zeig, J. K. (1980). *A Teaching Seminar with Milton H. Erickson.* New York: Brunner/Mazel.

Zeig, J. K., & Geary, B. B. (1988). Seeds of strategic and interactional psychotherapies: Seminal contributions of Milton H. Erickson, M. D. Submitted for publication.

Interventions for Anxiety

Chapter 10

From Panic to Peace: Recognizing the Continua

Russell A. Bourne, Jr.

Russell A. Bourne, Jr., Ph.D. (University of Virginia), has been Director of the Counseling Center at Randolph-Macon College in Ashland, Va., since 1976. Additionally, Dr. Bourne, a clinical psychologist, is a founding member of the Virginia Ericksonian Institute, and conducts a private practice. As a faculty member at the Third and Fourth International Congress on Ericksonian Approaches to Hypnosis and Psychotherapy, he presented a paper and led an advanced workshop. He has taught numerous undergraduate and graduate courses and conducts a variety of workshops for educators and mental health professionals. Bourne has published in the areas of developmental psychology, hypnotherapy, and psychodiagnosis.

Essentially all aspects of human experience, or human nature, may be regarded as occurring along certain continua. Regardless of whether the experience or quality of interest is something objectively measurable (i.e., height, weight, muscular strength) or subjectively evaluated (i.e., degree of anger, sadness, animation), it can be viewed conceptually as occurring to a greater or lesser extent in different individuals, or in the same individual at different times or under different circumstances.

Many persons who experience the subjective discomfort and the physiological excesses that accompany anxiety or panic states often forget the fact that the behavior(s) and internal state(s) present at the time of distress are primarily different only in degree from related states that they previously experienced without accompanying discomfort or upset. A major premise of this chapter is that the recognition of the appropriate continuum of experience by the patient will provide a context in which to employ hypnotic approaches to treatment predicated on Milton H. Erickson's ideas of utilization. In particular, this chapter discusses approaches to treatment applicable directly to those persons experiencing a variety of anxiety disorders and/or panic states.

REVIEW OF GENERALIZED ANXIETY DISORDERS AND PANIC STATES

Given that there is a tendency, even in the professional community, to refer occasionally to these two disorders as if they were indistinguishable from each other, a brief comparison is offered.

Anxiety is differentiated from panic or fear in that anxiety is a chronic state of arousal, whereas fear and panic are acute states (Barlow et al., 1984). The presence of anxiety as a feeling state is accompanied by one or more visceral reactions, usually of a cardiovascular or gastrointestinal nature. Common symptoms include palpitations, sweating, nausea, vomiting, nervous stomach ("butterflies"), diarrhea, frequent urination, shallow or constricted breathing, and tightness in the chest. Complaints of muscle tension, spasms, or headache are also common. Generally speaking, any given individual patient will not exhibit all of the above symptoms, but will find the same cluster of symptoms recurring (Hoehn-Saric, 1981). Although these complaints are characteristic of anxiety and panic states according to the revised third edition of the *Diagnostic and Statistical Manual of Mental Disorders* (APA, 1987), panic disorder is characterized by at least three attacks, in three weeks, of discrete periods of apprehension or fear, with at least four of the following 12 symptoms being present:

Dyspnea (difficult or labored breathing)
Palpitations
Chest pains
Choking or smothering sensations
Dizziness, vertigo or unsteady feelings
Feelings of unreality
Paresthesias (unpleasant tactile sensations—tingling, burning, prickling, etc.)
Hot and cold flashes

Sweating

Faintness

Trembling or shaking

Fear of dying, going crazy, or doing something uncontrolled
during an attack (APA, 1987)

These symptoms are in contrast to generalized anxiety disorder, in
which the presence of a "free-floating" anxiety is continuous for at
least one month, with symptoms of motor tension, autonomic hyperactivity, apprehensive expectations, and vigilance and scanning (APA,
1987). The second major difference between a generalized anxiety disorder and a panic disorder seems to be in the area of severity of somatic symptoms. Specifically, generalized anxiety disorder sufferers
usually experience a persistent anxiety with vague symptoms of autonomic origin, whereas panic disorder sufferers frequently report more
severe physical distress, in particular, headaches, palpitations, and res-
piratory symptoms (Anderson, Noyes, & Crowe, 1984; Breier,
Charney, & Heninger, 1985).

These diagnostic differentiations are significant to the premise of
this chapter only to the degree that the symptoms experienced by the
patient are utilized in the construction of appropriate hypnotherapeutic interventions. The fact that differential diagnosis has been confirmed (Klerman, 1986) reinforces the necessity of dealing with those
who present with a broad range of anxiety symptoms on as individual
a basis as possible when employing the approaches to be described in
this chapter.

THE NEED FOR TREATMENT OPTIONS

Currently, most treatment approaches with anxiety symptoms are
either pharmacological or behavioral. The specific pharmacological basis of therapeutics relevant to anxiety disorders is covered in several
recent articles (Barlow et al., 1984; Curtis, 1985; Klein, 1984; Klerman,
1986; Shrader & Greenblatt, 1983). Pharmacological intervention is
rather widespread within the psychiatric and general medical commu-
nities; however, research by Barlow (1984) indicated that "the evidence
of benzodiazepines in treating chronic anxieties is generally very
weak. Documentation exists only for short-term (2-4 weeks) thera–
peutic effects, and marked symptoms of physical dependence and
withdrawal have been verified with long-term use." Furthermore,

Anderson et al. (1984) reported that nearly half of the patients in a large study of panic disorder and generalized anxiety disorder sufferers had received medical (i.e., pharmacological) treatment for their disorder. Certainly, more treatment options are necessary, considering an estimate that between 2 percent and 5 percent of the general population has had or will experience significantly distressing anxiety symptoms. A report of recent follow-up studies indicated that less than 25 percent of the patients with anxiety disorders report full recovery (Breier et al., 1985). Given that Barlow and Beck (1984) also quoted results from a Gallup poll noting that between 30 percent and 40 percent of the general population reported having experienced symptoms of marked anxiety within the most recent year, it becomes all the more desirable to investigate alternative methods of treatment.

Hypnosis has been shown to be an effective therapeutic intervention for a variety of psychological and biological problems. Recently, there have been further investigations for its use in the treatment of anxiety (Andrews, 1985; Anderson et al., 1984; Barlow & Beck, 1984); the management of pain associated with cancer and medical procedures (Kellerman et al., 1983; Labaw et al., 1975); its utility in managing extreme emotional behavior (Swartz, 1981); and interpersonal and/or marital difficulties (Lankton & Lankton, 1983); physiological control (Rossi, 1986); as well as research specific to its use with anxiety (Van Pelt, 1975a; Gilligan, 1987) and fear (Mills & Crowley, 1986).

ERICKSONIAN APPROACHES

Erickson continually provided clarification of trance phenomena and the use of hypnosis and hypnotherapy for the development of interpersonal and/or intrapsychic change (Erickson, 1980; Erickson & Rossi, 1979; Erickson, Rossi, & Rossi, 1976; Haley, 1985). Though he provided a number of conceptual definitions of hypnosis, one that is particularly appropriate to the topic of this chapter was afforded in an address to the Clinical Society of Hypnosis in Topeka, Kansas (personal tape recording, 1960): "Hypnosis is a state. . . . that you induce in a person by the process of employing their patterns of behavior so that they can become aware in a special way."

Erickson was remarkably adept at identifying (1) the salient patterns of a person's dysfunctional and distressing behavior; (2) those patterns that offered a clue to the person's inner resources; and (3) the utilization of those patterns in a variety of ways to induce trance, facilitate change, and promote self-reliance.

Ericksonian hypnotherapy is most singularly distinguished from other approaches to psychotherapy by the practitioner's full appreciation and subsequent utilization of the "realities" of the patient. (See Gilligan, 1987, for a thorough discussion of the cooperative principles of Ericksonian hypnotherapy.) It is this cooperation with patients, and utilization of their individual responses, that permits them to move from panic to peace in a way that truly recognizes and validates the continua of all human experience.

It is appropriate to note at this point that the ideas suggested in this chapter are unaffected by theoretical bias. Whether the reader presumes a psychoanalytic conceptualization of anxiety (i.e., a struggle for control of unacceptable impulses and the resultant inability of an individual to discharge anxiety manifest from conflicts between instinctual demands and the personality's attempt to socialize itself, Fenichel, 1945), or the behaviorally oriented theory (i.e., an overconditioning of autonomic responses to noxious stimulation to nonspecific stimuli, thus resulting in a manifestation of "anxiety responses" to nonthreatening circumstances, Wolpe, 1973), the approaches offered for consideration require no change in the personality theory beliefs of the practitioner. What is required is an appreciation for the fact that when a person becomes insensitive to situational changes (environmental or biological) and begins responding in a fixed pattern (emotionally or behaviorally), that person will usually come to identify this pattern as being problematic. The Ericksonian approach to therapy fosters the notion that the same responses that are problematic in one situation may be expressed in different situations in ways that are comfortable for the patient and may even be generative for the person's psychological development.

Generally, it is felt that the ability to respond with anxiety is appropriate and beneficial to mental health, to a certain degree, and is a normal accompaniment to growth and change. The ability to tolerate and manage anxiety is necessary to allow for trying new things and finding one's own identities and meanings in life. However, these ideas alone, when shared with patients, are usually not sufficient to create a personal appreciation for the sensations and symptoms that have been so distressing! Instead, the symptom/symptom complex must be either diffused or reframed through a variety of interpretations. The patient is encouraged to increase the frequency of expression of the symptom while paying particular attention to increasing the *diversity* of contexts in which the symptom is expressed.

As many other psychotherapists have written (Erickson, 1980; Haley, 1984; Lankton and Lankton, 1983; Watzlawick et al., 1974), at times it is beneficial to encourage patients to "do their symptom better"; however, this is not usually enough to produce true generative change. Gilligan (1987) amplified this idea, observing that it is not therapeutic simply to request that patients do their symptoms more often (i.e., to repeat the expression of the symptom complex—"doing more of the same only harder"). Rather, it is requisite that patients learn to express their symptoms in *many* new ways and in *different* contexts. (To ask them to do more of the same, while forgetting to expand the realm of expression and/or context in which the symptom is expressed, may, in fact, be counterproductive.)

THREE VARIATIONS OF UTILIZATION

Three approaches to the task of heightening patients' recognition of the continua phenomenon are offered. The first approach focuses on the patient's actual physiologic symptomatology and utilizes associational strategies for the development of trance phenomena, recontextualization of the symptom complex, and development of greater self-assurance. The second approach relies upon metaphorical construction/transformation of the symptom complex and utilizes associational phenomena to increase the probability of dissociational responses being developed. The primary purpose of this approach is to provide the patient with symptom relief through recontextualization, and self-control. Finally, the third approach utilizes self- and other referenced future-paced modeling and associational techniques to facilitate symptom relief and self-reliance. Each approach relies, to a certain degree, on the development of a personally meaningful trance, and, therefore, practitioners should pay particular attention to the processes of "creating the context" (Gilligan, 1987) and "promoting readiness" (Bourne, 1988) that are tailored appropriately for each individual patient.

It is important to begin this process by having patients recall how their symptom complex has been expressed in past situations that were nondistressing. That is, when have the behaviors that are currently identified as "problematic" been experienced in a positive context and/or self-valuing fashion? If all symptomatic behavior is, indeed, part of the normal range of human experience, one way to assist patients in understanding and recontextualizing their current problematic behavior is to develop ways that expand their appreciation for the past diversity of expression they have experienced for a given behavior.

Since most of the symptom behavior addressed is, in part, physiologic in origin, a comment about the centrality of breathing is warranted. Breathing seems to be one of the most naturally rhythmic processes that humans experience, and it is a process that is affected by, or may affect, nearly every other human experience. Wilson (1986) provides a nice discussion of the use of breathing awareness and the control of anxiety and panic states. If breathing is to be addressed separately from other symptom behaviors, it is important to note that asking patients to concentrate on breathing, without further directives, may cause them to experience even greater dysrhythmia. It is important to specify whether one is asking that patients focus initially on their inhaling or exhaling response. When one concentrates on the exhale, there is a tendency to relax and allow the body to become quieter and more sedate. If awareness and concentration are focused on the inhale, the body tends to become more aroused and alert. If a patient's panic is manifest in a withdrawal trance, then to ask him or her to relax and breath (i.e., focus on the exhale) may encourage the inhibition of the arousal that is actually desired. In that case, it would be more beneficial to ask the individual to focus on the inhale.

UTILIZATION OF PHYSIOLOGIC SYMPTOMATOLOGY

The major symptoms characteristic of generalized anxiety disorder and panic disorder are usually interpreted as suggestive of autonomic arousal (Barlow et al., 1984; Benson, 1975; Brown, 1977; Wilson, 1986). This arousal, in all likelihood, has been interpreted positively at some point in the client's past. When the physiologic symptoms are used as the basis for the continuum construction, the patient is directed to recall past memories/experiences in which responses parallel to those of the distressed state were present *but* which were experienced in a non-distressed or positively connotated state. The symptomatic behavior, which may be autonomic (or may seem automatic), begins to be recontextualized as the patient elicits associations to past situations and circumstances in which these behaviors were present without accompanying anxiety or panic. Table 1 offers a few examples of symptom parallels.

Many persons who have experienced intense anxiety or panic will report that they want to be with someone they know or be somewhere that is familiar to them in order to feel safe and protected. It is possible to build on this wish by showing them the familiarity of their symptom complex by connecting it to past and familiar memories. That is, since they desire familiarity, the notion that their symptoms have been present before in other contexts can offer a "meta-familiarity" to them. When presented in trance, this connection may become long lasting.

When generating ideas and examples for use with patients' physical symptoms, it is important to have them define the "chain of events"

Table 1
Examples of Context Variability of Physiologic Symptoms*

Current Symptom	Parallel Past Experiences
Dizziness	Spinning around and being silly as a child; whirling around on a dance floor
Faintness	Being surprised or "giddy" with excitement
Feelings of unreality	Time distortions (time passing quickly when with a favorite friend/loved one or engaged in a favorite activity)
Hot and cold flashes	Experiencing a chill while being warmed by a fire; leaving a sauna/steambath and appreciating the changed temperature
Paresthesias	Wind burn on the face while skiing, bike riding, etc., or having one of the extremities "fall asleep" while engaged in a pleasant activity (watching TV, cuddling with a loved one, etc.)
Sweating/labored breathing	Physical exertion of a positive nature or from a valued activity

*These examples are presented merely to suggest possibilities; those chosen/developed must be appropriate to and consistent with the individual experiences and memories of the patient.

that usually results in their anxious state. Panic and/or anxiety may be elicited after the presentation of any number of cues associated with either painful experiences or the anticipation of repeated panic states. Once they have learned to sense the beginnings (the initial links in the chain), they can begin their trance and in so doing can start to diffuse and recontextualize the symptom complex automatically.

Often the initial presentation of suggested activities or events that seem natural to the evocation of their symptomatic behavior will induce a light trance. At this time, the astute practitioner should begin to pay close attention to the ideodynamic responses (including those minimal behaviors that result from specific ideas and thought patterns) generated. These behaviors offer the therapist cues for understanding the current unconscious processes of the patient, and also serve as a mechanism for eliciting desired emotional states and/or physiologic modifications. That is, when one begins to think about a certain event (pleasant or unpleasant), one will demonstrate behavior that is congruent with those thoughts. To paraphrase Gilligan (1987), when people think about a happy event, they begin to *look* a little happier; and when they remember an anxious experience, their breathing may begin to constrict and other individually specific responses to anxiety will be experienced. By eliciting past memories of behaviors, experiences, or situations in which the patient's symptom complex was present *without* the current level of anxiety or panic, the patient may no longer easily view the particular symptomatology as representing a static state of being.

Trance is used in the beginning of therapy to assist in the formation of useful associations. Later it may be used for the identification of variable contexts, and as a means for integrating these new associations and learnings. This wider appreciation for a person's biological response capability, and the awareness of the diversity of situations and contexts in which one is able to respond physiologically, usually heightens a patient's sense of self-appreciation. It also provides the patient with a larger context in which to view any further manifestations of his or her individual symptomatology. The following abbreviated case example of this application of Erickson's ideas of utilization may be helpful in understanding the general use of this approach.

Case Example: A woman in her late 40s came to therapy with complaints of feeling panic and fright whenever she found herself alone in her house during the late afternoon or early evening hours. Her husband's work schedule was varied, and occasionally he did not arrive home on time (usually around 6:00 P.M.) as expected. She would then "discover" herself rocking back and forth with little sense of body control. She had tried sitting down, reading, sleeping, and pacing, all to no avail. During the second therapy session, a light trance state was established and she was asked to revivify the experience of rocking her child when he was young and . . .

> . . . to become aware of the rhythm
> of swaying to and fro . . . gently,
> peacefully . . . rocking your son
> and enjoying . . . the comfort of providing
> him comfort . . . and security
> through movement . . . the gentle movement of
> rocking . . . slowly . . . and peacefully . . .

As she became increasingly aware of these memories, the focus was gradually shifted and she was encouraged to experience the weight of her child in her arms and on her lap. The symptoms of distress and panic she had experienced earlier became reframed and recontextualized as a variation of potentially pleasant sensations, and then diffused with the attentional shift from one kinesthetic sense (movement) to another (weight). Subsequent trance experiences included further symptom diffusion and sensory shifts as auditory (chair squeaking, environmental sounds) and olfactory ("unique/special" fragrance of her child, other smells—baby powders, lotions, etc.) memories were accessed. As therapy continued, she was able to employ this approach when at home in order to interrupt the panic sequence that usually began with her erratic and nervous rocking motion.

METAPHORICAL TRANSFORMATION OF THE SYMPTOM COMPLEX

Most people have had sufficient life experiences to provide a variety of memories and examples of behaviors analogous to those represented by their distressing physiologic symptoms. However, for some people this approach may be very difficult because their specific symptomatology may not lend itself as easily to the associational strategies described above. Also, for some people the idea of focusing upon their physical symptoms is either too alien or possibly too threatening to enable them to use the first approach. It then becomes necessary to offer a symbolic or metaphorical reconceptualization of their problem state in order to provide a one-step-removed approach to managing their anxiety. This may be done with a variety of visual, auditory, or kinesthetic images. Table 2 offers examples for metaphor construction.

Table 2
Examples of Metaphor Possibilities for Continuum Construction

Sensory Channels

Visual	Color spectrum	(i.e., blue to green)
	Light intensity	(i.e., bright to dim)
	Acuity	(i.e., sharp or defined to dull or blurred)
	Shape	(i.e., square to circle; polygon to lesser polygon)*
Auditory	Volume	(i.e., high to low)
	Tone	(i.e., bass/deep to treble/sharp)
	Rhythm	(i.e., undulating to erratic)
Kinesthetic	Temperature	(i.e., hot to cold; cold to frozen)
	Pressure	(i.e., firm to soft)†
	Movement	(i.e., fast to slow; dysrhythmic to rhythmic)
	Location	(i.e., permanent to variable; blurring distinctions or boundaries to isolating distinctions or boundaries)

Cross-Sensory/Multiple Sensory Shift

Visual-visual	(i.e., blue hexagon to pink circle)
Visual-auditory	(i.e., harsh bright light to deep bass tone)
Visual-kinesthetic	(i.e., red color to warm temperature)
Auditory-auditory	(i.e., loud bass tone to clear low treble tone)
Auditory-kinesthetic	(i.e., discordant rhythm to soft pressure)
Kinesthetic-kinesthetic	(i.e., cold hard pressure to warm soft slight touch)

Symbolic Regulators

Dials	(i.e., television channel selector)
Gauges	(i.e., thermometer)
Clocks	(i.e., having the secondhand become the minute hand)
Switches	(i.e., on/off or rheostat)
Animals	(i.e., wing movement of a soaring hawk or of a frenetic hummingbird)
Motors	(i.e., blades on a ceiling fan or propellor on a boat engine)

*As Watzlawick (1984) described the idea of an unresolved remnant, it is important to appreciate that not all *hard* or rigid pieces may be removed (i.e. going from a hexagon to a circle), however, they may be reduced (i.e., hexagon to a triangle).

†Of course there are many gradations to each possible metaphor and the actual symbolic selection is limited only to the imagination and flexibility of the practitioner. In the example of kinesthetic pressure, one patient constructed his continuum around the image of bedding variation, i.e., the feather tick mattress he recalled from his youth, to the very firm orthopedic mattress that he currently used, with the firm yet soft and conforming support of a waterbed mattress representing his desired state at mid-point on the continuum.

Essentially, the first step is to identify or associate the symptom complex with a particular metaphor of the patient's choosing. The symptom is then placed upon a continuum for that metaphorical image, and polarities are determined. Although this may be done before or during actual trance work, some clients have difficulty with speech during the trance state and, thus, for them it is preferable to do this in preparation for, rather than during, trance. After determining the defined ends of the continuum (or at least the one to which movement is desired), trance is induced. The patient is then assisted in the development of associational and dissociational responses to the chosen image and the symptom complex respectively. The following abbreviated case example may be helpful in understanding the general use of this approach.

Case Example: A 33-year-old man was referred by his family physician after complaining of intense feelings of pressure and anxiety that seemed to come over him with little warning and for no apparent reason. During the first therapy session, his language and style seemed to suggest that he was a "highly visual" individual. He had difficulty describing his physiologic symptoms with any kinesthetic specificity, and when asked what the distress might sound like if it were a sound, he seemed genuinely puzzled, and even annoyed! When asked what his distressing bodily feelings might look like were they to be presented in visual form, he immediately reestablished rapport and said that often he felt as if his symptoms were "a deep, and bright red shape of many jagged ridges or spikes," and that this "sounded crazy" to him. When requested, he was able to define the visual opposite of that experience as a pale blue, softly contoured oval. This became the image upon which the trance was focused. He was asked to keep his eyes open and to focus on the imaginary visual representation that he had chosen for his symptom (a red jagged-edged shape) and to allow that image to occupy nearly all of his visual field. Once that had been accomplished, the following was said:

> Allow yourself to focus on the red image . . . with all of its jagged edges . . . and notice how you can begin . . . to see the central part of that object with your primary vision, and still maintain an awareness of the extreme edges of the jagged spikes, with your peripheral vision . . . Continue to employ your peripheral vision and focused vision simultaneously. Be aware of what you can see out of each corner of your eyes . . . while still focusing upon the red image. It might be surprising . . . to notice how that red image can begin to change its color . . . only slightly at first . . . almost imperceptibly. And, as you become increasingly aware of that

> moderate color shift . . . from red to a slightly lighter shade . . .
> maybe a little pinkish . . . you can notice how your vision
> has softened around the edges . . . and that those spikes and rid–
> ges have become a little blurred . . . maybe even just a little
> blunted. . . . And as those spikes and ridges become softened . . .
> notice how the space between them begins to fill with that lighter
> shade. . . . I don't know if it's truly a bluish pink . . . or maybe a
> slightly lighter shade of reddish blue . . .

This process was continued as he progressively went deeper into trance and was assisted in altering the shape of that intensely anxiety-associated image to one he defined as being its opposite. Subsequent therapy sessions were devoted to the recreation of the soft blue contoured oval with different experiential channels (kinesthetic and auditory) being employed in order to widen his personal response set. Specifically, he was assisted in the trance state to develop auditory (a low melodious tone) and kinesthetic (warm, gentle, stroke on the back of the neck) responses to accompany his blue oval.

FUTURE PACED MODELING

This third approach to utilization incorporates basic techniques of modeling and rests upon the premises of self-fulfilling prophecy and self-determination. As Watzlawick (1974) noted, people's ability to "act and think as someone else might" in a given situation, or to act "as if" they believe or feel differently from their stated beliefs, may greatly influence their subsequent behavior, cognitions, and emotions. It seems that in many ways, we do, indeed, possess the ability to "create our own reality." For some patients, this idea is best communicated during the trance state as they are encouraged to image how another person, without the particular distress they are experiencing, would respond to their circumstances, or, to image how they might feel, or what they might do, at the termination of the anxiety-evoking circumstances.

The major purposes of this approach are to offer symptom relief and to promote self-reliance. Therefore, it is important to remember that the seemingly specific behaviors/experiences/feelings to be suggested may actually be nonspecific in nature. Ericksonian approaches to hypnotherapy are generally regarded as more permissive and more interactional than those of traditional hypnosis. Thus, the Ericksonian practitioner will usually select a general class of behaviors when wanting to facilitate a response (particular or general) in the patient. Once the class of hypnotic responses is determined, any given response within that class is validated. Therefore, when seeking to assist the patient with future-paced modeling relevant to anxiety reduction, it becomes critically important to suggest, and permit, a variety of acceptable responses in the patient. Table 3 provides examples of question structures and formations designed to elicit future-paced modeling.

Table 3
Examples of Questions for Future-Paced Modeling

OTHER REFERENCED

"How does someone who is X do/feel/experience Y?"

"What would someone who is X do/feel/experience in Z?"

    where X = a major trait or characteristic
           Y = minor behaviors or sensations
           Z = a particular situation

EXAMPLES: "How does someone who is confident walk up the step to board an airplane?"

            "What would someone who is comfortable do while he or she sat in a plane waiting for take-off?"

SELF-REFERENCED

"How would you experience X in A?

"What would you do/feel/experience in A?"

    where X = a major trait or characteristic
           A = a situation equivalent to the (desired) polar end of the anxiety continuum *or* the conclusion of the anxiety-provoking situation

EXAMPLES: "How would you experience comfort as the plane trip ended?"

            "What would you experience as you stepped from the plane and began walking down the steps?"

Most people have some general ideas of how others (who seem more capable, confident, secure, comfortable, relaxed, bright, accomplished, ad nauseam) would respond without distress in the situation or context that they find particularly distressing. It is possible to have them project and integrate this more generally "competent" image through associational approaches to trance. Each of us possesses the ability to project ourselves mentally into the future in order to determine how we might feel about a decision we make today, or how we might feel at the conclusion of a future activity or event. In so doing, we develop a "future memory" for our psychophysiologic state of being. (This idea is similar in nature to those referred to by Yapko, 1985, as "hypnotically created pseudorealities.") It is also possible to create a "future memory" vicariously by imagining the psychophysiologic state of another person who is either participating in, or experiencing the conclusion of, a particular activity, situation, or set of circumstances.

When employing this approach, it is best to use a variety of questions that access major and minor traits/characteristics, behaviors, and emotional experiences/sensations, across a diverse set of interpersonal and private circumstances. The following abbreviated case example may be helpful in understanding the general use of this approach.

> *Case Example:*   A 20-year-old female college student scheduled an appointment for therapy because of feelings of self-doubt and pervasive generalized anxiety. She was a participant in her college honors program, and was beginning to worry that the expectations of her by the faculty were exceeding her capabilities. Additionally, she was questioning whether she truly belonged in an honors program even though she had received national recognition as a Harry S. Truman Scholarship finalist.
>
> During the third therapy session, she reported that the upcoming final interview for the Truman scholarship was causing her significant distress. She was an attractive, socially poised, and articulate young woman who was open to an almost incidental comment that we might use trance as a method of providing relief from her current state of distress. She reported that she had employed meditational techniques in the past, and that she knew somewhat how to relax herself and "go inside." After a very nice trance was established, she was asked
>
> > to go inside and wonder just how someone who is confident . . . would walk through that door for a very important meeting . . . And what would someone who is experiencing all the poise and assurance they need, do with their hands . . . while they are hav-

ing that very important conversation? . . . And be very curious. . . . about how that someone, or perhaps even another person, who experiences similar confidence, would experience feelings of relaxation in their shoulders . . . and in their neck. And how would they focus their attention on the matters at hand while remembering that they can breathe, comfortably and securely . . . letting the body respond as an integrated physiological self . . . while the mind allows those people at that meeting . . . to note just how capable that person really is

These ideas were elaborated over the next several minutes, at which point the focus of the trance was slightly shifted and the patient was asked

to imagine how you would feel . . . as you leave that interview room . . . and wonder right now . . . what level of sensation . . . might be present in your hands and . . . whether the comfort, or the confident feelings, will be more prominent in your mind . . . And I think it would be a very good thing . . . for you to see yourself leaving that room, imagining how you might turn around with that special look . . . and acknowledge your pleasure at having been permitted to participate in such a very respectful gathering . . . And now I know . . . that it would be only typical . . . for you to want to tell someone about that experience. . . . And I really think you should . . . because they will be as interested as you are in just how well you did. . . . And they might even be amused . . . as you might be . . . in wondering about that bit of anxiety . . . that was present with you . . . before you entered that room, and even hung around a while after you were there . . . So please go right ahead and tell them that, too . . .

This session was held on the day before her scheduled interview. Three days following the interview, the young woman came to the office to report that she thought the interview had gone very nicely, although she was a bit puzzled by her feeling at a midpoint during the interview that "this really isn't as intimidating as I thought it might be. In fact, it almost seems a little familiar."

SUMMARY

The approaches to the treatment of anxiety and panic states outlined in this chapter are founded on two primary beliefs. First, all aspects of human experience (behaviors, sensations, cognitions, emotions, etc.) may be regarded as occurring along certain defined continua, and the particular continuum upon which any aspect of human experience is placed is best determined (class and location) by the patient. Second, the ideas of utilization (as suggested by Erickson and expanded, in particular, by Gilligan) form the basis for essentially all effective psychotherapeutic intervention. As Gardner (1974) noted, the most common source of failure in the patient/therapist relationship is the therapist's inability to "resonate" with the patient's experiences. It is, indeed, this ability to value, appreciate, and utilize (for the patient's benefit) whatever a particular individual brings to the therapist that makes therapy succeed.

How do we begin to understand and appreciate another human being? The following simple and direct observation by Milton Erickson (personal tape recording, 1960) offers an appropriate beginning: "It is your willingness to look at the other person and to be fully interested in what they are saying to you—by expression, by gesture, by movement, by blankness of expression, or by whatever means they have."

REFERENCES

American Psychiatric Association (1987). *Diagnostic and Statistical Manual of Mental Disorders, Third Edition, Revised.* Washington, D.C.: APA.

Anderson, J., Noyes, R., & Crowe, R. (1984). A comparison of panic disorder and generalized anxiety disorder. *The American Journal of Psychiatry, 4,* 572–575.

Andrews, G. (1985). Treatment outlines for the management of anxiety states. *Australian and New Zealand Journal of Psychiatry, 19,* 138–151.

Barlow, D., & Beck, J. (1984). Psychosocial treatment of anxiety disorders: Current status, future direction. In J. B. Williams & R. L. Spitzer (Eds.), *Psychotherapy Research: Where Are We and Where Should We Go?* New York: Guilford.

Barlow, D., Cowen, A., Waddell, M., Vermilyea, B., Klosko, J., Blanchard, E., & Di Nardo, P. (1984). Panic and generalized anxiety disorders: Nature and treatment. *Behavior Therapy, 15,* 431–449.

Benson, H. (1975). *The Relaxation Response.* New York: William Morrow.

Bourne, R. (1988). Promoting readiness for trance in treatment: The preparatory phase of hypnotherapy. *Ericksonian Monographs, (Vol. 4).* New York: Brunner/Mazel.

Boutin, J., & Tosi, D. (1983). Modification of irrational ideas and test anxiety through rational stage directed hypnotherapy. *Journal of Clinical Psychology, 39,* 382-391.

Breier, A., Charney, D., & Heninger, G. (1985). The diagnostic validity of anxiety disorders and their relationship to depressive illness. *The American Journal of Psychiatry, 142,* 787–797.

Brown, B. (1977). *Stress and the Art of Biofeedback.* New York: Harper and Row.

Curtis, C. (1985). New findings in anxiety: A synthesis for clinical practice in 1985. *The Psychiatric Clinics of North America: Symposium on Anxiety Disorders, 8,* 169–175.

Erickson, M. (1980). *The Collected works of Milton H. Erickson on Hypnosis (4 Vols.).* In E. L. Rossi (Ed.), New York: Irvington.

Erickson, M., & Rossi, E. (1979). *Hypnotherapy: An Exploratory Casebook.* New York: Irvington.

Erickson, M., Rossi, E., & Rossi, S. (1976). *Hypnotic Realities.* New York: Irvington.

Fenichel, O. (1945). *The Psychoanalytic Theory of Neurosis.* New York: W. W. Norton.

Gardner, G. (1974). Hypnosis with children. *The International Journal of Clinical and Experimental Hypnosis, 22,* 20–38.

Gilligan, S. (1988). Symptom phenomena as trance phenomena. In J. Zeig & S. Lankton (Eds.), *Developing Ericksonian Therapy.* New York: Brunner/Mazel.

Gilligan, S. (1987). *The Therapeutic Trances: The Cooperation Principle in Ericksonian Hypnotherapy.* New York: Brunner/Mazel.

Gordin, R. (1981). Effects of hypnosis, relaxation training, or music on state anxiety and stress in female athletes. *Dissertation Abstracts International, 42,* 598–599.

Granone, F. (1976). The importance of behavior therapy using hypnosis in psychosomatic medicine. *International Journal of Clinical and Experimental Hypnosis. 24,* 369.

Haley, J. (1973). *Uncommon Therapy.* New York: W. W. Norton.

Haley, J. (1984). *Ordeal Therapy,* San Francisco: Jossey-Bass.

Haley, J. (1985). *Conversations with Milton H. Erickson. (3 Vols).* New York: Triangle Press.

Hare, N., & Levis, D. (1971). Pervasive ("free-floating") anxiety: A search for a cause and treatment approach. In S. Turner, K. Calhoun, & H. Adams (Eds.), *Handbook of Clinical Behavior Therapy.* New York: Raven.

Kellerman, J., Zeltzer, L., Ellenberg, L., & Dash, J. (1983). Adolescents with cancer: Hypnosis for the reduction of the acute pain and anxiety associated with medical procedures. *Journal of Adolescent Health Care, 4,* 85-190.

Klein, D. (1984). Psychopharmacologic treatment of panic disorder. *Psychosomatics, 25,* 32–35.

Klerman, G. (1986). Current trends in clinical research on panic attacks, agoraphobia, and related anxiety disorders. *Journal of Clinical Psychiatry, 47* (6 suppl.), 37–39.

LaBaw, W., Holton, C., Tewell, K., & Eccles, D. (1975), The use of self-hypnosis by children with cancer. *The American Journal of Clinical Hypnosis, 17,* 233–238.

Lankton, S., & Lankton, C. (1983). *The Answer Within: A Clinical Framework of Ericksonian Hypnotherapy.* New York: Brunner/Mazel.

Linial, A. (1977). An investigation of a treatment of anxiety: A comparison of the relative effects of hypnosis and progressive muscle relaxation. *The International Journal of Clinical and Experimental Hypnosis, 18,* 15–24.

Marks, I. (1985). Behavioral psychotherapy for anxiety disorders. *The Psychiatric Clinics of North America, 8,* 25–35.

Mills, J., & Crowley, R. (1986). *Therapeutic Metaphors for Children and the Child Within.* New York: Brunner/Mazel.

Rossi, E. (1986). *The Psychobiology of Mind Body Healing: New Concepts of Therapeutic Hypnosis.* New York: W. W. Norton.

Shrader, R., & Greenblatt, D. (1983). Some current treatment opinions for symptoms of anxiety. *The Journal of Clinical Psychiatry, 44,* 21–29.

Stanton, H. (1984). A comparison of the effects of an hypnotic procedure and music on anxiety level. *Australian Journal of Clinical and Experimental Hypnosis, 12,* 127–132.

Swartz, C. (1981). Managing desperate emotional behavior with hypnosis. *Canadian Journal of Psychiatry, 26,* 555–557.

Van Pelt, S. (1975a). Hypnosis and anxiety. *Journal of the American Institute of Hypnosis, 16,* 10–15.

Van Pelt, S. (1975b). Hypnosis and panic. *Journal of the American Institute of Hypnosis, 16,* 39–46.

Watzlawick, P. (1978). *The Language of Change.* New York: Basic Books.

Watzlawick, P. (1984). Self-fulfilling prophecies. In P. Watzlawick (Ed.), *The Invented Reality: How Do We Know What We Believe We Know?* New York: W. W. Norton.

Watzlawick, P., Weakland, J., & Fisch, R. (1974). *Change: Principles of Problem Formation and Problem Resolution.* New York: W. W. Norton.

Weissman, M., & Merikangas, K. (1986). The epidemiology of anxiety and panic disorders: An update. *Journal of Clinical Psychiatry, 47*, 11–17.

Wilson, R. (1986). *Don't Panic: Taking Control of Anxiety Attacks.* New York: Harper and Row.

Wolpe, J. (1973). *The Practice of Behavior Therapy.* New York: Pergamon Press.

Yapko, M. (1985). The Erickson hook: Values in Ericksonian approaches. In J. Zeig (Ed.), *Ericksonian Psychotherapy, (Vol. I).* New York: Brunner/Mazel.

Chapter 11

A Hypnotherapeutic Approach to Panic Disorder

Harriet E. Hollander

Harriet E. Hollander, Ph.D., directs the Hypnotherapy Training Program at the University of Medicine and Dentistry of New Jersey—Community Mental Health of Piscataway. She is an Associate in the Department of Psychiatry.

This chapter presents a clinically based description of a three-phase treatment approach to panic disorder and associated anticipatory anxiety states. The treatment approach utilizes Freudian concepts of defense against anxiety (Freud, 1932), Erickson's conversational techniques for hypnotic induction (Erickson, 1980), and a phenomenological and existential perspective on the meaning of anxiety, control, and freedom in the context of this limiting condition (Merleau-Ponty, 1962; Sartre, 1947; Solomon, 1972). It describes the author's clinical experience, which has proven useful in treating anxiety disorders.

DESCRIPTION

Panic disorder is a distinct clinical entity manifesting the classical features first described by Freud in 1895, who called it anxiety neurosis (Freud, 1895). The symptoms vary little among patients. They experience overwhelming feelings of terror and a fear of dying or going mad. Acute somatic discomfort, which can mimic a cardiac episode, includes chest pains, choking sensations, dyspnea, parasthesias, dizziness, sweating, palpitations, and hot and cold flashes. Fear of recurring panic attacks may play a role in the development of an associated condition of agoraphobia and in general anxiety states. Persons with anxiety conditions are susceptible to, but do not necessarily develop, panic disorder (DSM-III-R, A. P. A., 1987).

PSYCHOBIOLOGICAL PERSPECTIVES

Freud viewed anxiety neurosis or panic from a psychobiological perspective. He wrote that heredity might render persons susceptible to this disorder, while suggesting that sexual dissatisfaction might be the precipitating trigger. Freud also observed that there were some cases in which panic attacks could not be reduced to psychological factors. In his later writings, Freud (1932) conjectured that panic attacks might originate in separation anxiety. The child unable to contain libidinized excitement arising from fear of abandonment changes it to panic. Subsequently, individuals develop a fear of their fear of separation.

Current biological approaches generally assume a diathesis for panic disorder. Research exists to support Freud's observation of a positive family history, notwithstanding the methodological problems associated with estimating social influence of close relatives who also have the disorder (Crowe, Noyes, & Pauls, 1983).

The work of Klein et al. (1978) provides evidence supporting Freud's observation that separation anxiety constitutes a specific etiology for panic disorder. Klein found that 20 to 50 percent of adult panic patients report school phobias or other pathologic-separation experiences in childhood. He suggests that panic patients have inadequate defense mechanisms for coping with separation.

The classic biologic investigation in panic disorder is by Pitts and McClure (1967). They found that an infusion of sodium lactate triggered panic in susceptible individuals but not in normal controls. This research finding, combined with the work of Klein, cited above, points to biological vulnerability triggered by a situational context in which separation anxiety plays a prominent role. It is currently hypothesized that this biological vulnerability may in part reflect hypersensitivity of noradrenergic receptors. Many medications effective against panic down-regulate post-synaptic B adrenergic receptors.

The biological perspective is further strengthened by the fact that medication can alleviate panic. Individuals who suffer from panic attacks respond positively to tricyclics and monoamine oxidase inhibitors, even when not depressed (Gorman, Liebowitz, & Klein, 1984). Klein et al. (1978) have shown that treatment with imipramine alone reduced the frequency of panic attacks and phobic sequelae to panic more effectively than placebo.

As is the case with any mental disorder that is an expression of biological, situational, and intrapsychic factors, medication is a limited remedy. Although antidepressants such as imipramine are effective in many cases of panic, symptom breakthrough with the use of drugs alone is not uncommon. Medication does not always relieve the general anxiety state associated with panic disorder and anticipatory fears that panic will often persist. Patients lose confidence when medication fails to prevent panic episodes; they are seldom content to rely solely on medication to manage their bewildering condition. They turn to psychotherapy.

PSYCHODYNAMIC PERSPECTIVES

Freud (1895) did not consider psychoanalysis to be a useful mode of treatment for panic. His view is sustained today. Insight-oriented therapy is not regarded as an effective intervention for panic or phobia, although Stoeri (1987) proposed that patients who can transcend their need for immediate action-oriented relief can be helped by psychoanalysis. Freud's conceptualization of anxiety is central to the understanding of panic, even if traditional psychoanalytic methods do not bring relief. Freud (1932) saw anxiety as a dynamic means of informing consciousness of danger. The role of the unconscious is to signal the conscious of danger and also to alert defenses against it.

It is true that panic is characterized by its apparent sudden and seemingly unprovoked onset. But the dangers that trigger panic are subtle and not always discernible. Though certain events can be easily observed, such as school phobias, fear of leaving home, or agoraphobia, often the threats that can trigger a panic sequence occur sometime before the panic event. Frequently, a trigger event is related not to threat of actual physical separation but to the subtler threat of separateness in the separation/individuation sequence. Fear of death or of the consequences of violent rage are also aspects of the separation/individuation process. Experiences involving these emotions may trigger panic attacks.

Freud's psychodynamic formulation of the ego's defense against anxiety is of major importance in understanding panic. It may be that

unconscious defenses against anxiety are brought into play when individuals are threatened by the developmental processes of separation/
individuation. These defenses may temporarily prevent the awareness
of anxiety when associated with interpersonal sequences that lead to
separateness. As this chapter tries to demonstrate through clinical
examples, it is the particular somatic nature of the maladaptive defense pattern against awareness of anxiety, employed by persons vulnerable to the disorder, that culminates in the panic attack, rather than
a linear process in which a specific anxiety experience is the trigger.

Specifically, this chapter suggests that patients who are vulnerable
to panic engage in a dysfunctional defense pattern against anxiety that
involves a kind of somatic dissociation. Such patients tend to complain
that they are unaware of their body sensations. However, careful observation reveals that these patients are in fact responding to subtle
nuances of a psychodynamically significant situation. Moreover, when
anxious, these individuals demonstrate some peculiar patterns of
breathing. They hold their breath and frequently seem to try to push
speech past their breathing. Chest muscles appear constricted. Other
individual signs of somatic tension are observable. It would seem that
panic symptoms are the ultimate physiologic reaction to this state of
somatic disequilibrium.

Psychoanalytic theory does provide the framework for understanding the special role of anxiety and unconscious defense in panic.
However, psychoanalytic treatment, with its singular emphasis on
treatment through the verbalization of experience, is limited conceptually in intervening to modify nonverbal symptoms of experiential
conflict.

PHILOSOPHICAL PERSPECTIVES

Philosophic ideas usually play a minor role, if any, in modern scientific approaches to the understanding of mental disorders. Although
the disciplines of philosophy and psychology were once closely linked,
they took divergent paths at the end of the 19th century. Psychology
became an experimental discipline under Wundt and retained the scientific tradition even when it expanded into a clinical profession
(Husserl, 1970).

Philosophers eschewed laboratory methods advocated by the new
psychology. Husserl (1970) rejected an approach that studied human
beings and their perceptions and sensations as an objective, "mundan-

ized" aspect of the physical world. In fact, Husserl, the father of phenomenology, defined the task of philosophy as the analysis of consciousness. The questions he pursued were ontological and had their origin in Descarte's *Meditations* (1968). Philosophy sought to understand the origin of self. Self was associated with consciousness. Reality and truth of the external world are represented in consciousness, through the mechanisms of perception.

Heidegger (1949) extended Husserl's theories. He saw a contradiction in the idea of consciousness or self, as a thing apart from the world yet able to grasp its reality. He located consciousness in-the-world (*Dasein*), thereby laying the foundation for modern system theory, which recognizes the unity of self–world interaction. A modern philosophical perspective can offer patients a cognitive framework for understanding the reality of panic. Philosophy is still a discipline that seeks to define what is real. From a philosophical viewpoint, panic is real; it exists; it is not "unreal" because it is a "mental phenomenon."

Philosophical questions are intuitively expressed by patients. For example, some patients subscribe to a 17th century Cartesian mind-body dualism. They are of the opinion that mind is a mysterious realm not understood by science. Taking their panic symptoms as an instance, they believe mind and body can betray them by responding so dramatically to events not represented in consciousness. They complain that their will is paralyzed. Patients with panic can relate to Kierkegaard's (1849) formulation, "Despair is the result of willing to be the self he is not."

Questions about panic resemble existential challenges. Is this suffering intended? Does panic exist to inform consciousness of some failure to act or is panic the effect of defective bodily governance, requiring, like an old-fashioned clock, some readjustment of wheels and weights? Can panic be transcended by action, choice, reflection? Is it me? Not me? Can it be analyzed separately from the self that experiences it, reflects on it, creates it?

Treatment interventions are accepted by patients when the therapist refers to phenomenological, ontological, and existential ideas. For example, panic can be interpreted ontologically: Anxiety is explained as a process by which the self develops, differentiates, and becomes autonomous.

The modern existentialists provide a philosophical framework into which panic can be placed. For example, Sartre (1947) believed that man creates himself through action. Consciousness enables him to reflect on his actions and on the sense of self that follows choice as consciousness reflects on its own operation. For existentialists, consciousness registers the many constraints on action. These include "the gaze" or interpersonal judgments of others. Freedom is achieved when an individual consciously reflects on the choices available within the perceived limits of the situation. Therapeutically, this means that for the patient with panic, anxiety constrains actions, but the patient has choices. The signals of anxiety can be either opportunities for defensive evasion or to undertake conscious reflection on the meaning and implication of events that are occurring in his or her world. Choice follows awareness.

Merleau-Ponty (1962), an existentialist of Sartre's generation, hypothesized a body consciousness that exists in-the-world. For him, the body consciousness can absorb and reflect knowledge of the world and the self. His phenomenological concept of body consciousness differs from the concept of cognitive consciousness that Sartre described. But it is consistent with the concept of a body consciousness intuitively utilized in Ericksonian approaches.

Ericksonian approaches to hypnotherapy are particularly adapted to individuals suffering from panic. Ericksonian approaches can integrate psychobiological, psychodynamic, and existential perspectives in different phases of treatment through the utilization of conversation and metaphorical inductions. The next section describes the three-stage treatment framework in which this occurs. The first treatment phase centers on the immediate crisis presented by the panic symptoms. The therapist works to interrupt the defensive sequence that culminates in panic by teaching the patient to utilize simple trance and rhythmic breathing patterns. A sense of hope for recovery and an experience of symptom relief is the goal in this phase.

The second phase of treatment focuses on the etiology of the panic. The emphasis is on identifying the sequence of subtle interactions that lead the patient to resort to maladaptive somatic patterns of breathing and tension that culminate in panic breakout. Panic is placed in a phenomenological and an existential perspective. The meaning of panic to the self is explored.

The third phase of treatment is given to working with the ontological meaning of the patient's resistance to letting go of panic symptoms after mastering techniques for containing symptoms. Panic symptoms are interpreted within a framework of meaningful self–world interaction.

Treatment Stage I

A number of themes that will recur throughout therapy make their first appearance in the initial stage of treatment. The most important theme is the existential distress expressed in the face of powerlessness to control terrifying, overwhelming, life-disruptive symptoms. Attention is paid to the patient's complaints of the persistence of generalized anticipatory anxiety. The therapist recognizes that in initial stages of treatment, patients will offer a well-rehearsed, cognitive account of some difficult life situation or traumatic event of psychological conflict. The themes of separation/individuation, rejection, death, and rage are prominent. The therapist may also note that phenomenologically the link between affectively laden themes and the occurrence of panic is missing. There will be little doubt that the temporal separation between a psychic trigger and eruption of panic contributes greatly to the patient's sense of unpredictability and overwhelming loss of control when panic strikes. However, the therapist must consider the possibility that the patient is not ready to accept the reality of a link between his or her emotional experiences and the physical reality of a panic attack.

Therapists are faced with a paradox. They are asked to accept the phenomenological validity of intense fear dissociated from any identifiable source. The patient fantasizes that in an unconscious, hypnotic state, the therapist will teach the patient simple ways to command the panic to stop, bypassing the self and the awareness of the reason for the panic response. Yet the patient does not want the therapist to be fooled. The patient wants the therapist to find the missing etiological link. The patient wants to be in control of psychic events that may be triggering panic. The patient wants to make conscious, meaningful sense of the seemingly senseless physical symptoms of the disorder.

A tactful way to release patient and therapist from the therapeutic bind created by the defense of dissociation is to begin by protecting the defense of dissociation and addressing the patient's request for symptom relief. The therapist deliberately postpones exploration of the etiology of panic for a later stage of treatment. The therapist explains that after the patient learns to control panic, then etiological factors, which contributed to the general level of stress, will be explored at leisure. Hypnosis is not offered as a quick-fix technique for panic, but as a way to access the inner self that will find the most appropriate mechanisms of control.

The control technique taught in early sessions is the use of rhythmic breathing followed by light trance. The technique is introduced when the therapist observes the maladaptive somatic defense pattern the patient uses to ward off awareness of anxiety. Typically, the patient exhibits some breath holding, increased rate and pressure of speech, tightening of abdominal muscles, and neck tension. Efforts by the therapist to interact *verbally* to reduce this tension are likely to fail. This maladaptive pattern of defense, which the patient with a susceptibility to panic uses to ward off awareness of anxiety, is responsible for the generalized state of tension that eventually breaks out in a full-blown panic episode. Teaching the patient to be consciously aware of this maladaptive pattern makes control of the panic episode possible and builds up hope of recovery.

To interrupt the defensive patterns, the therapist first elicits the patient's maladaptive somatic pattern of response to panic. A mild form of somatic defense pattern can usually be elicited by simply requesting the patient to retell the experience of having a panic attack. Then the therapist heightens recognition of the self-generated body tensions. Next the therapist introduces rhythmic breathing and trance. These interventions should be started on a conscious level and then used as a transition for trance work. Breathing and relaxation techniques are repeated with the patient during trance work.

The therapist encourages the patient to practice the newly learned breathing and trance techniques to control panic. The patient is asked to continue any other support that previously has been useful, including the use of medication and reliance upon the support of friends and family. In fact, family members are often encouraged to come to therapy sessions to learn techniques for assisting patients to terminate panic quickly. The following section includes an excerpt from an initial interview and illustrates the treatment approach for treatment stage I.

The Case of Maureen   Maureen, a 59-year-old married school teacher, had taken early retirement in order to enjoy some leisure time with her husband, who was ten years older than she. Her career had been successful. She had taught elementary school in an area of the city where most of the students came from economically stable backgrounds and were motivated to succeed in school. According to her description, she had been well liked by her students and had made several close friends among her teaching colleagues. She had just moved into a small home near the seashore, as she and her husband had planned. However, within a month of leaving her old neighborhood and job, she experienced the first of her panic episodes. Panic continued for a period of two weeks during the first episode. She took medication prescribed by her internist, but when she tried to discontinue the medication, the symptoms recurred.

One other factor is pertinent. Her father had recently died of cancer. Her mother, who had been an invalid with an unspecified diagnosis (possibly panic disorder), had recently suffered a mild heart attack. The mother moved in with Maureen and her husband. She had her own room, bath, and a small, separate kitchen in the house. In the city, they had lived within two blocks of each other. Maureen assured me there was not much that had qualitatively changed in their relationship, only that her mother was now physically closer. By implication, she told the therapist that surely this change could not be responsible for her panic symptoms. Family members had all agreed that this arrangement was appropriate as her mother was anxious about being left alone in the house following her cardiac episode. Maureen had twin sons who had married sisters. The couples lived near each other in a neighboring state, several hours away. Both couples had young children. Maureen and her husband usually visited them, as travel was difficult for the young parents with their babies. Maureen hoped that as the children grew older, her sons and their families would visit her at the seashore.

Maureen's mother did not accompany them on these out-of-state trips. She feared travel might be too stressful physically. She expressed concern about being left alone if Maureen and her husband planned an overnight stay away from home. Maureen acknowledged some concern over her mother's demands, but felt they were not unreasonable, given her mother's age and physical condition.

Maureen's physician recommended that she seek psychotherapy in order to gain some insight into possible stress factors affecting her condition.

M: I know I sometimes get frustrated with the demands my mother puts on me to not leave her alone, but she did have a scare with that heart attack.

T: Heart attack?

M: Well, they found some changes in her blood test. They said it was an episode or something. She was in the hospital for a week. They put her on medications and told her not to lift heavy things and to watch her food. They gave her a diet that was low in salt and fat.

T: And she gets a little nervous when you leave the house?

M: Yes. But usually one of us stays. He likes to get up late and work on the accounts for awhile. I go to the supermarket, which is near the house, and then we have breakfast. On Sundays, I go to Mass first and then he goes later. But one Sunday a neighbor stayed with her . . . We've been using our house for years for vacations so we know the year-round people . . . and Don was with me when I began to have the panic . . . I thought it was a heart attack or something . . . and then the next time he was at home with her and I was in the supermarket when I began to feel faint and dizzy. It was horribly embarrassing because I knew I wasn't having a heart attack but

I couldn't stand. They had to call the manager to get me a chair. Don had to get me and drive me home. I've had a couple of them since. The medicine helped, but when I stopped taking it, I had two more attacks, and then a third. I'm beginning to be afraid to leave the house . . . just like my mother. The doctor says I can take the medicine if I am having an attack. But this isn't the way I want to live. It's not the way we planned our retirement.

[Patient's voice rises, chest tenses. She holds her breath as she speaks and gets into the "recital."]

T: Maureen, let me interrupt you here. It sounds like you wonder whether something between you and your mother might be related to the panic attacks. I want to tell you right now that you can be sure it's not that simple. No one knows why some people get panic attacks and others don't. Now everybody gets old [patient becomes very attentive]. These days, with better medicine and good care, many people like yourself have to care for an aging parent. You'll want your children to care about you then, too. But all that is another matter and we can deal with those issues later. Perhaps, if you like, I can share with you some ways that others like yourself have found . . . for your information . . . But for now, you have this condition . . . and you don't like it . . . and there are things you can learn to do to live with it . . . a lot more comfortably . . . Would you like to learn what to do? [Patient has begun a light trance at this point. Chest tension has subsided. Breathing is more regular.]

Now what I'd like you to do is this. Just continue with what you are doing, especially noticing that you are breathing very regularly . . . your ability to do that is the most important part of your preventing those uncomfortable symptoms. Don't speak. Just keep breathing that way [patient smiles]. That's right. And now, without changing your breathing, you can just start describing to me every detail of one of those terrible episodes. . .

M: [realerts and begins to describe episode in market] Well, I was just standing at the delicatessen counter, waiting for the boy to slice some coldcuts and . . . [She begins to rush her speech and hold her breath, though somewhat more moderately.]
T: Remember, you have to breathe and tell the story while you relax that chest because this is the way you will abort that panic. Stop it. Start by breathing.
M: Breathing? [just beginning to comprehend that the therapist is quite serious about these instructions]. Well, that what's so hard to do when I'm having the attack.
T: That's correct. And you may have to just experience that choking and chest discomfort for a moment or two, and say to yourself, 'I've got to stand it, and I'll just let myself relax and then slowly start to

breathe calmly, comfortably.' Like now, and you have just seen that breathing is involuntary, but also under your control. So just practice it now with me.

[This time the patient follows instructions and the therapist continues to coach her.]

T: Now what you are doing on your own has many different names. Some people call it becoming desensitized. For others, it's like entering a light trance state. Some people call it self-hypnosis, just going inside . . . getting really comfortable until your body establishes a normal state of equilibrium . . . breathing . . . relaxing . . . taking your time . . . letting the breathing just happen naturally . . . by itself, and you won't get dizzy if you let your eyes close just a few seconds . . . just long enough to feel good. . . feel sure that you *can* breathe . . . rest . . . let your body experience that normal equilibrium state . . . just close them long enough to review how you can do this little exercise. That's right. And then just let yourself realert.

M: Yes. I could just do that before an attack, if I start to get a warning, and I could also take my pills if I need them.

Treatment Stage II

The second stage of treatment begins when the patient reports some success in aborting panic or limiting symptoms during an attack. The patient begins to have hope of mastering the disorder with behavioral techniques. Receptivity increases to exploring ways to resolve psychological conflict or life problems, though these problems are still seen as only indirectly linked to the panic attacks that arise independently of events occurring in conscious mental life.

Maureen, in the above example, reported that she had experienced the onset of panic in church. She became dizzy. Disregarding what people observing her might think, she focused on her breathing, closed her eyes, allowed herself to relax and drift into light trance. After about ten minutes, the uncomfortable sensations diminished. She went home, rested, and felt well the next day.

As she grew more skillful in recognizing her own self-generated breathing dysfunction, she became responsive to suggestions in trance concerning the relationship with her mother.

T: Maureen, you have learned a great deal about control. You have mastered a very nice pattern of breathing. That's right. And would you say that as you review the routine of your day you have a little bit of nice confidence about that comfortable breathing?

Now you know about learning and teaching. And you are very devoted to your mother, are you not? And you know that the new learning . . . about cardiac care is different . . . a need to do different things . . . and it really is very interesting to hear how the doctors do it now. Tell heart patients to exercise more. Get out more.   Encourage activity. Discourage helplessness. I don't know if a daughter can teach a mother. Help her to learn new ideas. . . how to breathe . . . how to let go.

Shortly thereafter, Maureen embarked on new caretaking arrangements for her mother. She and her husband resumed trips together during the day and to visit the children overnight. She was delighted with her sense of power and control. Therapy concluded as her psychosocial adjustment improved.

When panic has been of long duration, the situation in therapy is quite different. Clients want to examine the mechanism of their disorder, to explore its etiology. They want to control it. In fact, as they gain confidence in their skill to protect themselves, they ambitiously seek emotional control over all of life's vicissitudes. The therapist can help deflect this dubious quest for stoic imperturbability by providing a philosophical framework for understanding the purpose of anxiety.

The therapist now integrates ontological concepts with hypnotic experience. Patients are exposed to a philosophical perspective on the self. Philosophically, self is an active agent that represents reality in consciousness (Hursserl, 1970; Merleau-Ponty, 1962; Sartre, 1947). Psychodynamically, the self, or ego, utilizes anxiety as information that danger exists (Freud, 1932).

In trance, the patient learns to connect to a body consciousness (Merleau-Ponty, 1962), to an awareness of boundaries to a sense of self that chooses, and experiences freedom in choice (Sartre, 1947). The patient's Cartesian mind-body split, expressed in the wish to control physical symptoms by the exercise of mental willpower, is identified with the philosophy of Descartes. In trance, the patient rediscovers the self that can doubt. *Cogito ergo sum.* Hypnotic trance then recapitulates the Cartesian proof. The doubting patient discovers evidence of self, enhanced by memory, imagery, and affect.

Philosophical and dynamic concepts of self take on experiential meaning through trance. Age regressions and revivification techniques help the patient connect to the self in past and present experiences. In hypnosis, the patient weaves philosophical theory and psychodynamic insight into new experiences. Revived traumas, parental injunctions, and suppression of affective responsivity are reexamined in an altered here-and-now state to which the patient responds adaptively.

Hypnotic trance makes *constructive* use of the patient's ability to dissociate. Patients can visualize aspects of the self conversing, taking action at different ages and in different interpersonal contexts. They can observe the onset of defensive breath holding or hyperventilation in response to anxiety stimulated by significant others in their family, by colleagues at work, by peers. The patient, by directing the scene, can alter it. Self reflects on the experience of self. The self chooses among options.

For example, a patient gained insight into the source of her body dissociation from positive feelings as she visualized her father's gestures. She recalled that he was unable to be comfortably affectionate. His hug was not a hug but a push that kept her at a distance. She could feel the similarity to her response to her husband. She had developed a dissociative pattern that prevented her from responding to her husband's signals of intimacy. She either complained unrealistically of his coldness (separateness) or initiated panic after a period of closeness. Through trance her tolerance for closer physical contact increased.

The patient in trance undergoes distinct experiences—somatic relaxation, time distortion, age regression, posthypnotic responsiveness, heightened suggestibility, and amnesia. At the same time, certain aspects of trance are parallel to the experience of patients in psychoanalytic treatment. For example, Freud observed that the unconscious contains "contraries" or opposites that express some common core element. In trance, when unconscious processes are vividly accessed, patients represent these opposites or contraries in various ways. They can be projected symbolically as warring colors, as aspects of self at different ages, as aspects of self in interaction with family, colleagues, peers.

The self creates the self in an existential sense (Sartre, 1947) as it resolves the conflict of opposites in the trance. Choices seem easier in trance. Action, the basis for self-knowledge according to Sartre, meets less resistance in trance than in conscious states. A sense of existential freedom accompanies a choice that resolves conflict in the therapeutic trance. An existential sense of self-mastery is experienced on an unconscious level. New understandings are expressed posthypnotically in consciously made behavior choices. For a deeper appreciation of this process, the reader is referred to Erickson (1980), Erickson and

Rossi (1979), Carter (1983), Gilligan (1987), and Hollander, Holland, and Atthowe (1988).

Excerpts from the treatment of Janet illustrate the integration of philosophical and psychodynamic concepts in a hypnotherapeutic intervention in stage II. Janet was helped to reframe her mind-body ideas, and to connect with ego resources that she had as a child. The therapist helped Janet to access forgotten aspects of self and to project choices into the future.

> *The Case of Janet*   Janet, a 39-year-old married woman, was the only daughter of a chiropractor and a nurse. She was born to middle-aged parents long after they had given up hope of having children. As a child she had been subjected to a regimen of health care and training that bordered on psychological abuse. Her childhood was marred by parental concerns about her health. She was forced to take tonics and vitamins of dubious value all through childhood in order to prevent illness. Her parents washed and examined her with an obsessional concern for germs, and had little recognition of the need for body privacy and autonomy. As a child she suffered from school phobia.
>
> Janet succeeded in completing graduate school as a social worker and married a research scientist. Her first child died of crib death. She entered a support group to subdue her guilt; her parents implied that the child's death was in part a result of carelessness on her part because of her failure to repeat their child-rearing practices. But Janet had determination and resiliency. She gave birth to a second child, a healthy boy, whom she described as physically healthy, socially adjusted, and performing well in school. Janet exercised great control in trying not to burden her son with the many anxieties she felt about his health. She currently sought therapy for panic that began several months after a hysterectomy for a malignant growth, which was successfully removed. Her anxiety would have seemed legitimate except that she admitted to a long history of panic attacks that predated her surgery. She also complained of chronic generalized anxiety between panic attacks. This anxiety was expressed in hypochondriacal concerns. She frequently examined herself for bruises, fearing that she might have scratched herself unknowingly and that a fatal infection would result. She could not refrain from demanding that her husband reassure her about her state of health. He bore her repetitive inquiries with great patience since she apologized for her compulsive requests. Her inability to contain her hypochondria increased her self-contempt. In the first session, Janet describes her interest in therapy.

> SESSION 1   *J:* I went to the other therapist for 18 months but nothing changed. I believe I can lick this. There was a woman in the hospital who was a faith healer. She told me I would recover from my cancer if I could get my mind healed. I survived that. I know I can get mental

control over the panic. But I need your help. You have to reach my unconscious mind.

Trance was utilized in the initial session of treatment to provide a dramatic experience of relaxation, comfort, safety and feeling of well-being. The patient was specifically encouraged to observe and value her own developing confidence in creating a rich trance experience. Janet mastered trance and breathing techniques over the next several months. She reported general improvement in her chronic anxiety state and less preoccupation with fear of dying. She suffered no full-blown panic episodes. The second phase of treatment provided Janet with insight into the etiology of her hypochondriasis in the family situation. Trance was utilized to give Janet an opportunity to visualize herself in new roles when interacting with her parents. Fears still actively associated with home visits, yielded to hypnotic relaxation and reconstruction of the typical sequence of parental advice giving and submission by the patient. Janet recreated, in hypnosis, her parents' controlling, intrusive behavior. With her new breathing techniques, she relaxed, shifted among her hypnotic images and redirected the outcomes to their provocative behavior.

In reality, she began to respond to her parents more assertively. She rediscovered a sense of personal power that had been present but often inaccessible to her. Hypnotherapy was also used to make changes in her body consciousness in order to address the deeper roots of her hypochondriasis. Although initial therapeutic gains included a reduction in her pattern of demanding constant reassurance from her husband that she was not dying, specific body preoccupations persisted. In trance, she discovered that she had an impaired body image. Since childhood, she had felt physically awkward and dissociated from body feelings and functions. She had felt particularly gauche and awkward during adolescence. Since her surgery, she felt betrayed by her body and distrustful of it. Yet at another deeper level, which she identified as an inner level of self, she could identify a sense of personal "wholeness" despite her hysterectomy.

Trance in the second stage of therapy was used to access this sense of wholeness. Therapy sessions included Janet's husband. His willingness to explore and experience a sense of self in trance permitted and affirmed similar efforts on her part. His positive affirming role in her life provided a clearer philosophical contrast to the belief system of her family.

Trance suggestions were simple and did not vary at Janet's own request. She wanted to become aware of and connect with her body and her inner feelings. Trance laid the foundation for strengthening a sense of self that could grow, develop, choose and react autonomously, supported by a sense of physical integrity.

Out of trance, Janet would contrast the deep positive feelings she was beginning to acquire through her body consciousness with negative memories from early in her childhood. In trance, she remembered a sense of mastery that had been interrupted and surpressed.

When Janet reoriented from trance, the therapist would often offer an intellectual focus for her conscious mind. Janet had an excellent background in history and literature. The therapist would refer to Descartes' utilization of his doubts about the existence of consciousness as the proof he found for the existence of a self that can doubt. The therapist referred to modern existentialist ideas about freedom and being. In doing so, the therapist indirectly directed Janet to dissociate herself from injurious parental injunctions.

These interventions, directed to her conscious awareness, were woven into trance inductions. Janet was able to experience a continuity with conscious cognitive aspects of her therapy experience while trance provided the opportunity to explore aspects of her unconscious functioning.

A significant incident during the second phase of therapy illustrates the integration of functional breathing patterns, utilization of body consciousness, and the exploration of specific aspects of a traumatic event related to individuation of the self.

After several months of treatment, Janet came into her therapy session in a state of agitation. She had detected some nipple soreness and could not rid herself of the idea that she might be developing breast cancer. She wanted to use trance to reduce her anxiety, to visualize her situation objectively, and to lessen her sense of stress, which she believed could trigger serious illness. In trance, she went back to a frequently repeated experience. To make sure she moved her bowels, both parents used to watch her on the training stool. Their lack of trust in her bodily functions gave rise to her hypochondriasis.

SESSION 20   *J:* I need to do deep trance . . . if ever I needed mental control it is right now.
   T: All right, I'll just talk to you a little now, and you can let yourself go into trance, anyway you like, just let that breathing come easily.

Now you know the question of mind and body goes back a long way in philosophy. You remember Descartes said 'I think, therefore I am.' He proved you have a self. And everyone in growing up finds that self, taking care to mind your body. Can you see or sense yourself?

[J. goes into trance.]

J: They are watching me.
T: What is happening?
J: They are watching me on the potty. But I won't go.
T: And now what's happening?
J: They're getting mad.
T: How are you feeling?

J: I don't care. I know I'm right. I'm wearing my yellow dress and I get up and walk away. I feel good. I don't have to panic. Just remember, call the doctor, tell him.

T: How do you feel now?

J: Free. Not guilty. I can decide, take care of my body, don't need to listen to them. Don't have to control my mind either. Very free . . . Really me.

The following week Janet reported that she had visited the doctor. He was objective and supportive of her concern, but found no need for tests. She was declared to be in good health.

Treatment Stage III

As the patient masters techniques for diffusing the symptoms of panic and gains some insight into the significant themes that may raise anxiety, he or she must consider termination. Often there is a recurrence of panic in this phase. Several interpretations are possible. Termination revives separation issues that have played a significant role in the lives of panic patients. Or, as with any behavior undergoing a process of extinction, spontaneous recovery occurs as a lawful phenomenon.

However, a more fundamental issue may be present. Intuitively, patients resist giving up a symptom that has had a significant function in the maintenance of their psychological equilibrium. Their "body consciousness" recognizes that anxiety, like physical pain, plays a role in human survival. Therefore, clinically, patients respond to a psychodynamic or existential interpretation of their resistance. They are reluctant to part with uncomfortable, frightening symptoms because they do not want to give up the choice of having panic. Panic has served them well. When they are deaf and blind to the distress (stress) in their lives, their somatic consciousness has given them a clear, albeit violent, signal. The signal is that the self has to take some action leading to change. One patient described panic as feedback to "stop," "look," and "listen" to the self. Panic is a message.

The third stage of therapy helps the patient accept the necessity and inevitability of anxiety. Patients recognize that they now command a wider range of responses to signals of anxiety that will usually protect them from a full-blown attack. If one should occur, it has a signal function and is not a sign of failure in control.

The following brief example shows how patients come to live with their special vulnerability to panic.

The Case of Harold   Harold had worked through problems that triggered panic. The death of significant others in his life had created a fear of closeness. He feared a heart attack for himself because of family history, but put himself under excessive pressure at work. A year in therapy had improved his mental status greatly; he had reached a point at which he was gaining a great deal of satisfaction from life. The therapist observed that he might now begin to rely on his unconscious to protect him from full-blown panic, since he was now protecting himself from stress consciously in so many effective ways. He responded by having three panic attacks that week, despite the fact that he was still taking medication at the same level as originally prescribed.

The therapist backtracked and suggested that panic was an important tool for survival and adaptation. "Panic," the therapist suggested, "informed his consciousness and probably should not be permanently abolished." Harold replied, "Yes, I don't want anyone to control my panic, not even my own unconscious. I want to have the choice of having panic or not, as long as I know I can control it before or after it starts. I'm not afraid of it anymore."

SUMMARY

Panic results from a maladaptive somatic defense against anxiety in vulnerable individuals. Patients can be taught to use rhythmic breathing succeeded by trance to limit uncomfortable, frightening physical symptoms. They learn to identify how themes of separation, individuation, rage, and death may trigger anxiety and lead to self-generated maladaptive body defenses of breath-holding and physical tension that culminate in seemingly spontaneous panic attacks. They learn to see anxiety as a psychologically valid representation of events that require adaptive responses. Panic is seen as having a meaningful existential function in the preservation of the self.

REFERENCES

Carter, P. M. (1983), The Parts Model, Unpublished doctoral dissertation, International College, Santa Monica, Calif.
Crowe, R. R., Noyes, R., Jr., Pauls, D. L., et al. (1983). A family study of panic disorder. *Archives of General Psychiatry, 40,* 1065–1069.
Descartes, R. (1968). *Meditations.* La Salle, Ill.: Open Court.

Diagnostic and Statistical Manual of Mental Disorders (3rd Ed., revised) (1987). Washington, D.C.: American Psychiatric Association.

Erickson, M. H. (1980). In E. L. Rossi (Ed.), *Collected Papers of Milton H. Erickson* (4 vols.). New York: Irvington.

Erickson, M. H., & Rossi, E. L., (1979). *Hypnotherapy*. New York: Irvington.

Freud, S. (1895). On the grounds for detaching a particular syndrome from neurasthenia under the description "Anxiety Neurosis." In *The Standard Edition* (Vol. III). London: Hogarth Press.

Freud, S. (1932). Anxiety and instinctual life. In *The Standard Edition* (1962), Vol. XXII. London: Hogarth Press.

Gilligan, S. G. (1987). *Therapeutic Trances*. New York: Brunner/Mazel.

Gorman, J. M., Liebowitz, M. R., & Klein, D. F. (1984). *Panic Disorder and Agoraphobia*. Kalamazoo, Mich.: The Upjohn Company.

Heidegger, M. (1949). *Existence and Being*. Chicago, Ill.: Henry Regnery Co.

Hollander, H., Holland, L., & Atthowe, J., Jr. (1988). Hypnosis: Innate ability or learned skills? Steve Lankton (Ed.) *Ericksonian Monographs no. 4*. New York: Brunner/Mazel.

Husserl, E. (1970). *The Crisis of European Sciences and Transcendental Phenomenology*. Evanston, Ill.: Northwestern University Press.

Kierkegaard, S. (1849). The sickness unto death. In R. S. Bretnall (Ed.), *S. Kierkegaard Anthology* (1936). Princeton, N.J.: Princeton University Press.

Klein, D. F., Zitrin, C. M., & Woerner, M. (1978). Antidepressants, anxiety, panic and phobias. In *Psychopharmacology: A Generation of Progress*. M. A. Lipton, A. D. Mascio, K. F. Killum (Eds.), pp. 1401–1410, New York: Raven Press.

Klein, D. F., Zitrin, C. M., Woerner, M. G., & Russ, D. C. (1983). Treatment of phobias. *Archives of General Psychiatry, 40* (2), 139–145.

Merleau-Ponty, M. (1962). *The Phenomenology of Perception*. New York: Humanities Press.

Pitts, F. N., Jr., & McClure, J. N., Jr. (1967). Lactate metabolism in neurosis. *New England Journal of Medicine, 277*, 1329–1336.

Potter, W. Z. (1986). Introduction: Norepinephrine as an "umbrella" neuromodulator. *Psychosomatics 27* (supplement), 5-9.

Sartre, J. P. (1947). *Existentialism*. New York: Philosophical Library.

Solomon, R. C. (Ed.) (1972). *Phenomenology and Existentialism*. New York: Harper & Row.

Stoeri, J. H. (1987). Psychoanalytic psychotherapy with panic states: A case presentation. *Psychoanalytic Psychology, 4* (2), 101–113.

Chapter 12

Anxiety as a Function of Perception: A Theory About Anxiety and a Procedure to Reduce Symptoms to Manageable Levels

David L. Higgins

David L. Higgins, M. A., is a psychotherapist in private practice in San Diego. He specializes in brief therapy for anxiety disorders. He has conducted workshops at three of the five San Diego Conferences on Strategic and Hypnotic Interventions and was a presenter at the Third International Congress on Ericksonian approaches.

THE NATURE OF ANXIETY

Anxiety is one of the most difficult psychological terms to define, yet it is one of the most widely used. In addition to specific disorders characterized by chronic and debilitating anxiety listed in the revised third edition of the *Diagnostic and Statistical Manual of Mental Disorders* (APA, 1987), including generalized anxiety disorder, panic disorder, phobias, obsessive-compulsive disorder, and post-traumatic stress disorder, anxiety is mentioned as a symptom of most other disorders. Symptoms of anxiety also accompany a large variety of physiological disturbances, such as withdrawal from substances (barbiturates, alcohol, amphetamines, caffeine, cocaine, nicotine, etc.) and organic anxiety syndrome (DSM-III-R, p. 113).

Popular views of anxiety compare it with fear. This position states that fear consists of four elements (Rosenhan & Seligman, 1984; Sue,

Sue, & Sue, 1986): (1) cognitively, the individual expects danger; (2) physiologically, the individual experiences internal and external changes as the autonomic nervous system begins to mobilize the body maximizing its chances for survival; (3) emotionally, the individual feels apprehension, terror, or dread; and (4) behaviorally, the individual tries to adapt to, or flee from, the feared situation (Selye, 1976; Rachman, 1978). The elements of anxiety, according to this position, are identical to those of fear except for the cognitive element: The anxious individual does not expect a specific danger but rather that "something bad" (unspecified) will happen (Rosenhan & Seligman, 1984). Whether referring to clinical studies or personal observations, theorists agree that anxiety is an "unpleasant state" linked to some source of psychological arousal. It involves an involuntary focus on the concepts of danger or threat (Beck & Emery, 1985) and a sense of uncertainty about the outcome of an event (Garber, Miller, & Abramson, 1980). It is important to note that the individual cannot always point to specific reasons for his or her anxiety-based symptoms (Santrock, 1983).

Although there are similarities in experiencing fear and anxiety, the symptoms are triggered in different ways. For example, in phobias and post-traumatic stress syndrome, there is a specific object or event that triggers the symptoms. In contrast, in panic disorder, which consists of one or more panic attacks, and in generalized anxiety disorder, which is chronic and generally less severe, no specific event or object appears to be the cause. In all anxiety disorders, the anxious feelings are disproportionate to the amount of danger objectively present (Rosenhan & Seligman, 1984).

In spite of the discomfort it causes, anxiety, like other generally negative experiences, has positive aspects. In manageable amounts, anxiety seems to be useful in motivating an individual to perform well (Lugo & Hershey, 1981), to limit excessive striving behavior that might prove harmful to the individual (Beck & Emery, 1985), and as a factor in determining social responsibility and conscience (Gerow, 1986).

Whereas anxious individuals may not be consciously aware of why they feel tense, they can usually distinguish among different levels of anxiety (Taylor, 1983). Low levels of anxiety may help to make us more alert and aware of what is going on. Low and moderate levels of anxiety generally produce higher scores on complex learning tasks and problem solving than do either high levels or no anxiety at all (Lugo & Hershey, 1981; Beck & Emery, 1985). Some anxiety appears to mobilize individuals psychologically and physically for effective action. Although an acceptable level of anxiety may lead to constructive changes in behavior, too much anxiety can cause negative emotional symptoms that can hinder a person's growth (Schwab et al., 1970). Thus, there appear to be optimal anxiety levels for functioning effectively depending on the level of demand and the context under consideration. However, it is often difficult for an individual to determine and then maintain the optimal level of anxiety for a particular event. The threshold between too much anxiety and not enough varies significantly from individual to individual.

The author's conceptualization of anxiety differentiates between the reaction to an actual threat of physical or psychological harm in the moment and an imagined threat that is based on expectations rooted in an internalized belief or value system (Yapko, 1985). The author believes that individuals often have an idea of why they are anxious, although they may not be able to categorize it consciously. Difficulty in recognizing and expressing the source of the anxiety frequently appears to come from a degree of awareness that there is no real threat, or from an internalized value judgment such as, "It is silly or crazy to be afraid of that." Such self-condemning thoughts may prevent the person from being able to directly identify the source of the anxious feelings in order to do something about them. For example, most individuals are, to some degree, afraid of speaking in public, of performing publicly, or of being tested. Such sources of anxiety are known, acceptable, and can easily be expressed. However, fears of abandonment or of losing one's support system are too broad and nonspecific for many adults to readily recognize and acknowledge. Without a specific association or source for the anxiety, it is experienced as "floating" or undefined.

Although some individuals seem to seek out anxiety-producing activities such as mountain climbing or sky diving, most persons experience anxiety, whatever the cause, as so unpleasant that they quickly try to get rid of it, or avoid it altogether in any way they can. However, in the effort they are apt to make things worse for themselves because of their focus on the unpleasant symptoms rather than recognizing and addressing the underlying cause(s).

One way an individual may attempt to reduce anxiety is to blame it on another (projection) and then expect him or her to do something to help make the anxious feelings go away. The anxious person may be hostile and even violent toward another at one moment, and then cling to that person as a source of security the next. If the anxious individual perceives the other person (mother, father, lover, boss) as responsible for both anxiety and psychological or physiological survival, then the degree to which this is seen as fact will determine the extent of his or her anxiety. If that person threatens to withdraw support if the anxious individual does not do as told, and if the anxious individual is not sure whether he or she can, the result is feeling a high level of distress and experiencing anxiety as intensely as if someone were actually threatening his or her life. Thus, an attempt to relieve anxiety by shifting its cause and cure to another person can result in making the symptoms even worse.

Often the feelings of anxiety are lessened or avoided through drugs, alcohol, sexual promiscuity, or other reactive behaviors (Lugo & Hershey, 1981). However, many positive or constructive behaviors are also motivated by a need to control or avoid the psychological discomfort of anxiety. Such behaviors are usually accompanied by the illusion that what one chooses to do will be so pleasant and so rewarding as to keep the anxiety permanently at bay. This, of course, is wishful thinking. Behaviors engaged in to allay anxiety, whether judged positively or negatively, may actually prove effective in reducing the feelings of anxiety. However, at the same time, they will prove to be either functional or dysfunctional in terms of how they affect the general well-being of the individual. In any case, the motivation to act is provided by a need to move away from the present or potential discomfort of anxiety. If successful in reducing the anxiety state, any avoidance behavior will be strengthened (Mischel, 1981) and may eventually become "the only way to be." Many behaviors can effectively relieve anxiety in one context, but exacerbate other situations (Beck & Emery, 1985) creating even more anxiety as the negative spiral tightens.

The Multiple Dimensions of Anxiety

As noted earlier in this chapter, most theories of anxiety suggest that it is experienced on physiological, behavioral, affective, and cognitive levels. The cognitive level in particular appears to be more influential in creating anxious feelings than the others (Beck & Emery, 1985). Since anxiety is experienced on multiple levels, it is a complex experience that can also be associated with other disorders, especially depression (Burns, 1980; Garber, Miller, & Abramson, 1980; Beck &

Emery, 1985). Anxiety seldom exists without at least some symptoms of depression and vice versa. Some symptoms are unique to anxiety, others to depression, but many are shared by both disorders (Garber, Miller, & Abramson, 1980). Further, chronic anxiety, because of its apparent uncontrollability (Garber et al., 1980), can lead to a client's becoming depressed (Beck & Emery, 1985).

Like depression, anxiety has a number of basic themes (Garber, Miller, & Abramson, 1980; Beck & Emery, 1985; Yapko, 1988). In his book *When Living Hurts: Directives for Treating Depression* (1988), Michael D. Yapko listed what he referred to as dimensions of depression. Anxiety can be described in the same way. These dimensions are as follows:

Physiological. Anxious individuals may suffer disturbances similar to depression in sleep, appetite, sex drive, and increased sympathetic nervous system arousal, as well as the more classic symptoms specific to anxiety, such as rapid heart beat, faintness, sweaty palms, itching, shaking hands, shallow or rapid breathing, fidgeting, eyelid twitching, loss of appetite, and frequent urination (Garber, Miller, & Abramson, 1980; Beck & Emery, 1985; DSM-III-R, 1987).

Cognitive. Anxious individuals may experience indecision, confusion and rumination, and be hypervigilant. They may be self-conscious, unable to control their thinking, experience blocking, and lose objectivity and perspective. Further, they may anticipate that something bad will happen either to themselves or to significant others. They may have a fear of losing control, a fear of not being able to cope, and they may experience repetitive fearful ideations (Beck & Emery, 1985; DSM-III-R, 1987).

Behavioral. Anxious individuals may commit aggressive or destructive acts, engage in some form of substance abuse, display a generalized impulsivity, indulge in acting-out or compulsive behavior, and behave perfectionistically or in ways that are inconsistent with personal values. They may experience restlessness, avoidance, speech disfluency, or be unable to relax. In addition, these individuals may display an array of other behaviors such as nail biting, pacing, knuckle cracking, hair pulling, or finger tapping (Beck & Emery, 1985; DSM-III-R, 1987).

Affective.   Some of the experiences similar to depression are loss of sense of humor, poor self-esteem, feelings of inadequacy, loss or avoidance of social attachments, and increased irritability and anger. In addition, anxious individuals may be edgy, impatient, experience uneasiness or a "wound up" feeling (Beck & Emery, 1985; DSM-III-R, 1987).

Relational.   In relationships anxious individuals may experience considerable difficulty with others. They are often highly reactive and inappropriately scapegoat themselves or others. Further relational difficulties can arise from excessive approval-seeking behaviors and, at the same time, being hypercritical of others. Often anxious persons have diffuse or rigid personal boundaries, a narrow range of skills in communicating, are incongruent in the way they relate to others, and often alternate between seeking and avoiding power (Beck & Emery, 1985; DMS-III-R, 1987; Yapko, 1988).

Symbolic.   Anxious individuals can experience illusions, fantasies, images, or recurring dreams that can seriously distort perceptions of reality. In addition, they may look for causes and interpretations of their anxiety to the symbolism or esoteric dogma of religions, cults, and "Life Change" seminars. The values encouraged by such organizations often become the basis for unrealistic comparisons and perfectionist ideas that exacerbate anxious individuals' attitudes that they are not capable of performing adequately in a number of life events (Garber, Miller, & Abramson, 1980; Beck & Emery, 1985).

Historical.   In cases of both depression and anxiety, there is often a history of specific personal failures, or inconsistent demands and expectations from significant others (Maslow, 1968). These clients often have a narrow range of what they feel are successful personal experiences to draw upon as a basis for judging their abilities to handle future events. Further, anxious individuals are often governed by a rigid, perfectionistic, parental value system that they have integrated as their own (Yapko, 1985). In addition, they may continuously experience what they perceive as uncontrollable aversive events (Beck & Emery, 1985).

When anxious individuals repeatedly encounter negative experiences perceived as unavoidable or out of control, they may feel helpless. Such cumulative experiences often trigger depression (Abramson, Seligman, & Teasdale, 1978; Garber, Miller, & Abramson, 1980). As a result, they may begin a pattern of avoiding similar contexts in which the outcomes could actually be controlled and are, in fact, well within the limits of their current skills (Beck & Emery, 1985). Avoidance or escape behaviors become strengthened when they are successful in reducing the anxiety state (Mischel, 1981), despite the fact that they may reinforce passivity.

Contextual. Perceived characteristics of an actual or imagined context can trigger feelings of anxiety. Predictable reactions of intense anxiety can become associated with specific persons or groups of people, objects, places, a variety of sensory stimulations, and particular times (i.e., early evenings, weekends, holidays). The anxious reactions appear to be constructed from fragments of memories or beliefs that relate in some negative way to the anticipated experience (Ellis, 1975; Burns, 1980; Beck & Emery, 1985).

THE ROLE OF PERCEPTION IN EXPERIENCING ANXIETY

The word "perceive" is defined in The Random House Dictionary (1980, p. 652) as follows: "1) to become aware of by means of the senses and 2) to understand or form an idea of." Perception is defined as: "1) the act of perceiving and 2) immediate or intuitive recognition" (p. 652). The act of perceiving may rely on information that is not factual, but is, instead, illusory.

To many psychotherapists, illusion is unacceptable. In their view, staying in touch with reality is the hallmark of mental health. (See Martin Seligman's comments on this subject in Chapter 1.). People who hold too many illusions, especially about important things, are viewed as less well adjusted (Taylor, 1983).

It is widely recognized that people's lives are often based on misconceptions and misperceptions. Attitudes, memories, and thoughts relating to future events are, to a large degree, illusory simply because they have not yet happened. Most of life is experienced either in memory or projections into the future based upon the past. Some illusions produce feelings of hope, happiness, or excitement; others produce anxious feelings and/or depression.

Dynamic Factors that Engender an Individual's Perceptions

From the cognitive position, a person experiences his or her life through positive or negative cognitive evaluations that may or may not be valid (Ellis & Harper, 1975; Beck, 1976; Burns, 1980; Beck & Emery, 1985).

Family Myths and Composite Judges.   Persons close to the anxious individual can have considerable effect on how he or she responds in any given setting (Schachter, 1964).

Many of a person's beliefs and values are handed down by significant adults in his or her life as they are growing up. In essence, the child accepts without question the opinions and beliefs of those who seem to have absolute power. After reaching adulthood, anxious individuals often reference childhood experiences and check how they are doing in a particular situation through comparisons with a personally created composite larger-than-life figure. This metaphorical internal judge is created from an endless array of beliefs, myths, opinions, "shoulds," "oughts," "cannots," "must nots," views of personal potentials, and shortcomings accumulated over the years from parents and other significant relationships (Ellis & Harper, 1975; Burns, 1980; Beck & Emery, 1985; Yapko, 1985).

Values.   Integrating the hodgepodge of unquestioned family myths and biased opinions, the anxious person will have built a set of values used to judge self and others as he or she moves from one context to another (Yapko, 1985). If the comparison is not favorable, the individual may experience considerable feelings of anxiety but may not be able to determine why (Beck & Emery, 1985).

Locus of Control.   A factor that plays a significant role in the experience of anxiety is whether an individual perceives the ability to control elements in anticipated circumstances (Garber, Miller, & Abramson, 1980). This perception appears to be largely influenced by the individual's evaluation of his or her previous performances in similar circumstances. It is also influenced by having internalized arbitrary evaluations offered by an accepted authority ("the composite judge") such as "you're stupid," "you'll never amount to anything," "you don't have the mental skills to succeed," or "people who feel that way are crazy."

If the individual has experienced success or simply believes that he or she will be capable of meeting a demand, i.e., has a sense of internal control (Yapko, 1985, 1988), then anxiety levels are apt to be lessened. Higher levels of anxiety generally occur when the individual feels that his or her fate is decided by the situation (externally controlled) (Garber, Miller, & Abramson, 1980; Beck & Emery, 1985).

Difficulty with Contingencies. After repeatedly experiencing acute anxiety in a variety of contexts, the individual may develop an overall sense of becoming less and less able to competently manage anticipated episodes. Anxious persons seem to have lost, or perhaps never have had, the ability to generalize their skills in one area to deal effectively with contingencies in another (Garber, Miller, & Abramson, 1980). As a result, they may require that everything be carefully planned or resolved to the last detail, before they will take the risk of starting any new undertaking.

A Distorted Sense of Responsibility and Control. Clients who suffer from anxiety often seem to feel that they should be able to do something about almost everything that happens in their world, and, in some cases, even in the world at large.

Usually related to this distorted sense of responsibility is their belief that were they not so inadequate, they could do something about the issue at hand. Thus, they often feel guilt because some personal myth tells them that they should be more effective (Ellis & Harper, 1975; Beck & Emery, 1985). There is often little awareness that events frequently happen by chance, or are beyond the influence of any single individual.

A Distorted Sense of Personal Ability. Especially when working with anxious children, the author has observed that they often have little or no sense of mastery over the elements in their environment. It is frequently true that they have minimal control over what happens to them, and thus they have not yet developed a repertoire of skills to handle changing situations effectively. As a result, they are often frustrated and frightened by how powerless they really are.

This childhood feeling of powerlessness and ineptitude is easily accessed and it may serve as the referent from which the anxious adult perceives an inability to manage an anticipated situation. As a result, resources are perceived to be either limited or nonexistent. A common lament of these individuals is, "I have never made good things happen. I can't make good things happen now, and I never will be able to make good things happen."

As a defense against the discomfort of anxiety, individuals may develop an attitude of arrogance or bravado that places them in situations that are beyond their immediate capabilities. This can set them up for repeated failures, further anxiety, and often depression as well. (Even individuals who enjoy considerable financial and professional successes in their chosen fields may experience considerable daily anxiety over the possibility of being exposed as fraudulent or not as effective as their public image portrays them to be) (Clance, 1985).

THE PERCEPTION MODEL OF ANXIETY

According to Paul Watzlawick (1984), human beings live life in an "as if" world. He predicted that by behaving "as if" a reality exists or will exist, it will come to exist. Anxiety seems to be most often felt when the person references an unsuccessful past experience and projects those results onto the outcome of a future event. Confidence and anxiety are each the result of personal perceptions—believed in imaginings—of how an individual will perform in a specific future context. If one imagines doing well in a given context, then feelings of confidence, comfort, and healthy anticipation result. If, on the other hand, an individual evaluates himself or herself in a negative way and has images of performing in an undesirable manner, he or she may experience considerable anxiety and display a number of behaviors intended to reduce the discomfort (Beck & Emery, 1985).

Individuals construct images of themselves both as they are, and as they ideally should be (Rogers, 1961; Maslow, 1968). Such images are formed through an accumulation of social values and from observing the results of personal performances in a variety of contexts. In addition, people have a tendency to create an image of what significant others think they are, and should be (Morris, 1985).

Based on this premise, feelings of anxiety can be created by making a comparative evaluation of those three perceptions (i.e., who they are, who they should be, and what others think they should be) while imagining their future performance in a particular context or in relationship to others. The comparisons are among: (1) how individuals imagine they will perform; (2) how individuals perceive they should perform; and (3) how individuals perceive others think they should perform. The degree of anxiety experienced, from mild to severe, appears to depend on two further evaluations: (1) the degree of separation between the above three perceptions, and (2) how crucial the results of the anticipated performance will be to their psychological or physiological well-being.

If individuals conclude that their present abilities compare unfavorably with what they think they should be, or what others think they should be, they will experience some degree of anxiety. The severity of anxious feelings depends on how badly individuals expect they will do in a situation, how much control they will have in a particular event, and how critically they will be judged afterward. The second factor affecting the degree of anxiety has to do with their anticipation of harmful consequences in a dangerous situation. These fears are relatively primitive and are closely related to the person's automatic protective functions (Beck & Emery, 1985). An individual may determine that a situation poses too much of a threat to his or her psychological or physical well-being and therefore decide against participating in it. This determination may or may not be valid, perhaps based on superstition or past unsuccessful experiences rather than on immediate, rational examination of the activity, the place, or the circumstances. If the outcome of the episode is evaluated to be a matter of "life or death" and there is no perceived ability to assert control over the situation, people will experience severe anxiety, even panic (Beck & Emery, 1985; Garber, Miller, & Abramson, 1980).

This simplified concept of anxiety has proved, in the author's practice, to be easily understood by anxious individuals. Explaining anxiety in this way helps to take some of the mystery out of clients' feelings, and gives them a sense of direction. It is made clear from the outset that a change in the individual's perception of personal abilities, personal expectations, and others' expectations, or the importance of the outcome, will result in a change in the level of anxiety.

Initial clinical focus, then, is on helping clients to reduce their feelings of anxiety to a manageable level by (1) increasing their capability more accurately to evaluate their ability to perform, and then to take necessary, reasonable action; (2) reevaluating the importance of how others judge them in each context; and (3) reevaluating the significance of the outcome of each event.

PERCEPTION AS AN INTERVENTION

Anxious clients often look for change in the wrong places because their experiences and values have incorrectly prescribed where and how to look. As they enter therapy, they may imagine having to perform in new contexts confined by rigid values, old information, and previously ineffective techniques. The client is guided in the direction of change, is offered life-enhancing tools, and is encouraged to look for changes in a different place and in a different way than in the past.

Goal: The overall objective in the perception model is to empower clients to use better what they already know, and use better skills they already have. In a manner consistent with this objective, clients are offered a selection of alternate views and abilities that they can personalize and add to their existing resources.

The initial goal of treatment is to help decrease feelings of anxiety to a tolerable level as soon as possible. Longer-term therapeutic goals are to provide a series of gentle, gradual changes so the client feels safe and in control while letting go of familiar, if not effectual, values and techniques (Yapko, 1985). To this end, hypnotic, strategic, and cognitive approaches are directed in the course of therapy toward the many levels and aspects of anxiety previously discussed.

A Place to Start

Human beings prefer nonambiguous to ambiguous situations and have been found to cope better with painful or threatening stimuli when they feel that they can exercise some degree of control, rather than be passive or helpless victims (Garber, Miller, & Abramson, 1980; Rubin & McNeil, 1985). The fact that events tend to be less anxiety provoking when the individual can, in some way, control them implies that an effective place to start is to give clients an uncomplicated technique whereby they may begin to assume control over some aspect of their anxiety. This technique would be aimed at an achievable target—one that a client can immediately conceive of as possible.

The process described in the following is directed primarily at the cognitive facet of anxiety and has proved to be effective in the early stages of treatment. Although other facets of anxiety discussed previously are addressed in later sessions as well, this early intervention helps to give the client an immediate sense of control and considerable relief of troublesome symptoms. Thus encouraged, the client is more easily engaged in treatment.

A Specific Intervention: An Empowering Message

This intervention consists of three parts: (1) information gathering and planning, (2) an initial trance (relaxation and reframing), and (3) a didactic explanation of the perception theory of anxiety and the perception alteration process.

Identifying What the Client Perceives.   The initial step in this process is to learn from the client, "This is what I perceive to be true about me and my world, but this is what I want to be different about me and my world. This is how I have previously tried and failed, and this is the amount of energy I am now willing to invest." Since an individual reacts to each experience with an appraisal of his or her ability to cope, and that evaluation translates into self-confidence or a sense of vulnerability (Beck & Emery, 1985), this is an important piece of information as it helps to determine what the client perceives as his or her strengths and weaknesses.

Furthermore, it is important to understand when developing a treatment plan that clients' established beliefs, values, and rituals clearly affect their perspective on a particular course of action. What one individual might consider an exciting new opportunity may seem an intolerable waste of energy to another because the anticipated payoff is not considered valuable enough to invest the effort. This is often particularly true when the client has been managing his or her feelings of anxiety with some kind of short-term coping mechanism. In clinical practice, clients regularly present promiscuous sex and a variety of readily accessible social drugs, including alcohol and cigarettes, as tools they have used to reduce their feelings of anxiety. It is important for the client to know that there is little the clinician can immediately offer to compete with those activities for intensity, swiftness, and sureness of effect. However, hypnosis and other strategic techniques can, in time, help develop the skills and opportunities for the individual to experience comparatively acceptable highs and lows, without the expense and the pain caused by drugs or other dysfunctional behaviors.

The First Trance.   After gathering as much information from clients about their cognitive style, developmental background, world, and self-views (Yapko, 1985, 1988) as seems comfortable during a conversational inquiry, the author usually continues the first session by inducing a trance. The process is framed as a hypnosis training session that will familiarize the client with the sound of the author's voice and any changes that might occur in the client's experience as a result of trance. The primary purposes of the first trance process are to have clients experience relaxation and discover their ability to control how they feel, even if only for 20 to 30 minutes, and to make good use of any client expectations that something positive will happen by experiencing trance (Yapko, 1984). The secondary purposes are to (1) seed ideas about the possible existence of alternatives that the client may not be aware of at the time, but may effortlessly discover at some unexpected moment; (2) build an expectancy that internal resources will be rediscovered even though they may have been forgotten or overlooked; (3) suggest that a sense of control over the smallest, least significant segment of life is a very good indicator that things are not completely out of control—a center from which to expand skills; (4) suggest that since balance and rhythm seem to exist in all segments of nature, then perhaps if the client slows down and stops for just a while, it may be possible to experience a similar balance and rhythm in his or her life; and (5) reframe anxiety as a creative energy that is essential for survival. The reframing of anxiety continues in the following vein:

> And like any other energy, too much can cause some damage . . . it needs to be metered carefully to be used most effectively . . . in order to be this anxious, you must be a very creative person . . . dull people are hardly ever anxious . . . isn't it nice to know that you have so much creative energy at your personal disposal . . . you can choose a level of anxiety that is just right for you for now . . . put the rest somewhere safe in your imagination . . . reserve it for later . . . in case you need it . . . you will soon learn just the right amount . . . to use in all kinds of different undertakings . . .

"Wonderings" are presented hypnotically that refer to the duration and intensity of the client's feelings of anxiety, ". . . and I wonder how much anxiety is just enough for you . . . and I wonder how much anxiety is too much . . . I wonder how long you have to feel anxious before an event in order to control the outcome," and so forth. The trance session usually lasts 20 to 30 minutes, and an audiotape is made of the process. The individual is instructed to listen to the tape at least twice a day in a restful place as a way of developing greater familiarity with trance. The client is instructed not to expect any overwhelming results, "maybe just a couple of unanticipated changes or personal discoveries." Before ending the session, the client is told that during the next session he or she will be taught a little bit about how and why some people experience feelings of anxiety, often for no apparent reason.

It is possible that a client may come to therapy in such an agitated state that he or she might not be able to concentrate sufficiently to experience even a light trance. If the clinician determines that this is the case, trying to induce a formal trance would be contraindicated. An unsuccessful attempt to experience trance at this juncture could exacerbate the client's feelings of not being able to do anything about the feelings. However, the procedure may be presented in a calm, absorbing conversational form with positive results.

Explanation and Perception Alteration.   A portion of the second session consists of explaining the perception theory of anxiety to the client. "This is why some individuals experience anxiety . . . if this theory were to apply to you, how would you describe the reason you feel anxious?" The author uses original materials that visually illustrate an anxiety-producing perception, a comfort-producing perception, and a perception of what would be ideal. During this discussion, ~~Technique~~ the client is asked to describe how he or she visualizes events. Since undesirable visual images often stimulate verbal cognitions resulting in increased anxiety, and the identification of this cognitive process can help clients to gain mastery (Beck & Emery, 1985), clients are asked to describe where they experience pleasant visualizations, where they experience worrisome visualizations, when they are feeling anxious, and where they visualize the circumstances occurring that cause those feelings. This process helps the client become aware that some kind of imagining process often precedes emotion, whether happy or sad, even when it is so rapid that it is not possible to define it consciously (Beck & Emery, 1985).

There are numerous facets of anxiety on a number of different dimensions at which therapy may be effectively directed. The next stage of the technique is intended to help the client experience change by inducing images that will facilitate more effective behavior or thought patterns (Beck & Emery, 1985). The client is asked to visualize a situation in which he or she feels comfortable, in other words, with little or no anxiety. While visualizing the situation in an entirely individual way, the client is asked a series of questions: "How do you view yourself in the situation?" "Where do you think you should be?" "How should you be performing?" "How much does what others think matter?" "How important is the outcome of the event?" "What do you think will happen if you fail perfectly?" "What are the results that previously have happened, or what is expected to happen as a result of the events of this pleasant, anxiety-free visualization?" Finally, they are asked, "Which of those perceptions seems to be most important in deciding that the event is safe and pleasurable." The client is then asked, "If that situation were to become anxiety-provoking, which of those perceptions would change first?"

The following is an example of a very simple yet effective process to help the individual experience a greater degree of control over his or her anxious feelings. It can be used as a metaphor and is described to the client or included as a segment of a formal trance process. It is begun by asking the client to visualize the event with a gauge or dial in the upper-right-hand corner of the visualization area that reads from 1 to 10, with 1 representing absolute comfort and 10 panic. The session continues with such suggestions and questions as:

> "You can find tolerable, manageable, just right amounts of anxiety that would be somewhere in the middle . . . of course, you have to determine that measure for yourself . . . notice your feelings and adjust the dial to match . . . where on the dial or gauge does it read you anxiety to be? How much anxiety does the dial register when the process is going just right? Now focus on the perception that you think is the most important in this visualization. What does the dial read now? Change it back . . .

"Dial of Anxiety"

The process continues until the client can control, in his or her imagination, how the dial reads by changing one perception of the event.

When the client is feeling comfortable with the process, the instructions continue:

> Now visualize, in the same manner, a scene or event in which you feel just a little anxious . . . adjust the dial to match your

> feelings . . . notice the reading on the dial when your anxiety is manageable for you . . . now go back and visualize the pleasant scene . . . adjust the dial again . . . now turn the dial up, just past the tolerable mark and notice your feeling as you visualize the scene . . . now adjust it down to comfortable . . . notice changes in feeling . . .

The client is asked to go back and forth from a pleasant visualization to a moderately uncomfortable one, repeating the process until he or she discovers the ability to adjust the amount of anxiety associated with the visualized event simply by mentally adjusting the dial or gauge.

After a minimal amount of practice with the procedure, clients have learned to adjust the amount of anxiety they feel about a particular event by visualizing it at full anxiety and then mentally turning down the dial to what they have determined to be a tolerable level.

This particular procedure is most effective with people who can easily visualize. Unfortunately, not all anxious clients are able voluntarily to control their visualizing or to focus on any one thought for very long (Beck & Emery, 1985). If the clinician senses that this is the case, then the specific process described above may be altered without losing its impact. One way to do this would be to help clients access and describe metaphorically in their own words how they experience anxiety and then to determine to what degree they are experiencing it. The suggestion would be for them to experiment with their own methods of taking control of the unpleasant feelings, using the dial technique as an example of a metaphor that works for some people.

As skill in being able to consciously alter anxiety increases, clients also learn to not be anxious about feeling anxious. As they become more comfortable with independently altering feelings, they are taught to invite the discomfort in, measure it, time it, and get to know it in detail, rather than constantly trying to avoid it. This process has proved effective in giving clients a sense of control over their anxiety at a very early stage of treatment.

Once clients have been able to experience a degree of control over the immediate symptoms, they are more capable of working with some of the other more psychodynamic aspects of their anxiety such as the role of their overall self-confidence in determining their anxiety; how a change in context from private to public or from one public context to another can affect their evaluation of themselves; how automatic thinking based on perfectionistic values and experiences can develop a theme of physical or psychological vulnerability (Beck & Emery, 1985); how their cognitions, both in verbal form and visual images, often center on some theme of personal or psychological catastrophe; and how their concept of "inadequate performance" in a variety of situations often makes them feel vulnerable to negative evaluation and rejection.

Therapy continues by gently confronting and replacing clients' dysfunctional perceptions about themselves and their abilities in a variety of contexts. They are guided both to gain an understanding of how others evaluate them and to alter the importance of those evaluations. Finally, they are taught how they may more realistically evaluate the anticipated psychological or physical outcome of specific events.

CONCLUSION

The perception-based theory of anxiety has proved to be an effective way for clients to better understand their feelings of anxiety and how they evaluate themselves in a variety of contexts. The easily mastered, yet powerful, beginning exercises based on the theory are first steps in helping clients to recognize alternative ways of perceiving their world (which underlies their anxiety), and to gain a new sense of mastery over some contextual contingencies.

Though it is not intended to be an instant anxiety cure in itself, the author has observed that clients exhibiting a variety of anxiety-related symptoms such as smoking, use of mind-altering drugs, compulsive overeating, compulsive sex, performance anxiety, floating anxiety, and phobias have benefited from this easily mastered initial procedure. It is seen as an early step compatible with longer-term therapeutic processes that may involve reframing or reconstructing clients' lifelong values, accessing clients' existing resources, and helping them to build new, more effective, relevant skills.

REFERENCES

Abramson, L. Y., Seligman, M. E. P., & Teasdale, J. (1978). Learned helplessness in humans: Critique and reformulation. *Journal of Abnormal Psychology, 87*, 32–46.
American Psychiatric Association (1987). *Diagnostic and Statistical Manual of Mental Disorders* (3rd ed., rev.). Washington, D.C.: American Psychiatric Press.
Beck, A. T. (1976). *Cognitive Therapy and Emotional Disorders*. New York: International Universities Press.
Beck, A. T., & Emery, G. (1985). *Anxiety Disorders and Phobias: A Cognitive Perspective*. New York: Basic Books.

Burns, D. (1980). *Feeling Good: The New Mood Therapy*. New York: Morrow.

Clance, P. (1985). *The Impostor Phenomenon*. New York: Bantam Books.

Ellis, A., & Harper, R. A. (1975). *A New Guide to Rational Living*. Englewood Cliffs, N.J.: Prentice-Hall.

Garber, J., Miller, S. M., & Abramson, L. Y. (1980). On the distinction between anxiety and depression: Perceived control, certainty, and probability of goal attainment. In J. Garber & M. E. P. Seligman (Eds.), *Human Helplessness: Theory and Applications* (pp. 131–169). Orlando, Fla.: Academic Press.

Gerow, J. R. (1986). *Psychology: An Introduction*. Glenview, Ill. Scott, Foresman.

Lugo, J. O., & Hershey, G. L. (1981). *Living Psychology*. New York: Macmillan.

Maslow, A. H. (1968). *Toward the Psychology of Being*. New York: Van Nostrand Reinhold.

Mischel, W. (1981). *Introduction to Personality*. San Francisco: Holt, Rinehart & Winston.

Morris, C. G. (1985). *Psychology: An Introduction*. Englewood Cliffs, N.J.: Prentice-Hall.

Rachman, S. J. (1978). *Fear and Courage*. New York: Freeman.

Random House Dictionary, The (1980). New York: Ballantine Books.

Rogers, C. (1961). *On Becoming a Person*. Boston: Houghton Mifflin.

Rosenhan, D. L., & Seligman, M. E. P. (1984). *Abnormal Psychology*. New York: Norton.

Rubin, Z., & McNeil, E. B. (1985). *Psychology: Being Human* (4th ed.). New York: Harper & Row.

Santrock, J. W. (1983). *Life-Span Development*. Dubuque, Iowa.: Wm. C. Brown.

Schachter, S. (1964). The interaction of cognitive and physiological determinants of emotional state. In L. Berkowitz (Ed.), *Advances in Experimental Social Psychology*, vol. 1. New York: Academic Press.

Schwab, J. J., McGinnis, N. H., Norris, L. B., & Schwab, R. B. (1970). Psychosomatic medicine and the contemporary social scene. *American Journal of Psychiatry*, 126, 108–118.

Selye, H. (1976). *The Stress of Life*. (2nd ed.). New York: McGraw-Hill.

Sue, D., Sue, D. W., & Sue, W. (1986). *Understanding Abnormal Behavior*. Boston: Houghton Mifflin.

Taylor, S. E. (1983, Nov.). Adjustment to threatening events. *American Psychologist*, 1161–1173.

Watzlawick, P. (1984). *The Invented Reality*. New York: Norton.

Yapko, M. D. (1984). *Trancework: An Introduction to Clinical Hypnosis*. New York: Irvington.

Yapko, M. D. (1985). The Erickson hook: Values in Ericksonian approaches. In J. K. Zeig (Ed.), *Ericksonian Psychotherapy* (Vol. I, pp. 266–281). New York: Brunner/Mazel.

Yapko, M. D. (1986). Depression: Diagnostic frameworks and therapeutic strategies. In M. D. Yapko (Ed.), *Hypnotic and Strategic Interventions: Principles and Practice*. New York: Irvington.

Yapko, M. D. (1988). *When Living Hurts: Directives for Treating Depression*. New York: Brunner/Mazel.

Application: sign. of thinking process (p. 248)

Caused: p 251-254   *p. 254 (3 perceptions)*

Chapter 13

Trance-Forming Anxiety: Hypnotic and Strategic Approaches to Treatment

Christopher J. Beletsis

Christopher J. Beletsis, Ph.D., has been conducting training programs on Erickson's approaches to hypnosis and therapy for the past nine years. He presented at the Second and Third International Congresses on Ericksonian Approaches to Hypnosis and Psychotherapy in Phoenix in 1983 and 1986, and has been a faculty member of the Erickson Institute of San Diego's conferences on Hypnotic and Strategic Interventions in 1985, 1986, 1988, and 1989.

Beletsis has two published chapters, one entitled "An Ericksonian Approach in the Treatment of Alcoholism," and the other entitled "Balance: A Central Principle of the Ericksonian Approach." He is currently finishing editing a book by Drs. Gilligan and Carter entitled The Winds of Change.

In addition to his teaching and writing activities, Beletsis maintains a private practice in San Diego.

Anxiety disorders are the most frequently found disorders in the general population. They are described at length in the revised third edition of the *Diagnostic and Statistical Manual of Mental Disorders* (American Psychiatric Association, 1987), which notes that, "The characteristic features of this group of disorders are symptoms of anxiety and avoidance behavior" (p. 235). Most individuals experience occasional anxiety and avoidance, but are able to manage them without much difficulty. However, many people suffer acute episodes of intense anxiety (panic disorders) or chronic feelings of anxiety and worry (generalized anxiety disorders). These and other anxiety disorders are characterized by unrealistic anxiety and worry, and an array of physical symptoms such as trembling, palpitations, chest pains, shortness of breath, and difficulty sleeping (American Psychiatric Association, 1987, p. 238). Anxiety disorders can cause severe problems and limit one's experience, thus indicating a need for psychotherapy.

Hypnosis has particular value as a therapeutic tool for treating anxiety disorders due to its focus on relaxation and its ability to shift attention to more pleasant experiences. Hypnosis is also a high learning state since the individual in trance tends to be very focused and absorbed, yet operating with little or no conscious interference. By facilitating easier and fuller access to experiences, trance greatly aids in the development and integration of resources and changes. Milton H. Erickson, M.D., a pioneer in the field of hypnotherapy, contributed greatly to the development of short-term strategic approaches to therapy (Haley, 1973). Strategic therapy complements the use of hypnosis, and is especially effective for treating anxiety disorders because of its solution-oriented approach to problems, and the more active role assumed by the therapist.

The purpose of this chapter is to present a conceptual framework for the treatment of anxiety. The model focuses on five hypnotic and strategic approaches effectively used by the author in the treatment of anxiety: (1) guided self-hypnotic processes (e.g., a tool for relaxation, learning, and integration); (2) developing resources (e.g., comfort, security, confidence, etc.); (3) paradoxical strategies (e.g., prescribing or encouraging symptoms); (4) reframing (e.g., protection, attention, motivation, etc.); and (5) belief system/self-image changes (e.g., "It's okay to relax," or "I deserve to relax"). Specific applications of these techniques will be illustrated by case examples.

It seems important to clarify at the outset some of the assumptions made in this chapter. First, anxiety is seen as an active, ongoing self-hypnotic process. Self-hypnosis is one's ability to develop and become absorbed in a particular experience. The trances we develop may be generative, relaxing, and therapeutic, or they may be limiting and self-devaluing (Gilligan, 1987). Many clients suffering from anxiety disorders have unrealistic and excessive worry, which they make increasingly worse through negative thoughts and internal images. As the feelings of anxiety increase, the negative thoughts and images continue and the negative self-hypnotic cycle perpetuates itself. Thus, the experience of "anxiety" refers to a complex set of internal experiences a person is having. It is important to find out specifically how this unique client experiences anxiety. Questions that elicit personal experience and meaning are: What triggers the anxiety? Are the triggers internal or external? How is the anxiety maintained? What, if anything, is its positive value or function? What visual images are seen right before and during episodes of feeling anxious? What is the client saying to himself or herself? Where does the client feel anxious? Where does he or she never feel anxious? What does the client believe about anxiety? What behaviors does it motivate? What does it stop the client from doing? This information helps the therapist develop treatment approaches that respect and utilize the client's idiosyncrasies.

Second, it is assumed that the client can learn to recognize and interrupt the triggers and symptoms of anxiety at an early stage. Such information can be utilized to lead to some other, more desirable response. People can learn to shift the locus of control (Yapko, 1988) of anxiety from external (i.e., feeling out of control and perceiving that anxiety happens *to* them) to internal (i.e., recognizing that they have choices and that they can influence the subjective state they are in).

Third, the symptoms of anxiety can be accepted and utilized by the therapist as a basis for trance development and therapy. This principle of utilization is central to hypnotic and strategic approaches, and is elaborated upon in later sections of the chapter especially in the section on paradoxical strategies.

The remainder of this chapter focuses on the five approaches delineated earlier as the basis for treating anxiety.

GUIDED SELF-HYPNOTIC PROCESSES

Clients can be guided through a self-hypnotic process in order to develop a relaxed state during the session. Upon reorienting from trance, clients often report that it was the most relaxed they have been for awhile, but may complain that they cannot become that relaxed on their own. Thus, self-hypnosis can be taught as a tool for clients to use outside of therapy to relax, shift their attention to pleasant experiences, and develop a more resourceful state of being. As clients learn to use this self-hypnotic process effectively, they develop a greater awareness of their breathing, degree of body comfort, and internal images and dialogue. They can then begin to use those new awarenesses as a basis for self-hypnosis and thus help themselves intervene when anxiety begins to develop.

One can begin guiding clients through the self-hypnotic process (Grinder & Bandler, 1981) by the second or third session. Once they have learned how to develop comfortable trance experiences in the safety of the therapy session, they can begin practicing at home. This process fosters their independence, and promotes the feeling that they can influence their experience in a positive fashion. Hypnotic work can then be more easily used during later phases of therapy.

The following is a step-by-step set of instructions for the client of the self-hypnotic process that the author uses.

1. Find a safe, comfortable place where you will not be disturbed. It is best if your entire body, including your head, is supported by a chair, couch, or pillows.
2. Set a time limit of up to 30 minutes. Use an alarm clock or have someone check on you so that you do not have to worry about the time as you enjoy the self-hypnotic trance.
3. Identify and consider your goal. What would you like to achieve during this time? Start out with relaxation. Once you have developed the skill of self-hypnosis, you can use it to assist you in other ways, such as developing such resources as self-appreciation, confidence, or creativity.
4. Begin the self-induction by fixing your eyes on one spot. Next focus on your breathing, allowing yourself to breath fully and freely, and make any necessary adjustments of your body for more comfort. Then make statements to yourself of whatever you are aware of seeing, hearing, or feeling, such as: "I am aware of the sounds in the background; I'm aware of my body being supported by the chair; I can feel my feet resting on the floor; I'm aware of the tension in my chest; I'm aware of the color of the wall," and so on. Make three statements of things you see, three statements of things you feel, and three statements of things you hear. Then make two statements of each, then one statement of each, and then close your eyes. With your eyes closed, repeat the process of three-two-one statements of what you see, hear, and feel.
5. Allow your body to rest and your mind to wander as if in a dream. If your goal is to relax, you may imagine a very peaceful scene or

remember forgotten pleasant experiences. If your goal is to feel confident, you may imagine times in your past when you could feel confident. The more you practice, the easier it will become.

6. Come back again by making statements about what you are aware of, or by hearing the alarm clock and feeling awake and refreshed, as if after a good rest.

Self-hypnosis is a skill that can be developed by anyone, but needs to be practiced regularly. Guiding clients through several trance experiences, as well as making a tape of an induction for them to use at home, helps develop their skill and comfort about going into trance, and thus makes it easier for them to use it outside the therapeutic context.

Breathing fully, freely, and regularly is very important. When intense fear or anxiety occurs, breathing becomes restricted and irregular, and the chest becomes tight. Learning to breath deeply helps ensure relaxation, learning, and integration.

The client's ability to breathe and develop a pleasant, relaxing trance is one resource he or she may use when beginning to feel anxious. Developing other resources is also valuable in the treatment of anxiety. This is discussed in the next section.

DEVELOPING RESOURCES

Erickson's therapeutic approaches were based on an assumption that clients have sufficient resources to generate meaningful changes (Gilligan, 1987), but that those resources or choices are dissociated from the context(s) in which they are needed. One of the basic goals of therapy is to develop resources and integrate them into the problem context(s) so that clients can experience more options in their lives and, thus, more of a connection to their potential wholeness. "Resources," as used here, refers to generative abilities and feelings that individuals have but are not always capable of using. Examples include confidence, comfort, assertiveness, security, and self-esteem.

Erickson (1980) noted that "The importance of trance induction as an educational procedure in acquainting patients with their latent abilities has been greatly disregarded" (pp. 36–37). In discussing the value of using trance for developing and integrating resources, Erickson continued:

The induction and maintenance of a trance serve to provide a special psychological state in which patients can reassociate and reorganize their inner psychological complexities and utilize their own capacities in a manner in accord with their own experiential life. (p. 38)

The first step is to identify a resource to develop.

In treating anxiety, it is valuable to help clients develop an experience of "safety and security." This resource, although general and seemingly basic, is very useful for facilitating therapy, and is often desperately needed by clients. It is especially effective for working with chronically anxious and fearful clients, since they frequently have no apparent frame of reference for "safety" and may not have experienced much comfort. Safety and security are a primary complementary experience of anxiety and fear, thus helping to provide the supportive balance (Beletsis, 1986) needed by the client to fully explore the anxiety.

Safety and security need to be developed both externally and internally, and tend to go hand in hand, each making the other easier to experience. A secure environment, meaning a safe, comfortable office and the establishment of a trusting therapeutic relationship, is beneficial in three main ways. First, it fosters the development of rapport between the therapist and client, creating a relationship in which the client can be open and honest. Second, it creates a context in which the client can develop an internal experience of "safety." And finally, it focuses the therapy on building resources and solutions.

One way to begin developing safety and security is to ask the client questions that evoke the experience. These include: When did you feel safe and secure in the past? What seems to be getting in the way of having that experience currently? What would it be like if you could feel safe and secure now? What images, feelings, sensations, sounds, smells, posture, or beliefs are associated with safety and security? What are some of the ways that you could express or have expressed feeling safe and secure? Asking about the opposite of feeling safe and secure can also help to define the resource.

Using trance to develop experiences more fully is very beneficial, and is accomplished through the increased absorption and sharper focus on aspects of a particular experience. These include the richness of sensory details, the increased ability of the client to shift into the past or future, and the increased responsiveness and creativity that result from the unconscious processing of suggested experiences.

One client with whom the author worked had been diagnosed as having AIDS. He was understandably very anxious and fearful, but anxiety greatly diminished his ability to deal effectively with his relationships, daily activities, and even his own health. Additionally, a concern was that the resulting stress would further supress his immune system functioning (Siegel, 1986). After the first interview, the next couple of sessions involved helping him develop an experience of safety and security in trance, a state that he could then elicit self-hypnotically when he needed to. There were several steps in this process. First, resources of safety and security were created in the office by using pillows for support and warmth, and by having him choose a comfortable place for both of us. Next, he was asked several general questions, similar to those mentioned above, about his experience of safety and security. He was focused in detail on an especially safe and secure experience in his past. He described a special room with a very comfortable couch, a warm blanket, and a beautiful view of a garden. The room was in a relative's home in a different country, and he reported feelings of love and support in connection with his relative. While in trance, he experienced being in the room and feeling very safe and relaxed, and he began to remember other details about which he had forgotten. The experience was developed and strengthened in further trance sessions and discussions, until he eventually reported that he could elicit that relaxed state easily. This gave him "a place to go to relax" when he began feeling anxious, and it helped improve the quality of his life.

Integration of resourceful behaviors, attitudes, feelings, and beliefs is an essential aspect of psychotherapy, and may demonstrate or determine its lasting effectiveness. Often, clients have an important insight or they acknowledge that a particular change or additional resource would benefit them greatly, but then fail to use what they have identified as helpful as a natural and lasting part of their experience and identity outside the therapeutic context.

Integration is a natural process in which resources and learnings are consolidated, leading to increased feelings of self-worth and an increased ability to achieve one's goals. With guidance, support, and practice, changes that seem difficult to make at first become increasingly easy until they are natural, flowing, and automatic. Erickson often used stories during trance to evoke "early learning set" experiences (Erickson & Rossi, 1979), such as learning to count and learning the alphabet, to remind clients' unconscious minds that they have the ability to learn and change even though it may seem difficult.

Once experiences of positive resources have been discovered and developed, they provide sources of internal support and thereby make it easier to work more directly and deeply with the anxiety and fear. Supporting, respecting, and utilizing all parts of a client, even "problematic" ones such as anxiety, is an essential guideline for this approach, and is the basis for the paradoxical strategies discussed in the next section.

PARADOXICAL STRATEGIES

Techniques used to encourage or exaggerate symptoms, behaviors or communications, such as symptom prescription (Watzlawick, 1974), are known as "paradoxical." Paradoxical techniques, pervasive in hypnotic and strategic approaches to therapy, are the basis of "utilization" (Haley, 1967; Erickson & Rossi, 1979; Gilligan, 1987), a central principle of the Ericksonian approach. Utilization is accepting and using whatever the client offers as the basis for therapy and the development of trance. Erickson (Haley, 1967) discussed the "utilization of anxiety by a continuance and a transformation of it" (p. 397).

The utilization approach assumes that all aspects of a person, even problematic ones such as anxiety, have value (Carter, 1982, 1983; Beletsis, 1986). Therefore, the therapist is not attempting to get rid of symptoms or behaviors. Instead, the focus is initially on accepting and developing experiences, and then on transforming and integrating them, even those that are labeled "resistant" or "problematic." Most people attempt to stop or devalue anxiety, thereby never accepting the experience or allowing it to develop fully. This paradoxical technique of accepting and developing a symptom in therapy serves three main purposes. First, by accepting the anxiety and encouraging its development in therapy there is less resistance, since the client is being instructed to continue to do what he or she is already doing (Haley, 1973). Second, it provides an opportunity for the therapist to discover any positive functions of the symptom. This is elaborated upon in the next section. Third, one may teach the client methods to control the anxiety by first learning to exaggerate it and express it in a variety of different ways.

Anxious clients experience conflict between wanting to feel self-assured and safe but actually feeling anxious and afraid. One approach to resolving this conflict is to develop a full experience of each side (Carter, 1983; Beletsis, 1986). In the same ways that other resourceful experiences, (discussed earlier) are developed, the experience of anxiety can also be developed. Once these oppositional experiences have been accepted and developed, they can be integrated.

Grinder and Bandler (1976) wrote about the process of integration. They said:

> The therapist's task in working with a client's incongruencies is to assist the client in changing by integrating the parts of the client which are in conflict, the incongruencies which are draining his energies and blocking him from getting what he wants. Typically, when a client has parts which are in conflict, no part is successful, but each sabotages the others' efforts to achieve what they want . . . Integration is a process by which the client creates a new model of the world which includes both of the formerly incompatible models in such a way that they are coordinated and function smoothly together, both working to assist the client in getting what he wants from life. (p. 44)

The value and integrity of this approach are especially evident when working with intense fear or anxiety. When clients get stuck or begin to withdraw, they are signaling that it is time to shift to the complementary experience (Gilligan, 1985), one chosen by them. It may be safety, security, or some similar experience. The more fully safety and security are developed, the easier it becomes to work with the anxiety-evoking experience. The result of shifting back and forth between complementary parts is a connection of resources to problems, or integration.

One paradoxical homework assignment found to be particularly effective is to instruct clients to pay attention to their anxiety at a specific time each day. They are encouraged to feel it, experience it noncritically, and ask it what it wants for them. Asking what the anxiety wants *for* them begins to imply or suggest that it may somehow be valuable or useful to them. By encouraging the symptom in this fashion, the therapist creates a situation in which "resistance" would mean not being anxious since the task is to be anxious. It also changes the client's relationship with the symptom from one in which the anxiety is out of control and the client is fighting to control it, to one in which the client actively produces the anxiety while attempting to explore and value it. Erickson (Haley, 1985) said, "Encourage them to act in a symptomatic way . . . Then they don't have to fight against their symptoms" (pp. 273–274). Many clients suffering from anxiety disorders have a difficult time going into a therapeutic trance. Therefore, it is recommended that the therapist first train them in self-hypnosis and develop resources before suggesting this homework assignment.

Paradoxical strategies are most effective when the therapist is truly caring and compassionate, communicating a deep support of the client's growth, and when the client believes that the approach will help. During most paradoxical interventions, the secondary gains, or "value" of anxiety become evident. Identification of value in symptoms is the basis for reframing techniques, discussed in the following section.

REFRAMING

"Reframing" (Watzlawick, 1974; Bandler & Grinder, 1982; Carter, 1983) presupposes that there is already a frame—i.e., an interpretation or perspective—associated with some symptom or "problem." Most often, clients with a symptom (such as anxiety) consider it a useless problem, and seek therapy to get rid of it. Creativity and choice are generated, in part, by having a variety of different perspectives or "frames" about something. In exploring a symptom such as anxiety, a general guideline for the therapist to keep in mind is that anxiety is functional. It is a form of communication, or signal, and is potentially valuable.

Since anxiety may have some valuable intention, it can provide a direction for the client. The author often asks clients, "If your anxiety could talk, what would it say it wants you to do?" One client reported that his anxiety wanted him to "slow down" and take care of himself. Another client, who suffered from panic disorders, became anxious when she felt alone. Through reframing and therapy, she learned to use her anxiety to let her know when it was time to call someone or be with a friend. (Ultimately, she was preparing for another relationship, and needed therapy to help with those preparations.) A third client, who had been in a car accident, subsequently experienced severe anxiety and fear whenever he had to drive in a car. He recognized that his anxiety wanted to ensure his protection. In each case, once the intention of the anxiety had been accepted and looked upon with positive value, it subsided.

In relationships, a client may become anxious in order to induce somebody to respond in a particular way; i.e., to get attention or love, or to be taken care of. In such cases, anxiety results from the client's lack of ability to get appropriate needs met in a healthier way. Therefore, the anxiety is a communication to the self that an important need is not being met. Once seen within this positive frame, the client can be assisted in developing appropriate ways of getting needs met.

Frequently, individuals have negative beliefs and images about themselves—they are not capable or lovable, do not deserve to have what they want in life. As these self-limiting messages become clear, they too can be transformed in therapy through the types of reframing strategies described in this section, and through the techniques described in the next section.

BELIEF SYSTEM/SELF-IMAGE CHANGES

An individual's belief system and self-image greatly influence his or her actions and capabilities (Dilts, 1987), and thus results. If an individual goes into a situation believing that he or she is inadequate, and then imagines being rejected, these underlying beliefs and assumptions contribute to the development of anxiety. The client is considered to have an anxiety disorder (Beck, 1987) "when there is no objective threat; his assessment of the dangerousness of a problematic situation is erroneous or exaggerated" (p. 153). In discussing the cognitive therapy of anxiety, Beck said,

> Patients may judge themselves too harshly due to a belief that they are inadequate; they may fail to generate plans or strategies to deal with problems because of a belief that they are helpless; or they may reason on the basis of self-defeating assumptions. (p. 149)

When people have self-limiting beliefs and assumptions, there is a potential for a negative self-fulfilling prophecy, which, unfortunately, usually comes to pass. This reinforces the anxiety and poor self-image. These beliefs, no matter how inaccurate or exaggerated, become the foundation for self-image. There are several ways to intervene at this level.

First, the subjective model the client has can be directly challenged and expanded by using questions (Bandler & Grinder, 1975) such as: How do you know? What stops you? Do you really believe that would happen? What would happen if you did? The intention of this type of questioning is to facilitate reality testing in a way that encourages clients to acknowledge and incorporate more realistic beliefs.

Second, it can be effective to find counterexamples of the beliefs and behaviors targeted for therapy. For example, the author treated an 11-year-old boy and his mother for symptoms of anxiety associated with family issues. The boy's father had abandoned him three years earlier, which left him with conflicting feelings of love and hate toward his father. He was very fearful and anxious that his mother would leave him, too. He had frequent nightmares of his mother's "going away," and he was overly concerned with her whereabouts. During one session, as mother and son sat facing each other holding hands, he described his nightmares, sadness, and fears of her leaving. She heard him, acknowledged what he was saying, and with tears in her eyes, she hugged him. Then she made clear eye contact and told him that she loved him, had no intention of leaving him, and very much wanted to raise him and watch him grow. She pointed out that it would probably be *him* who would leave *her* when he became old enough to go to college and wanted to be on his own. He smiled, hugged her, and told her he loved her. She had effectively countered his beliefs, leading to a resolution of his symptoms.

Finally, hypnosis can be used to develop and strengthen the clients' self-images and identities by having them experience themselves in the future (Haley, 1967; Grinder & Bandler, 1981; Gilligan, 1987) with all the changes complete. For example, a client may imagine himself or herself two months in the future saying, "I'm capable and lovable," and actually feel very secure and confident, and then imagine approaching a previously anxiety-producing situation and handling it without difficulty. This process helps give the client a frame of reference, similar to role playing, for successfully integrating a new self-image and using therapeutic changes.

CONCLUSION

Anxiety is woven throughout an individual's emotional life cycles, and is associated with many different psychological problems. This chapter has presented a framework for how the author approaches the treatment of anxiety. It presented five techniques that have been found especially effective. It should be noted that although these techniques have been discussed separately, they often overlap and are used simultaneously.

The principle of accepting and utilizing the client's unique experience cannot be overemphasized. It is important that changes be developed and integrated in a way that is appropriate for each individual. Erickson spoke about developing a new technique for each individual, and frequently worked with clients to develop small changes that could be built upon (Haley, 1973). The guiding principles of utilization and tailoring therapy to the unique individual communicate many qualities, such as flexibility, support, trust, compassion, determination, appreciation, curiosity, hope, and creativity. These are qualities that underlie successful psychotherapies.

REFERENCES

American Psychiatric Association (1987). *Diagnostic and Statistical Manual of Mental Disorders* (3rd ed., rev.). Washington, D.C.: American Psychiatric Association.

Bandler, R. (1985). *Using Your Brain for a Change*. Moab, Utah: Real People Press.

Bandler, R., & Grinder, J. (1975). *The Structure of Magic* (Vol. I). Palo Alto, Calif.: Science and Behavior Books.

Bandler, R., & Grinder, J. (1979). *Frogs Into Princes*. Moab, Utah: Real People Press.

Bandler, R., & Grinder, J. (1982). *Reframing*. Moab, Utah: Real People Press.

Beck, A. (1987). Cognitive therapy. In J. Zeig (Ed.)., *The Evolution of Psychotherapy* (pp. 149–163). New York: Brunner/Mazel.

Beisser, A. (1970). The paradoxical theory of change. In J. Fagan & I. Shepherd (Eds.), *Gestalt Therapy Now* (pp. 77–80). Palo Alto, Calif.: Science and Behavior Books.

Beletsis, C. (1985). An Ericksonian approach in the treatment of alcoholism In J. Zeig (Ed.), *Ericksonian Psychotherapy* (Vol. II) (pp. 359–372). New York: Brunner/Mazel.

Beletsis, C. (1986). Balance: A central principle of the Ericksonian approach. In M. Yapko (Ed.)., *Hypnotic and Strategic Interventions: Principles and Practice* (pp. 57–73). New York: Irvington.

Carter, P. (1982). Rapport and integrity for Ericksonian practitioners. In J. Zeig (Ed.), *Ericksonian Approaches to Hypnosis and Psychotherapy* (pp. 48–57). New York: Brunner/Mazel

Carter, P. (1983). The parts model. Unpublished doctoral dissertation, International College, Santa Monica, Calif.

Dilts, R. (1987). Workshop Outlines. Ben Lomond, Calif.: Dynamic Learning Publications.

Erickson, M. (1980). Hypnotic psychotherapy. In E. Rossi (Ed.), *The Collected Papers of Milton H. Erickson on Hypnosis* (Vol. IV) (pp. 35–48). New York: Irvington.

Erickson, M., & Rossi, E. (1979). *Hypnotherapy: An Exploratory Casebook*. New York: Irvington.

Erickson, M., Rossi, E., & Rossi, S. (1976). *Hypnotic Realities*. New York: Irvington.

Gilligan, S. (1985). Generative autonomy: Principles for an Ericksonian hypnotherapy. In J. Zeig (Ed.), *Ericksonian Psychotherapy* (Vol. I) (pp. 196–239). New York: Brunner/Mazel.

Gilligan, S. (1987). *Therapeutic Trances: The Cooperation Principle in Ericksonian Hypnotherapy.* New York: Brunner/Mazel.

Grinder, J., & Bandler, R. (1976). *The Structure of Magic* (Vol. II). Palo Alto, Calif.: Science and Behavior Books.

Grinder, J., & Bandler, R. (1981). *Trance-Formations.* Moab, Utah: Real People Press.

Haley, J. (1967). *Advanced Techniques of Hypnosis and Therapy.* New York: Grune & Stratton.

Haley, J. (1973). *Uncommon Therapy.* New York: Norton.

Haley, J. (1985). *Conversations with Milton H. Erickson, M.D.* (Vol. I). New York: Triangle Press.

Polster, E. & M. (1973). *Gestalt Therapy Integrated.* New York: Vintage.

Satir, V. (1978). *Your Many Faces.* Millbrae, Calif.: Celestial Arts.

Siegel, B. (1986). *Love, Medicine and Miracles.* New York: Harper & Row.

Watzlawick, P., Weakland, J., & Fisch, R. (1974). Change: *Principles of Problem Formation and Problem Resolution.* New York: Norton.

Watzlawick, P., (1978). *The Language of Change.* New York: Basic Books.

Yapko, M. (1988). *When Living Hurts: Directives for Treating Depression.* New York: Brunner/Mazel.

Therapeutic Approaches for Anxiety and Depression

Chapter 14

The Treatment of Anxiety and Depression in Pain States

Robert Schwarz

Robert Schwarz, Psy.D., is the Director of the Institute for Advanced Clinical Training in Philadelphia. He is also a senior clinical instructor at Hahnemann University. Schwarz is in full-time private practice. He was a consultant for the oncology unit of Mercy Catholic Medical Center. He was a faculty member at the Third and Fourth International Congresses on Ericksonian Approaches to Hypnosis and Psychotherapy. His paper on "The Use of Posthypnotic Suggestion in the Hypnotherapy of Pain" was published in the Ericksonian Monographs. He is currently coauthoring a book on post-traumatic stress disorder.

Pain is a complex psychological construct that involves sensory, affective, and evaluative aspects (Melzack & Wall, 1982). The treatment of the sensory aspects of pain have been described elsewhere (Erickson, 1967; Barber, 1982; Schwarz, 1984; Sacerdote, 1970, 1982). In order to effectively discuss the psychological treatment of anxiety and depressive issues in pain states, it would be heuristic to have a psychological epistemology of pain that accounts for these issues. The definition of pain that is used in this chapter was derived from previous definitions (Melzack & Wall, 1982; Mersky et al., 1979; Sternbach, 1968), and specifically addresses the roles that mediating variables such as anxiety and depression have in perception of pain. Pain can be defined as follows:

1. It is subjective experience that is mediated by idiopathic variables of the individual within the context of his or her environment.

2. A necessary but not sufficient condition for the presence of pain is a noxious somatosensory experience, that may or may not be due to actual injury.
3. Individuals can be said to be "in pain" if, and only if, they experience suffering (measured in terms of negative affect and aversive drive) as a perceived consequence of the sensory experience (Schwarz, 1984, p. 4).

The key aspects of this multiple-part definition for our purposes here are the first and third. Both anxiety and depression influence the subjective experience of pain. However, they themselves are influenced by other variables. In the first part of this chapter, key mediating variables that are relevant to the generation or prevention of anxiety and depression in pain states are discussed. In the second part of the chapter, treatment approaches that attenuate negative affect and aversive drive are presented.

THE ROLE OF ANXIETY AND DEPRESSION AS PART OF PAIN

The intimate connection between anxiety and pain has often been discussed (Beecher, 1956, 1960, 1966; Chapman & Feather, 1973; Hill et al., 1952a, 1952b, 1955; Melzack & Wall, 1982; Schalling, 1976; Erickson, 1967; Sternbach, 1968). The unequivocal finding is that the more anxious or fearful a person is, the more likely that person will experience suffering as a perceived consequence of a noxious somatosensory experience. What are the mediating variables that increase anxiety for a person in pain? We will consider three variables: meaning and context, controllability, and individual psychodynamics.

The role of depression as a factor in pain has also been discussed (Mersky & Spear, 1967; Sternbach, 1974; Violin, 1982). The question considered here is whether or not depression causes the pain state, or is a function of being in pain. In the clinical setting, the answer can be either or both. Each patient must be assessed as a unique individual, again considering the variables of meaning and context, controllability, and psychodynamics as they pertain to depression.

Meaning and Context

In a classic study, Beecher (1956) compared a matched sample of 150 civilian surgical patients with 150 wounded soldiers. He found that soldiers experienced far less pain and requested significantly fewer narcotics than the surgical patients even though their injuries were much worse. He concluded that differences in meaning and context for the two groups accounted for the finding. The civilians shifted from a relatively calm and routine life to undergo major surgery, whereas the soldiers were released from a dangerous and highly unpleasant environment to the safety of the hospital. The different meaning derived from these disparate contexts led to a relatively high level of anxiety for the surgical patients and relatively low levels of anxiety for the soldiers. It is the difference in anxiety levels that produced the divergence of pain experience for the two groups.

The "actual" difference in context is not the only variable. There is a great deal of internal appraisal and attribution that occur for the person. Generally, these processes occur at a nonconscious, nonvolitional level (Leventhal & Nerenz, 1983). Some of the patterns of appraisal are relatively common and predictable, whereas others can be highly idiosyncratic.

Contextual and attributional factors that generally influence the amount of anxiety and depression patients feel include:

1. The degree of danger associated with the pain (e.g., terminal versus nonterminal illness).
2. The degree of loss, current and anticipated (e.g., disfigurement or loss of functioning).
3. The intensity and duration of pain.
4. The degree of unexpressed dystonic emotions (e.g., anger or guilt).
5. The degree of perceived controllability or the lack thereof.
6. The degree of social support vs. isolation (e.g., can the patient talk to doctors, nurses, or family about the pain experience or other dysphoric feelings).
7. Associational links to prior experiences of pain or illness and the meaning of those experiences.

One may quickly recognize that the preceding variables can be highly interdependent. For instance, the degree of danger (especially in terms of death) can be related to the degree of anticipated loss. The degree of unexpressed emotions may be related to the lack of social support. Furthermore, these variables can influence other factors (as seen in Figure 1). One example is that as intensity and duration of pain increase, so does psychological regression.

Treatment Issues.   Once the clinician has understood the contexts of patients' situations as well as how patients have appraised their situation, specific treatment goals can be set. Although much of this presentation is focused on hypnotic interventions, it is vital for clinicians to place hypnosis within an overall psychological approach to pain management (Barber, 1982). These include systemic interventions (e.g., with family or hospital personnel), occupational interventions (e.g., having the patient engage in meaningful activities), educational interventions, and cognitive-behavioral interventions.

Controllability.   Perhaps one of the most salient features of clinical pain, from the point of view of patients, is the resulting sense of helplessness and lack of control they feel. The more severe and the more the chronic the pain, the more frustrated and helpless patients will tend to feel. The desperation involved in such a plight is keenly described by Sternbach (1968, p. 83): "We implore others to help us, to take the hurt away . . . We beg forgiveness, we say we are sorry. We ask God for help, we ask him to save us . . . We are ready to promise anything, if only someone will save us." The problem for the patient in chronic pain occurs when no help comes. When patients lack information about their condition, i.e, the nature and meaning of their pain, it contributes to their perceived lack of controllability. Perhaps it is safe to say that a chronic pain condition is one of life's naturally occurring "learned helplessness" laboratories. Seligman (1975) has amply described the resulting depression that occurs when animals and people are in such aversive and uncontrollable situations.

Patients experience a *lessened subjective sense of suffering* when they are given a cognitive response they believe can influence the aversiveness of an event. This is defined as "cognitive control" (Thompson, 1981). Hypnosis is one such cognitive response.

Treatment Issues.   One of the connotative aspects of pain in Western culture is that it is personally uncontrollable, except perhaps by medication. Hypnosis counters this helpless view and offers patients a sense of control and self-efficacy. Hypnotherapy patients are taught that they are in control and are using hypnosis to reduce their own pain, and their unconscious minds have the ability to alter pain perception. Patients are taught to use self-hypnosis to reinforce the learning.

Often, the doctor also feels helpless and out of control with respect to the patient's pain or illness. Hypnosis can open up a special interpersonal channel that allows patient and doctor to remain in contact despite what might otherwise seem a desperate, hopeless, and anxiety-laden situation for both parties (Spiegel & Spiegel, 1978).

One can quickly see how context, attribution of meaning, anxiety, depression, and lack of controllability interact (see Figure 1). The goal for therapy is to break the negative deviation amplification circuit* in which most patients find themselves and replace it with a positive feedback loop.

Pain as a Functional Equivalent for Anxiety, Depression, and Other Dysphoric Affects

Pain as a functional disease is a complicated topic. It has been dealt with in the literature from a number of different frames of reference. Among these are the role of childhood experiences in terms of social modeling (Craig, 1978); lack of affection, overt aggression, and battering (Engel, 1959; Violin, 1982); the role of hypochondriasis (Engel, 1959; Pilowsky, 1978); and depression (Mersky & Spear, 1967; Sternbach, 1974; Violin, 1982).

This section deals with both psychogenic pain that exists *because* of psychodynamic issues, or pain that is *exacerbated* by psychodynamic issues. In a general psychoanalytic theory of pain, Szasz (1957) proposes that pain is due to the perception of a threat to the integrity of the body, regardless of whether or not the threat is "real." In "organic pain," one can find objective evidence of danger. In "psychogenic pain," there is no observable evidence of danger. In the latter case, the perception of danger is usually based on idiosyncratic unconscious processes. The pain may be linked with dangers associated with aggression, sexuality, dependency, or other conflicted issues. Generally, most pain cases are a combination of organic and psychological factors.

Physical trauma and the ensuing pain can disrupt the psychic equilibrium of an individual. For instance, people who characteristically

---

*In this context, this is a circuit of interacting intrapsychic and interpersonal variables through which patients repeatedly cycle. After each cycle the effect of the interaction of the variable increases in the same direction.

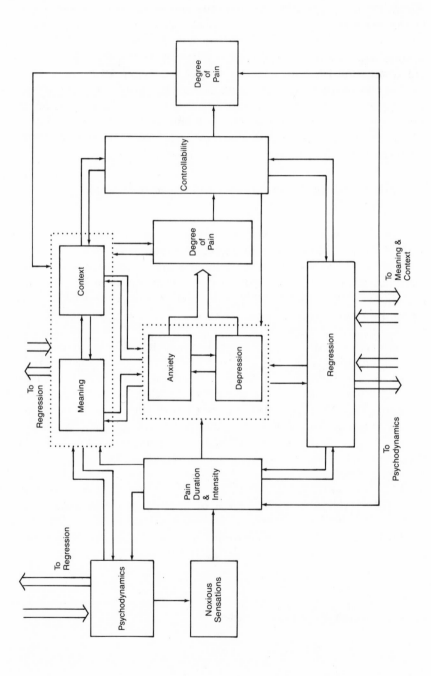

Figure 1. Schematic of Interaction of Selected Variables of Pain Perception

sublimate their hypochondriacal tendencies may become obsessed with their painful bodies after an accident. Sometimes the event that causes the person pain may have a particularly conflictual meaning for the patient. For example, a mother who survives a car crash in which her three-year-old son dies (where she was the driver) may use physical pain to assuage her guilt. In other situations, the pain or the illness associated with the pain may act as a lightning rod for current conflicts or reactivated old conflicts. An example of the former is a case in which a single mother had many problems with her teenage daughter. She would frequently become furious with her daughter, and would either try to say nothing to her, or would uncontrollably fly into a rage. In either case, her back pain would flare up as a result of her problems with anger.

An example of a reactivated conflict is the case of a man who was dying of cancer who had developed a crush on his private-duty nurse. The pattern that appeared most relevant was that when his father was very ill, he had been having an affair with his father's private-duty nurse. At one point, his father had suffered a complication while his son was off with the nurse. The father almost died. It was postulated that his crush on his current private-duty nurse reactivated his guilt about his father's private-duty nurse, which, in turn, exacerbated the pain.

Freud stated that "the ego is first and foremost a bodily ego" (1923 / 1960, p. 16). It is not a coincidence that our language has many expressions that equate pain with some type of emotional suffering. For instance: "Mr. Smith is a pain in the neck"; "This is such a headache"; or "It hurts me to hear you say that." When the affects become particularly powerful or are highly conflicted, the body can become the central channel for the communication of emotional suffering.

Pain has been described as a functional equivalent of unexpressed anger turned against the self (Engel, 1959; Pilowsky, 1978; Sacerdote, 1970), as well as a form of self-punishment to relieve excessive guilt feelings (Engel, 1959). Pain tends to bind the negative affect so that the patient can avoid painful emotions (Sternbach, 1974). The author's clinical experience supports these assertions.

Another important consideration is that extended pain, especially severe pain, is a significant stressor. It exerts a tremendous regressive pull on the patient. As Sternbach (1968) pointed out, the patient pleads for help from God and the doctors, who unconsciously may represent the compassionate all-good parent who can kiss the hurt away. There tends to be an unconscious fantasy of being punished associated with pain. The pain, in part, represents the damage that the angry, all-bad parent might inflict, which can potentiate anxiety and increase suffering. Despite pleading for help, promising to be good, and saying one is sorry, the pain does not stop. The good parent does not come to the rescue. Therefore, there is the fantasy that one is bad, unloved, and abandoned. (In some instances, these patients may cause sufficient anxiety and helplessness in doctors and family members that external support is fostered for this fantasy.) These private cognitions intensify depressive affect and perceived pain. As is discussed later, these dynamics can often be seen in clear terms with cancer.

Treatment Considerations.   Four general goals can be derived from the previous discussion. First, pathological regression needs to be prevented or reversed. Hypnosis may be particularly suited for this job, because the archaic involvement during hypnosis (Shor, 1962)* serves to prove to the patient that the all-good parent still cares; therefore, the patient must still be worthwhile and not abandoned. Second, patients can be taught how to differentiate emotional suffering from physical pain. Third, patients' psychodynamic conflicts can be resolved. Fourth, if the conflicts cannot be resolved, they can be utilized in such a manner as not to leave the patient incapacitated (Erickson, 1954). For instance, it is important to note that many pain patients demand medication, even though the medication does not work. Therefore, one can infer that it is "the act of giving" medicine that has symbolic meaning (e.g., the good parent kissing the hurt away). Since it is "the act of giving" that is important, one might well give something nontoxic such as relaxation or hypnosis.

INTERVENTION STRATEGIES

The following are interventions that influence the emotional aspects of pain without directly modifying the pain sensations (unlike interventions such as analgesia, anesthesia, and dissociation). In the clinical

---

*Shor measures archaic involvement along three dimensions: (1) the extent to which during hypnosis archaic object relations are formed on to the person of the hypnotist; (2) the extent to which a special hypnotic relationship is formed on to the person of the hypnotist; (3) the extent to which the core of the subject's personality is involved in the hypnotic process (p. 314).

situation, both types of interventions are used. In theory, one would expect a synergistic effect. Clinical experience seems to bear this out.

Education and Respect for the Patient

The importance of respecting the patient has been consistently discussed in works on Ericksonian therapy (Lankton & Lankton, 1983; Erickson & Rossi, 1979; Zeig, 1985). An aspect of respect that is not discussed often is the right of people to have information about what is happening to them. Patients often complain that doctors never explain anything because they are too busy. Not only is patient education an important initial intervention, but the avoidance of this aspect of treatment can be an iatrogenic source of increased dysfunction.

Most people do not understand how their nervous system processes pain. One of the better ways to establish rapport with someone with a nonacute pain condition is to spend some time to find out:

1. What they know about the physical reason for their pain;
2. Their existential understanding of their condition (e.g., God gave me cancer because I have been bad);
3. What they know about pain's function, and how they can influence their experience of it.

Once this information has been gathered, the clinician can spend time educating patients about their condition. Two universally important points of discussions are:

1. The signal function of pain (Sternbach, 1968; Szasz, 1957), and how when all that can be done and has been done about the pain, there will no longer be any need for the pain (Thompson, 1983).
2. A modified explanation of the gate control theory of pain (Sacerdote, 1982) and what this means about how people can learn to control their pain through psychological methods. Alternatively, endorphins can be discussed as another way the body can control pain. It should be noted, though, that there is little evidence that hypnotic pain control is mediated through this mechanism (Schwarz, 1984).

The results of these initial interventions are fourfold:

1. Rapport with the clinician is strengthened. Often, no one has talked to patients about their *pain condition*. If the patients are involved, they are likely to feel respected as partners in the treatment instead of feeling dejected and abandoned, anxiously wondering why the doctor will not talk to them. Taking the time to listen and explain the situation helps decrease patients' sense of isolation. Furthermore, patients' sense of self-worth can be strengthened (after all, "the doctor" took the time to explain things).
2. Anxiety resulting from erroneous beliefs about the medical situation can be attenuated because they can be identified and corrected.
3. The deviation amplification circuit of stress, anxiety, and regression, which synergistically creates even more stress, anxiety, and regression, can be interrupted with the infusion of information, a sense of hope, and a sense of respect and partnership in the relationship.
4. Interventions that will be used later can be seeded (Zeig, 1985) during this early phase of therapy. For instance, the concept that the unconscious mind can protect a person can be discussed in conjunction with the gate control theory of pain. In addition, other idiosyncratic information given to the clinician by the patient can certainly be utilized later in treatment.

Separating Emotional from Physical Pain

Clinicians can start the process of differentiating emotional suffering from physical pain during the evaluation phase of treatment. Just getting patients to focus on the different affective components of the pain response (like any problem) will tend to disrupt the symptom. One intervention involves asking patients to rate pain and suffering separately. After asking patients to rate the "pain" on a 0–10 scale, therapists can then ask how much the pain bothers patients on a 0–10 scale (Barber, 1983). In some cases, the second rating will be higher than the first. In this event, the groundwork has been laid for a discussion and/or treatment on the dysphoric affect. If the opposite case occurs, clinicians can explore with patients how they are already managing their pain, and build upon those natural resources. For example, one woman stated that she would moan in a low tone to help distract herself from her pain. She did not respond well to visual imagery. However, she did respond well to suggestions about listening to music and other auditory stimuli.

A second intervention involves asking patients whether or not they notice how their feelings and thoughts affect their pain. If they reply in the affirmative, then these issues can be discussed and interventions planned. If patients do not notice how their mental activity influences their experience of suffering, the therapist can use pain-focusing techniques (Sachs et al., 1977). Patients (in trance) are instructed to focus on their pain while they experience different thoughts, feelings, and images. The task is to differentiate which forms of mental activity increase or decrease the pain. Pain-reducing thought processes can be strengthened through hypnotic or strategic interventions.

A third approach consists of offering suggestions and metaphors to separate emotional pain from physical pain. Two examples of suggestions include:

> Over the next week you can begin to recognize how your emotional state affects your body. And as you begin to notice your pleasant emotions and the emotions that hurt, you can realize how they are different from the sensations that your body experiences. And even as you are learning this, your body can know that it does not need to hurt, even if your feelings hurt.

Or;

> A tear can mean many things. And yet, water trickling down skin can be a soothing sensation. And so, your conscious mind can appreciate the softness of the water on your cheek, while your unconscious mind can notice the sadness you are feeling.

A third example involves a metaphor told to one patient about the Little Prince (Sainte-Exupery, 1971) who needed to know the difference between a baobab tree, whose roots could *crush* his planet (she had a "crushing" pain), and a rose bush, which can evoke various feelings in observers, even though it is hard to tell the difference between a rose bush and a baobab tree at first. At the next session, the patient talked about her emotional hurts for the first time.

Symbolic Hypnotherapy

Anxiety and depression can be treated symbolically in a number of ways. One of the problems with depression and anxiety states is that they are generally amorphous feelings for patients. To remedy this

problem, patients can be asked to form concrete symbols for their feelings. For instance, they can be asked to identify a color and / or a shape
that is a symbol for their fear or depression. They can then be asked to
alter the symbol.

For example: One patient with cancer had a severe medication reaction. She was extremely scared. She was asked to see the fear in her
mind's eye. It was suggested that it would have a color and a shape.
She responded that it was a blue square. A pink circle was defined by
her as a symbol for being calm. She was able to shrink the square and
round the edges, but she could not change the color. It was then suggested that she *attack* that blue square with pink cannon balls. (It was
postulated that she had a great deal of anger that she was not expressing.) A simile of watching snow fall on black pavement and wondering when it would begin to stick, as well as many other suggestions,
were used to build up an automatic response. She was also asked to
become very involved in watching the pattern of the cannon ball splat-
ter, and how the color would change. It was interesting to note that
this intervention did nothing to alter the medication reaction. However, it had a profound effect on her emotionally. Not only did it
significantly reduce her fear about this incident, she stated that it convinced her that she really did have the ability to control her experience. She almost never had pain after this episode despite the cessa-
tion of high doses of narcotics.

Another patient with cancer was taught the technique of hypno-
plasty (Sacerdote, 1982) to help her manage her anger. She felt her
anger belonged to her, and that it was unfair to give it to anybody
else. She was taught to imagine a ball of clay. The absorptive characteristics of clay were described to her. She was then asked to model,
shape, or pound the hypnotic clay and let the clay absorb her anger.
Next, she was told to throw it away somewhere so that the contami-
nated clay would not bother her any more. Posthypnotic suggestions
were offered to the effect that every evening she go into a trance, get
some new clay, and work out her anger. Her immediate response upon
orienting from the trance was to state that her pain was gone, even
though no direct hypnotic work was performed on her pain.

Sometimes it may be better to address highly conflicted material
indirectly through the use of symbols. In this manner, clinicians can
avoid increasing patients' anxiety by making unconscious material
conscious. One particular area in which the author has done this is in
terminal patients' beliefs about death. Lori, a 29-year-old patient, made

several comments wondering why she was being punished by having cancer. She felt she must have done something wrong, and somehow deserved it. However, she refused to talk further about this concern. During one session of hypnosis to achieve pain control, she was asked to notice the development of a soft fluffy feeling on top of the area in pain. Once this feeling started to develop, it was further described as a "white cloud kind of feeling." The following progression occurred:

1. The white cloud feeling was defined as "special."
2. The idea of fantasies about floating on a white cloud was developed.
3. The ideas of blue sky and a special golden-colored light were elaborated.
4. Associations to peaceful, happy, and calm emotions were developed.

She responded to this symbolic suggestion of being in heaven by entering a deeper trance than she had on previous occasions. Upon reorientation, she commented that her pain was reduced and that she felt calmer than usual. She did not comment on the experience except to say that she liked it a great deal. However, two days later she did talk about her feelings about heaven.

Finally, the procedures involved in trance ratification can be framed as a symbol of the patient's deeper potentials for control. The more autonomous and unusual the ratification behavior (e.g., arm levitation), the more confident and reassured patients will be in the use of hypnosis to overcome pain.

Building Ego-Supportive Affective States

Elton et al. (1980) described a "secret room" technique in which patients are asked to imagine finding a secret door in the corridors of their minds that leads to a secret room that they design for maximal pleasure, satisfaction, comfort, and security. Once in the room by themselves with the door closed, it is suggested that they are completely safe. As the image is described to the patient, many ego-strengthening suggestions are given. It is important to note that most of these suggestions are along affective dimensions. These include decreased anxiety and depression, and increased peacefulness, safety, security, hopefulness, and self-esteem. The emphasis is not on directly eliminating the pain. Rather, it is on dissociating the pain from the self, and surrounding the self in an ego-supportive affective environment.

It does not appear to be necessary to choose a room for patients. Many of the author's patients have chosen places that are outdoors. In such cases, the same type of ego-supportive suggestions are given. These suggestions can also be symbolically expressed through the characteristics of the images. For instance, one patient chose a scene on a cliff by a waterfall. The suggestion was given to the patient that the massive rock would somehow lend its strength and ability to the patient to remain stable and solid. Finally, since the patient needs a way to get to the secret place, the author usually employs a descending ten-step version of the rapid induction analgesia (Barber, 1977) technique. As the patient is walking down the steps, many analgesia suggestions are given. Upon reaching the bottom, the patient can find himself or herself at the secret place.

Sacerdote (1977) described two types of hypnotically elicited mystical states. He differentiated introvertive and extrovertive types. The introvertive mystical state is induced through suggestions that patients experience themselves as "surrounded in every direction by wider and wider transparent concentric luminous spheres of serenity and cheerful calmness. . . " (p. 314). Many suggestions are given for increasing relaxation, calmness, serenity, and peace. In the extrovertive experience, patients are led on a difficult climb to the top of a symbolic mountain. A beautiful scene covering all sensory modalities is described. Patients are told that they can see valley after valley and mountain ranges. Suggestions for an expanded sense of time and the future are offered. The goal is to "enable patients to deal in entirely new ways with the problems of guilt and punishment, of life and death" (p. 316).

Binding and Delimiting Dysphoric Affective States

Paradoxically, one of the better ways to achieve successful pain control with patients who have a great deal of anxiety and depression involved in their pain is to suggest the development of a circumscribed amount of discomfort (Barber, 1982; Erickson, 1967, 1983). The addition of a novel yet noxious sensation accomplishes several functions.

1. It is a stimulus that can compete with the pain for the person's attention.
   a. If a person is in intense pain, and the clinician comes in and says that he or she will take away that pain (especially if other doctors have failed), the patient is not likely to take the hypnotist seriously. However, if the hypnotist says that he or she wants the person to develop a new discomfort, the patient is going to become quite involved emotionally, even if it is to resist the development of pain (Erickson, 1983).
   b. Many people tend to react with all-or-nothing repsonses. If they feel any discomfort at all, they interpret that as being in pain; therefore, a residue or return of even 10 percent of the original pain can lead to a reinstatement of the full pain response. A substitute noxious sensation tends to prevent such an occurrence.
2. Prescribing sensations that are noxious can bind anxiety, guilt, sadness, and other dysphoric affects for people who express these emotions somatically. If the patient is likely to do this, it is far better that he or she have a new mildly noxious sensation than intense pain.

   For example, Erickson worked with a woman named Cathy who had a great deal of pain secondary to her breast cancer. Erickson stated:

   > I explained to her with profound apologies that even though I had relieved the pain of her cancer by this numbness, I would have to confess that I was going to be an absolute failure in one regard. I would not be able to remove the pain from the site of the surgical scar area. Instead of removing the pain, the best, the very best that I could do would be to leave the scar area with an annoying, disagreeable, great big mosquito-like feeling. It would be something awfully annoying; something she would feel helpless about; something she would wish would stop. But *it would be endurable* . . . (Erickson, 1983, p. 172)

In this example, Erickson suggested an itch, to which the affects of annoyance, helplessness, and the wish for "it" to stop were securely bound. In many ways, the "it" seemed to be a symbol for cancer or death. Binding the dysphoric affect to the suggested pain allowed it to be expressed symbolically without either spreading over the body or increasing in intensity.

The case of Cathy (Erickson, 1983) also demonstrates the other principles. In her waking moments, Cathy would chant "Don't hurt me! Don't scare me!" Erickson got her attention by chanting in the same cadence, "I am going to hurt you. I am going to scare you." His initial suggestions were that he wanted her to feel other noxious sensations (a burning in her foot).

Since a "small" amount of residual pain is framed as not treatable, noxious post-session sensations have a high probability of being tolerated by patients and considered merely *residual* pain. The larger remaining portion of pain relief would be protected from the deleterious effects of doubting. Dissociating a small amount of remaining pain from the large amount of pain control may actually serve as a suggestion to notice how much relief was achieved (Erickson, 1983).

Reframing Interventions

There are a number of different definitions of reframing (Bandler & Grinder, 1982; Lankton & Lankton, 1986; O'Hanlon, 1987). In this chapter, reframing is broadly defined as those interventions that are used to influence the attributional processes of the individual. In colloquial terms, the clinician suggests to the patient, "Perhaps it would be more beneficial if you look at 'X' in this helpful way instead of in that hurtful way."

Hypnosis as more control. It is often said that it is important to clear up patients' misconceptions about hypnosis. A common patient concern is the fear of loss of control. This issue can be thoroughly reframed by teaching patients that hypnosis gives them more control over their bodies' functioning than they normally have. Clinicians can use common examples, or specific instances in patients' experiences where they controlled pain unconsciously (e.g., not noticing a cut, losing a headache at a movie). It can be explained that the unconscious mind can control pain by closing the gate, or by releasing endorphins, and so on.

For example, a patient had to undergo minor surgery without anesthesia. One aspect of the hypnotic intervention was the utilization of the patient's desire to be in control as well as his tendency to be rebellious at times. It was suggested that he would really enjoy watching and listening to the doctor be so perplexed by *his ability* to be so pain-free without any chemical anesthetic. He would get a tremendous sense of satisfaction from knowing that he, the patient, did the pain control without any help from the doctor. In response to these suggestions, the patient grinned like a Cheshire cat. Since the rebelliousness and need for control were discharged in this productive manner, it was easy to strengthen the trust he had in the doctor relative to the surgical aspect of the procedure.

Altering painful attributions. Patients often create various frames of reference or attributions of meaning that foster a continued pain response. The first job of the clinician is to identify those attitudes, attributions, or frames of reference that are preventing a more adaptive response. For instance, if pain is associated with a terminal illness, then a person may believe that since the illness is uncontrollable, the pain must also be uncontrollable. There are a range of interventions to address these issues. The most direct would be simply to talk with patients, and offer direct suggestions and reassurance. The most indirect would be the use of complex metaphors. The use of metaphor to influence attitudinal and psychodynamic issues is discussed elsewhere (Lankton & Lankton, 1983, 1986).

In many instances, psychodynamic issues are a part of the pain problem. If pain has become a significant part of the current equilibrium, then the possibility of the alleviation of pain is likely to cause anxiety because of the threatened disequilibrium. One way to address this issue is through simple reframing metaphors.

Mary was an 18-year-old young woman referred because she suffered from headaches every day for the past five years. The relevant aspect of her treatment was the need to reframe the inevitable anxiety-provoking situations she would have to face once she no longer had the headaches that previously helped her avoid them. Mary had stated that she wanted to be a biologist. The reframing intervention consisted of telling her that when scientists solve one problem, they know that many more problems and questions will arise. A scientist anxiously looks forward to the new questions that are a natural part of the process of growth.

CANCER, PUNISHMENT, AND THE FEAR OF DEATH

In this section, the special issues of pain secondary to cancer are discussed in order to further illustrate the principles previously described. In the following case examples, both the patients knew they were terminally ill. Both patients had unexpressed, and probably inexpressible, concerns about punishment and a fear of death. The many hypnotic skills taught to these patients were not fully utilized until these emotional issues were resolved.

Case 1:   Lori, a 29-year-old woman, had a very difficult time discussing her concern about dying. She was on heavy doses of narcotic medication. Nevertheless, the pain continued. The use of the symbols for heaven with this patient have already been discussed. A few days later, she started to talk of her concerns about getting into heaven. She felt that she must be being punished for something terrible she had done. Otherwise, why would she be suffering like this now? Although she did not state this, it seemed clear that her reasoning was that if God was going to punish her here on earth, then she was never going to get into heaven. While in trance, the following reframing intervention was made. It was pointed out to her (in more detail than described here) that many of the prophets and the saints suffered a great deal while they were on earth. Yet they were chosen messengers of God, and had a special place in heaven. This perspective resulted in a reduction in her pain and a marked reduction in her depression.

Case 2:   Al was a 63-year-old cancer patient who had achieved a good deal of pain control. However, after several weeks of treatment, his medical condition temporarily worsened. He was stabilized, but could no longer control pain, even with the author's help. Referencing a recent conversation with Al, the author asked him (while in trance) if he felt he needed to suffer to make up for his sins. He nodded that he did. Al was asked if he felt that pain with a suffering rating of 2 was enough pain for his purposes. He said it was not. A pain with a rating of 4 was designated as sufficient. Al was asked if an hour of pain at a level of 4 would be enough. He said it would. At this point, many suggestions were offered about "having an hour of pain a day, which is 60 minutes. . . . Probably some days 50 minutes would be enough, or an hour, or three-quarters of an hour, certainly no less than 30 minutes . . .," and so on. Then it was repeated in many different ways that there were only 24 hours in a day, and that the other 23 hours could be pain-free. The time of day was negotiated (with binds of comparable alternatives) when his private-duty nurse was working. It was also suggested that Al not cheat, that he should not ask for any aspirin for that 30 minutes to an hour in order to make sure that he got all the suffering he needed to make up for his transgressions. It was also suggested that he should not

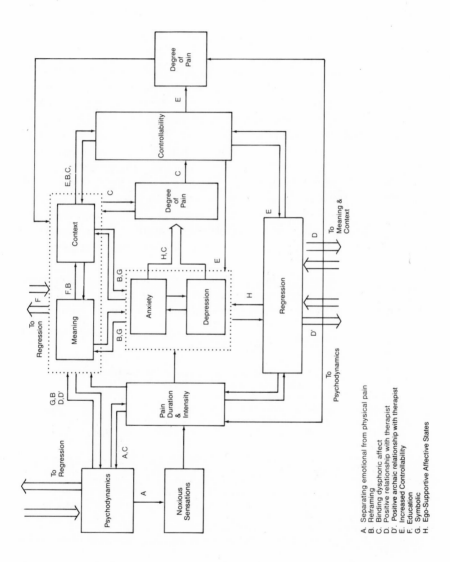

Figure 2. Schematic Points of Action of Interventions on Variables of Pain Perception

complain to others during the period of time he was using to atone. The immediate result of this intervention was that the pain disappeared. His nurse reported that sometime between 11:00 A.M. and noon Al would usually appear to be wincing, but that he never complained of pain. She further reported that it never seemed to last for more than an hour.

SUMMARY

Anxiety and depression both influence the subjective experience of pain. However, they are themselves influenced by other variables, such as context, attribution of meaning, controllability, and psychodynamics. A diagnosis of the idiosyncratic interaction of these variables for a given patient is an important aspect of the design of hypnotic and nonhypnotic interventions. The treatment approaches that have been discussed include respecting and educating the patient, separating emotional from physical pain, binding dysphoric affect, symbolically manipulating anxious and depressive mentation, building ego-supportive affective states, and reframing. These approaches can be related to the underlying variables that modify the experience of pain. In Figure 2, the hypothesized sites of therapeutic effect have been demarcated.

It is also hypothesized that the special therapeutic effect of hypnosis on pain comes from a synergism derived from the modality's ability to influence the sensory, affective, and evaluative aspects of pain.

REFERENCES

Bandler, R., & Grinder, J. (1982). *Reframing: Neurolinguistic Programming and the Transformation of Meaning*. Moab, Utah: Real People Press.

Barber, J. (1977). Rapid induction analgesia: A clinical report. *American Journal of Clinical Hypnosis, 19,* 138–147.

Barber, J. (1982). Incorporating hypnosis in the management of chronic pain. In J. Barber & C. Adrian (Eds.), *Psychological Approaches to the Management of Pain.* New York: Brunner/Mazel.

Barber, J. (speaker) (1983). *Hypnotic Alteration of Pain Perception* (audio cassette No. P317-D-4). Phoenix: Milton H. Erickson Foundation.

Beecher, H. K. (1956). The relationship of significance of wound to pain experienced. *Journal of the American Medical Association, 161* (17), 1609–1613.

Beecher, H. K. (1960). Increased stress and effectiveness of placebos and "active drugs." *Science, 132,* 267–268.

Beecher, H. K. (1966). Pain: One mystery solved. *Science, 151,* 840–841.

Chapman, C. R., & Feather, B. W. (1973). Effects of diazepam on human pain tolerance and pain sensitivity. *Psychosomatic Medicine, 35* (4), 330–339.

Craig, K. D. (1978). Social modeling influences on pain. In R. A. Sternbach (Ed.), *The Psychology of Pain.* New York: Raven.

Elton, D., Burrows, G. D., & Stanley, G. (1980). Chronic pain and hypnosis. In G. D. Burrows & L. Dennerstein (Eds.), *The Handbook of Hypnosis and Psychosomatic Medicine.* Holland: Elsevier.

Engel, G. L. (1959). "Psychogenic" pain and the pain prone patient. *American Journal of Medicine.* 899–918.

Erickson, M. H. (1954). Special techniques of brief hypnotherapy. *Journal of Clinical and Experimental Hypnosis* (2), 109–129.

Erickson, M. (1959). Hypnosis in painful terminal illness. *American Journal of Clinical Hypnosis,* 1 (1), 117–121.

Erickson, M. (1967). An introduction to the study and application of hypnosis for pain control. In J. Lassner (Ed.), *Proceedings of the International Congress for Hypnosis and Psychosomatic Medicine.* Berlin / New York: Springer-Verlag.

Erickson, M. (1983). *Healing in Hypnosis.* E. L. Rossi, M. Ryan, & F. Sharp (Eds.). New York: Irvington.

Erickson, M., & Rossi, E. L. (1979). *Hypnotherapy: An Exploratory Casebook.* New York: Irvington.

Freud, S. (1960). The ego and the id. In J. Strachey (Ed. Trans.), *The Standard Edition of the Complete Psychological Works of Sigmund Freud.* New York: Norton. (Original work published, 1923.)

Hill, H. E., Bellevill, R. E., & Wikler, A. (1955). Studies on anxiety associated with the anticipation of pain: II. Comparative effects of phenobarbitol and morphine. *Archives of Neurology and Psychiatry,* 73, 602–608.

Hill, H. E., Kornetsky, C. M., Flannery, H. G., & Wilker, A. (1952a). Studies on anxiety associated with the anticipation of pain: I. Effects of morphine. *Archives of Neurology and Psychiatry,* 67, 612–619.

Hill, H. E., Kornetsky, C. M., Flannery, H. G., & Wilker, A. (1952b). Effects of anxiety and morphine on discrimination of intensities of painful stimuli. *Journal of Clinical Investigations,* 31, 473–480.

Lankton, S., & Lankton, C. (1983). *The Answer Within: A Clinical Framework of Ericksonian Hypnotherapy.* New York: Brunner / Mazel.

Lankton, S., & Lankton, C. (1986). *Enchantment and Intervention in Family Therapy: Training in Ericksonian Approaches.* New York: Brunner / Mazel.

Leventhal, H., & Nerenz, D. R. (1983). A model for stress research with some implications for the control of stress disorders. In D. Meichenbaum & M. Jaremko (Eds.), *Stress Reduction and Prevention.* New York: Plenum.

Melzack, R., & Wall, P. (1982). *The Challenge of Pain.* New York: Basic Books.

Mersky, H. (chairman) and IASP Subcommittee on Taxonomy (1979). Pain terms: A list with definitions and notes on usage. *Pain,* 6, 249–252.

Mersky, H. (1978). Pain and personality. In R. A. Sternbach (Ed.), *The Psychology of Pain.* New York: Raven.

Mersky H., & Spear, F. G. (1967). *Pain: Psychological and Psychiatric Aspects.* London: Baillierc, Tindall & Cassell.

O'Hanlon, W. H. (1987). *Taproots: Underlying Principles of Milton Erickson's Therapy and Hypnosis.* New York: Norton.

Pilowsky, I. (1978). Psychodynamic aspects of the pain experience. In R. A. Sternbach (Ed.), *The Psychology of Pain.* New York: Raven.

Sacerdote, P. (1970). Theory and practice of pain control in malignancy and other protracted or recurring painful illnesses. *International Journal of Clinical and Experimental Hypnosis,* 17, 160–180.

Sacerdote, P. (1977). Applications of hypnotically elicited mystical states to the treatment of physical and emotional pain. *International Journal of Clinical and Experimental Hypnosis,* 25, 309–324.

Sacerdote, P. (1982). Techniques of hypnotic intervention with pain patients. In J. Bar-

302 *Brief Therapy Approaches to Treating Anxiety and Depression*

ber & C. Adrian (Eds.), *Psychological Approaches to the Management of Pain.* New York: Brunner/Mazel.

Sachs, L. B., Feuerstein, M., & Vitale, J. H. (1977). Hypnotic self-regulation of chronic pain. *American Journal of Clinical Hypnosis, (2),* 106–113.

Sainte-Exupery, A. (1971). *The Little Prince.* New York: Harcourt Brace.

Schalling, D. (1976). Anxiety, pain and coping. In I. Sarason & C. Spielberger (Eds.), *Stress and Anxiety* (Vol. 3). New York: Wiley.

Schwarz, R. (1984). The hypnotherapy of pain: A study of clinical methodologies. Unpublished doctoral dissertation.

Seligman, M. P. (1975). *Helplessness: On Depression, Development, and Death.* San Francisco: W. H. Freeman.

Shor, R. E. (1962). Three dimensions of hypnotic depth. *International Journal of Clinical and Experimental Hypnosis, 10,* 23–38.

Spiegel, H., & Spiegel, D. (1978). *Trance and Treatment.* New York: Basic Books.

Sternbach, R. (1968). *Pain: A Psychophysical Analysis.* New York: Academic.

Sternbach, R. (1974). *Pain, Patients and Treatment.* New York: Academic.

Szasz, T. (1957). *Pain and Pleasure.* New York: Basic Books.

Thompson, K. (speaker) (1983). *Pain Control in Traumatic Situations* (audio cassette No. P320-24AB). Phoenix: Milton H. Erickson Foundation.

Thompson, S. C. (1981). Will it hurt less if I can control it? A complex answer to a simple question. *Psychological Bulletin, 90* (1), 89–101.

Violin, A. (1982). The process involved in becoming a chronic pain patient. In R. Roy & E. Tunks (Eds.), *Chronic Pain: Psychosocial Factors in Rehabilitation.* Baltimore: Williams & Wilkins.

Zeig, J. (1985). *Experiencing Erickson: An Introduction to the Man and His Work.* New York: Brunner/Mazel.

Chapter 15

Hypnotic Treatment of Depression with the Use of Dissociation and Submodalities

Norma Barretta, Philip Barretta, and Joseph A. Bongiovanni

Norma Barretta, Ph.D., is a clinical psychologist in private practice in San Pedro, Ca. She is a Fellow of the American Society of Clinical Hypnosis. Philip Barretta, M. A., is a marriage, family, child counselor in private practice in San Pedro, Ca., and a special member of the American Society of Clinical Hypnosis.

The Barrettas' are well known national and international trainers in neurolinguistic programming and Ericksonian hypnosis.

Joseph A. Bongiovanni, M. A. (Loyola Marymount University) also has a B. A. in music from California State University, where he served as composer in residence for the theatre department for two years, winning both local and national recognition for his work. He is a certified trainer in the Carkhuff Communications Model. He has led several workshops focusing on interview skills utilizing neurolinguistic programming, and has completed his practitioner training in NLP.

This chapter describes how a dissociative process is used therapeutically to change patient responses by manipulating sensory submodalities. This hypnotic technique allows the therapist to intensify and expedite the process of therapeutic learning by the patient. The structure of this hypnotic approach is examined, and case histories are presented as examples of its successful use in the treatment of severe depression.

Dissociation has long been considered a basic component of trance induction, and as such is assumed to be familiar to the reader (Erickson & Rossi, 1979). Dissociation serves to depotentiate the habitual framework and belief systems of the client. It does this by allowing the patient to avoid kinesthetic involvement and thus to have a more comfortably objective experience in reviewing past events. Submodalities may be defined as that vast array of dimensions one holds within each major sensory modality. The general quality and specific degree of experience of the submodalities are unique both to the individual and to the particular context under consideration.

The chief distinction between modalities and submodalities is as follows: Modalities are those primary sensory channels through which we represent and "map" our reality. These include visual, auditory, kinesthetic, and olfactory/gustatory channels. Submodalities are the qualities and component characteristics of those larger representations and processes, such as brightness, distance, loudness, timbre, texture, and temperature.

For example, one can compare a melody played by a flute with the same melody played by a violin. Although the representation is virtually the same in terms of content, the quality of sound of a violin is considerably different from that of the flute, even at the same registers. In this case, one could say that the timbre of the instruments are submodalities of the pitches produced. A partial listing of submodalities grouped according to modality follows in Table 1:

Table 1. Submodalities, Grouped According to Modality

Visual	Kinesthetic	Auditory	Olfactory/gustatory
Light	Pressure	Volume	Sweet
Distance	Cold	Tonality	Sour
Size	Warm	Speed	Acrid
Focus	Smooth	Pitch	Salty
Brilliance	Clammy	Timbre	Bitter
Contrast	Rough	Resonance	Flowery
Color	Mushy	Tone	Smoky

Just as a thesaurus adds quality and dimension to language, submodalities enhance awareness of experiential processes, allowing just the right description of the event at hand, whether it is in consciousness or not.

How do submodalities, which usually serve to make experience associative, facilitate the seemingly diametric process of dissociation? A simple answer to the question is evident in the previous example of submodalities of the flute and violin. Those components that allow one the internal representation of the sound of a flute or violin are the associative submodalities of the auditory experience that is symbolically (i.e., linguistically) coded "flute" or "violin." Other sensory modalities and submodalities may also be associated, and would serve further to intensify the coding of the representation.

To facilitate further explanation of the submodalities, let us refer to the coded experiences as beliefs labeled "violin" and "flute." To be specific, assume the belief under examination is one labeled "violin." We can recall and identify all the submodalities associated with that belief in order to make certain that we have an accurate representation of our belief "violin." We check all modalities that may have also coded information into this particular experience. When the search is complete, we are congruent in the belief "violin." It matches that framework we have habituated and identified, and we then know what the belief "violin" is. Equally important, however, is that we also know what it is *not!* Remember, the submodalities are unique both to the experience under consideration and to the individual.

In order to begin a submodal shift in this "violin" example, we could examine some of the submodalities that are associated with the experience. Let us say that one of them is a clear vibrato. A shift could begin by re-representing that submodality—not as a clear vibrato, but rather as dry and muted. As we change the associated submodalities of an experience, we also change the habitual framework that helps to code and support the belief.

The dissociative process utilizes the uniqueness of the specific combination of submodalities as the basis for facilitating change. The belief "violin," which has been identified and coded through the submodalities, can be changed by the switching of the currently operating submodalities. By taking what we know to be the associated submodalities of the coded experience "violin" and changing them, we begin to change the belief "violin."

The "violin" example demonstrates some of the principal mechanics of dissociation and the therapeutic use of submodalities. It must be remembered that most belief systems are multi-modal, meaning they contain representations in more then one modality. This also means that such habituated frameworks are capable of containing many submodalities. The process used in maintaining these beliefs are generally not varied, but instead are quite rigid—i.e., looped between modalities.

In the case of depression, it appears that the rigid and dysfunctional loop is between the auditory and kinesthetic modalities. Severely depressed individuals may reflect the rigidity of their position by presenting a posture that is visibly tight, restricted, and constrained. When asked how they feel, they may reply, "stuck," as indeed they are. Such patients will also tend to talk to themselves in a manner that reinforces their self-deprecation and negative feelings, quite literally giving them more about which to talk negatively and to feel badly. The submodalities that operate in a severely depressed individual are usually as rigid as his or her beliefs. Thus, by changing submodality representations, the process of dissociation can be greatly expedited.

It should be noted that dissociation is part of the much larger process of hypnosis. The shift in conscious awareness that dissociation provides sets the stage for the unconscious search and projective process that will lead to the target state of a utilizable hypnotic response. The following case anecdote of Hillary is provided as an example overviewing the complete process. A more detailed example appears in the second case anecdote, Jim.

HILLARY

Hillary was first seen during an acute episode of severe depression following a suicide threat at the dental office where she was employed. She had locked herself in a bathroom and for the greater part of the day had threatened suicide. Although her co-workers pleaded with her not to take any rash action, they were well aware that the medicine chest in the bathroom contained more than an ample supply of medication that might allow her to carry out her threat. The dentist for whom she worked hesitated to call paramedics or police, believing that it might be detrimental to his practice if he were unable to "talk her down." Hillary's co-workers talked with her throughout the day, unable to convince her to come out of the bathroom. Later in the afternoon, the dentist promised to drive Hillary to our offices, whereupon she agreed to leave the bathroom.

Her appearance was that of someone who had obviously been crying most of the day. Her mascara had run, her posture was slumped forward, her hair was in disarray, and her visual focus was fixed downward. She presented a blunted affect, and did not volunteer any immediate verbal response.

By behavioral mirroring, the therapists, Philip and Norma Barretta, were able to meet Hillary at her existing point of reality, seeing and feeling the world to some degree as if through her eyes. Experiencing her world in this way, Philip and Norma could become aware of Hillary's modality representation. It was learned that Hillary's experience was definitely not significantly visual. It became apparent that in order to effect positive change, they would have to help move Hillary out of the kinesthetic-auditory loop and into more of a visual mode.

After a short period of mirroring Hillary, Norma made the following statement: "You know, Hillary, if I looked as bad as you do at this moment, I would want to kill myself, too."

Upon hearing this, Hillary looked up for a moment, directly into Norma's eyes. She then immediately returned to her original posture. At this point Philip asked: "How are you going to do it?" She looked up slightly and responded, "Oh, I don't know. Pills, I guess." Philip replied, "I can teach you a faster way. That's too slow." Hillary looked up, holding her stare a bit longer, but ultimately returning to her previous position without comment. Norma then asked her: "Who would you like to have find the body?" Hillary took a deep breath, sighed, and said: "Oh, I don't know." At this point, Philip and Norma both jumped up, made a loud noise by clapping their hands together, and literally screamed at her: "What? You're going to waste one perfectly good suicide and you don't have somebody to find the body? Put it off until we decide."

At this point, Hillary looked up at the two therapists and laughed aloud. Norma touched Hillary's knee as Hillary laughed, to "anchor" the feeling of laughing. Since Hillary was still seated, her eyes were necessarily directed upward in order to make eye contact. This visual information-processing eye positioning and the accompanying feeling of lighthearted laughter also became "anchored," meaning that it was established as a conditioned response that could be elicited again. It could be elicited by Norma's touch as well as by having Hillary look up. Hillary responded to the outburst by saying: "You are both crazy!", at which point Philip and Norma returned to a seated position and quietly said: "Well, we're not the ones who locked ourselves into a bathroom. We're not the ones who threatened suicide all day, and we're not the ones sitting in this office looking as bad as you do right now." Hillary sat back in her chair and replied: "You're right, I'm the crazy one."

Now both therapists knew that their client was now in a position actually to begin therapy. The thrust of their initial efforts was to initiate *some* change in her view of the world, to brighten it up, and to help her see that there was something to experience other than the depressive state in which she had been stuck for a quite long time.

As therapy proceeded, information gathered from Hillary indicated that her depression seemed to deepen whenever she went to a home she owned in another part of the country. The depression that seemed to be triggered at her second home continued even upon her return to southern California, and would remain for several weeks. As the therapists explored what, if anything, might have triggered the depressive episodes, they noticed that Hillary's nostrils consistently flared in response to questions about the second home. Although Hillary seemed to have no conscious awareness of what she was experiencing, it seemed apparent that she was recalling some olfactory memories because the response was always the same. Philip then suggested that she talk about the smells in the house.

At this point, Hillary immediately went into a severely depressed state. She began to sob and describe how she felt when she was in that house. The preponderance of depressive memories was triggered by several olfactory submodalities, including mustiness, smoky odors, dog smells, and, particularly, the smell of the bedspread and draperies in her bedroom. Working hypnotically, Hillary was given suggestions for kinesthetic comfort and dissociation. A suggestion was made that she could brighten up the house with new wallpaper, paint, drapery, and carpet. The renovation project provided a specific means by which she could change the multiple submodalities that seemed to serve as triggers for her depression. She agreed, and after having done so, she reported that her new experience of the house triggered a completely different subjective response. After that report, Philip pointed out to Hillary how the smells had driven her depressed states. She considered the information and then immediately reverted to her previously depressed affect. Both therapists then began attaching positive and desirable feelings to the "new" smells that now were to be found at the other house. In doing so, the negative anchor and depressing effect of the undesired submodality was eliminated.

A three-year follow-up indicated that Hillary had a more positive outlook, a different perspective on her life, and a clearer view of what she could do to keep herself functioning in a happier state. She had brightened her life picture for herself, had taken charge of the feelings that used to interfere with her ability to function, and had reduced the internal auditory dialogue. It would seem that the greatest changes began to occur after Hillary literally changed the smells of her second home. She constantly commented how different that house smelled whenever she went there after the redecorating.

Discussion of Hillary

The case of Hillary provides an excellent example of how submodalities can dramatically intensify a coded experience and combine with submodalities of other sensory modes in order to become a trigger for complete sets of behaviors. Hillary's depression had persisted for over ten years, remaining impervious to therapeutic approaches that did not involve the examination of unconscious processing driven by submodalities. Her numerous episodes of suicidal ideation ended only after the pernicious auditory-kinesthetic loop had been interrupted and the olfactory submodality triggers remodeled.

Through the dissociative process, the ability to choose was restored to Hillary's unconscious so that she could decide between the limited smells of depression and the unlimited smells of happiness. Hillary, we're pleased to say, found that happiness made more "scents," and in so doing, won by a nose.

JIM

Jim was a 38-year-old man who reported that he could not recall a single moment in his life that had not been traumatic. Jim's father was an alcoholic and had left the home when Jim was still an infant. Jim was reared by his mother, who was extremely strict and often used the threat of "hellfire, brimstone and eventual damnation" in disciplining him. She blamed Jim for everything unfortunate that happened in her life. High academic standards were set for Jim, and severe beatings were the consequence for any grade below an "A." He was constantly referred to as "the boy."

Jim was often called into his mother's room to rub her feet, a task he found demeaning. During these foot-rubbing sessions, his mother would tell him, ostensibly "for his own good," how stupid, ugly, and evil he was. This constant denigration was intended to "save" Jim from the fires of hell. All through these episodes, Jim reported having done his best to be a "good boy." Not unexpectedly, nothing Jim did won the approval of his mother, nor did it end her constant demeaning of him.

As was the case with Hillary, Jim had a depressogenic auditory-kinesthetic loop functioning. In his case, the voice he heard in his thoughts was that of his mother. As with Hillary, the loop had to be broken before new information could be presented. The "nagging" voice of his mother was relatively easy to disengage by changing the submodality associated with it. While Jim was comfortably dissociated with a strong kinesthetic anchor established for safety, he was asked to hear his mother speaking in the voices of various cartoon characters. The positive result was that Jim found uncontrollable humor in her verbalizations, rather than recrimination.

Since Jim could not recall any positive past experiences in his personal history, one had to be constructed using submodalities. Jim was asked to use someone whom he knew to serve as a model for such an experience. He chose a neighbor who had been very active in woodworking and had invited Jim to help in a woodworking project. Unfortunately, Jim had become so concerned with achieving perfection in the project that he was not able to enjoy the "fun" of doing it. Nonetheless, the neighbor had provided an excellent male model for Jim. The neighbor was a kind and gentle "family man" who treated Jim respectfully and sympathetically. As Jim put it, "He was nice to me and gave me hope that not everyone in the world is as critical and mean as my mother was."

First, a visual and auditory representation of Jim's model [the neighbor] was constructed. Jim was told that he could pretend to borrow the positive resources his model had. Next, Jim was asked to construct a picture of his neighbor on a television screen in front of him. He was then instructed to change the various submodality distinctions. He was asked to increase the brilliance of the picture, sharpen its contrast, enhance its focus, increase its size, and so forth. He was also asked to adjust the sound on this television set, changing the neighbor's voice in speed and pitch and later in character. At times, Jim had the neighbor sound like cartoon characters (such as

Bugs Bunny or Mickey Mouse) or actors (such as Cary Grant or Clark Gable). All of this was done while Jim was comfortably dissociated. It was later discovered that the cinema had been an avenue of escape for Jim as a young man, and the utilization of auditory submodalities served to help facilitate Jim's search for positive resourceful states from those experiences. Jim was instructed to continue playing with his imaginary TV until he appeared able to manipulate the picture of his neighbor in every possible way. At no time was this a problem for Jim because he was able to maintain the dissociated state. Once Jim became adept at controlling his TV, he was instructed to make the picture of his neighbor very tiny and put it in the lower-right-hand corner of the screen. He was then directed to return it to fill the entire screen with every potential resource as fully developed as possible. Jim was then asked to return the picture to its tiny size and hold it steadily in the lower-right-hand corner. This he did easily, having been provided with ample practice opportunities. Next, he was instructed to put a picture of himself at his lowest emotional point onto the full screen. Once again, Jim was asked to change the focus, the sound, the contrast, and the like until it was apparent to the therapists that he could manipulate this picture as easily as the others. At this point, Jim was instructed to focus on the little picture held steady in the lower-right-hand corner and then to have it rapidly blow up, pushing the other image completely off the screen and out of the picture. To facilitate this, Norma made both a "swishing" noise and an extended-arm motion as a nonverbal suggestion to fill the screen.

By this time, Jim had entered trance and begun processing the new experience. He was asked to intensify the submodalities of the picture, and even make the resourceful neighbor three dimensional. He was then asked to step into the picture and fully to experience being in it. The process was repeated: first, the picture of the less-than-resourceful Jim filling the large screen, then again "blown out" by that of the fully resourceful neighbor. When this became easy for Jim to do, he was told to step into the picture and replace his neighbor in a fully resourceful state.

Following the third repetition of this exercise, Jim was no longer able to recall the unresourceful picture of himself. He now experienced himself as fully associated with those submodalities of the resourceful neighbor.

A one-year follow-up on Jim indicated that he had found the ability to enjoy himself and had reaffirmed his own self-worth and resourcefulness. He reported minimal incidents of depression, and demonstrated his capacity to pursue a much happier, more functional life.

Discussion of Jim

Jim's depression was driven by strong internal auditory inputs originating in his traumatic childhood. He had no positive experience that he could call upon in order to build resources from within himself. Furthermore, he felt that it was "unsafe" to do so, as a result of the severe conditioning imposed upon him by his mother.

In this instance, therefore, resources had to be "borrowed." Jim had to be taught how to manipulate the sounds in his head and how to change the pictures for his own benefit. This therapeutic work was done while Jim was in a dissociated state; thus, he was able to feel comfortable and safe as he changed the sounds and the pictures. In a dissociated state, Jim could take full control and manipulate the auditory and visual submodalities he experienced.

When Jim had developed enough skill, he was reassociated so that he could experience the good feelings that accompanied his new pictures and sounds. He was now "in charge."

SUMMARY

Using dissociation to enhance the reframing of responses by manipulating the submodalities can be a relatively rapid and effective means to bring about change in even the most severely depressed individuals. Once the kinesthetic dimension of experience is safely protected by dissociation, the client can begin the process of change and discover more beneficial choices. The use of submodalities facilitates not only the examination of the undesired feelings, but also a far more comprehensive reassociation of the desired emotional response.

REFERENCES

Andreas, S., & Andreas, C. (1987). *Change Your Mind and Keep the Change* (1st ed.), Moab, Utah.: Real People Press.

Bandler, R., Andreas, S., & Andreas, C. (Eds.) (1985). *Using Your Brain for a Change.* Moab, Utah.: Real People Press.

Bandler, R., & Grinder, J. (1976). *The Structure of Magic (Vol. I).* Palo Alto, Calif.: Science and Behavior Books.

Bandler R., & Grinder, J. (1976). *The Structure of Magic (Vol. II).* Palo Alto, Calif.: Science and Behavior Books.

Bandler, R., & Grinder, J. (1979). *Frogs into Princes: Neuro-linguistic Programming* (1st ed.). Moab, Utah.: Real People Press.

Dilts, R., Grinder, J., Bandler, R., and DeLozier, J. (1980). *Neurolinguistic Programming (Vol. I): The Study of the Structure of Subjective Experience.* Cupertino, Calif.: Meta Publications.

Erickson, M., & Rossi, E. (1979). *Hypnotherapy: An Exploratory Casebook.* New York: Irvington.

Haley, J. (Ed.) (1967). *Advanced Techniques of Hypnosis and Therapy: Selected Papers of Milton Erickson, M.D.* New York: Grune & Stratton.

Laborde, G. Z. (1983). *Influencing with Integrity: Management Skills for Communication and Negotiation.* Palo Alto, Calif.: Syntony Publishing.

Laborde, G. Z. (1988). *Fine Tune Your Brain: When Everything's Going Right and What to Do When It Isn't.* Palo Alto, Calif.: Syntony Publishing.

Chapter 16

When Doesn't the Problem Happen?

Jane E. Peller and John L. Walter

Jane E. Peller, A.C.S.W., is Co-director of Consultations in Chicago. She is an assistant professor in the Department of Social Work at Northeastern Illinois University (Chicago).

John L. Walter, A.C.S.W., is Co-director of Consultations in Chicago. He is also practicing brief therapy at the Evanston Hospital in Evanston, IL.

How often it happens that our ongoing clients come into our offices and tell us about how they continue to feel depressed or anxious. As they continue to report their stories and feelings, they appear to be performing an induction on themselves as they elicit increasingly negative experiences and feelings. Their "symptomatic" trances become deeper as they recount and report on how bad they feel. The worse they feel, the more negative memories come up, spiraling in a vicious cycle.

If therapists do not do something to interrupt clients at those times, the induction continues and then clients feel worse and remain seemingly trapped. Unfortunately, the clients play out these negative inductions on themselves every day and reinforce the negative labels they have attached to the experiences. Eventually, they are convinced that not only do they *feel* that way, but that they *are* that way.

However, this type of "induction" need not continue. Basic to Ericksonian approaches is the principle of utilization (Erickson & Rossi, 1980; de Shazer, 1985; Lankton & Lankton, 1983; Dolan, 1985; Gilligan, 1987; O'Hanlon, 1987). Milton H. Erickson utilized the responses of his subjects not only to induce trance, but also to create workable, realistic solutions to their problems. He often elicited experiences from the client, sometimes from contexts other than the problematic one, in which the client either did not experience the problem or was somehow able to solve it. These experiences were used as resource states for the client as well as a source for further intervention.

This chapter describes one way of duplicating Erickson's approach. It is not a work on depression or anxiety, but rather a description of a method for eliciting more positive "inductions" in place of the old "depressed" or "anxious" trance states. There are several assumptions inherent in this approach. (For a more expanded description of this approach, see *Keys to Solution in Brief Therapy* and *Clues: Investigating Solutions in Brief Therapy* by Steve de Shazer.)

ASSUMPTIONS REGARDING THERAPEUTIC CHANGE

The Advantages of Focusing on the Positive

Focusing on "the positive" facilitates further change. Basic to this assumption is the constructivist statement that there is no meaning inherent in anything in and of itself apart from the observer (von Glaserfeld, 1984; von Foerster, 1984; Watzlawick, 1984; Maturana & Varela, 1987). If this is assumed, then it follows that observers with a positive frame can construct more positive meanings or realities.

More simply put, if a client can be seen as performing a negative induction on him or herself by eliciting continuous negative thoughts and feelings, then it follows that by eliciting positive thoughts and feelings, a client can create a more positive induction. With the elicitation and selective perception of positive thoughts and feelings, a client builds a resource state with more associations to similar states. More positive frames are then used to perceive surrounding events, and, therefore, more positive events are found.

Another way of stating this assumption is to say that talking about change leads to further change. Clients describe problems and change in a way that is greatly shaped by the interaction between the client and therapist. Clients' descriptions of a problem or solution are affected by the assumptions and direction of the questions of the therapist. Carefully worded questions can help construct the desired reality.

As helpers, our interviews or sessions are more successful when they guide the client to a different set of options for defining or responding to the problem. Gingerich, de Shazer, and Weiner-Davis

(1987) found in their research on clinical interviewing that when counselors focused on change by eliciting times of previous or present changing, clients reported times of which they were aware as well as times of which they had not previously thought. Clients spoke of times they had solved or were currently solving the problem. The research shows clients may have previously dismissed these times of problem-solving as insignificant. However, through the focusing by the interviewer, clients began to see these behaviors as significant toward lasting solutions and to recall even more examples.

By asking such questions as, "Are there recent times when this was less of a problem?" or "When doesn't the problem happen?" clients can be guided into more positive areas. In answering these questions, clients search for experiences of some success and can begin to associate success to even more contexts. People often feel differently as they speak of positive times, and may even become positively revisionist about the "bad" times. (For a more expanded explanation of these questions and question sequences, see Lipchik, 1988.)

Speaking about change evolving in the future can also promote change. The book *The Inner Game of Tennis* (Gallwey, 1974) speaks to the advantages of creating images of success or of visualizing what one wants to do. The assumption is that providing a visual, auditory, or kinesthetic representation of the desired change provides a conceptual model as well as an experience that can be built upon or imitated.

A client may be told, "Let's say that this is the last session and your problem is either resolved or you are more confident that you are on track to solving it. What are you doing differently?" We can facilitate clients' identifying resources and expectations as they project themselves into the future. In responding, they are likely to describe concretely what they will be doing or thinking differently. With this approach, there is the presupposition that *they will* solve the problem.

Exceptions Suggest Solutions

There are exceptions to the problem that may be used to construct solutions to the problem (de Shazer, 1985, 1988). However, clients may initially not be aware of exceptions to the problem or that the exceptions contain potential for change.

All of us are inadvertent victims of our constructions. Events or experiences are constructed or selected in a manner consistent with the frame through which we approach them. Similarly, those experiences that are different are not selected.

We perceive the events of the day as if we have developed rules about what is to be perceived from the random events around us. Many times these frames or rules become so pervasive that events or behaviors that are different from one's frame of reference are not selected. It is as if we do not even see them because they do not fit.

Experiences that are outside of the frame are not different enough to stand out or be marked as different or exceptional. Along Bateson's line of thinking, they may not be different enough to make a difference (Bateson, 1972). Even though they may be exceptions to the pattern or to what is expected, they may be marked only as flukes, random, or too small to be significant.

Clients create contexts and representations of the problem whereby they simply do not recognize or give credit to those exceptional times when the problem does not occur.

De Shazer (1988) described a client who had been doing cocaine on a daily basis for quite some time and came in for treatment in order to stop this abuse. In the course of the interview, she mentioned that she had not used cocaine in the past three days. This was an exception to the daily pattern of using the drug. However, she did not see this as exceptional or significant because she assumed the real solution to be something else. These three days simply did not count in her experience, negated by her assumption that the "real" solution would be no longer wanting the drug. So, every time she did not use cocaine it did not count because she was aware that she still wanted it.

Consistent with this assumption, she was looking for someone to make her not want cocaine anymore. She thought that as long as she still liked it and wanted it, there was no way she could stop using it. So, in effect, the context she created for these three days of no cocaine was one of "no significance."

Another example of clients overlooking solutions was a couple who sought therapy for recurring fights. Their conflicts were about the past affairs each had had and whose fault it was that they had happened. Each honestly thought that the way to solve the problem of hurt feelings and resentment was to "talk it all out." But each time they attempted to talk, it resulted in their fighting and feeling so bad that they ended up being unable to talk about almost anything. Further, they assumed that if they could not talk this problem out, their relationship was hopeless. Thinking that it may be hopeless, they were that much more desperate the next time they attempted to talk it out.

Since they thought the "real" solution was to talk out the events of the past and resolve them by reaching some agreement on whose fault it was, they were rigidly constructing their experience around this assumption. Consequently, they missed other events going on outside of that pattern because the other experiences appeared to not be relevant to their notion of *the* solution.

In the course of the interview, this couple mentioned going on a bike ride together and having a relaxed time. This was different for them to share, but they were not sure how to explain how it happened. As observers outside of this couple's relationship system and not sharing their assumption about how to solve the problem, this seemed significantly different from their usual patterns. Rather than assuming that the divisive issues had to be resolved first and that they had to be resolved through constant but fruitless discussion, we thought they would have a better chance of re-establishing trust by doing something other than talking about the problem. Since they were looking for resolution only through what they thought to be the solution, the impact of having fun on the bike ride was not a difference that made a difference to them.

The therapists assumed that the bike ride was a meaningful difference and a possible route to what they stated they wanted, which was evolving trust again in their relationship. During this time of bike riding, they agreed they had fun and that "trust" was not a problem. They were not thinking about it, nor were they talking about it. They agreed that they would be on the right track to solving the problem if they continued to have more times like they had during the bike ride.

In this instance, the contrast of the usual problem time with the episode of the exception provided the contextual difference that was helpful in constructing a goal and designing interventions for this couple. They appeared to believe that their resolving this issue from the past would lead to more trust. The direction of this thinking was reversed by suggestions that their noticing or creating more trusting times would result in the issue of the past becoming less of a problem. The couple was instructed not to do anything different but merely to observe any other times in their relationship that they enjoyed or wanted to keep. Further interviews elicited differences of context or meaning that enabled them to have good times. Even some fights were marked as good because they were productive and centered on how to accomplish something they both wanted, e.g., how to get their daughter to do her homework. Naturally, as they noticed more good times and how each contributed to making them happen, they decided that what was in the past was better left in the past.

Small Change Is Generative

Small changes can lead to larger changes. At first glance, many problems can appear to be very complex and difficult and therefore require very complex and powerful solutions. However, this is not necessarily the case because a small change in a pattern can lead to continuous changes or generative change.

One example involves a client named Jim who sought therapy to deal with panic attacks. He was encouraged to seek therapy because his constant anxiety and anticipatory fears of further anxiety were becoming intolerable to his live-in girlfriend. Jim stated that he was especially afraid of his anxiety because his father had been hospitalized for several years for anxiety and eventually committed suicide. Jim feared that this trait was something passed down to him from his father and that he could end up hopelessly hospitalized too. Despite all of his efforts to control his anxiety or to identify its causes, it appeared to be getting worse. Jim thought that it was not only a very serious problem, but also a very complicated one. He assumed it would take a great deal of courage to get over his fears.

Jim was a camera repairman, and since the beginning of these panic attacks, he had become so anxious at work that he noticed his hands shaking. This caused him to become even more worried that perhaps he could not be steady enough with his tools to repair the fine instruments. An episode of missoldering camera wires convinced him that his anxiety was becoming so bad that it was interfering with his performance and that he might lose his job. He quit his job soon after for fear of making further mistakes.

Jim was obviously in a downward spiral of anxiety and panic. He sought medication because it had been the solution his father had sought, and was an approach consistent with what he thought was a biologically based problem. His girlfriend, who had previously been diagnosed as manic-depressive and was accustomed to the use of medication, concurred with his solution of medication and rest. However, even after a course of prescribed medication, he was just as fearful. His girlfriend was now becoming less understanding of his being immobilized.

Each day Jim saw further evidence of his problem. In the interviews, he could barely remember what it was like to feel good, much less confident to face his fears. Jim saw this as a very complicated and difficult problem, and, therefore, was overwhelmed by the thought of how to solve it.

Utilizing the principle that small change can lead to larger change, Jim was instructed to be very cautious about his problem and not to expect too much too soon. Instead, he was advised to take things one step at a time, and even to break his steps down into much, much smaller pieces. He was then instructed that the next time he was aware of feeling anxious or panicky, he was to *do* something, anything, rather than think.

This suggestion was enough to initiate a break in the pattern of perseveration and panic. He came back and reported that one time he decided to go for a walk, another time he decided to go to his photography class rather than stay home and feel bad, and still another time, when both he and his girlfriend were in a "blue funk," he suggested they go out and listen to some live music. He stated that such decisions sometimes made the feelings go away, not all the time, but sometimes. However, his actively doing something broke the cycle of his internal dialogue enough times to lead to his *doing* more. With this initial success he was able to continue building more of a representation of progress.

Resources are Within

People are assumed to have all the resources they need to solve their problems (Gilligan, 1987; Lankton & Lankton, 1983). This Ericksonian assumption reaffirms the belief that people are not defective, but rather can solve their problems if helped into a different direction. Similar to other models (Anderson, Goolishian, & Winderman, 1986; Weakland, Fisch, Watzlawick, & Bodin, 1974) the authors believe that the problem is not in the person or in the system, but rather the problem is the problem. Therefore, the focus of therapy is on developing a solution rather than on the deficits of a person or dysfunctions in a system.

Clients are Cooperating

De Shazer (1984), Gilligan (1987), and others have stated that clients do not resist change or therapists as helpers. Clients attempt to solve their problems according to the way they have defined or framed it and in the way they think change takes place. If they do not accept suggestions, it is not because they are "resistant." Rather, the suggestion simply does not fit with their notion of how change takes place. Thus, in "resisting," they are cooperating and showing how they can be helped by providing feedback about how they change and what therapists do that does or does not work. The onus, therefore, is on helpers to be flexible enough to find ways to cooperate with clients and their view of the world.

Wholism

The notion of wholism states that any change anywhere in a system necessarily affects the entire system (Fisch, Weakland, & Segal, 1982). Any change in interaction, whether between people or in the recursive way that someone attempts to solve a problem, affects the system as a whole. This notion supports the "ripple effect" of small changes, as no interactional system is ever exactly the same once change has begun. Any change in the interaction will ripple into other interactions as well.

Wholism also allows helpers to solve problems, even ones that would traditionally be defined as "family" problems, by working with only one person. Any change by one person will necessarily and inevitably affect the interactions with other relationship members.

A CASE EXAMPLE INCORPORATING A SOLUTION-FOCUS

With the above assumptions, the overall goal in treatment is to join the client in constructing a solution. The authors do this by implanting assumptions into interviews and by the interventions suggested. The following case example demonstrates this approach.

People Lovers: Wanda, a 30-year-old single woman, came alone into therapy because of her depression. She reported that she had been "coping" with depression all her life. When questioned about this, she described herself as an "insecure" person who felt "needy" about everything in her life. She stated that she had been a "depressed" person for as long as she could remember, and that she was able to mask it by being "deceptive" with others. She thought she had to be deceptive in order to be liked. Because of this "problem," she reported that she often acted deceptively even toward her lover in order to maximize acceptance and affection. She, therefore, was the one in the relationship who consistently ended up "approaching the other" for affection and reassurance. This frame of reference and subsequent negative self-induction had become so strong for Wanda that even when she considered doing, acting, or feeling differently, i.e., positively, she perceived it as being "deceptive."

Following the assumption that there are exceptions to the problem, Wanda was asked if there were times when these problems did not occur. Wanda acknowledged that there were many times that her friends told her that she was not insecure. Additionally, Wanda reported that she was not deceptive with people about whom she did not care. However, these things did not matter to her, because all she could notice from her self-limiting frame of reference were the times she was deceptive, insecure, and needy for attention.

Wanda's initial goals in therapy were to "increase her self-confidence and improve her self-image." However, these were not specific enough goals to be helpful in constructing solutions. It was necessary to know concretely what she would be doing, thinking, or saying to herself when the problems were solved. When asked, "If this were the last session and the problem was solved, or you were confident that you were on the right track to solving the problem, what would you be doing differently?," she replied that she would not be working so hard in trying to get her lover to show her how much he cared. Such effort always reminded Wanda of her feeling "insecure" and "needy." Instead of being the "approacher," Wanda said she wanted to be "saying what was on her mind, listening more and being more receptive."

When asked if this ever occurred now, she stated that she did respond in the desired way on occasion. As a matter of fact, her lover, Frank, was sitting in the waiting room during our session. Wanda had told him what was on her mind, which was that she wanted him to come along for support. However, Wanda decided not to push her request and that if he did not want to come with her, that was all right. Then she dropped the subject. "How did you do that?", she was asked. She responded, "I bit my tongue," meaning she stopped herself from increasing the level of demand on Frank.

This was an exception to the pattern of Wanda's approaching Frank to get affection. Consistent with the assumption of building on the exception to the problem, Wanda was asked how she thought of doing that. She did not know. Questioning revealed that there were several times when Wanda "bit her tongue." In fact, when she did, Frank was more responsive in the relationship. When he was more responsive in the relationship, Wanda did not feel the old familiar insecure and needy feelings.

Clearly, Wanda had all the resources she needed to solve the problem, but because actions such as "biting her tongue" did not lead either to her lover's responding totally in the way Wanda wanted him to or in Wanda's feeling more self-confident, these solutions were not perceived by her as making a difference. Since they did not make a difference, Wanda did not recognize that it might be useful to do more of such behavior.

In accordance with the model of building on clients' strengths and the things they are already doing positively, the authors decided to give the following intervention:

> We are very impressed with your sensitivity, commitment to the relationship, and your honesty in the session with us. In fact, for someone who reports being so deceptive, we find you to be very open and honest. We aren't quite sure how you figured out that it was better to "bite your tongue," but it seemed to work and we are very impressed by the fact that you stumbled onto a possible workable solution. However, we need more information and we want you to watch for what happens between now and the next session that you would like to continue to have happen between the two of you.

As predicted, Wanda returned the next week with reports of success. When she "held back by biting her tongue," Frank approached more. In fact, he bought her a gift one day. Even though Wanda had not directly been told to bite her tongue, by the use of suggestive questions and building on the exception to the problem in the intervention, Wanda was able to remember and select an already-existing workable experience and use it to begin to solve her problem. When people have something that is already working, but it is outside of their usual frame of reference and/or their experience, reassurance from the therapist may be all that is needed for the client to do more of what works. Given this, and the assumption of cooperation, the second intervention focused on telling Wanda to do more of her solution and to watch for how she overcame the temptation to approach Frank when she did not think it was likely to be responded to as desired. The veiled statement in this intervention was that there are times when approaching is likely to succeed and there are times when it is not.

By the third session, six weeks after the initial visit, it became clear that Wanda was utilizing the exception to the pattern as a solution. She was saying what was on her mind, and listening and being receptive to different opinions from Frank. For example, Wanda left a note for him one day simply saying how much she loved him and that she would talk to him later. Wanda was asked how this was different from before, and she stated enthusiastically that she would have declared at least 100 times "I love you," and asked whether he loved her, too. Subsequently, Wanda just went on with her daily events instead of waiting around and becoming depressed and/or anxious about the anticipated response from Frank.

At this point, the assumption that a small change can lead to further changing prompted the question, "As these changes continue, what else in your life will be different?" Wanda responded that she did not think other things would be different. This was interpreted as Wanda's maintaining her frame of herself being an "insecure person" or "insecure personality." In other words, she was not recognizing the pattern of this exception as an ultimate solution to the more global problem of her "insecure personality." Wanda needed a new label to fit the new behaviors so that the new behaviors could generate further new behaviors. The third intervention focused on this missing link:

> We are very impressed with what you have done since we saw you last. We were really expecting that you were not going to be able to keep up these changes of pulling back. But we have to say that we question something you said about being an insecure personality. To us, you are what we call a "people lover." They are people with a lot of love within them and, therefore, a lot of love to give to others. They love to be with people, to talk, etc. Unlike others, who need to be alone a lot, people lovers have little need for alone time. People lovers, however, often have one problem: Mistakenly, they think that when people don't give as much or in the same way, it means there is something wrong with them. They think it is a message about themselves instead of understanding that people lovers are rare rather than common. So, one of the things that happens is that non-people lovers get overwhelmed by people lovers. We just want you to think about this.

Wanda immediately took this to heart. She spontaneously responded with: "It is really good to know that being a people lover is just a part of my character and not something I have to do something about. It is a relief to hear that it is not an insecurity factor."

She returned two weeks later and said, "I told Frank what you said, and he said that he knew all along that I was a people lover. And so I said to him, "Well, why didn't you tell me that before? It could have saved me a lot of grief." For two weeks Wanda had been viewing herself as a people lover, someone who was extremely caring. She decided that if someone, like her lover, did not want her attention at that moment, she could give her attention to someone else until he was ready. For example, Wanda decided that since people who were not people lovers need time alone, Wanda would give Frank time for himself. Consequently, Wanda began to contact friends at various times instead of "waiting around" for Frank. As Wanda continued to do this, Frank did not feel pressure from Wanda to be with her all the time. Frank was then more able to approach Wanda and take the initiative in the relationship with her.

Since Wanda had initially stated that she wanted to have self-confidence and increased self-esteem, the authors wanted to know if these changes could be tied into these global frames. Wanda thought it would be a very high probability.

Follow-up contact, at three months and then again one year later, showed a continuation of the changes with a new way of thinking about herself as a people lover. Her friendships had improved, apparently because she was no longer complaining to them about her relationship and she also had developed enough confidence to change jobs.

Discussion

This case exemplifies how exceptions to the problem can be used to create a solution and interventions toward that end. The exceptions-to-the-problem pattern were those times that Wanda did something other than approaching or seeking reassurance.

Initially, efforts toward seeking assurance were framed by Wanda as evidence of being insecure and needy. Exceptions were already existing within her range of personal resources, and were not something she or the therapists had to create. Interviewing was directed toward successes rather than following either the client's original frame or the direction someone else might have used if it was assumed that the client did not have resources. If the therapist had joined Wanda in her frame of the problem, countless more examples of her being insecure and needy, and therefore depressed and anxious would have been jointly constructed. Even if clients believe that there are absolutely no exceptions to the problem, it is only true from their self-limiting reality and point of view. As outsiders to their frame of reference, the authors subscribe to a view that predisposes us to look even further for the exceptions.

A solution was negotiated in the course of therapy as one of maintaining "people lover" behavior. Whereas Wanda initially used a problem-maintaining label, "insecure personality," as her guideline for making decisions, she now uses the more positively adaptive description of herself as a "people lover" as her guide.

What seemed to Wanda to be a very complicated, severe, and long-standing problem of insecurity and depression was viewed differently by the authors. Insecurity, deceptiveness, neediness, low self-esteem, lack of self-confidence, depression, and fear of losing her relationship were all labels she used to explain her "approaching" behaviors.

In this case, by changing her frame and label, she was enabled to recognize and more deliberately utilize behaviors that she already had that were successful. Sometimes clients need only to change behavior and a new frame of reference emerges; other times clients need only to

change the frame and the behaviors emerge. With Wanda, it was helpful to do both. To have presented a new frame within the first session
would not have been successful because Wanda first had to have successes on which to put the new label.

This case also demonstrates the wholistic nature of interactions. By
helping Wanda change the way she interacted with Frank, he was enabled to develop a view of Wanda that he liked, i.e., that of Wanda
being a "people lover." It was not necessary to meet directly with
the lover, or to even send him a message to change the interactional
system.

In conclusion, the authors' experience in using a solution focus is
that searching for the positive suggests to the client that there are
things that he or she is doing that already work and are useful in
solving a given problem. The presenting complaints of anxiety and
depression are no exception to this.

REFERENCES

Anderson, H., Goolishian, H., & Winderman, L. (1984). Problem determined systems:
     Towards transformation in family therapy. *Journal of Strategic and Systemic Thera-*
     pies, 5 (4), 1–13.
Bateson, G. (1972). *Steps to an Ecology of Mind.* New York: Ballantine.
de Shazer, S. (1984). The death of resistance. *Family Process, 1,* 11–16.
de Shazer, S. (1985). *Keys to Solution in Brief Therapy.* New York: Norton.
de Shazer, S. (1988). *Clues: Investigating Solutions in Brief Therapy.* New York: Norton.
Dolan, Y. (1985). *A Path with a Heart.* New York: Brunner/Mazel.
Erickson, M., & Rossi, E. (1980). *The Collected Papers of Milton Erickson.* New York:
     Irvington.
Fisch, R., Weakland, J., & Segal, L. (1982). *Tactics of Change.* San Francisco: Jossey-Bass.
Gallwey, W. (1974). *The Inner Game of Tennis.* New York: Random House.
Gilligan, S. (1987). *Therapeutic Trances: The Cooperation Principle in Ericksonian Therapy.*
     New York: Brunner/Mazel.
Gingerich, W., de Shazer, S., & Weiner-Davis, M. (1987). Constructing change: A re-
     search view of interviewing. In E. Lipchik (Ed.), *Interviewing* (pp. 21–32). New
     York: Aspen.
Lankton, S., & Lankton, C. (1983). *The Answer Within: A Clinical Framework of Ericksonian*
     Hypnotherapy. New York: Brunner/Mazel.
Lipchik, E. (Ed.) (1988). *Interviewing.* New York: Aspen.
Maturana, H., & Varela, F. (1987). *The Tree of Knowledge.* Boston: New Science Library.
O'Hanlon, W. (1987). *Taproots.* New York: Norton.
von Glaserfeld, E. (1984). An introduction to radical constructivism. In P. Watzlawick
     (Ed.), *The Invented Reality* (pp. 17–40). New York: Norton.
von Foerster, H. (1984). On constructing a reality. In P. Watzlawick (Ed.), *The Invented*
     Reality (pp. 41–62). New York: Norton.
Watzlawick, P. (1984). *The Invented Reality.* New York: Norton.
Weakland, J., Fisch, R., Watzlawick, P., & Bodin, A. (1974). Brief therapy: Focused prob-
     lem resolution. *Family Process, 13,* 141–168.

because I know it is possible to feel a variety of different sensations in your body. The question, of course, is how to *allow that to happen*, how to *experientially remember* different possibilities. To answer that question, I'm going to ask you to participate in an experiment, a very simple and safe experiment. The experiment involves first allowing yourself to take a few deep breaths and relax. You don't have to move. . . . you don't have to talk . . . you don't have to try to do anything at all except remain absorbed here with me and here with you and hear me here suggesting possibilities there for your unconscious to hear there and develop now at your rate, in your own style . . . that's it . . .

If these sorts of suggestions do not adequately absorb attention, the therapist usually needs to enter the client's reality a bit more. This might involve identifying and experientially elaborating the content of the person's ongoing awareness. In depressed individuals, this might be a repetitive voice incanting, "I can't do it . . . Nothing will work," or an overwhelming bodily feeling of emptiness. The emotional attachment to such content makes them ideal for developing trance. For example, the following approach was used with another depressed client:

You don't believe it is possible . . . you sense that no one thing will work . . . and I disagree and I agree . . . I believe it is possible . . . and I believe that no one thing will work . . . and you don't believe it is possible . . . and I don't believe it is possible for just one feeling to work . . . and we are different and yet we can agree on certain things . . . and we are the same in other ways, yet we can disagree on certain things . . . you don't believe it is possible, and do you also believe that feelings can develop and remain independently of belief? . . . do you believe that the heavy feeling can operate independently from your conscious concerns? . . . I believe, and we agree and we may disagree that no one thing will work . . . at least two of us, at least two feelings . . . a feeling of heaviness that is traditional, and who really knows what we should believe about a companion feeling . . . I don't know and you don't believe it is possible . . .

These communications, delivered in a soft, sensitive, yet intense manner, served to absorb the person's attention. Like all effective hypnotic communications, they did not deny the person's present reality but suggested how that reality could be expanded in different ways.

2. *Distribute attention to three to four areas.* Once therapist and client are experientially joined, attention is distributed across three to four areas of the body. The idea here is that the analytical mind organizes experience in a linear, sequential fashion, whereas the experiential mind is capable of simultaneous, parallel processes. Shifting attention to multiple foci thus diminishes the former and augments the latter, thereby naturally developing a receptive trance. A straightforward version of the technique is evident in the following transcript:

> . . . and so as you continue to hear my voice here, what a nice thing to know that your unconscious mind has an unconscious body . . . and that unconscious body can communicate in its own way in so many different ways . . . and what do I mean by that? Simply this . . . Your hands (look meaningfully at hands) . . . Your hands can communicate yes or no, your hands can communicate with feeling, your hands can communicate yes or no, your hands can communicate with feeling, your hands can communicate with sensation . . . and I don't know which sensation might begin now to develop in those hands . . . the right hand . . . or the left hand . . . sensation . . . heaviness . . . or perhaps lightness . . . I don't know . . . all I know is that your unconscious mind can let your unconscious body communicate in a way that's right for you . . . And how do your hands feel now?
>
> *Client:* A little heavy.
>
> *Therapist:* That's right . . . your unconscious can initiate and develop and work with a feeling of heaviness in your body . . . And you don't know and I don't know how that feeling might spread or intensify . . . all I know is that you really needn't let your hands hog all of the action . . . because you've got a variety of different body sensations available . . . and as you hear me here unconsciously with me, your ears may also begin to develop sensation . . . everybody's entitled to the pleasant surprise of comfortable ears . . . your hands can be there, feeling that heaviness, and your ears can be there, discovering their ability to develop sensation . . . and how do your hands feel now?
>
> *Client:* The heaviness is moving up the arms.
>
> *Therapist:* That's right . . . your unconscious really can have moving and secure sensations. And how do your ears feel?
>
> *Client:* I don't feel my ears.
>
> *Therapist:* You don't consciously sense your ears yet. You really can let some feelings recede and others come forward unconsciously, a little more. And as your unconscious body experiments with shifting sen-

sations, shifting feelings, shifting priorities, I'm wondering about your unconscious ability to develop sensation in your eyelids . . . That's it . . . even as they blink . . . blink . . . blink . . . that's it . . . we can both wonder what feelings develop in those eyes unconsciously moving up and down, up and down, up and down . . . your unconscious can learn to respond to certain behavioral cues with automatic satisfying feelings . . .

As Gilligan (1987) described, the nonverbal communications accompanying such suggestions should be congruent with the suggested feeling. For example, a feeling of lightness is suggested with upward inflections and soft tone, heaviness is mentioned with downward inflections and a sinking voice, and so forth.

In this way, attention is shifted to at least three areas of the body. This reorganizes awareness in the body, from a diffuse yet chronic feeling in a symptom area (e.g., chest or stomach), to a shifting and alive pattern of sensations in different parts of the body. In a very real sense, this brings the experiential body back into relationship in the world, a crucial development for a person wanting to change.

3. *Emphasize the hypnotic response as a mastery ability.* As with any hypnotic development, the therapist ratifies any sensation alterations and frames them as general mastery abilities that may be used in different ways (e.g., for symptom relief).

That's right . . . you really can let your unconscious mind and your unconscious body respond . . . you don't have to try to understand it . . . you don't have to try to control it . . . because you can comfortably enjoy the knowledge that sensation can develop in your body in a variety of different ways . . . *your unconscious mind has the ability to express a variety of different sensations* . . .

4. *Elaborate the mastery theme in multiple dimensions.* Having introduced the key mastery theme ("your unconscious has the ability to express a variety of sensations"), the therapist now elaborates the variety of ways in which mastery may experientially develop. Different parameters include:

what (numbness, tingling, warmth, coolness, etc.)
when (now, five minutes, when your unconscious is ready, etc.)
how (slowly, quickly, surprisingly, comfortably, etc.)

where (arm, head, wrist, stomach, etc.)
with whom (all alone, with therapist, with spouse, etc.)

For example:

> And so as you continue to experientially sense that ability to ex-
> press sensation in a variety of different places . . . what a nice
> thing to know that you can do so in many ways . . . for example,
> your unconscious body can develop sensations of heaviness or
> numbness . . . very real numbness . . . or lightness . . . real light-
> ness lifting now . . . so many different possibilities, some of which
> you will say "no" to, some of which you will say "yes" to, each
> of which you can respond to in a way that fits the needs of the
> self . . . the needs of the self . . . the sensations of the self . . .
> expressed over time . . . your unconscious really can work over
> time . . . developing sensations now, a little more . . . a little bit
> later . . . a little trance later in those areas where you want, you
> need to develop new sensations . . . at those times, in those places,
> with those individuals, in those areas that best fit your overall de-
> velopment as a human being . . .

5. *Receive and ratify feedback in hypnotic frames.* During the course of
hypnotic explorations, the therapist continually observes and occasionally inquires about the client's ongoing responses. Each response is
defined as a legitimate unconscious response and encouraged to further
develop.

If the client can talk while remaining comfortably in trance, this can
be done straightforwardly. For example:

Therapist: And what sensations are you aware of now?
Client: [pause] The hands are very heavy.
Therapist: Your unconscious is continuing to develop that feeling of
   heaviness in the *hands*, Brenda, the hands, *all in the hands.* [This is a
   suggestion for a lifting of the heavy feelings in the chest.] That's
   right, your unconscious really does have the ability to develop that
   heavy sensation in your hands . . . and who really knows how and
   when and where that comfortable heaviness, that secure heaviness,
   will continue to develop . . . perhaps the heaviness will move up
   the arm . . . perhaps it will spread to the head slowly . . . I don't
   know . . . all I know is that your unconscious can let that feeling

develop in a way and at a rate that is meaningful for you as an individual . . .

If talking tends to disrupt trance, a "refractionation" technique (Gilligan, 1987) involving a series of brief trances might be used. That is, a five-to-ten minute trance might be followed by a five-to-ten minute discussion of the client's responses, followed by a deeper trance utilizing the information, followed by further waking state feedback, and so forth.

Another possibility is to request that ideomotor finger signals indicate when sensation begins to hypnotically develop. When a finger lifts, the hypnotist then proceeds with general ratification:

> That's it . . . your unconscious really can express itself in so many comfortable ways . . . your unconscious can recognize and communicate the onset of useful sensations in a variety of fashions . . . and that sensation that is beginning to develop can really develop comfortably . . . perhaps it will spread . . . perhaps it will intensify . . . perhaps it will remain the same . . . I don't know . . . all I know is that you can enjoy discovering how your unconscious mind can activate and utilize sensation for your own developmental learnings . . . and you can learn so much from that feeling . . .

Note that these general communications apply to virtually any sensation development.

6. *Elaborate hypnotic responses: stories.* During the course of a therapeutic trance, it is common for a client's attention to gradually narrow from multiple possibilities to one or two actualities. Thus, the client usually responds to the many suggestions given by the hypnotist by developing a few responses that are especially meaningful. These responses can be elaborated as resources relevant to the therapy goals. For example, the depressed client described above presented complaints of heaviness in the chest and, in a parallel fashion, responded hypnotically with heavy hands. The therapist can use the hypnotic response (heavy hands) to experientially change the symptomatic response (heavy chest). An excellent technique in this regard involves the use of metaphorical stories that symbolically suggest pathways for change. For example:

And as those hands continue to develop that special feeling of heaviness, what a nice thing to know that your unconscious mind knows so much about developing new relationships and new learnings . . . and such learnings can happen in so many ways . . . For example, Mary and Joe were going to have a baby . . . They came to see me, and you could note *all the changes* that had already occurred in her body . . . her *body image was no doubt changing* as well . . . and Mary and Joe wanted to *use hypnosis* to have that baby . . . they wanted to use hypnosis to *feel comfortable*, to stay comfortable, to allow the life deep within Mary to continue to grow and emerge at the right time . . . so I said to them, "That's right, you really can learn how *your unconscious mind can work for you in many different ways*" . . . And Mary was especially concerned about handling any pain during the delivery . . . and so I asked her where she sensed she needed help with developing comfort and security in her body . . . She indicated her belly, so I let her know in no uncertain terms that she really shouldn't discriminate against herself, that she really had a *whole body* of possible learnings to draw on and that there was no need to emphasize only that area . . . that any place of discomfort could be joined by other *areas of comfort*, to weave a new pattern of perhaps puzzling but nonetheless compelling *comfort and absorption* . . . Mary developed a nice deep trance and I continued to emphasize that the feelings in her belly should be joined and modulated by the feelings in other parts of her . . . and she discovered in trance that her hands could begin to be numb and tingling at the same time . . . she learned in trance how to let the feelings in her hands connect with the feeling in her stomach, to let the inner feelings move outside when needed . . .

This story further elaborated how peripheral resources (hands) could be joined with troublesome areas (belly) to generate new responses. In doing so, it provided the client with experiential opportunities to reconnect and reframe the feeling in her solar plexus to the healing properties of the whole body.

7. *Future pacing.* Once a hypnotic resource has been linked to a symptomatic response in trance, posthypnotic suggestions are given to ensure that linkage will generalize to other situations. The general idea, related directly or indirectly (e.g., stories), is that when the symptomatic response occurs in the future, the new hypnotic resource can be simul-

taneously activated to provide a more satisfying experience. For example:

> And so it is satisfying to know that the unconscious can apply learnings in so many ways, in so many areas, at so many times . . . And I really don't know when, and you consciously don't know when, your unconscious will decide to apply these new learnings in those situations where you need them . . . perhaps your unconscious will select out a time tonight, when you feel safe and secure, to begin to activate the comfortable sensations of heaviness in your hands, not to mention your chest, not to mention your sense of lightness, not to mention your chest, not to mention your solar plexus . . . begin to activate those new feelings of heaviness to connect you with a center of comfort, with a center of hypnotic learning, with a center of breathing deeply and comfortably, with a center for dreaming . . . I don't know if it will be tonight . . . whether you will be alone or with others . . . all I know is that your unconscious mind can take the time to learn from those feelings of heaviness in a way that surprises your conscious mind . . .

Thus, the suggestions predict the return of the symptomatic response (heaviness), but within a therapeutic framework of the new learnings. This is the common Ericksonian technique of claiming the symptomatic response as grounds for therapeutic learnings.

8. *Self-appreciation.* Before concluding trance, several minutes of self-appreciation can be suggested. Besides being a therapeutic process in and of itself, it provides a transition between trance and the waking state.

> And so as you continue to consolidate these new learnings, as you continue to allow your unconscious mind, with each breath you take, to know a little deeper that you really can trust and develop your future in accord with inner needs . . . what a nice thing to know that you can take a few moments of clock time, all the time in the world, to simply enjoy yourself . . . to thank yourself . . . to feel that sense of security . . . that sense of knowing that you can always return to this place of comfort . . . this place of learning . . . this place of appreciating the needs of the self and trusting the resources of the unconscious mind . . .

9. *Reorient.* Reorientation is now accomplished in a straightforward fashion:

> And you can keep those resources as you begin to allow yourself to slowly reorient out of trance, back here into the room . . . taking all the time in the world in the next several minutes . . . perhaps wanting to count from 5 to 1, to allow yourself to gradually reorient . . . gradually reorient . . . gradually orient . . .

10. *Post-trance suggestions.* Most subjects remain in an extremely receptive state for five to ten minutes after trance is formally ended. This period is an excellent time for gently emphasizing key ideas. As Gilligan (1987) discussed, techniques for accomplishing this include stories, jokes, and embedded suggestions. As in any intimate relationship, the underlying connection between therapist and client is maintained, even as attention gradually expands to include other stimuli and topics.

In using this ten-step method, the therapist should remain sensitive to the cooperative nature of the hypnotic relationship. Though both therapist and client share an interest in increasing the client's ability directly to experience bodily sensation, neither knows exactly how this will happen. As Erickson (personal communication, 1977) noted:

> All I know (during hypnotic work) is that I've got an unconscious mind . . . and they've got an unconscious mind . . . and we're sitting in the same room together . . . therefore, trance is inevitable . . . I don't know how . . . I don't know when . . . I don't know why . . . but trance is inevitable . . .

Similarly, the therapist uses this method with a deep confidence in the client's natural ability to experience bodily sensations. The 10-step method is one guide for realizing this ability, another is the client's values and ongoing responses. Blending the two by modifying the method to include the client's contributions will produce the best results.

Complementing Hypnotic Work with Tasks

As a rule, work done in trance should be balanced by work done outside of trance (Gilligan, 1987; Lankton & Lankton, 1983; Yapko,

1988). In this regard, the above hypnotic method may be complemented by tasks designed further to reconnect the depressed or anxious person experientially. For example, the author typically directs such individuals to join some sort of *movement classes*, such as dance therapy, Feldenkreis lessons, yoga, or martial arts. Since it is virtually impossible to be depressed or anxious when immersed in gentle, rhythmic movement processes, such classes are very helpful in reuniting mind and body. Another type of task concerns *social activities*. Following Erickson's (in Rossi, 1980) premise that the social environment provides innumerable opportunities for therapeutic growth, clients are asked to wonder (in and out of trance) about which social resources (persons, places, things, events) might be helpful in developing desired solutions. For Brenda, the depressed client described earlier, tasks included (1) going to the park every other day and (2) becoming involved in an extensive job search (writing letters, getting interviews, and so forth). For another client with similar goals, regular communication with his wife and children became important. Such straightforward tasks are often essential to consolidating and extending the resources revivified in trance.

Another type of task is self-hypnosis. The author teaches most clients self-hypnosis, and then directs them to use this skill to further learnings developed in the sessions. For example, Brenda practiced the hypnotic sensation alteration process nightly for 15 to 20 minutes, developing a ritual that replaced her depressive routine. Self-hypnosis may also be used to rehearse performances in upcoming events (job interviews, family meetings, social gatherings), and to imagine different futures.

Other types of tasks worth mentioning are those that are silly, paradoxical, ambiguous, or otherwise unusual (Lankton & Lankton, 1986). Such tasks may be especially useful in disrupting the rigid mental sets characterizing depressed or anxious individuals. For example, Brenda was given the assignment of carrying around two books, one a heavy and exceedingly dry treatise on depression, the other an edited volume of futurist predictions. Each time she felt depressed, she was to hold the books and sense which one felt more "familiar," then decide from which she would like to read a page. The task puzzled her, and also began to orient her more to thinking about the future.

These and other tasks build on the bodily feelings revived by the hypnotic method. They provide avenues for depressed and anxious persons to channel their attention and opportunities to increase their social participation. In doing so, they constitute important therapeutic techniques for steering individuals back onto their primary path of developmental growth.

GENERATING VARIETY IN OTHER PARAMETERS

Thus far, how therapists may operate as variety generators in the area of bodily sensation has been examined. Of course, this principle of "do it more, do it better" can be applied in other areas as well. This section overviews how variety may be generated in some of these other areas.

Images of the Future

Earlier it was noted how the vision of the future held by a person influences his or her experience and expression in the present. Unfortunately, depressed and anxious individuals are typically attached to a singular, unsatisfying image of the future. This image is often based on past failures so that, to paraphrase a pop philosopher, such individuals are navigating down the freeway of life with eyes rigidly locked on the rear-view mirror. Thus, the task of the therapist is to orient attention back to the road to the future. It is often difficult to do this straightforwardly with clients in waking states, since their rigid response sets render them impervious to considering or committing to new possibilities. The best interventions, therefore, bypass the limits of the conscious mind.

An excellent method in this regard is the psuedo-orientation in time technique developed by Erickson (1954), wherein it is suggested that the desired future has already transpired. The client is then asked to "review" the experiences that have enabled this satisfying future to develop. One version of this technique (see Gilligan, 1988a) involves hallucinating a "rainbow arc" of crystal balls. Hypnotized clients first envision a positive future state within a "crystal ball" located in the lower right peripheral field. They then regress to an early memory that their unconscious selects as useful in developing the future crystal ball. The regression memory is placed in a crystal ball in the lower left peripheral field, and a slightly later memory (relevant to achieving the future crystal ball) is then accessed and placed in the next crystal ball in the left-to-right arc. In this way, a series of "memories" from early childhood to present to "future" is developed as a bridge leading to the desired future state. It is an excellent technique, as it allows both a vision of a satisfying future and a means to frame depressing events as leading to that future. Thus, depression is used as a vehicle of growth rather than as an enemy to be purged.

If clients have difficulty generating a sense of the future while in trance, a process one might call *parallel hallucinating* may be used. This method, a modified version of Erickson's (1964) "my friend John" technique, involves therapists using their hypnotic abilities to "hallucinate" the "future self" of the client in the office, alongside the therapist and client. This future self is introduced into the conversation, with the goal being to elicit contributions from the client on the topic. For example, Patrick was a young man unresponsive to suggestions for imaging a desired future. As he continued to complain about feeling hopeless, the therapist selected a spot in the office and became curious as to how a satisfying future self would appear. An image gradually emerged, and the therapist continued in the following way:

Client: . . . so I just don't feel I have any support.

Therapist: (with intense absorption to spot in room): Do you know what color hair she has?

Client: (disrupted and bewildered) What?

Therapist: (maintaining absorption) Her hair? It looks beautiful to me. What do you think?

Client: (still bewildered) I don't understand what you're talking about?

Therapist: The woman. This woman. (gesturing to hallucination) You do want to have a relationship, do you not?

Client: (looks sad) Yeah, but what are you doing?

Therapist: I'm asking the unconscious to look into your future, and I seem to see you with someone you can trust.

Client: (looks very absorbed but still sad, head drops) That's not possible.

Therapist: (looking with hypnotic intensity at client) You consciously don't believe now that it's possible. But I'm here to let you know that it *is* possible . . . I can see it *there*.

Client: (looking increasingly hypnotically absorbed) She wouldn't stay with me long.

Therapist: (continuing to hypnotically absorb client) Yes, you need to think in small chunks. You need to appreciate that some skills do need to continue to develop. You do need to stay connected with resources. And I guess that's why you're here. (client entranced) It's good to know that you have much to learn. Just as it's essential to know what you want. (pause) What color hair does she have?

Client: (pause) Brown.

As this brief excerpt illustrates, therapists can use their own hypnotic abilities to shift primary attention to the future. As a future self is imaged and introduced by the therapist, it can stimulate the client to operate in similar fashion. Note that the therapist acknowledges considerations raised by the client, but does not let them interfere with the primary task of imaging a desired future.

A third method for generating images of viable futures involves *"chunking down" strategies*. This is especially useful with depressives, who tend to think in global, generalized images (Yapko, 1988). For example, Linda was depressed over her inability to actualize any of her future-oriented images, which tended to feature dramatic, life-changing events such as major career achievements and marrying a "Tom Selleck"-type character. She was asked in trance to "feel free to limit herself" to decidedly bland and minor images of achievement. These images—e.g., planting a garden, taking a class—provided reference structures for realistic and satisfying changes.

A related strategy is to ask clients hypnotically to generate different "puzzle pieces" of a satisfying future across multiple trances. For example, John, a middle-aged lawyer afraid to make commitments, was asked in trance to let his unconscious reveal just one "puzzle piece" as a clue to a satisfying future. His conscious mind was baffled and disconcerted about the image of a key that developed. This technique was repeated a half dozen times during the following three weeks, with a different image emerging each time. An integrating trance was then developed wherein it was suggested that all the "clues" would fit into a viable image of the future, one that his unconscious could share with him at a rate and in a style appropriate for his overall development. This technique is especially useful with clients like John, whose conscious minds (and their learned limitations) interfere with the envisioning of viable futures.

These and other methods are useful in generating variety when clients are stuck in a single (unsatisfying) image of the future. They do not attempt to take away the limited orientation of the client, but rather expand the range of possibilities to include additional choices.

Images of the Past

Just as depressed and anxious clients become rigidly entrenched in invariant images of the future, so do they attach to singular representations of the past. Thus, the therapist's skill as variety generator also applies to stimulating multiple images of the past. One technique involves hypnotically regressing clients to events before the depressing or anxious process set in. For example, Margaret and Michael entered therapy after 20 years of marriage. Their mutual experience was overshadowed by the memory of Michael's affair and Margaret's attempted suicide three years before. They could revivify few events before this time and felt hopeless about the future. Part of the therapy included regressions to their first meetings together, involving passion, pleasure, and hope. These memories were emphasized as vital resources, and further hypnotic communications involved wondering aloud about how such feelings could "trickle" into the future. Thus, hypnosis was therapeutically used to dislodge the clients' fixation to the tragedies and to reorient them to the resources of having experienced positive times together.

The psychological relationship to one's past can also be hypnotically altered through the age-progression techniques noted above. For example, Stella felt depressed after being fired from her job as a newspaper photographer. She was hypnotically progressed a year into the future, and asked to review how her values associated with certain events (such as the job firing) had changed over the past year, as new experiences transpired. As she envisioned herself working as a freelance photographer, she felt thankful about leaving her newspaper position for this new, more satisfying career.

A final technique concerns the type of memories revivified by clients. Depressed individuals all too often orient to sad or somber memories (Gilligan & Bower, 1984). One straightforward intervention is to ask clients, in both trance and waking states, about preferences and pleasures quite unrelated to the symptomatic process. Therapists may interrupt clients' depressive talk with inquiries about favorite flowers, sports, colors, movie stars, and so forth (see Gilligan, 1987). Similarly, clients may be given tasks, such as listing favorite values, and then asked to attend to them actively. In doing so, clients' images of the past become more balanced and their possible futures are expanded.

These techniques assume that the values assigned to the past reflect the values of the self's present state. Thus, shifting the perspective of the viewing state may shift the values assigned to past events. This new representation of the past enables greater freedom in the present and future.

Intensity

The intensity a feeling holds may also be varied for therapeutic gain. By learning to increase and decrease intensity, a person gains a sense of mastery and participation in the process (Erickson, 1967 / 1980). To develop this learning, therapists may use the sorts of rating scales commonly employed in hypnotic pain control processes (Erickson, 1967 / 1980; Sacerdote, 1982). The author usually introduces several such scales to depressed and anxious clients: the first has to do with degree (1–10) of depression or anxiety felt, the second with the degree (1–10) of security felt. A symptomatic event is accessed and the person is asked: On a scale of 1 to 10, how depressed do you feel? How secure do you feel? Hypnotic interventions such as resource accessing, story telling, sensation alterations, and so forth, are then introduced and the person's ratings again obtained. Just as in the sensation alteration procedure outlined above, the therapist ratifies each ratings shift with general comments about "the unconscious ability to change that feeling and to change that feeling about the feeling in meaningful and appropriate ways."

As a person develops changes in intensity ratings, specific possibilities may be explored. For example, clients may learn to increase and then decrease a feeling of anxiety, while keeping feelings of security constant. The tables are then turned, with security varied while intensity of feeling is maintained. Such operations enable a person to master the process of increasing and decreasing intensity, while also demonstrating how, for example, security may be maintained even when depression temporarily increases. This distinction allows individuals to stay connected with themselves (i.e., not to give up) when a symptomatic event is reaccessed.

For example, Mark developed intense feelings of anxiety before public speaking engagements. He felt such feelings to be involuntary and interpreted them as evidence of impending failure. In therapy he learned to shift the intensity of the anxiety up and down, while increasing his sense of security. This process enabled him to join and remain comfortable with the feelings of anxiety that began to develop at his next presentation.

Physical Context

A person may be stuck in a certain experience by virtue of performing it in the same physical context time and time again. This can be determined by straightforwardly inquiring as to *where* a symptom is expressed. If it occurs in the same place repeatedly, varying that physical context may enable new possibilities to emerge. For example, Rebecca was a middle-aged secretary who complained of feeling "empty and blue." Living alone, her symptoms were most acute each evening when she would plop herself into a chair and stare at the television. A set of interventions concentrated on having her practice "the ability to feel empty and blue" in various physical locations, including in a meditation room at home, at the library, and in the park. Of course, her feelings varied with the context shifts, as they invariably will, and new ways of being then became available.

Another client, Robert, complained of overeating. This frequently involved consuming large amounts of peanuts while watching television. He was directed to build a "goober shrine" in his spare room at home, and was assigned a certain "goober ritual" to practice in front of the shrine upon returning home from work each night. This ritual, which he found hilarious, disrupted his "goober mania," whereupon trance work was used to develop alternate ways of "feeling and filling" his inner needs.

Social Others

A final variable worth noting is *social others*. Therapists may identify *who is present* when a person feels depressed or otherwise symptomatic. If clients are typically alone, they may be directed to express their symptom with others. For example, Mary was a hard-working professional wife and mother who complained of binge eating. She felt guilty and sad about not spending enough time with her husband, just as she felt depressed about her uncontrollable snacking. She was directed to schedule a 30-minute "binge" walk early each morning with her husband. She was to carry sundry snacks with her during this time, offering them to her husband along with the cryptic inquiry, "Do you want more?" She was then to ask herself the same question while keeping her husband "in the back of her mind." Carried out over a two-week interval, this strategy of "doing her symptom" in a different social context (with her husband, on a walk) elicited a variety of emotional responses from her. She stopped binging and began to pay more attention to her marriage. Both she and her husband cut back on professional commitments and sought couples therapy.

Variability may also be introduced when the symptom is performed by two or more people. Don and Paul were a gay couple expressing dissatisfaction in their sexual relationship. Don would want to "get right to it" and finish sex within minutes, whereas Paul felt he often needed over an hour to open up emotionally. Their different timings would frequently result in disruptive arguments during sex. They were given the simple task of setting aside an hour each evening for an experiment. The experiment would begin with them taking "up to 60 seconds, no more" for a gentle kiss. Don was then to take a deep sigh, walk into his study and lock the door, and spend the next 45 minutes engaged in his pleasurable hobby of reading poetry and writing in his journal. Meanwhile, Paul was to remain on the bed fantasizing slowly and sensuously, knowing in the back of his mind that 45 minutes would not be quite enough time. After 45 minutes, Don was to reenter the room and receive a kiss from Paul, whereupon both could wonder how they might "come together emotionally." This task of social separation enabled satisfying sex to develop for both of them. Interestingly, after a week Paul began to "cheat" and surprise Don in his office before the time was up.

These two brief examples indicate how a fixed social relationship may block the natural process of developmental change. As this parameter is varied, new possibilities reveal themselves and more satisfying ways of being may emerge.

SUMMARY

In exploring the process of human change, it becomes apparent that many parameters are involved in the construction of an experiential reality: bodily sensation, images of the future, images of the past, and so forth. When these parameters are free to vary according to changing needs and situations, developmental growth is possible; but when they become rigid and invariant, sensitivity to the vital "now" of the experiential self is lost and problems typically develop. In this view, the therapist operates as a variety generator in promoting flexibility and change across different aspects of experience. Although we have identified some of these parameters, many others exist—time (when, how long), frequency (how often), cognitive frame (what it means), attribution (why it happened), and so forth. The task of the therapist is to identify those values that are rigidly and dysfunctionally fixed for a given client, and to introduce interventions that will support and expand his or her range of expression. As variability increases, so does the connectedness of the symptomatic expression to its larger (social, organismic, or psychological) contexts. This recontextualization enables the symptom to operate as part of a solution to the challenges of developmental growth. And this, first and foremost, is the commitment of therapy.

REFERENCES

de Shazer, S. (1982). *Patterns of Brief Family Therapy: An Ecosystemic Approach.* New York: Guilford Press.

Erickson, M. H. (1954). Psuedo orientation in time as a hypnotherapeutic procedure. *Journal of Clinical and Experimental Hypnosis, 2,* 261–283.

Erickson, M. H. (1964/1980). The "Surprise" and "My-Friend-John" techniques of hypnosis: Minimal cues and natural field experimentation. *American Journal of Clinical Hypnosis, 6,* 293–307. Reprinted in E. L. Rossi (Ed.) *Collected Papers of Milton Erickson, Volume I.* New York: Irvington Press.

Erickson, M. H. (1967/1980). An introduction to the study and application of hypnosis for pain control. In J. Lasner (Ed.), *Hypnosis and Psychosomatic Medicine.* New York: Springer-Verlag. Reprinted in E. L. Rossi (Ed.), *Collected Papers of Milton Erickson, Vol. IV.* New York: Irvington Press.

Gilligan, S. G. (1987). *Therapeutic Trances: The Cooperation Principle in Ericksonian Hypnotherapy.* New York: Brunner/Mazel.

Gilligan, S. G. (1988a). Psychosomatic healing in Ericksonian hypnotherapy. *Hypnose und Kognition, 5,* 25–33.

Gilligan, S. C. (1988b). Symptom phenomena as trance phenomena. In J. Zeig & S. Lankton (Eds.), *Developing Ericksonian Therapy: State of the Art.* New York: Brunner/Mazel.

Gilligan, S. G., & Bower, G. H. (1984). Cognitive consequences of emotional arousal. In C. E. Izard, J. Kagan, & R. Zajonc (Eds.), *Emotion, Cognitions and Behavior.* New York: Cambridge Press.

Gilligan, S. G., & Kennedy, C. M. (in press). Solutions and resolutions: Ericksonian hypnotherapy with incest survivor groups. *Journal of Strategic and Systemic Therapy,.*

Lankton, S. R., & Lankton, C. (1983). *The Answer Within: A Clinical Framework for Ericksonian Hypnotherapy.* New York: Brunner/Mazel.

O'Hanlon, B., & Wilk, J. (1987). *Shifting Contexts: The Generation of Effective Psychotherapy.* New York: Guilford Press.

Pearce, J. C. (1981). *The Bond of Power.* New York: E. P. Dutton.

Pribram, K. H. (1971). *Languages of the Brain: Experimental Paradoxes and Principles in Neuropsychology.* Englewood Cliffs, N.J.: Prentice-Hall.

Rossi, E. L. (Ed.) (1980). *Collected Works of M. H. Erickson, M. D. Vol. IV.* New York: Irvington Press.

Sacerdote, P. (1982). Techniques for hypnotic intervention with pain patients. In J. Barber & C. Adrian (Eds.), *Psychological Approaches to the Management of Pain.* New York: Brunner/Mazel.

Siddle, D. (1983). *Orienting and Habituation: Perspectives in Human Research.* New York: Wiley.

Yapko, M. D. (1988). *When Living Hurts: Directives for Treating Depression.* New York: Brunner/Mazel.

Name Index

Abramson, L. 8, 15, 26, 246, 248, 249, 250, 251, 252, 253, 255, 256
Alloy, L. 26
Alper, T. 202
Anderson, H. 320
Anderson, J. 209, 210
Anderson, K. 13
Andrews, G. 210
Atthowe, J. 239

Bailey, S. 13
Bandler, R. 121, 124, 180, 267, 272, 273, 275, 296
Bandura, A. 202
Barber, J. 281, 284, 290, 294
Barlow, D. 208, 209, 210, 213
Bateson, G. 317
Beck, A. 67, 96, 110, 120, 136, 185, 186, 188, 189, 190, 191, 192, 246, 248, 249, 250, 251, 252, 254, 255, 257, 259, 260, 261, 262, 274
Beck, J. 210
Beecher, H. 282
Beletsis, C. 269, 271, 272
Benson, H. 213
Bernard, C. 53
Blumberg, E. 53
Bodin, A. 320
Bourne, R. 212
Bower, G. 343
Bradshaw, J. 77
Breier, A. 209, 210
Brown, B. 213
Burns, D. 193, 248, 251, 252
Burns, M. 24
Burrows, J. 53

Carter, J. 20
Carter, P. 239, 271, 273
Chaplin, J. 66
Chapman, C. 282
Charney, D. 209
Cheek, D. 35, 43, 45

Clance, P. 254
Cosby, B. 7
Covi, L. 185, 186, 191, 192, 193
Craig, K. 285
Crowe, R. 209, 227
Crowley, R. 150, 210
Crutchfield, C. 62
Cuatrecasas, P. 36
Curtis, C. 209

Delbruck, M. 36
Delozier, J. 124
Descartes, R. 41, 47, 51, 230, 237, 241
de Shazer, S. 314, 315, 316, 317, 321, 328
Dewey, J. 19
Dilts, R. 274
Dolan, Y. 314
Duszynski, D. 53
Dwyer, C. 23

Eisenhower, D. 20
Ellis, A. 67, 96, 252, 253
Elton, D. 293
Emery, G. 67, 185, 186, 188, 189, 190, 192, 246, 248, 249, 250, 251, 252, 254, 255, 257, 259, 260, 261, 262
Engel, G. 285, 287
Erickson, M. 46, 91, 107, 108, 113, 114, 115, 119, 120, 121, 124, 125, 129, 135, 151, 152, 155, 169, 175, 189, 195, 196, 208, 210, 212, 215, 223, 226, 238, 265, 268, 270, 271, 276, 282, 288, 289, 294, 295, 296, 304, 314, 338, 340, 341, 343, 344
Evans, E. 31, 53

Farmer, J. 62
Farrar, W. 37
Feather, B. 282
Fenichel, O. 211
Fezler, W. 177
Fisch, R. 320, 321
Fleming, B. 185

349

Flood, J. 45
Ford, G. 20
Frankenhauser, M. 55, 56
Freud, S. 76, 226, 227, 228, 237, 287
Friedman, S. 52

Gallwey, W. 316
Garber, J. 246, 248, 249, 250, 251, 252, 253,
    255, 256
Gardner, G. 223
Garvey, M. 31
Geary, B. 186, 188, 190
Gendron, D. 53
Gerow, J. 246
Gilligan, S. 152, 155, 188, 191, 195, 210,
    211, 212, 215, 223, 238, 265, 268, 271,
    272, 275, 314, 320, 321, 328, 329, 330,
    333, 338, 343
Gingerich, W. 315
Girgus, J. 13
Gleick, J. 62
Goldstein, A. 36
Goolishian, H. 320
Gordon, D. 121
Gorman, J. 228
Greenblatt, D. 209
Gregory, I. 175
Grinder, J. 121, 124, 180, 267, 272, 273,
    275, 296

Haley, J. 106, 124, 130, 151, 155, 187, 188,
    189, 190, 200, 210, 212, 265, 271, 273,
    275, 276
Hamilton, M. 193
Harper, R. 252, 253
Havens, R. 107, 114
Heidegger, M. 230
Heninger, G. 209
Herkenham, M. 37
Hermann, P. 20–21
Hershey, G. 246, 248
Hill, H. 282
Hills, C. 50
Hoehn-Saric, E. 208
Hofstadter, R. 19
Hogg, J. 185, 189, 190, 192
Holland, L. 239
Hollander, H. 239
Hollon, S. 31, 185, 186, 187, 188, 191, 192,
    193
Hornykiewicz, O. 41
Hoving, T. 30–31
Hughes, J. 36
Humphrey, H. 19, 20
Husserl, E. 229, 237

Iker, H. 53
Insel, T. 46
Iversen, L. 37

Johnson, L. 20–21
Jung, C. 43, 46, 172

Kamen, L. 17, 23
Kanner, L. 171
Kellerman, J. 210
Kennedy, J. 21
Kierkegaard, S. 230
Kissen, D. 53
Klein, D. 209, 227, 228
Klerman, G. 209
Klopfer, B. 53
Koriath, J. 51, 59
Kroger, W. 177

Labaw, W. 210
Landers, D. 59
Lankton, C. 115, 119, 121, 150, 176, 210,
    212, 289, 296, 314, 320, 338
Lankton, S. 115, 119, 121, 150, 176, 210,
    212, 289, 296, 314, 320, 338
Leshan, L. 53
Leventhal, H. 283
Levy, S. 22
Lewinsohn, P. 185, 202
Liebowitz, M. 228
Lindholm, E. 59
Lipchik, E. 316
Lipman, R. 186, 192
Livingston, K. 41
Lowney, L. 36
Luborsky, L. 12
Lugo, J. 246, 248
Lustman, P. 193

Maclean, P. 41
Madanes, C. 120, 151, 155, 200
Maier, S. 7
Maslow, A. 250, 254
Masson, J. 76
Maturana, H. 50, 62, 315
Maxwell, R. 50
May, R. 55
McClure, J. 227
McEwen, B. 40
McNeil, E. 256
McPhee, J. 30
Melzack, R. 281, 282
Mergenhagan, S. 37
Merleau-Ponty, M. 226, 231, 237
Merskey, H. 281, 282, 285

Metalsky, G. 15
Miller, H. 67, 77
Miller, S. 246, 248, 249, 250, 251, 252, 253, 255, 256
Mills, J. 150, 210
Minuchin, S. 77
Mischel, W. 248
Mishkin, M. 41
Morawska, E. 29
Morley, J. 45
Morris, C. 254
Murphy, S. 193
Musetto, A. 91

Nerenz, D. 283
Newton, I. 51
Niewenhuys, R. 37, 41
Nixon, R. 19, 20
Nolen-Hoeksema, S. 13, 15, 17, 30
Noyes, R. 209, 227
Nunn, T. 53
Nuwer, M. 41

Oettingen, G. 16, 29
O'Hanlon, W. 107, 296, 314, 328, 329
Olds, J. 41

Packard, N. 62
Paget, J. 53
Pal, B. 36
Papez, J. 41
Paul, S. 37
Pauls, D. 227
Pearce, J. 327
Pert, C. 36, 37, 41
Peterson, C. 10, 12, 15, 16, 22, 24
Petrie, H. 41
Pilowsky, I. 285, 287
Pitts, F. 227
Pribram, K. 41, 330

Rachman, S. 246
Rodin, J. 23
Rogers, C. 254
Rosen, S. 121, 125
Rosenbaum, M. 193
Rosenhan, D. 245, 246
Rossi, E. 35, 36, 40, 43, 45, 46, 55, 56, 113, 114, 120, 122, 129, 130, 152, 155, 175, 189, 210, 239, 271, 289, 304, 314, 339
Rossi, S. 120, 175, 210
Ruth, D. 185, 186, 191, 192, 193
Rubin, Z. 256
Ruff, M. 37
Rush, A. 67, 185, 186, 188, 189, 190, 192

Russell, P. 50
Ryan, M. 40, 113, 114, 122, 129, 130, 152

Sacerdote, P. 281, 287, 289, 292, 294, 344
Sachs, L. 291
Sainte-Exupery, A. 291
Salameh, W. 92, 102
Samudzhen, E. 52
Santrock, J. 246
Sartre, J. 226, 230, 237, 238
Satir, V. 77, 151
Schachter, S. 252
Schalling, D. 282
Scharrer, B. 41
Scharrer, E. 41
Schmale, A. 53
Schmitt, F. 36, 37, 38, 40
Schulman, P. 18
Schwab, J. 247
Schwarz. R. 281, 282, 289
Segal, L. 51, 62, 321
Seligman, M. 5, 7, 8, 10, 12, 13, 15, 16, 17, 18, 22, 23, 24, 29, 67, 110, 120, 124, 245, 246, 251, 284
Selye, H. 52, 246
Semmel, A. 10, 15
Shashoua, V. 40
Shaw, B. 67, 185, 186, 187, 188, 189, 190, 191, 192, 193
Shaw, R. 62
Sherman, S. 142
Shor, R. 287
Shrader, R. 209
Siegel, B. 270
Simons, A. 193
Simonton, C. 53, 54
Smeltzer, D. 175
Smith, G. 45
Snow, H. 53
Snyder, S. 36
Solomon, R. 226
Spear, F. 282, 285
Spiegel, D. 285
Spiegel, H. 285
Stanton, M. 186, 188, 190
Sternbach, R. 281, 282, 284, 285, 287, 289
Stevenson, A. 20
Stever, J. 185
Stoeri, J. 228
Sue, D. 246
Sue, D. W. 246
Sue, S. 246
Swartz, C. 210
Sweeney, P. 13
Szasz, T. 285, 289

Taylor, S. 246, 251
Teasdale, I. 8, 31, 251
Thomas, C. 53
Thompson, K. 289
Thompson, S. 284
Thornton, D. 185
Trotter, R. 110
Truman, H. 19
Turkevich, N. 52

Vaillant, G. 24
Van Pelt, S. 210
Varela, F. 50, 62, 315
Violin, A. 282, 285
Visintainer, M. 22
Volpicelli, J. 22
von Baeyer, C. 10
von Foerster, H. 62, 315
von Glaserfeld, E. 315

Wahl, L. 37
Wahl, S. 37
Waldo, M. 185
Wall, P. 281, 282
Walshe, W. 53
Watzlawick, P. 124, 151, 212, 217, 219,
    254, 271, 273, 315, 320

Weakland, J. 320, 321
Weber, R. 37
Weiner, H. 36
Weiner-Davis, M. 315
Weingartner, H. 45
Weinstein, M. 202
Wetzel, R. 193
Whiteley, J. 67, 96
Wilk, J. 328, 329
Wilson, R. 213
Winderman, L. 320
Winnicott, D. 171
Wolpe, J. 211

Yalom, I. 185, 192, 193, 196
Yapko, M. 51, 56, 120, 121, 122, 123, 125,
    126, 127, 131, 134, 137, 138, 141, 144,
    145, 151, 187, 190, 191, 195, 199, 221,
    247, 249, 250, 252, 253, 256, 258, 266,
    338, 342
Youngren, M. 185

Zeig, J. 50, 106, 107, 115, 119, 121, 122,
    124, 135, 151, 176, 186, 188, 190, 199,
    289
Zullow, H. 16, 19

Subject Index

ACAs (Adult Children of Alcoholics) 77, 138
Affective dimension 136–138, 248, 250
  intervention 136–138
  symptoms 136, 250
Age progression 114–115, 133, 187, 190, 195, 343
Age regression 130, 174, 175, 178, 187, 195
Agoraphobia 227, 228
AIDS 270
AMACs (Adults Molested as Children) 76
Amnesia 46, 114, 176, 187
Anchor 142, 156, 307
Anecdotes 113, 116, 120, 121–122, 124, 199, 310
Anger 14, 69, 72, 90, 95–96, 136, 137, 287
Anxiety 16, 50, 78, 84, 130, 207, 211, 214, 215, 228–229, 242, 243, 245–262, 264–276, 344
Anxiety disorder 110, 208, 210, 226, 245–246, 265, 274
Arithmetical progression 129
Artistic metaphor 157
"Artists" metaphor 137–138
Assignments, homework 91, 93, 113, 339
Attention disorder 172, 182
Attributional style 5–32, 202, 283, 285, 296
  and achievement 6, 10, 17–21, 25, 26
  and depression 6, 10, 12–13, 16, 17, 25, 26, 110, 111, 202
  and health 7, 10, 17, 21–25, 26
  origin of 29–31
Attributional Style Questionnaire 10–11, 14–15, 18, 22, 29
  children's version, 13, 15
Auditory-kinesthetic looping 306, 309, 310
Autohypnosis 47, 113, 178, 202, 265, 273, 284
Autonomic nervous system 37, 55, 213, 246
Avoidance 248, 249, 251, 264

"Baby-step" metaphor 156
Beck Depression Inventory, 192
Behavioral dimension 133–135, 248, 249
  intervention 134–135
  symptoms 133–134, 249
Binding Dysphoric Affect 294–296
Bipolar depression 13, 65, 74
Bodily sensation 330–338, 339
Boundaries 90, 250
Braiding process, 151, 156–169
Breast cancer 22
Breathing 213, 229, 231, 233, 236, 241, 243, 266, 268
Breathing technique 235–236, 243
Brief treatment 108
Bulimia 153–155

Cancer 51, 53, 54, 210, 292, 298–300
Catecholamines 14, 25
CAVE 11–12, 19, 21, 22, 24, 29
Cell receptors 36, 40
Ceremony 56–61
  the making of the mask 60–61
  the talking circle 58–60
  the water ceremony 57–58
Child abuse 76–77, 179–180, 197
Childbirth 46
Childhood depression 13, 15, 17, 92, 157, 171–182
Children 15, 17, 30, 171–182
Choice 53, 231, 237, 238
"Chunking Down" strategies 342
"Circus" metaphor 132–133
Cognitions 186
Cognitive dimension 131–133, 248, 249
  intervention 132–133
  symptoms 131–132, 249
Cognitive distortions 67, 96–97, 111, 123, 125, 131, 136, 185, 190, 274, 289
Cognitive Theory of Depression 67, 185–186, 202, 252

Cognitive therapy 16, 31, 184, 185–186, 188
    in groups 184–203
    procedures 96–97, 112–113
    process of change in 16, 31, 186, 188, 274
Collaborative empiricism 189
Composite judge 252
Confusion technique 195
Consciousness 43, 45, 47, 57, 230
Constructivism 51, 315
Contextual dimension 142–144, 251
    symptoms 142–143, 251
    intervention 143–144
Contraindications 122–123, 131, 134, 200
Control 6, 54, 191, 232–233, 236, 241, 242, 248, 253, 256, 258, 260, 261, 266, 272, 282, 283, 285, 293, 297
Cooperation 211, 329
Creative thought 60, 62, 120, 122, 124
Crisis intervention 134
Critical incident 31
"Crystal Ball" technique 340
Culture and depression 27–29, 56
Cybernetic 36, 41, 44, 47
"Cycles" metaphor 129–130

Deframe 152–153, 329
Depression
    attentional processes in 51, 330–333
    attributions in 12–13, 14, 110
    dynamics in 28, 53, 77, 110–112, 248
    symptoms of 25–26, 28, 50, 51, 65–67, 126–127, 172
    treatment of 17, 51, 91–103, 113–116, 124–147, 184–203
Depression, childhood 13, 15, 17, 92
Depression, conceptual models 67
Depressive types, proposed 67–69
    anxiety–linked 84–86
    boderline 82–84
    defeatist 70–72
    hysterical 74–76
    narcissistic 72–74
    oppositional 69–70
    parentified 76–82
    secondary 86–89
Diagnostic interview 173
Dissociation 96, 133, 175, 178, 180, 187, 218, 237, 268, 288, 294, 303, 304, 305, 310, 312
DSM III-R 65, 69, 73, 208–209, 227, 245, 249, 250, 264

"Early Learning Set" 270
"Einstein" metaphor 143–144
Emotion 36, 41, 45, 136–137
Empowering 152, 257
Endorphins 289, 296
Exceptions (to patterns) 316–319, 325
Existentialism 226, 230–231, 238, 243
Expectancy 258
Expectation(s) 55, 110, 112, 192, 193, 316
Experiential metaphor 57, 116, 123, 126
Experiments, disconfirming 188
Eye position 307

Family myths 252
Feeling Good 193, 201
Feeling-tone complex 43, 46
Feldenkreis movement 339
Feminine consciousness 43, 46–47
Flexibility 116, 135, 138, 346
Foresight 113, 114
Future, images of 8, 239, 340–342
Future orientation 102
    characteristics of 107, 109–110, 125
    definition of 109
    therapeutic goal of 110, 112–113, 116, 122, 125, 221, 239, 275, 328, 339, 340
Future pacing 212, 219–222, 336–337

"Garden of Eden" fantasy 174–175, 180
Gate Control theory of pain 289, 290
Generative change 155, 211, 212, 265, 319–320
Global thinking 103, 104, 111, 112, 125, 131, 132, 137, 202, 342
Grant study 24
Grief 93–94
Group psychotherapy 184–203
    inclusion/exclusion criteria for 192–193
    group size 192
Guilt 54, 72, 253, 287

Hamilton Rating Scale for Depression 193
Helplessness 7, 27–28, 52, 53, 70, 110, 122, 124, 131, 202, 250–251, 274
Hindsight 113, 114
Historical dimension 138–140, 250
    intervention 139–140
    symptoms 138–139, 250
Homeostasis 125

Hopelessness 8, 52, 70, 125, 131
Hopelessness Theory of Depression 8
Hormones 43, 45, 46, 56
Hypothalamus 41, 43, 44
Hypnosis 35, 46, 102, 113, 123, 126, 187,
    193, 208, 210, 221, 231, 232, 256, 257,
    258, 265, 284, 288, 293, 329
    in groups 191, 194–195, 202
    in treatment of anxiety 210–211, 215,
        231, 232–233, 240–241, 258–262, 265,
        270
    in treatment of depression 102, 113,
        115–116, 123, 179
    individual inductions 196–197
    taped inductions 202
Hypnotic imagery 55, 177, 290

Iatrogenic 152, 155, 289
Imagery 53, 55, 102, 103, 140, 142, 177,
    190, 237, 254, 265, 274, 275, 290, 316,
    340–342
Images of past 253, 342–343
Immune system 21–23, 53, 56, 270
    helper-suppression ratio 23
    t-lymphocytes 21–22, 23, 27, 28
Indications 122
Information substances 36–41, 43, 46
Information transduction 36, 41, 47
Insight 107, 116, 121, 127, 189, 196, 228,
    242, 270
Insight vs. Change therapies, 107
Intake interview 193
Integration 56, 93, 147, 157, 239, 265, 268,
    270, 271, 272, 275, 342
Intensity 343–344
Internal-external attributions 8
Interspersal techniques 175, 185
IS-receptor communication system 38,
    40

"Journey" metaphor 139–140

Labeling 151, 155, 187
Learned Helplessness 7, 67, 110, 284
Learning 45, 56, 57, 115–116, 190, 265,
    284, 304
"Life" metaphor 115–116
Life Reframing in Hypnosis 114
Limbic system 41, 43, 44
Little Prince, The 291
Living metaphor 157
Locus of control 8, 112, 143, 187, 252–253,
    266

Manic-Depression 13, 35, 180
Masks 60–61, 159–166
Mastery themes 76–82
Memory 41, 42, 56, 237, 251
Menstruation 43–44
Messenger molecules 36
Messenger RNA 42
Metaphor(s) 57, 91, 93, 102, 115–116,
    119–147, 150–169, 190, 199–200, 252,
    260, 291, 297
    indications and contraindications
        122–123
    use of 121–122, 190, 216–219, 291,
        335–336
Metaphorical atmosphere 35, 36, 41, 42,
    43, 47
Metaphorical task 115–116, 158
Mind/body communication 35, 36, 41, 42,
    43, 47
Mind-gene-molecule connection 35, 41,
    47
Modality representation 304
Modeling 310–311
Molecular biology 35, 37, 47
Monsters 157–166
Mood 43, 101, 190
Motivation 41, 99–100, 123, 193, 248, 265
Multiple Dimension Dissociative Model
    of Depression 126
Multiple embedded metaphor 176
Multiple level communication 56,
    120–121, 187
"Multiplex Experimental Ideas" 155
"My-Friend-John" technique 196, 341

Negative expectations 110, 116, 131
Negative triad of cognitive model 110
Neuroactive substances 37, 38
Neuro-Linguistic Programming 124
Neurotransmitters 37, 38, 55

Olfactory memory 308
Optimism 14, 15, 18–19, 20, 21, 22, 23, 26,
    27, 28
Ordeals and tasks 130, 187, 191, 200

Pain 46, 210, 242, 281–300
Panic 207, 208, 214, 215, 227, 228, 232,
    233, 236, 255
Panic disorder 208, 210, 226–243, 246, 264
Paradoxical 51, 56, 174, 265, 271, 272, 294,
    339
Parallel hallucinating 341

Parasynaptic system 38
Participatory model of health 50, 53, 57
Past temporal orientation 108
    definition of 109
    role in depression of 110–111
Past vs. present oriented therapies 107
Patterns of depression 110–111
Peptides 36, 37, 38
Perfectionism 87, 97–99, 134, 250, 261
Personal responsibility and control 54
Pessimism 6, 13, 14, 15, 16, 17, 18–19, 20,
    22, 23, 24, 111, 112, 116
Pharmacology 36
Phenomenology 35, 36, 38, 45, 155, 169,
    226, 230, 231, 232
Physiological dimension 127–131, 248,
    249
        intervention 128–131
        symptoms 127–128, 249
Positive expectations 112, 115, 125, 142,
    190, 258
Present temporal orientation
    definition of 109
    role in emotional problems of
        109–110
Primary representational system 109
Proteins 37
Providing a worse alternative 201
Pseudo-orientation in time 190, 195, 340
Psychoanalysis 47, 76, 188, 211, 228–229,
    231, 237, 238
Psychobiology 46, 47, 227, 231
Psychological complexes 43
Psychosomatic 35, 41, 74, 76, 78

"Quacker Island" 157–166, 169

"Rapid Induction Analgesia" Technique
    294
Rapport 120, 123, 127, 188, 289, 290
Reality testing 137
"Refractionation" Technique 335
Reframing 125, 136–137, 187, 190, 191,
    197–198, 211, 239, 257, 258, 265,
    273–274, 296–297, 329
Reframing rehearsal 197
Relapses 17, 181, 202, 242
Relational Dimension 145–147, 250
    interventions 146–147
    symptoms 145–146, 250
Renaissance paradigm, A 61, 62
Resources 119, 122, 125, 157, 169, 190,
    210, 262, 265, 268, 270, 272, 311, 315,
    320, 328

Responsibility 54, 69, 89, 97, 112, 145, 191,
    253
Rigidity 53, 111, 116, 124, 131, 189, 250,
    256, 306, 318, 339, 340, 342
Risks factors for depression 6, 10, 14, 27,
    126
Rosenbaum's Self Control Schedule 193
Rumination 16, 19, 20, 71, 131, 132, 133

Schemas 67, 186
School phobia 227, 228
"Secret Room" Technique 293
Seeding 102, 107, 125, 135, 140, 191,
    198–199, 258, 290
"Seeds" metaphor 107, 134–135
Self-fulfilling prophecies 115, 219, 274
Self-hypnosis 47, 202, 265, 266–268, 273,
    284
    children 178
Self-image 8, 274–275, 289
Separation anxiety 227, 228, 242, 243
Signal function of pain 289
Sleep disturbance 26, 127, 128, 129–131,
    157, 172, 201
Solutions 141, 190, 314, 316, 320, 326, 327,
    328
Specific-global attributions 8, 9
Spectator therapy 196
Spontaneous recovery 242
State-dependent memory,
    learning, and behavior (SDMLB) 40,
        42, 43, 44, 45, 46, 56
Storytelling metaphors 157, 335–336
Strategic psychotherapy 56, 124, 151, 184,
    188, 192, 256, 265
    characteristics of 124, 155
    commonalities with Ericksonian
        psychotherapy 187–190
Stress 53, 54
Submodalities 303–312
Sufis 57
Suicide 13, 82, 131, 133, 134, 193, 306, 343
"Symbiosis" metaphor 146–147
Symbolic dimension 140–141, 250
    metaphorical interventions 141–142
    symptoms 140–142, 250
Symbolic processing 124, 291–293, 294,
    335–336
Synaptic junctions 37–38, 40, 42
Systems approach 51, 62, 230, 321

Task assignments 113, 123, 126, 130, 133,
    135, 138, 140, 142, 144, 147, 188, 190,
    191, 200, 273, 330, 338, 339

Temporal orientation 106–117
  definition of 108–109
  diagnostic category 110–112
  influence on experience of 110–111,
    140
  influence on therapist orientation of
    108
  role in emotional disorders of
    108–112, 122, 125
Termination 201–202, 242
"Three Wishes" approach 175
Time bind 130
Trance 123, 124, 125, 128, 174, 175, 178,
    187, 189, 191, 194, 197, 210, 211, 214,
    215, 218, 231, 237, 238, 240–242, 257,
    265, 268, 291, 304, 314, 315, 330–339
Transformation (transformative) 51, 61,
    151, 155, 157, 169, 271
Tricyclic antidepressants 16, 227
"Tough-guy" attitude 159

Ultradian Healing Response 47
Ultradian rhythms 47
Unipolar depression (see Depression)
Unstable-stable attributions 8, 9
Utilization 187, 189, 208, 210–211, 212,
    215, 223, 271, 276, 290, 314
  of resistance 187

VAKOG (visual, auditory, kinesthetic,
    olfactory, gustatory) (examples of)
    304
Values 27, 134, 151, 247, 250, 252, 256,
    257, 261, 262, 273
Visualizations 55, 238, 259, 260–262, 290,
    316

"Web" metaphor 141–142
When Living Hurts 110, 115, 249
Wholism 321, 326
Will 53